SAP® ERP FINANCIALS QUICK REFERENCE GUIDE

SAP® ERP Financials Quick Reference Guide

SAP ECC 6.0

Surya Padhi

MERCURY LEARNING AND INFORMATION

Dulles, Virginia
Boston, Massachusetts
New Delhi

Publisher: David Pallai
MERCURY LEARNING AND INFORMATION
22841 Quicksilver Drive
Dulles, VA 20166
info@merclearning.com
www.merclearning.com
1-800-758-3756

This book is printed on acid-free paper.

Surya Padhi, *SAP® ERP Financials Quick Reference Guide: SAP ECC 6.0.*
ISBN: 978-1-936420-31-5

SAP® ERP Financials is the trademark(s) or registered trademark(s) of SAP AG in Germany and in several other countries.

The publisher recognizes and respects all marks used by companies, manufacturers, and developers as a means to distinguish their products. All brand names and product names mentioned in this book are trademarks or service marks of their respective companies. Any omission or misuse (of any kind) of service marks or trademarks, etc. is not an attempt to infringe on the property of others.

Library of Congress Control Number: 2012946010

131432

Printed in the United States of America

Our titles are available for adoption, license, or bulk purchase by institutions, corporations, etc. For additional information, please contact the Customer Service Dept. at 1-800-758-3756 (toll free).

The sole obligation of MERCURY LEARNING AND INFORMATION to the purchaser is to replace the book and/or disc, based on defective materials or faulty workmanship, but not based on the operation or functionality of the product.

This publication contains references to the products of SAP AG. SAP, R/3, SAP NetWeaver, Duet, PartnerEdge, ByDesign, SAP BusinessObjects Explorer, StreamWork, and other SAP products and services mentioned herein as well as their respective logos are trademarks or registered trademarks of SAP AG in Germany and other countries.

Business Objects and the Business Objects logo, BusinessObjects, Crystal Reports, Crystal Decisions, Web Intelligence, Xcelsius, and other Business Objects products and services mentioned herein as well as their respective logos are trademarks or registered trademarks of Business Objects Software Ltd. Business Objects is an SAP company.

Sybase and Adaptive Server, iAnywhere, Sybase 365, SQL Anywhere, and other Sybase products and services mentioned herein as well as their respective logos are trademarks or registered trademarks of Sybase, Inc. Sybase is an SAP company.

SAP AG is neither the author nor the publisher of this publication and is not responsible for its content. SAP Group shall not be liable for errors or omissions with respect to the materials. The only warranties for SAP Group products and services are those that are set forth in the express warranty statements accompanying such products and services, if any. Nothing herein should be construed as constituting an additional warranty.

This book is dedicated to my beloved wife, Sharmistha,
and my two precious angels, Seejal and Sheetal.

CONTENTS

PREFACE

This book is unique because of the following characteristics:

- Designed as a quick reference that covers the major sub-modules of financial accounting, controlling, and financial supply chain management;

- Covers the components you need to configure for a variety of projects and how to get results;

- Includes concepts of SAP® General Ledger (formally called New GL) and its configuration requirements;

- Covers configuration and use of financial supply chain management;

- Provides coverage of the most popular business processes and practices;

- Includes concise instructions and tips with a self-testing, question and answer format

We have divided the entire book into following chapters:

Chapter 1: An Overview of SAP® ERP Financials: Chapter 1 describes an overview of SAP applications and its components. Being a beginner to SAP you will come to know the various applications and components that are available in SAP;

Chapter 2: Financial Accounting and Controlling: Chapter 2 contains in detail SAP® FICO (Financial Information and Controlling) and its components. This chapter depicts many configuration steps and also guides users about the proper use of FICO components;

Chapter 3: SAP® General Ledger: Starting with mySAP® ERP ECC 5.0 and now in 6.0, SAP introduced SAP® General Ledger (previously called *New General Ledger*). In SAP General Ledger, SAP has packaged different components of the SAP applications in a single platform. This chapter provides a good understanding of SAP General Ledger and its configuration requirements;

Chapter 4: Financial Supply Chain Management: SAP® Financial Supply Chain Management takes care of various missing bridges of effective cash collection processes in the accounts receivable component of SAP financial accounting;

Chapter 5: Business Processes: This chapter depicts various business processes and the steps involved to carry out the transactions in SAP ERP Financials. These business processes involve various SAP modules and provide a very good functional knowledge about financial accounting, as well as controlling users and consultants;

Chapter 6: Reporting: This chapter starts with various reporting tools available in SAP for financial accounting and controlling, and ends with report writer and report painter functionality of SAP ERP Financials. Report writer and report painter provide functionality to build user-oriented documents with little technical knowledge.

We hope you will enjoy this book and be successful using SAP products.

S. Padhi
September, 2012

CHAPTER 1

AN OVERVIEW TO SAP® ERP FINANCIALS

In This Chapter

1.1 SAP and Its Products

SAP® Business Suite is an integrated application that enables enterprise to execute business processes and optimize resources. SAP Business Suite is designed to perform business-specific functions and work with other SAP and non-SAP products.

SAP Business Suite application provides industry specific solutions and comes with the following core solutions.

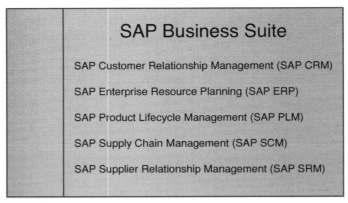

FIGURE 1.1 SAP Business Suite.

SAP® Customer Relationship Management (CRM)

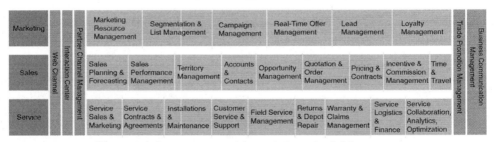

FIGURE 1.2 mySAP™ CRM solution map.© Copyright 2012. SAP AG. All rights reserved.

Customers are the most valuable asset of any business. One of today's most significant business challenges is retaining old customers while finding new customers.

SAP CRM Solution includes:

- Marketing
- Sales
- Service
- Contract center
- E-Commerce

SAP® Enterprise Resource Planning (ERP)

	End-User Service Delivery			
Analytics	Strategic Enterprise Management	Financial Analytics	Operations Analytics	Workforce Analytics
Financials	Financial Supply Chain Management	Financial Accounting	Management Accounting	Corporate Governance
Human Capital Management	Talent Management	Workforce Process Management		Workforce Deployment
Procurement and Logistics Execution	Procurement	Supplier Collaboration	Inventory and Warehouse Management	Inbound and Outbound Logistics / Transportation Management
Product Development and Manufacturing	Production Planning	Manufacturing Execution	Enterprise Asset Management	Product Development / Life-Cycle Date Management
Sales and Services	Sales Order Management	Aftermarket Sales and Service	Professional Service Delivery	Global Trade Services / Incentive and Commission Management
Corporate Services	Real Estate Management	Project Portfolio Management	Travel Management	Environment, Health, and Safety / Quality Management

FIGURE 1.3 mySAP™ ERP roadmap. © Copyright 2012. SAP AG. All rights reserved.

With the help of SAP ERP, a component of the SAP Business Suite, companies can improve their business process using the following elements:

- *SAP® ERP Financials* is comprehensive integrated financial management software that empowers finance and costing departments. Later in this book we will discuss Financial Information and Controlling (FICO) and Financial Supply Control Management (FSCM) component of SAP ERP Financials.

- *SAP® ERP Human Capital Management* is an integrated and complete solution for human resource processes.

- *SAP® ERP Operations* helps achieve operational excellence in key business areas such as procurement, logistic execution, product development, manufacturing, sales, and service.

- *SAP® ERP Corporate Services* application increases efficiency by providing solutions to corporate service functions.

SAP® Product Lifecycle Management (PLM)

Product Management	Product Strategy and Planning	Product Portfolio Management	Innovation Management	Requirements Management	Market Launch Management
Product Development and Collaboration	Engineering, R&D Collaboration	Supplier Collaboration	Manufacturing Collaboration	Service and Maintenance Collaboration	Product Quality Management	Product Change Management
Product Data Management	Product Master and Structure Management	Specification and Recipe Management	Service and Maintenance Structure Management	Visualization and Publications	Configuration Management
PLM Foundation	Product Compliance	Product Intelligence	Product Costing	Tool and Workgroup Integration	Project and Resource Management	Document Management

SAP NetWeaver

FIGURE 1.4 mySAP™ PLM solution map.

SAP PLM is part of the business suite, which gives organizations the unique ability to perform their essential business processes with modular software that is designed to work with other SAP and non-SAP software. In SAP PLM, one can:

- ▪ Create and deliver innovative products
- ▪ Optimize product development process
- ▪ Become more agile than one's competitors

SAP® Supply Chain Management (SCM)

Strategic Planning	Strategic Supply Chain Design			Strategic Sourcing	
Demand Planning	Forecasting & Lifecycle Planning		Promotion Planning	Consensus Demand Planning	
Supply Planning	Safety Stock Planning	Supply Network Planning & Outsourcing	Distribution Planning	Customer Collaboration	Supplier Collaboration
Procurement	Purchase Order Processing		Receipt Confirmation	Invoice Verification	
Manufacturing	Production Planning & Detailed Scheduling			Manufacturing Execution	
Warehousing	Inbound Processing	Outbound Processing	Cross Docking	Warehousing & Storage	Physical Inventory
Order Fulfillment	Sales Order Processing		Logistics Coordination	Billing	
Transportation	Transportation Planning		Transportation Execution	Freight Costing	
Visibility	Procurement Visibility	Manufacturing Visibility	Fulfillment Visibility	Transportation Visibility	Supply Chain Analytics

FIGURE 1.5 mySAP™ SCM solution map. © Copyright 2012. SAP AG. All rights reserved.

The SAP SCM solution automates customer-centric business processes across many aspects of an organization's operation. The SAP SCM application is a complete supply chain management application that enables collaboration, planning, execution, and coordination that empowers companies to adapt their supply chain process in an ever-changing and competitive environment.

SAP® Supplier Relationship Management (SRM)

Purchasing Governance	Global Spend Analysis		Category Management		Compliance Management
Sourcing	Central Sourcing Hub		RFx / Auctioning		Bid Evaluation & Awarding
Contract Management	Legal Contract Repository	Contract Authority	Contract Negotiation	Contract Execution	Contract Monitoring
Collaborative Procurement	Self-Service Procurement		Services Procurement	Direct / Plan-Driven Procurement	Catalog Content Management
Supplier Collaboration	Web-based Supplier Interaction		Direct Document Exchange		Supplier Network
Supply Base Management	Supplier Identification & Onboarding		Supplier Development & Performance Management		Supplier Portfolio Management

(SAPNetWeaver)

FIGURE 1.6 mySAP™ SRM solution map. © Copyright 2012. SAP AG. All rights reserved.

The SAP SRM application automates, simplifies, and accelerates procure-to-pay processes for goods and services. With SAP SRM, you can reduce procurement costs, build collaborative supplier relationships, better manage supply bases, and improve your bottom line with innovative offerings and a faster turnaround time to the market.

Along with that core solution, SAP has developed the following industry specific modules to cater to business specific requirements:

- Financial and public services
  - Banking
  - Defense and security
  - Healthcare
  - Higher education and research

- Insurance
- Public sector

- Manufacturing
  - Aerospace and defense
  - Automotive
  - Chemicals
  - Consumer products
  - Engineering, construction, and operations
  - High tech
  - Industrial machinery and components
  - Life sciences
  - Mill products
  - Mining
  - Oil and gas

- Service
  - Media
  - Professional services
  - Retail
  - Telecommunications
  - Travel and logistics services
  - Utilities
  - Wholesale distribution

Like other ERP packages, SAP is also a complex ERP in order to meet various business requirements as well as country-specific requirements. While no ERP can cover 100% of organizations' business requirements, SAP covers the standard functionality of almost all countries. The difference between the business requirements and functionality available within a ERP is called GAP. A customer chooses ERP, which reduces this GAP.

To meet business requirements, we now have two options:

1. When functionality is available, configure the system.

2. When functionality is not available, either we can customize or change the business process.

In this book, we will cover SAP ERP Financials FICO (**FI** – Financial Information & **CO** – Controlling, now commonly known as Management Accounting and FSCM.

CHAPTER 2

FINANCIAL ACCOUNTING AND CONTROLLING

In This Chapter

2.1 SAP® FICO

SAP® FICO is also mentioned as SAP FI/CO, where FI stands for *Financial Accounting* and CO stands for *Controlling*, now referred to as *Management Accounting*. There are two target groups that use accounting information:

1. *External users*: These users typically require information that conforms to legal requirements. This data is managed in the application component FI. Groups that would fall under this category are the federal government, state governments, financial institutions, and insurance providers.

2. *Internal users*: These users come from all levels within the company. They need information for the internal operations of the company. This information is contained in the application component CO.

The FI module is used to monitor and review the financial statements of a given entity. Financial reports used for external reporting purposes (such as balance sheets, profit and loss calculations, and cash flows) are created in FI. These external reporting requirements are based on the varying legal requirements set by the relevant financial authorities, usually prescribed through general accounting standards such as Generally Accepted Accounting Principles (GAAP) or International Accounting Standards (IAS). The FI module is called external accounting because it focuses on external reporting.

The application component CO contains all the functions for effective controlling of cost and revenue of an entity. CO covers all aspects of management. It is management oriented and management driven. It offers a broad spectrum of tools that can be used to compile information for the company management, which greatly exceeds that required by law.

Table 2.1 shows the differences between FI and CO modules.

TABLE 2.1

FI	CO
1. Reporting: Module generates reports	
Financial statements such as balance sheets, income statement, and cash flow statements.	Control reports such as cost center reports, profit center reports, and actual and plan reports.
2. Modules: Covers following sub-modules	
AA (Assets Accounting)	CEL(Cost Element Accounting)
AP (Accounts Payable)	CCA(Cost Center Accounting)
AR (Accounts Receivable)	IO(Internal Order)
BL(Bank Ledger)	ABC(Activity-Based Costing)
FM (Fund Management)	PC(Product Costing)
GL (General Ledger Accounting)	PA (Profitability Analysis)
LC (Legal Consolidation)	PCA (Profit Center Accounting) In SAP® G/L, this submodule form is part of FI.
SPL (Special Purpose Ledger)	
TM (Travel Management)	

TABLE 2.1 (*continued*)

FI	CO
3. Governing rules: Modules governed by International Accounting standards	
Country specific accounting rules such as US GAAP, UK GAAP, and India GAAP.	No such rule. Driven by management.
4. Organization Entities: Modules include following SAP Organization structure.	
– Company code	– Controlling area
	– Operating concern

The FI module comes with the following submodules. You will learn more about sub-modules later in this book.

The *General Ledger (FI-G/L)* records all relevant accounting transactions from a business point of view in the G/L accounts. In order to retain a clear overview, the G/L often contains collective postings. In such cases, the information posted is displayed in more detail in the subsidiary ledgers, which provide their information to the G/L in summarized form.

Accounts Payable (FI-AP) records all financial transactions with your vendor. This module often gets it data from procurement or Materials Management (MM).

Accounts Receivable (FI-AR) records all financial transactions for dealings with customers. Much of its data is obtained from Sales and Distribution.

Asset Accounting (FI-AA) records all accounting transactions relating to the management of assets starting from acquisition of assets to the sale or scrap of an asset. This submodule interacts with FI-AP, FI-AR, and G/L of FI modules, as well as MM modules.

Travel Management (FI-TM) manages, calculates, and supports travel costs, travel planning, and travel expenses. This submodule is tightly integrated with SAP HR and FI-AP because employees in SAP are treated as vendors.

Bank Ledger (FI-BL) supports the posting of cash flow, cash payments, and cash receipts.

All transactions posted to G/L expenses and revenue account directly or indirectly flow to controlling. Similarly, when cross object transactions happen between controlling objects, the system creates and FI posting. Figure 2.1 shows data flows between various submodules of FI.

Like FI, CO covers following submodules. However, we will cover those in more detail later in the book.

Cost and Revenue Element Accounting [CO-OM-CEL] is part of Overhead Cost Controlling. It provides classification of transaction items. These transactions are captured in various cost objects, such as a cost center or an internal order, depending on their cost or revenue element.

Cost Center Accounting (CO-CCA) is used for cost collection and provides information about where costs are incurred in your organization.

An *Internal Order (CO-IO)* is another kind of cost object used for a wide variety of purposes to capture costs and, in some cases, revenues within a controlling area.

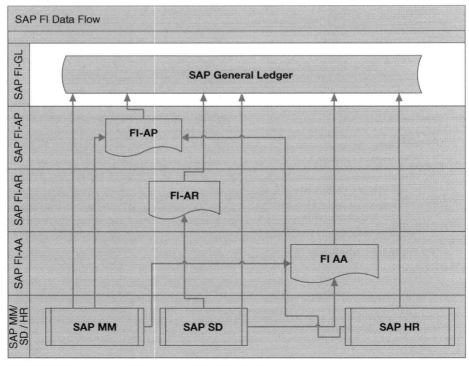

FIGURE 2.1 FI data flows. © Copyright 2012. SAP AG. All rights reserved.

Product Costing (CO-PC) takes care of all aspects of a product, from planning to tracking of costs. This submodule consists of following components:

- Product Cost Planning (CO-PC-PCP)

- Cost Object Controlling

- Actual Costing

If you are looking for multidimensional reporting tool, then *Profitability Analysis (CO-PA)* is the best solution. Through profitability analysis you can analyze market segments and profitability measures.

2.2 FI Enterprise Structure (SAP® FI-ES)

For external reporting, enterprise generates various statutory or mandatory reports, which are further driven by country and business specific requirements. As these reports are accessible to the public and refer to various segments of the user group, reports should be precise, understandable, and should comply with legal requirements.

In order to have efficient reporting in the initial stage of SAP implementation, you must lay down a FI foundation that is called FI Enterprise Structure. In this section, we will deal with various forms of organization within this foundation, their meanings, and how you can best use them.

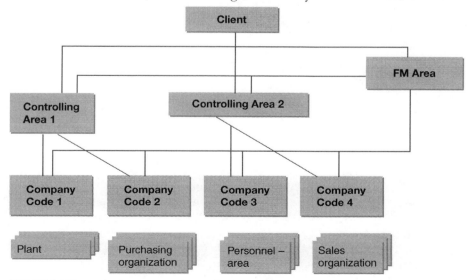

FIGURE 2.2 FI organization structure.Source: http://
help.sap.com/saphelp_46c/helpdata/en/b9/3e9d73417c11d189400000e829fbbd/content.htm

2.2.1 Client

- In mySAP™ ERP the client is the highest level of organization entity. When you are logging into the SAP system, you are entering as the client. All data and specifications are created or configured at client level. This minimizes duplicate data entry and maintenance of data. In an SAP server you can have multiple clients. Each one is an independent unit with separate master records and complete set of tables.

2.2.2 Company Code

- A company code is an independent balancing and legal entity from which you will generate balance sheets and income statements. All financial statements are created at company code level, therefore company code is the minimum structure required in mySAP™ ERP Financials. When a corporation is doing business in different countries, as per the country-specific law, entity needs to be registered in that country. In SAP, this is called a company code. In SAP, you can create a new company code or edit company code by doing the following:

  - ***Transaction Code***: OX02

    Or

  - ***R/3 IMG Menu***: IMG → Enterprise Structure → Financial Accounting → Edit, Copy, Delete, Check Company Code → Edit Company Code Data

    Or

  - ***mySAP ERP IMG Menu***: IMG → Enterprise Structure → Financial Accounting → Edit, Copy, Delete, Check Company Code → Edit Company Code Data

Question – 1

Name the organizational entities for which the profit and loss statement and balance sheet can be generated.

A. Company code

B. Profit center

C. Internal order

D. Cost center and profit center

2.2.3 Business Area

▪ Business area in SAP refers to a separate organizational unit meant for internal purposes that can be used across company codes within a client. If business areas balance sheet is active in transaction code OBY6 (menu path IMG → *Financial Accounting* → *Financial Accounting Global Settings* → *Company Code* → *Enter Global Parameters*), you can generate business area-wide balance sheet. To use business area, you first need to create a set of business areas that you are going to use. You can create by following either:

- *Transaction Code*: *SPRO*

  Or

- *R/3 IMG Menu*: *IMG → Enterprise Structure → Financial Accounting → Edit, Copy, Delete, Check Company Code → Edit Company Code Data*

  Or

- *mySAP ERP IMG Menu*: *IMG → Enterprise Structure → Financial Accounting → Edit, Copy, Delete, Check Company Code → Edit Company Code Data*

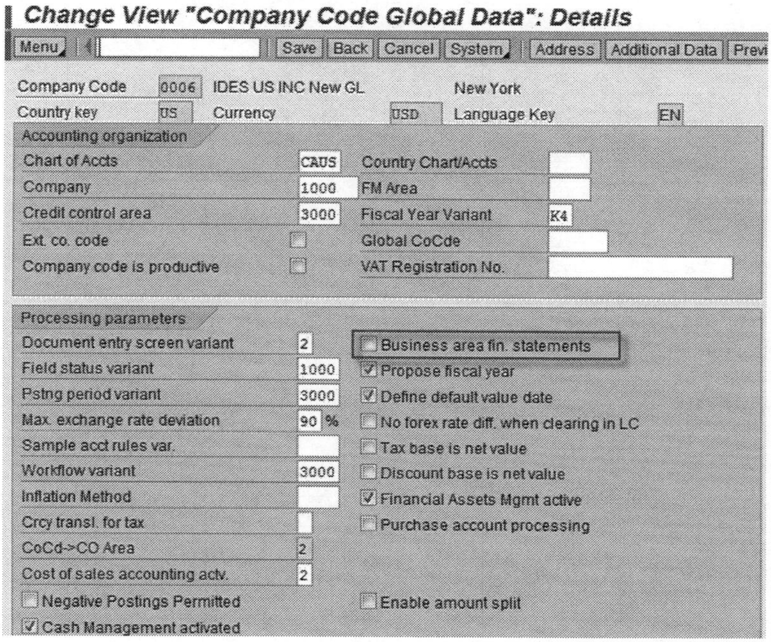

FIGURE 2.3 OBY6 company code global setting.

Question – 2

Business area is a legal entity for which you need to generate financial statements:

1. True

2. False

2.2.4 Fiscal Year

- Fiscal year (also known as financial year or accounting year) is a set of periods used to calculate legal entities' financial reports, such as balance sheet, income statement, and cash flow statement. The fiscal year of an entity does not coincide with calendar year. Figure 2.4 shows some of the commonly used fiscal years in various countries.

Year (an example ➜)		2011												2012										
Months	Jan	Feb	Mar	Apr	May	Jun	Jul	Aug	Sep	Oct	Nov	Dec	Jan	Feb	Mar	Apr	May	Jun	Jul	Aug	Sep	Oct	Nov	Dec
Posting Period ➜	1	2	3	4	5	6	7	8	9	10	11	12	1	2	3	4	5	6	7	8	9	10	11	12
Country⬇																								
United States of America																								
India (Income Tax Act)																								
India (Companies Act)❶																								
Australia																								
Canada																								
Hong Kong																								
China																								
Germany																								
Portugal																								
Taiwan																								
Egypt																								
Ireland																								
Japan (Government)																								
Japan(Non-Government)																								
New Zealand (Government)																								
New Zealand (Non-Government)																								
United Kingdom																								

❶ Law has not defined the start of the fiscal year, however fiscal year should consist 12 months

FIGURE 2.4 Country and fiscal year.

- In SAP, you will define fiscal year as a variant called fiscal year variant (FYV), which contains the definition of normal and special posting period. SAP comes with a few pre-delivered fiscal year, however, you can create your own fiscal year by doing the following:

  - ***Transaction Code***: OB29

    Or

- **R/3 IMG Menu**: *Implementation Guide (IMG) → Financial Accounting → Financial Accounting Global Settings → Fiscal year → Maintain Fiscal Year Variant (Maintain short end Fisc. year)*

  Or

- **mySAP ERP IMG Menu**: *Implementation Guide (IMG) → Financial Accounting (New) → Financial Accounting Global Settings (New) → Ledgers → Fiscal Year and Posting Periods → Maintain Fiscal Year Variant (Maintain short end Fisc. year)*

FV	Description	Year-depend	Calendar yr	Number of posting	No. of special peri
01	Calendar year, 4 spec. pe	☐	☑	12	4
IN	Calendar year, 4 spec. pe	☐	☑	12	4
K0	Calendar year, 1 spec. pe	☐	☑	12	
K1	Calendar year, 1 spec. pe	☐	☐	12	1
K2	Calendar year, 2 spec. pe	☑	☑	12	2
K3	Calendar year, 3 spec. pe	☐	☐	8	3
K4	Calendar year, 4 spec. pe	☐	☑	12	4
K5	Calendar year, 1 spec. pe	☐	☑	12	1
K6	Calendar year, 4 spec. pe	☐	☑	12	4
K7	Calendar year, 4 spec. pe	☐	☑	12	4
K8	Calendar year, 1 spec. pe	☐	☑	12	1
K9	Calendar year, 4 spec. pe	☐	☑	12	4

FIGURE 2.5 OB29 fiscal year variant.

- In total you can define 16 posting periods (12 normal posting periods, 4 special posting periods).

  - Normal Posting Period
  - Special Posting Period

- The system derives the posting period from the posting date. If the posting date is within the last normal period, you can post the transactions in one of the special periods.

- A fiscal year can be defined as a calendar fiscal year or as a non-calendar fiscal year.

- If the fiscal year's normal posting periods are the same months of the calendar year, then fiscal year is called *calendar year*. In other words, if the fiscal year is defined as the calendar year, the posting periods are equal to the months of the year. For example, in the standard SAP system K4 is a calendar fiscal year.

- For calendar year, you need to check the indicator "Calendar year" against the fiscal. This ensures that you do not need to maintain additional parameters of fiscal year.

Fiscal year variants				
FV	Description	Year-depend	Calendar yr	Number of posting
K4	Calendar year, 4 spec. periods	☐	☑	12

- If each fiscal year of a fiscal year variant has the same number of posting periods and always starts and ends on the same day of the year, then the fiscal year is an *independent fiscal year*. Otherwise, the fiscal year is designated as *year dependent*.

- All calendar fiscal years are year independent; however non-calendar fiscal years may or may not year dependent.

- In case of a non-calendar fiscal year, you can define the start and end of posting periods by assigning end dates to each period.

- You can define a year dependent period year by checking "Year-dependent" against the designated fiscal year.

- If one fiscal year is less than 12 normal postings, that fiscal year is called *shorten fiscal year*. A shorten fiscal year is always year dependent and followed or succeeded by a complete fiscal year. When you want to close your account before or after completion of fiscal year, that fiscal year would be called shorten fiscal year.

Case Study 2.1

Company B acquires Company A. Company B follows calendar year as fiscal year, while Company A follows April–March fiscal year. In order to facilitate smooth consolidation, Company B directs Company A to follow calendar fiscal year. In this situation, Company A will end its accounting year in December 2011 instead of March 2011. In this case, Company A prepares its financial statement after 9 months.

- Since fiscal year is a variant, you need to assign fiscal year variant to company codes. You can assign only one fiscal year variant to each company, however, a fiscal year variant can be assigned to more than one company code. You can assign a fiscal year variant to company code by using the following:

  - *Transaction Code*: OBBP

    Or

- **R/3 IMG Menu**: *Implementation Guide (IMG)* → *Financial Accounting* → *Financial Accounting Global Settings* → *Document* → *Fiscal Year* → *Assign Company Code to a Fiscal Year Variant*

    Or

- **mySAP ERP IMG Menu**: *Implementation Guide (IMG)* → *Financial Accounting (New)* → *Financial Accounting Global Settings (New)* → *Ledgers* → *Fiscal Year and Posting Periods* → *Posting Periods* → *Assign Variants to Company Code*

2.2.5 Posting Period

- Posting periods are defined in the fiscal year variants as *Posting Period Variant (PPV)* and used to differentiate business transaction from one period to the next.

- You can open and close posting period in order to prevent an unintended entry by the user group. Normally, the current posting period will be open at a particular point of time. At the end of each month, current and previous posting are open for posting.

- You can control open and close posting period with the combination of an account number range and account types.

- Similar to fiscal year, variant posting period variant is created at client level. You can assign posting period variant to any number company code in a client.

- If one posting period variant is assigned to more than one company code, you can control the opening and closing of posting periods simultaneously. This is suitable for centralizing the closing at the end of the month.

Change View "Posting Periods: Specify Time Intervals": Overview

New Entries

Var.	A	From acct	To account	From per.1	Year	To period	Year	From per.2	Year	To period	Year	AuGr
1000	+			1	2005	12	2012	13	2005	16	2012	
1000	A	1	ZZZZZZZZZZ	1	2005	12	2012	13	2005	16	2012	
1000	D	1	ZZZZZZZZZZ	1	2005	12	2012	13	2005	16	2012	
1000	K	1	ZZZZZZZZZZ	1	2005	12	2012	13	2005	16	2012	
1000	M	1	ZZZZZZZZZZ	1	2005	12	2012	13	2005	16	2012	
1000	S	1	ZZZZZZZZZZ	1	2005	12	2012	13	2005	16	2012	

FIGURE 2.6 OB52 open close posting period.

▦ Figure 2.6 shows attributes of posting period variant 1,000. While posting an FI transaction, whether it is originated in FI or other modules, system checks posting period variant at at document header level and at line item level.

▦ Document level check: Document header level check is the first level check initiated by the system with posting period and fiscal year assigned to posting period variant. Document level check does not check account types and account number ranges. Ensure that the document level check account type field is masked by "+." The posting period variant must contain at least one account type with "+" symbol.

▦ Every FI posting first passes through document level check to reach the second level check. At the second level check, line items are checked against account number range maintained in the "From account" and "To account" range, as well as against the fiscal year and posting period range.

▦ Second level check, or line item level check, is optional.

▦ You can authorize a specific group of person for posting to a particular posting period by assigning authorization group to the period interval(s) and user(s).

▦ Creation, maintenance of posting period, and its assignment to company code involves three steps:

- Define variants for open posting periods

- Open and close posting periods

- Assign variants to company code

▦ You can carry out these steps through:

- ***Transaction Code***: .....

    ...... *Define Variants for Open Posting Periods – OBBO*

    ....*Open and Close Posting Periods – OB52*

    ....*Assign Variants to Company Code – OBBP*

    Or

- **R/3 IMG Menu**: *Implementation Guide (IMG)* → *Financial Accounting* → *Financial Accounting Global Settings* → *Document* → *Posting Periods* →

  …..*Define Variants for Open Posting Periods*

  …..*Open and Close Posting Periods*

  …..*Assign variants to company code*

  Or

- **mySAP ERP IMG Menu**: *Implementation Guide (IMG)* → *Financial Accounting (New)* → *Financial Accounting Global Settings (New)* → *Ledgers* → *Fiscal Year and Posting Periods* → *Posting Periods* →

  ……..*Define Variants for Open Posting Periods*

  ……..*Assign Variants to Company Code*

  ……..*Open and Close Posting Periods*

- When entering a document you are entering a posting date. The posting date determines posting period and fiscal year.

2.2.6 Currency

- While creating company code, you need to define currency code for the company code. This currency is called *company code currency* or *local currency* in SAP, and all other currencies are interpreted as *foreign currency*. While entering a transaction, the system defaults currency code from the relevant company code. You can override the system default currency code by entering another currency (called as a *document currency*) and then the system translates the amount posted in foreign currency into company code currency.

- To translate transactions from foreign currencies into local currencies, the system uses currency translation rates. You can maintain currency transaction rates between currencies by following either of the following paths for exchange rate types:

  - **Transaction Code**: *SPRO*

    Or

- **R/3 IMG Menu**: *Implementation Guide (IMG) → SAP NetWeaver → General Settings → Currencies → Enter exchange rates*

  Or

- **mySAP ERP IMG Menu**: *Implementation Guide (IMG) → SAP NetWeaver → General Settings → Currencies → Enter exchange rates*

▪ Through exchange rate types, you can maintain different exchange rates for the same set of currencies.

▪ In SAP, exchanges rates are used for various purposes such as valuation of foreign currency transactions, translation of foreign currency transaction into local currencies, and planning.

▪ You can maintain relationships between currencies daily, monthly, and yearly. As maintenance of exchange rates is normal business practice, SAP has provided various tools in order to facilitate user communities. The tools include inversion, base currency, and exchange rate spread.

For each type of exchange rate, you can use any one of the methods listed previously. However, you can also use different conversion tools for different exchange rate types.

▪ Besides the previously mentioned maintenance tools, SAP has provided:

  - Program RFTBFF00 to import flat file directly into system.

  - Program RFTBDF07 and RFTBDF14 can be used with help of RFC (Remote Function Call) to transfer real-time data from external system into SAP.

▪ *Base Currency:* If you are adopting this tool, then you need to assign base currency to a exchange rate type, and then maintain this exchange rate between all other currency and base currency. The system will automatically calculate translation base currency and another currency.

▪ *Exchange Rate Spread*: Exchange rate spread is a link between the buying/selling rate and the average rate of two currencies. If you maintain exchange rate spread for exchange rate type, then you need to only maintain the average rate. Based on exchange rate, a spread system will calculate the buying/selling rate by adding and subtracting exchange rate spread to and from the average rate.

  - **Transaction Code**: *SPRO*

    Or

- **R/3 IMG Menu**: *Implementation Guide (IMG)* → *SAP NetWeaver* → *General Settings* → *Currencies* → *Maintain Exchange Rate Spreads*

  Or

- **mySAP ERP IMG Menu**: *Implementation Guide (IMG)* → *SAP NetWeaver* → *General Settings* → *Currencies* → *Maintain Exchange Rate Spreads*

▨ You can maintain exchange rates between two currencies through either direct quotation or indirect quotation, depending on business practice and market standards.

▨ In the case of direct quotation, one unit of foreign currency is quoted for the local currency, whereas in the case of indirect quotation, one unit of local currency is quoted for the foreign currency. For example, company code currency is USD and foreign currency is INR. When you are expressing the exchange rate between INR and USD it is called direct quotation. For example, 1 INR=0.02 USD. On the other hand, when you are expressing the exchange rate between USD and INR it is called indirect quotation. For example, 1 USD=45 INR.

- **Transaction Code**: *SPRO*

  Or

- **R/3 IMG Menu**: *Implementation Guide (IMG)* → *SAP NetWeaver* → *General Settings* → *Currencies* → *Enter Prefixes for Direct/Indirect Quotation Exchange Rates*

  Or

- **mySAP ERP IMG Menu**: *Implementation Guide (IMG)* → *SAP NetWeaver* → *General Settings* → *Currencies* → *Enter Prefixes for Direct/Indirect Quotation Exchange Rates*

Question – 3

Exchange rate types distinguish the exchanges to be considered for various purposes such as valuation, transaction, conversion, planning, etc.

1. True

2. False

Question – 4

The currency key you entered in the document header is for

A. The whole document

B. Each line item

C. A group of line items

D. None of the above

Question – 5

The local currency of a transaction

A. Can be entered by the user

B. Is always the company code currency

C. Is the currency of the chart of accounts

D. Is determined by the country field in the customer/vendor masters

Question – 6

Field status variants are company code dependent.

A. True

B. False

2.3 General Ledger (SAP® FI G/L)

2.3.1 Chart of Account

- Like fiscal year, *Chart of Account (CoA)* is also a variant created at client level, identified by a four character ID. CoA contains basic information of general ledger such as language, length of G/L account numbers, and creation of cost element. The length of a G/L number can be 1 to 10 characters.

- CoA must be assigned to every company code for which a general ledger master will be created. A CoA can be assigned to any number of company codes in a particular client.

■ In SAP, you will find several types of CoA: operational chart account, group chart of account, and country chart of account. A CoA can be classified as a group CoA, operational CoA, or country CoA.

■ The CoA assigned to company code is known as an *operational CoA*. While posting transactions, you choose a G/L account master record of operational CoA. You can assign a CoA to company code through any of the following:

- **Transaction Code**: OB62

  Or

- **R/3 IMG Menu**: *Implementation Guide (IMG) → Financial Accounting → General Ledger Accounting → G/L Accounts → Master Data → Preparations → Assign Company Code to Chart of Accounts*

  Or

- **mySAP ERP IMG Menu**: *Implementation Guide (IMG) → Financial Accounting (New) → General Ledger Accounting (New) → Master Data → G/L Accounts → Preparations → Assign Company Code to Chart of Accounts*

■ The CoA which is assigned to an operational CoA is called a *Group CoA*. You can assign a CoA to operational CoA through any of the following methods:

- **Transaction Code**: OB13

  Or

- **R/3 IMG Menu**: *Implementation Guide (IMG) → Financial Accounting → General Ledger Accounting → G/L Accounts → Master Data → Preparations → Edit Chart of Accounts List*

  Or

- **mySAP ERP IMG Menu:** *Implementation Guide (IMG) → Financial Accounting (NEW) → General Ledger Accounting (New) → Master Data → G/L Accounts → Preparations → Edit Chart of Accounts List.*

■ Figure 2.7 depicts the definition of an "INT" CoA. In the Figure 2.7 sample:

- The length of G/L account is 10.

- The maintenance language of the chart of account is "English."

- The integration will be a manual primary cost element for the relevant G/L account.

- The group CoA will be "CONS."

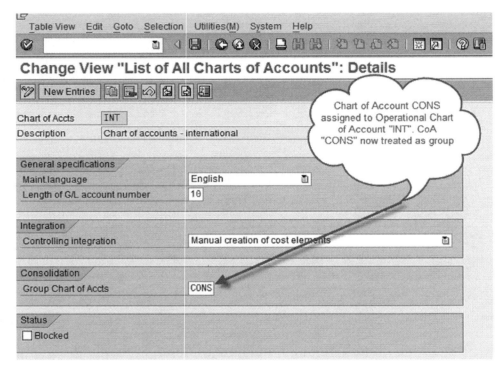

FIGURE 2.7 T.Code: OB13 chart of account definition.

- The block indicator is used to prevent the user from using this CoA. If the check box is active, you can't create a G/L account under this CoA. A block indicator is generally used when the CoA is not ready for use.

- If you enter a group CoA in the CoA, the system expects you to enter a group account number in the corresponding field in the G/L account definition, which becomes the required entry field.

Question – 7

You can assign a company code with

A. Three chart of accounts

B. Two charts of accounts

C. Only one chart of account

D. A chart of account called as operating chart of account

Question – 8

Which of the following statements is true? (multiple answers)

A. One company code can use multiple charts of accounts.

B. One chart of accounts can be used by multiple company codes.

C. A company code can have multiple operational chart of account.

2.3.2 Retained Earnings Account

▪ In customizing, you define at least one retained earnings account for your chart of account. When you define one retained account while creating a G/L master record, the system automatically assigns a retained earning account to a G/L account. If you define more than one retained earnings account, the system allows you to choose the right retained earning account for G/L account. You can define retained earnings account through either:

- *Transaction Code*: OB53

  Or

- *R/3 IMG Menu*: Implementation Guide (IMG) → Financial Accounting → General Ledger Accounting → G/L accounts → Master Records → Preparations → Define Retained Earnings Account

  Or

- *mySAP ERP IMG Menu*: Implementation Guide (IMG) → Financial Accounting (New)→ General Ledger Accounting (New) → Master Data → G/L Accounts → Preparations → Define Retained Earnings Account

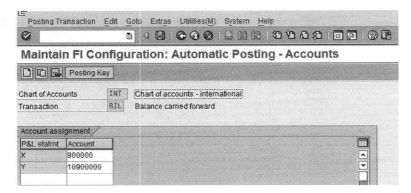

FIGURE 2.8 T.Code: OB53 retained earning account.

▪ As Figure 2.8 shows, we defined two retained account X – 900,000 and Y – 1,090,000, where X represents a retained account identifier and the corresponding G/L account is "9,0000."

▪ When you create a G/L account master under CoA "INT," the system expects that you will choose a retained account, i.e. either "X" or "Y."

Question – 9

The P & L accounts balance is transferred to a retained earnings account. You determine the retained earning account as part of the selection criteria when executing the Balance Carry Forward program.

A. True

B. False

2.3.3 Account Groups

▪ In order to facilitate the grouping of accounts that have the same attributes, you define account groups. You need to define at least two account groups: balance sheets accounts and income statement accounts. You can define G/L account groups through either:

• ***Transaction Code***: *OBD4*

    Or

• ***R/3 IMG Menu:*** *Implementation Guide (IMG) → Financial Accounting (New) → General Ledger Accounting (New) → Master Data → G/L Accounts → Preparations → Define Account Group.*

Or

- ***mySAP ERP IMG Menu:*** *R/3 menu Path: Implementation Guide (IMG) → Financial Accounting → General Ledger Accounting (New) → Master Data → G/L Accounts → Preparations → Define Account Group.*

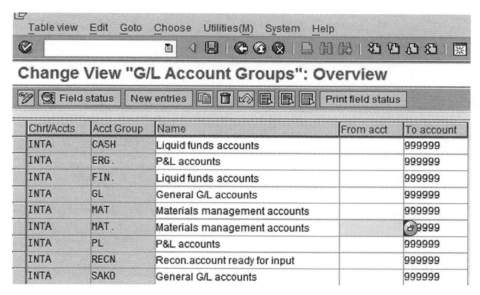

Chrt/Accts	Acct Group	Name	From acct	To account
INTA	CASH	Liquid funds accounts		999999
INTA	ERG.	P&L accounts		999999
INTA	FIN.	Liquid funds accounts		999999
INTA	GL	General G/L accounts		999999
INTA	MAT	Materials management accounts		999999
INTA	MAT.	Materials management accounts		999999
INTA	PL	P&L accounts		999999
INTA	RECN	Recon.account ready for input		999999
INTA	SAKO	General G/L accounts		999999

FIGURE 2.9 T.Code: OBD4 G/L account groups.

- Figure 2.9 demonstrates how various account groups are maintained for chart of account INTA. While creating the G/L master under CoA INTA, you need to select one of the account group maintained for this CoA.

- Account group controls the following attributes of a G/L account master:

  - The fields displayed in the master record

  - The number range of G/L accounts. By assigning number range to account groups, you are ensuring that the same types of G/L masters are created within the defined number range.

- Like the G/L account group, you will come across customer account groups and vendor accounts groups later in this book.

Question — 10

An account group(there may be more than one answer)

A. Defines the number range for a mater record

B. Uses a field status group to control the field layout for the maintenance of master records

C. Determines one-time accounts for accounts payable and accounts receivable

D. Is defined for every company code

2.3.4 G/L Mater Number Range

- In the G/L account group, you assigned the G/L number range. While creating the G/L master you type in the new G/L number and select the appropriate account group. The system then ensures that the account group and the account number matches those defined in OBD4. Note that the number intervals of G/L master records can overlap.

2.3.5 G/L Masters

- A G/L master has two segments: the chart of account segment and the company code segment.

- *Chart of account segment* contains general information that applies to and is available to all company codes that uses that G/L account. The CoA segment contains the following tab pages:

  - *Types/Descriptions*: This tab contains short and long descriptions of the G/L master, types of G/L accounts, information on whether this G/L is a balance sheet account or an income statement, account groups it belong to, group G/L account assignments, and the default trading partner. Figure 2.10 further illustrates this tab.

- In the CoA segment, you need to specify whether the account is a balance sheet account or a profit and loss account. During the year-end closing these two account types are treated differently. Balance sheet accounts are carried over to next year to the same account, while profit and loss accounts of the net balance are carried over to retain earning account.

  - *Key works/Translation*: In this tab, you will maintain the key words of the G/L account in other languages.

Change G/L Account Chart of accts data

G/L Account 98100 Accrued interest
Chart of Accts INT Chart of accounts - internatio   w. Template

| Type/Description | Key word/translation | Information |

Control in chart of accounts

| Account Group | General G/L accounts |
Sample account
○ P&L statement acct

   Detailed control for P&L statement accounts
   P&L statmt acct type
   Functional Area

◉ Balance sheet account

Description

| Short Text | Accrued interest |
| G/L Acct Long Text | Accrued interest |

Consolidation data in chart of accounts

| Trading Partner | |
| Group account number | 140200 | Other Current Assets |

FIGURE 2.10 T.Code: FSP0 G/L master chart of account segment-type/descriptions.

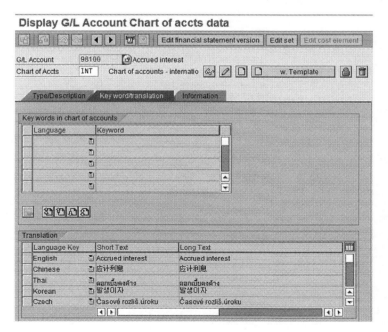

Display G/L Account Chart of accts data

G/L Account 98100 Accrued interest
Chart of Accts INT Chart of accounts - internatio   w. Template

| Type/Description | Key word/translation | Information |

Key words in chart of accounts

Language	Keyword

Translation

Language Key	Short Text	Long Text	
English	Accrued interest	Accrued interest	
Chinese	应计利息	应计利息	
Thai	ดอกเบี้ยคงค้าง	ดอกเบี้ยคงค้าง	
Korean	발생이자	발생이자	
Czech	Časové rozliš.úroku	Časové rozliš.úroku	

FIGURE 2.11 T.Code: FSP0 G/L master chart of account segment-key words/translation.

- *Information*: The system automatically updates some of the fields of this tab such as created on and created by. Besides these two fields you can see that there is a button to change document. If you select the "change document" button, the system will come up with Change Log.

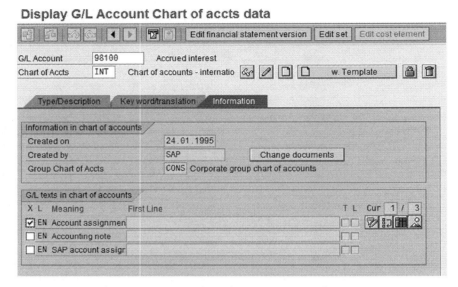

Display G/L Account Chart of accts data

FIGURE 2.12 T.Code: FSP0 G/L master chart of account segment-information.

- You can create chart of account segment using:

  - **Transaction Code**: FSP0

    Or

  - **SAP Menu:** SAP menu → Accounting → Financial Accounting → General Ledger → Master Records → G/L Accounts → Individual Processing → In Chart of Accounts.

- In order to use G/L account from the assigned chart of account, you must create a *company code segment* for that account. Adding a company code segment to the chart of account segment makes a complete G/L account. The company code segment contains information that is valid for relevant company code.

- You can create chart of account segment using:

  - **Transaction Code**: FSS0

    Or

- **R/3 IMG Menu:** *SAP menu* → *Accounting* → *Financial Accounting* → *General Ledger* → *Master Records* → *G/L Accounts* → *Individual Processing* → *In Company Code*

▪ When you execute T. Code FSP0, the system prompts you to enter company code, which brings up company-code specific information.

▪ Since each company code maintains its own company code segment data, company code data of same G/L accounts can be different for company codes using the same G/L account.

▪ Company code segment contains following tab pages:

- *Control Data*: This is one of the important tabs that controls much of information for a G/L master. A few of the important fields include account currency, whether the G/L is a reconciliation account or not, and whether line item management and open item management is active or not.

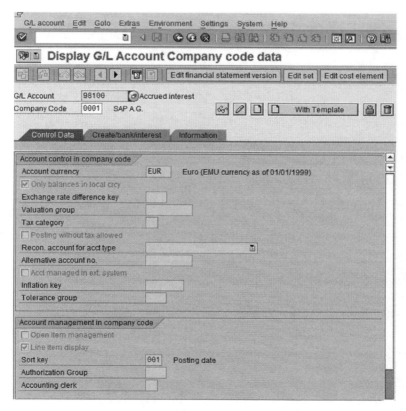

FIGURE 2.13 T. Code: FSS0 company code segment-control data.

- *Create/bank/interest*: This tab contains a few important fields relating to posting control such as:

  – Whether the manual posting is allowed

  – Field status group assignment, which controls fields ready for input while entering transactions

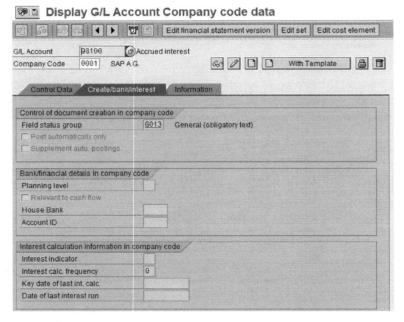

FIGURE 2.14 T. Code: FSS0 company code segment-create/bank/interest.

- *Information*: This tab holds some of the information relating to company code segment of the relevant G/L account.

▪ You can access both segments of a G/L account through either:

  - ***Transaction Code***: *FS00*

    Or

  - ***R/3 IMG Menu***: *SAP menu → Accounting → Financial Accounting → General Ledger → Master Records → G/L Accounts → Individual Processing → Centrally*

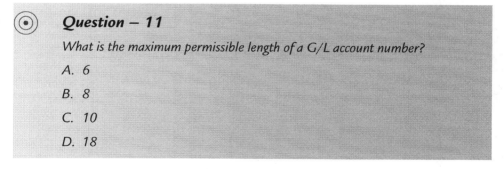

FIGURE 2.15 T. Code: FSS0 company code segment-information.

⊙ **Question – 11**

What is the maximum permissible length of a G/L account number?

A. 6

B. 8

C. 10

D. 18

2.3.6 Open Item Management

■ Open items are considered incomplete transactions that are offset by another transaction. For example, vendor invoice is an open item because this transaction will be offset by outgoing payment.

■ The balance of an open item managed account is always equal to the total of all other open items.

- The account with open item management must have line item display activated.

- You can activate or deactivate open item management when the G/L balance is zero. The activation or deactivation will have an effect on transactions posted after the activation or deactivation.

- You should activate open item management of the accounts where you are expecting an offset entry to complete the transactions, such as a:
  - Bank clearing account
  - GR IR account
  - Salary clearing account

- You can't archive a document that contains a line item with open item attributes. There are various ways you can clear a open items, such as:
  - While making an outgoing payment
  - While receiving an incoming payment
  - Through journal vouchers

- Open item clearing process always creates a clearing document. In SAP, you can see three types of clearing: post with clearing, automatic clearing, and clearing with another G/L.

- *Posting with clearing*: Normally this situation arises when you are posting incoming and outgoing payments. Incoming payments and outgoing payments clear one or more open items equal to the open items. You can carry out posting with clearing either manually or by using an automatic payment program.

- *Automatic clearing*: Automatic clearing is based on the configuration system subgroups, and clears open items of a G/L account.

- Through an automatic clearing program, you can clear open items of G/L accounts and sub-ledgers.

- All G/L accounts require that an automatic clearing process be set in configuration through either:
  - ***Transaction Code***: SPRO

    Or

- **R/3 IMG Menu:** *Implementation Guide (IMG) → Financial Accounting → General Ledger Accounting → Business Transactions → Open Item Clearing → Prepare Automatic Clearing*

  Or

- **mySAP ERP IMG Menu:** *Implementation Guide (IMG) → Financial Accounting (New) → General Ledger Accounting (New)→ Business Transactions → Open Item Clearing → Prepare Automatic Clearing*

Change View "Additional Rules For Automatic Clearing": Overview

New Entries

ChtA	AccTy	From acct	To account	Criterion 1	Criterion 2	Criterion 3	Criterion 4	Criterion
	D	1	99999999	ZUONR				
	D	A	Z	ZUONR	GSBER	VBUND		
	K	1	99999999	ZUONR				
	K	A	Z	ZUONR	GSBER	VBUND		
	S	0	999999	ZUONR	GSBER	VBUND		

FIGURE 2.16 T. Code: SPRO automatic clearing setup.

- Figure 2.16 depicts a client level automatic clearing configuration. You can make this configuration for all CoAs or a specific CoA. If you enter a CoA ID in the "ChtA" field, which is currently blank, the configuration will be specific to that CoA. The "AccTy" field contains account type indicator where D represents customer, K represents vendors, and S represents G/L accounts. The "From acct" field contains account numbers.

- The system provides five freely defined criteria to sum up open items for clearing along with the CoA and account types. If the sum of open item based on selection is zero, then the system clears those open items and creates a clearing document.

- Automatic clearing program doesn't clear:

  - Notes items

  - Statistical postings

  - Items with withholding tax entries

- *Clearing with another G/L:* In clearing with G/L type, you can clear entries of one account with credit entries of other accounts. You can reach this functionality through either:

- **Transaction Code**: F-04

   Or

- **SAP Menu**: SAP menu → Accounting → Financial Accounting → General Ledger → Posting → F-04 – Post with Clearing

---

⊙ Question – 12

What is meant by open items management in a G/L account master record?

A. Items on that account can never be cleared

B. Items on that account can be cleared

C. No balances are available for that account

D. None of the above

- mySAP ERP Financials provides a new transaction code: **FAGL_ ACTIVATE_OP** to activate the open item management attribute of a G/L master records, in case it was not activated while creating the G/L master records. This new transaction code is available from enhancement package 3 with software component EA-APPL (SAPK-60504INEAAPPL) and your activated business function FIN_GL_Cl_1. You can activate business function by using the following transaction code: **SFW5** or menu path IMG → Activate SAP ECC Extensions. Refer SAP Note: 1356457 for more functionality.

2.3.7 Line Item Management

- You can activate the line item management field in the control tab pages of the company code segment. This field controls how the transactions are updated and stored in the SAP tables.

- If this field is active, it ensures that posted line items are stored in a special index table so that you are able to see details and total transaction those are posted to the G/L accounts.

- As you are capturing additional data, you should activate this field when you don't have any other source/alternatives to get detail transactions.

- Some of G/L accounts for which you should not activate line item management include:

  - *Reconciliation accounts*: such as customer reconciliation accounts, vendor reconciliation accounts, assets reconciliation accounts and all alternative reconciliation accounts. Reconciliation accounts are control accounts. Detailed transactions are available in the subsidiary ledger.

- *Revue Accounts*: In these accounts posting happens through account determinations. In this case, detail transactions are available in the sales and distribution modules.

- *Material stock accounts*: These accounts detail inventory that is managed in material management modules.

- *Tax accounts*: When you are using an external tax system, detailed transactions are available in the external system.

▪ When creating a G/L master record, decisions have to be made about whether or not the account should be managed as a line item management. Once transactions are posted to a G/L account it is difficult and time consuming to change line item management attributes of G/L accounts.

⊚ ## Question – 13

What is meant by line item display in a G/L account master record?

A. Only line items can be displayed

B. Only balances can be displayed

C. Line items and balances can be displayed

D. None of the above

2.3.8 Account Currency

▪ When creating a G/L master record, you should select either one of the following currencies:

- Local currency – company code currency

- Foreign currency – currency other than company code currency

When you create a G/L master record, the system proposes local currency (company code currency) by default. If the account currency is local currency, the account can be posted to any currency. If the account is posted with foreign currencies, the system will translate foreign currencies into local currencies.

▪ Accounts managed in foreign currency can only be posted in foreign currency.

2.3.9 Document Concept in mySAP ERP Financials

▩ Every transaction that changes value in a company code is recoded in an accounting document called an FI document.

▩ Each accounting document in mySAP ERP Financials consists of at least two line items and a maximum of 999 line items.

▩ Each FI account document consists of a document header and line items. The document header consists of company code, document date, posting date, document currency, and document type, which are applicable to whole document. Line items consist of various attributes of posting line items such as G/L account number, amount per line items, and associated cost objects.

▩ In mySAP ERP an accounting document is uniquely identified by a combination of following:

  • Document number

  • Company code

  • Fiscal year

▩ You can view an accounting document through:

  • *Transaction Code:FB03*

    Or

  • *SAP Menu:* SAP menu → Accounting → Financial Accounting → General Ledger → Document → Display

▩ In mySAP ERP Financials, FI document are controlled by:

  • Document type

  • Posting key

  • Field status group (FSG) in the relevant G/L account

▩ A document that has already been posted cannot be deleted. However, you can correct the document through change document or by reversing the original document.

▩ The user can change certain fields at document header level and line item level of a document that has already been posted based on configuration.

- However, the system does not permit to changes to following fields:
  - Amount
  - Posting key
  - Gl accounts
  - Customer number
  - Vendor number
  - Asset numbers
- The system maintains the following information in the document change log:
  - Changed field name
  - Old value and new value
  - User who changed it
  - Date and time of such changes
- You can configure FI document change rule through either:
  - ***Transaction Code****: SPRO*

    Or
  - ***R/3 IMG Menu:*** *Implementation Guide (IMG) → Financial Accounting → Financial Accounting Global Settings→ Document*

    .... Document Header → Document Change Rules, Document Header

    ....Line Item → Document Change Rules, Line Item

    Or
  - ***mySAP ERP IMG Menu:*** *Implementation Guide (IMG) → Financial Accounting (New)→ Financial Accounting Global Settings (New) → Document → Rules for Changing Documents →*

    .... Document Change Rules, Document Header

    .... Document Change Rules, Line Item

Question – 14

In financial accounting a FI document date

A. Must be in the same period as the posting date

B. Must be in a period higher than the posting date

C. Must be in a period lesser than the posting date

D. Can be in any date independent of the posting date

Question – 15

When you execute automatic clearing program, the original documents are

A. Cleared and deleted from the system

B. Cleared, deleted, and archived from the system

C. Cleared in the system

D. None of the above

Question – 16

In financial accounting a residual posting

A. Generates a new line item

B. Reduces the value in the original invoice line item

C. Reverses the original line item

D. Generates a parking document

Question – 17

What is the maximum number of line items allowed in an accounting document?

A. 2

B. 50

C. 100

D. 999

> ## Question – 18
>
> *In financial accounting, a document currency*
>
> A. Can be any currency
>
> B. Must be the company code currency
>
> C. Is the controlling area currency
>
> D. Must be the currency defined in the G/L master

2.3.10 Document Types

- Document type controls the header part of a financial document while posting key and FSG controls line fields available for input while posting a transaction.

- Document types are used to differentiate business transactions, for example, customer invoices, vendor invoices, and assets posting.

- Document type in mySAP ERP controls the following important attributes of financial document:

  - Account types allowed for posting (customer, vendor, material, assets, and G/L accounts)

  - Document number ranges

  - Free test fields

- You can create or change FI document types through:

  - ***Transaction Code****: OBA7*

    Or

  - ***R/3 IMG Menu:*** *Implementation Guide (IMG) → Financial Accounting → Financial Accounting Global Settings → Document → Document Header → Define Document Types*

    Or

  - ***mySAP ERP IMG Menu:*** *Implementation Guide (IMG) → Financial Accounting (New)→ Financial Accounting Global Settings (New) → Document → Document Types → Define Document Types for Entry View*

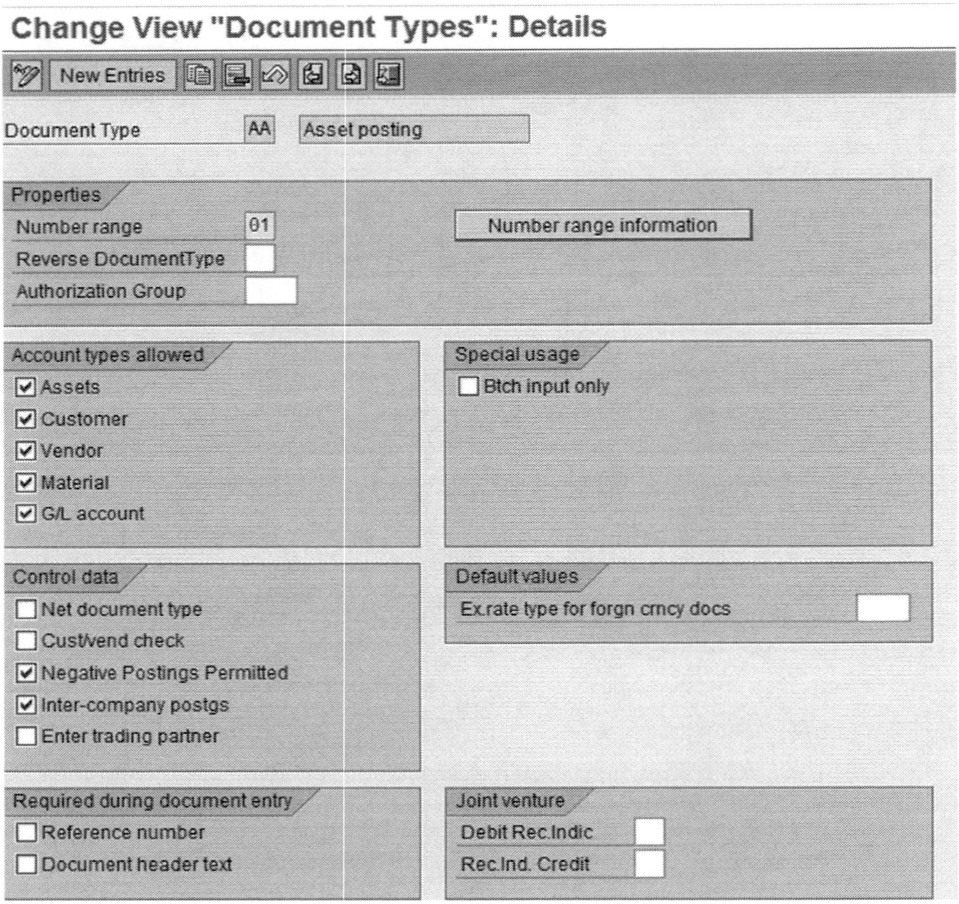

Change View "Document Types": Details

| 🖉 New Entries | 🖹 🖫 🖉 🖫 🖫 🖫 |

Document Type AA Asset posting

Properties
Number range 01   [Number range information]
Reverse DocumentType ☐
Authorization Group ☐

Account types allowed
☑ Assets
☑ Customer
☑ Vendor
☑ Material
☑ G/L account

Special usage
☐ Btch input only

Control data
☐ Net document type
☐ Cust/vend check
☑ Negative Postings Permitted
☑ Inter-company postgs
☐ Enter trading partner

Default values
Ex.rate type for forgn crncy docs ☐

Required during document entry
☐ Reference number
☐ Document header text

Joint venture
Debit Rec.Indic ☐
Rec.Ind. Credit ☐

FIGURE 2.17 T.Code: OBA7 create / change document types.

- Figure 2.17 depicts pre-delivered document type AA.
- Document types are client dependent, which means that once document types are created they are available across the company codes.
- A few standard SAP delivered types of document are:
  - AB (Accounts doc): used for all types of accounts
  - AA (Asset posting): used for assets related postings
  - DR (Customer invoice): used for customer invoice posting

- DZ (Customer payment): used for customer-incoming payment
- KR (Vendor invoice): used for vendor-invoice posting
- KZ (Vendor payment): used for vendor payment

■ The following types of documents are used for data transferred from other modules:

- WE (Goods receipt): Used to capture goods receipts data flows from MM modules
- RE (Gross inv. Receipt): used to capture logistic invoice verification data
- RV (Billing doc. transfer): used to capture sales related data from SD modules

■ All of these types of documents can be used as is or modified.

Question – 19

Which of the following statements is true? (multiple answers)

A. *One document type can use only one number range*

B. *One document type can use multiple number ranges*

C. *One accounting document created with multiple document types*

D. *One number range cannot be used by multiple document types*

2.3.11 Document Number Ranges

■ In mySAP ERP Financials, each FI document receives a unique document. This document may be an internal assigned number (called internal number range) or user assigned number (external number range).

■ *Internal document number range*: In case of internal document number ranges, document numbers are always numerical. When saving an FI document the system assigns the document a number from the assigned number range to a document type.

■ *External document number range*: When recording a business transaction, the user assigns a document number from the assigned number range to document type. In case of external number ranges, the document number can be alpha-numeric.

- You can create an FI document number range through:

  - **_Transaction Code_**: _FBN1_

    _Or_

  - **_R/3 IMG Menu:_** _Implementation Guide (IMG) → Financial Accounting → Financial Accounting Global Settings → Document → Document Number Ranges → Define Document Number Ranges_

    _Or_

  - **_mySAP ERP IMG Menu_**: _Implementation Guide (IMG) → Financial Accounting (New)→ Financial Accounting Global Settings (New) → Document → Document Number Ranges → Documents in Entry View → Define Document Number Ranges for Entry View_

Maintain Number Range Intervals

	Interval			

NR Object	Accounting document

Intervals

	No	Year	From number	To number	Current num	Ext		
	01	2011	1000000000	2999999999	0	☐		
	02	2011	0200000000	0299999999	0	☐		
	03	2011	0300000000	0399999999	0	☐		
	04	2011	0400000000	0499999999	400000000	☐		
	14	2011	0000000101	0000000200	107	☐		
	15	2011	0000000300	0000000399	0	☐		
	17	2011	0000000201	0000000299	202	☐		
	18	2011	0000000001	0000000100	11	☐		
	19	2011	0000000500	0000000599	506	☐		

FIGURE 2.18 T. Code: FBN1 FI document number range.

- Figure 2.18 depicts a number range maintenance screen. By checking the "Ext" check box against a number range, you are making that number range an external number range.

- The current number field of the Figure 2.18 shows the next available number in that number range group. In the case of an external number range group, this field will be blank.

- Each number range is represented by a number range ID, which you need to key in the document type maintenance screen as show in Figure 2.18 in the number range field.

- Document number ranges are company code dependent. Document number ranges can either be year dependent or year independent.

- *Year dependent number range*: These document number ranges are specific to a year. If the document number ranges are year dependent, you need to create an FI document number range before the beginning of each new year. Figure 2.18 depicts a year dependent number range valid for the year 2011.

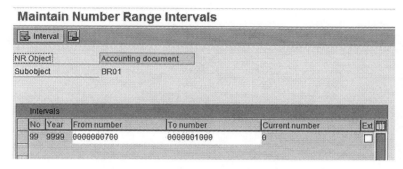

FIGURE 2.19 T. Code: FBN1 year independent number range.

- *Year independent number range*: Figure 2.19 depicts a year independent number range. By entering "9999" in the year field you can make a number range independent from the fiscal year. The FI document number range continues one year to the next.

- A number range can be assigned to multiple document types. In this case, document types share document number ranges.

- You can find number range gaps either through:

  - *Transaction Code*: S_ALR_87009880

    Or

  - *R/3 IMG Menu:*

    Or

  - *mySAP ERP IMG Menu*

Did you ever face document number range gaps? Here is the concept:

In some cases of number ranges, SAP uses a number range buffering concept. In buffering concept systems defined buffer numbers are allocated to the user and next number + buffer numbers to the second user, and so on. For example, User A logged into the system and initiated a COPA posting. While initiating the COPA transaction, the next available number is 1000000010, and the default buffering number is 110. This means the system will allocate 1000000010 to 1000000119 to User A and 1000000120 to 1000000229 to User B, and so on.

These buffer allocated numbers are stored in the shared memory of the application server. If you lose the shared memory for whatever reason, the system cannot utilize the number stored in the shared memory, and creates gaps between document numbers.

Number Range Object: Display

Change Documents

Object	COPA_IST	Number range object has intervals
Short text	Actual line items	
Long text	Nummer ranges for actual line items in profitability analys.	

Interval characteristics

Subobject data element	ERKRS
To-year flag	☐
Number length domain	BELNR
No interval rolling	☑

Customizing specifications

Number range transaction	KEN1		
Warning %	10.0		
Main memory buffering	☑	No. of numbers in buffer	110

Group specification

Group table	TVGAI	Maintain text
Subobject field in group table	ERKRS	
Fld NoRangeElement	VRGAR	Delete group ref.
Fields int./ext. no.range no.	NUMKI	NUMKE
Display element text	☑	

FIGURE 2.20 T. Code: SNRO number range buffering.

In the case of some number range objects, standard SAP comes with the number buffering switch on. You can turn the number range buffering off by unchecking "Main memory buffering" check box in transaction code SNRO or SAP menu → Tools → ABAP Workbench → Development → Other Tools → Number Ranges. Figure 2.20 T. Code: SNRO number range buffering shows the number range set up for actual COPA line items. The object name here is COPA_IST and the associated IMG transaction code for the number range maintenance is KEN1. As you can see, the number range buffering has been switched on, which also maintains what would be the number range buffer.

Refer to OSS Note 175047 – Causes for FI document number gaps (RF_BELEG) for more information. This number buffering concept is not only applicable to FI module, as it works with other modules as well.

2.3.12 Posting Keys

▪ Similar to document types, posting keys are created and maintained at client level. A posting key is a two character numeric ID which determines:

- Account types to which posting will be made

- Whether amount will be debited or credited

- Fields available for input

▪ The posting keys have been enhanced for the enjoy transactions. You use Dr. or Cr. instead of posting keys.

▪ The pre-configured SAP system comes with posting keys, however you can create your own posting keys through either:

- ***Transaction Code****: OB41*

  Or

- ***R/3 IMG Menu:*** *Implementation Guide (IMG) → Financial Accounting → Financial Accounting Global Settings → Document → Line Item → Controls → Define Posting Keys*

  Or

- ***mySAP ERP IMG Menu:*** *Implementation Guide (IMG) → Financial Accounting (New)→ Financial Accounting Global Settings (New) → Document → Define Posting Keys*

▪ The pre-configured posting keys are:

TABLE 2.2

Posting Key	Posting Key Desc.	Dr. / Cr.	Account Typevs
1	Invoice	Debit	Customer
2	Reverse credit memo	Debit	Customer
3	Bank charges	Debit	Customer
4	Other receivables	Debit	Customer
5	Outgoing payment	Debit	Customer
6	Payment difference	Debit	Customer
7	Other clearing	Debit	Customer
8	Payment clearing	Debit	Customer
9	Special G/L debit	Debit	Customer
11	Credit memo	Credit	Customer
12	Reverse invoice	Credit	Customer
13	Reverse charges	Credit	Customer
14	Other payables	Credit	Customer
15	Incoming payment	Credit	Customer
16	Payment difference	Credit	Customer
17	Other clearing	Credit	Customer
18	Payment clearing	Credit	Customer
19	Special G/L credit	Credit	Customer
21	Credit memo	Debit	Vendor
22	Reverse invoice	Debit	Vendor
24	Other receivables	Debit	Vendor
25	Outgoing payment	Debit	Vendor
26	Payment difference	Debit	Vendor
27	Clearing	Debit	Vendor
28	Payment clearing	Debit	Vendor
29	Special G/L debit	Debit	Vendor
31	Invoice	Credit	Vendor
32	Reverse credit memo	Credit	Vendor
34	Other payables	Credit	Vendor
35	Incoming payment	Credit	Vendor
36	Payment difference	Credit	Vendor
37	Other clearing	Credit	Vendor
38	Payment clearing	Credit	Vendor
39	Special G/L credit	Credit	Vendor
40	Debit entry	Debit	G/L account

TABLE 2.2 (*continued*)

Posting Key	Posting Key Desc.	Dr. / Cr.	Account Typevs
50	Credit entry	Credit	G/L account
70	Debit asset	Debit	Asset
75	Credit asset	Credit	Asset
80	Stock initial entry	Debit	G/L account
81	Costs	Debit	G/L account
83	Price difference	Debit	G/L account
84	Consumption	Debit	G/L account
85	Change in stock	Debit	G/L account
86	GR/IR debit	Debit	G/L account
89	Stock inward movement	Debit	Material
90	Stock initial entry	Credit	G/L account
91	Costs	Credit	G/L account
93	Price difference	Credit	G/L account
94	Consumption	Credit	G/L account
95	Change in stock	Credit	G/L account
96	GR/IR credit	Credit	G/L account
99	Stock outward movement	Credit	Material

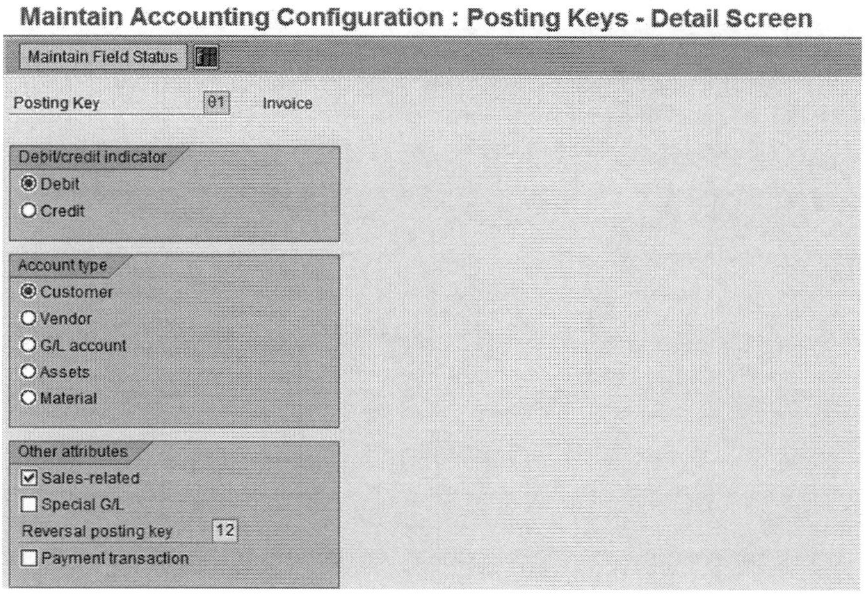

Maintain Accounting Configuration : Posting Keys - Detail Screen

Maintain Field Status

Posting Key   01   Invoice

Debit/credit indicator
⦿ Debit
○ Credit

Account type
⦿ Customer
○ Vendor
○ G/L account
○ Assets
○ Material

Other attributes
☑ Sales-related
☐ Special G/L
Reversal posting key   12
☐ Payment transaction

FIGURE 2.21 T. Code: OB41 posting key configuration.

- Figure 2.21 shows a configuration screen of pre-delivered posting key 01. Posting 01 is used for customer Dr. For example, if you are selling your product and posting the transaction into FI through enjoy transaction, then you would use posting key 01 to Dr. customer.

- In posting key configuration, you are determining attributes of posting keys:

  - Whether the posting is a Dr. or Cr. posting key

  - What type of accounts type will be posted with this posting key

  - Whether the posting key is sales related or not

  - What the reversal posting key would be

Question – 20

In the standard system, the posting key 40 refers to

A. *Credit to general ledger account*

B. *Debit to general ledger account*

C. *Debit to vendor account*

D. *Credit to vendor account*

2.3.13 Field Status Groups

- When entering an FI document, you can see various fields available for input. Fields available for input varies from G/L accounts due to the different field status group assignment to G/L accounts. For example, if you are posting to an expenses account, the system is expecting a cost object, while posting to a G/L account, the system doesn't need a cost object.

- In customizing, you can maintain or create a field status variant. The field status variant is created at client level and is assigned to a company code. A field status variant can be assigned to more than one company code.

- Field status variant consists of one or more field status groups. You can assign field status groups to a G/L account master.

- Field status groups consist of field groups where you can determine which fields are required, optional, displayed, or suppressed.

- Even though field status groups control fields of document entry screens, there are certain exceptions. These include:

  - If the business area used and business area financial statement is activated, then you can define whether the field is required or optional.

  - Even though the tax field is ready for input, you can enter only the G/L account relevant for tax. The field status hide cannot be combined with required.

  - If the document is posted to a subsidiary ledger, then the field status groups assigned to a reconciliation account control the fields.

- You can create and maintain field status variant through either:

  - ***Transaction Code****: SPRO*

    Or

  - ***R/3 IMG Menu:*** *Implementation Guide (IMG) → Financial Accounting → Financial Accounting Global Settings → Document → Line Item → Controls → Define Field Status Variants*

    Or

  - ***mySAP ERP IMG Menu:*** *Implementation Guide (IMG) → Financial Accounting (New) → Financial Accounting Global Settings (New) → Ledgers → Fields → Define Field Status Variants*

- Once you have created the fields status variant, you can assign fields status variant to company code through either:

  - ***Transaction Code****: SPRO*

    Or

  - ***R/3 IMG Menu:*** *Implementation Guide (IMG) → Financial Accounting → Financial Accounting Global Settings → Document → Line Item → Controls → Assign Company Code to Field Status Variants*

    Or

  - ***mySAP ERP IMG Menu:*** *Implementation Guide (IMG) → Financial Accounting (New) → Financial Accounting Global Settings (New) → Ledgers → Fields → Assign Company Code to Field Status Variants*

⊙ **Question – 21**

The fields available while posting a transaction are controlled through the field status group at

A. Posting key only

B. Field status of Posting key and G/L masters

C. Field status group in G/L master records only

D. None of the above

2.3.14 Employee Tolerance Group

▪ Employee tolerance group is used to restrict certain groups of employees from performing certain transactions for which they are not authorized. It is also used to authorize certain group of users to post an accounting entry up to certain monetary limit. In order to post transactions to FI, you need to have at least one employee tolerance group. Setting up an employee tolerance group is two-step process: define an employee tolerance group and assign an employee tolerance group to user.

▪ You can define an employee tolerance group through either:

- *Transaction Code*: OBA4

  Or

- *R/3 IMG Menu:* Implementation Guide (IMG) → Financial Accounting → Financial Accounting Global Settings → Document → Line Item → Define Tolerance Groups for Employees

  Or

- *mySAP ERP IMG Menu:* Implementation Guide (IMG) → Financial Accounting (New) → Financial Accounting Global Settings (New) → Document → Tolerance Groups → Define Tolerance Groups for Employees

▪ Once you have created an employee group you need to assign an employee through either:

- *Transaction Code*: SPRO

  Or

- **R/3 IMG Menu:** *Implementation Guide (IMG) → Financial Accounting → Financial Accounting Global Settings → Document → Line Item Assign User/Tolerance Groups*

  Or

- **mySAP ERP IMG Menu:** *Implementation Guide (IMG) → Financial Accounting (New) → Financial Accounting Global Settings (New) → Document → Tolerance Groups → Assign User/Tolerance Groups*

▪ Whether or not you use the functionality of an employee tolerance group, in order to post transactions into FI you need to configure a least one employee tolerance group.

▪ If you don't want to use an employee tolerance limit functionality, you can create a dummy employee tolerance group with "blank" as the group ID.

▪ Employee tolerance groups control:

  - The upper monitory limit per document

  - The upper monetary limit per line items

  - Maximum cash discount a user is able to grant

▪ Figure 2.22 depicts an employee tolerance group set up. Employee tolerance group is company code dependent and is always in the local currency.

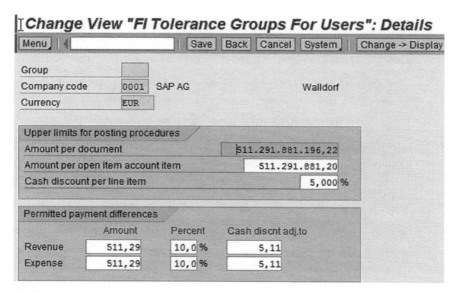

FIGURE 2.22 OBA4 employee tolerance group.

■ If the group ID is blank, you do not need to assign to any specific employee, but you do need to assign an employee tolerance group ID to user ID.

2.3.15 G/L Tolerance Group

■ The G/L tolerance group controls the permitted payment difference for clearing open G/L items. You can define this tolerance either in an absolute amount, a percentage, or both. When you define tolerance limit in an amount and a percentage, the G/L account system will consider the amount and the percentage while clearing.

■ You can create a G/L tolerance group through either:

- **Transaction Code**: OBA0

  Or

- **R/3 IMG Menu:** Implementation Guide (IMG) → Financial Accounting → General Ledger Accounting → Business Transactions → Open Item Clearing → Clearing Differences

  Or

- **mySAP ERP IMG Menu:** Implementation Guide (IMG) → Financial Accounting (New) → General Ledger Accounting (New) → Business Transactions → Open Item Clearing → Clearing Differences → Define Tolerance Groups for G/L Accounts

■ In order to clear a G/L account the system expects at least one G/L tolerance group. Like employee tolerance, you can create a blank tolerance group. If no tolerance group is assigned to G/L master record, then the blank tolerance group applies.

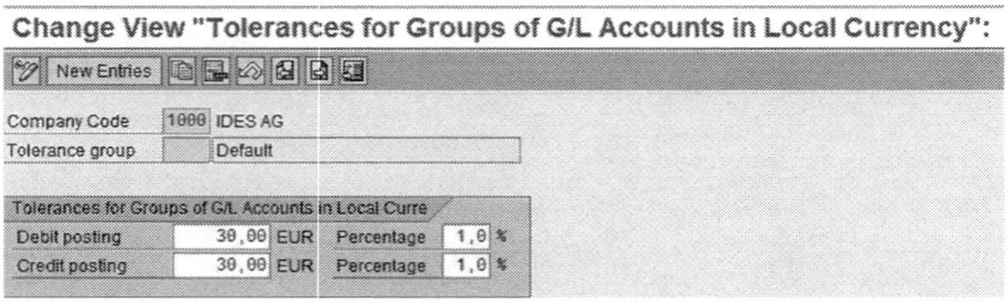

FIGURE 2.23 OBA0 - G/L tolerance group.

■ Figure 2.23 shows a pre-delivered G/L tolerance group for company code 1,000, where tolerance is defined as both an absolute amount and percentage.

■ Let us assume that you want to clear a Dr transaction of EUR 1,000.00 with Cr. transaction of EUR 980.00. In this case, in terms of absolute amount you can clear the open EUR 1,000.00 against EUR 980.00, but it doesn't fulfill tolerance in terms of the percentage. If you maintain both tolerance in terms of the amount and percentage, the system considers the minimum in both tolerances in order to clear an open item.

In order to activate G/L tolerance, you need to assign G/L tolerance group to G/L master in the control data tab. Figure 2.24 depicts the G/L tolerance group assignment in G/L master record. As you are assigning G/L tolerance group at company code level, you can assign different tolerance groups to G/L master for different company codes.

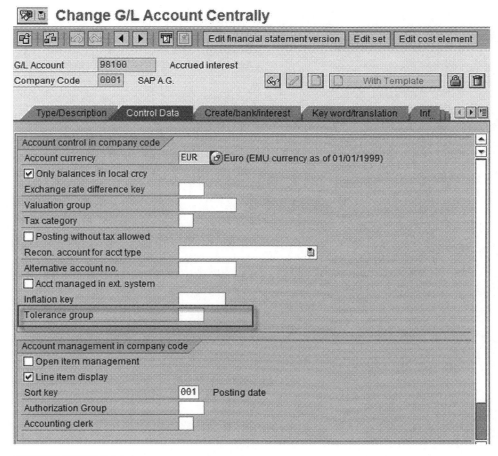

FIGURE 2.24 FS00 G/L tolerance group assignment.

2.3.16 FI Document Reversal

- SAP ERP doesn't allow you to delete a document once it is posted in order to make a correction. In order to make a correction, you need to reverse the FI documents. If the document is originated from another module, you need to reverse the source document in order to reverse the FI document.

- SAP ERP provides two types of reversals: normal reversal and negative reversal.

- *Normal Reversal*: When you are using normal reversal, the system posts credit for incorrect debit and debit for incorrect credit. There is no additional set up required for normal reversal.

- *Negative Reversal*: If configuration is available, you can perform negative reversal. In case of negative reversal, the system posts negative credit for incorrect credit and negative debit for incorrect debit.

- In order to use negative reversal, you need to configure the following two steps:

  - The company code must permit negative posting

  - Reversal reason code for negative posting

- You can configure negative posting permission through either:

  - ***Transaction Code***: *SPRO*

    Or

  - ***R/3 IMG Menu:*** *Implementation Guide (IMG) → Financial Accounting → General Ledger Accounting → Business Transactions → Adjustment Posting/Reversal → Permit Negative Posting*

    Or

  - ***mySAP ERP IMG Menu:*** *Implementation Guide (IMG) → Financial Accounting → General Ledger Accounting (New) → Business Transactions → Adjustment Posting/Reversal → Permit Negative Posting*

- You can configure reversal reason code for reversal posting through either:

  - ***Transaction Code***: *SPRO*

    Or

- **R/3 IMG Menu:** *Implementation Guide (IMG)* → *Financial Accounting* → *General Ledger Accounting* → *Business Transactions* → *Adjustment Posting/Reversal* → *Define Reasons for Reversal*

  Or

- **mySAP ERP IMG Menu:** *Implementation Guide (IMG)* → *Financial Accounting* → *General Ledger Accounting (New)* → *Business Transactions* → *Adjustment Posting/Reversal* → *Define Reasons for Reversal*

- SAP application provides two categories of reversal: individual reversal and mass reversal. Individual reversal is used for the reversal of an FI document individually, while mass reversal is used for the reversal of more than one document at a time.

- You can reverse a G/L, customer, or vendor document individually through either:

  - **Transaction Code:** *FB08*

    Or

  - **SAP Menu:** *SAP menu* → *Accounting* → *General Ledger* → *Document* → *Reverse* → *Individual Reversal*

- For mass reversal follow either:

  - **Transaction Code:** *F.80*

    Or

  - **SAP Menu:** *SAP menu* → *Accounting* → *General Ledger* → *Document* → *Reverse* → *Mass Reversal*

- When using the document reversal process, remember to update the original document with the reversal document number, so that you can relate the original document with the reversal document and navigate back and forth.

- You can't reverse a cleared document. If the document is already cleared by another document, you need to reset the clearing document before reversal.

- During the reset process, the system breaks the clearing relation between the documents. You can perform reset and reversal in one step. Follow either of the following options for reset and reversal:

- ***Transaction Code****: FBRA*

  Or

- ***SAP Menu:*** *SAP menu → Accounting → General Ledger →*
  Document → Reset Cleared Items

▪ The reversal system uses the reversal document type associated with the original document type. In Figure 2.17, you can see a field available for reversal document type.

▪ Since the document reversal process is automatic, the system is expecting an internal document number range in case of reversal document type.

2.3.17 Cross-Company Code Transactions

▪ Cross-company code transactions involve two or more company codes in a business transaction.

▪ In cross-company code transaction, the system posts a separate document for each company code with company code specific document numbers.

▪ Individual company documents are linked together by a cross-company document number.

▪ For example, the following types of transactions create cross-company code transactions:

- An employee works in different company codes for part of the time

- An employee changes company code during a payroll period

- One company code makes purchases for other company codes (central procurement)

- One company code pays invoices for other company codes (central payment)

- One company code sells goods to other company codes

▪ You can display cross-company code transactions through either:

- ***Transaction Code****: FBU3*

  Or

- **SAP Menu:** *SAP menu → Accounting → General Ledger → Document → Cross-Company-Code Transaction → Display*

■ You can reverse cross-company transactions through either:

- **Transaction Code**: *FBU8*

  Or

- **SAP Menu:** *SAP menu → Accounting → General Ledger → Document → Cross-Company-Code Transaction → Reverse*

■ Once you execute FBU8, the system displays whether all associated documents are reversible or not.

■ In order to process cross-company code transactions, you need to define cross company code clearing account through either:

- **Transaction Code**: *OBYA*

  Or

- **R/3 IMG Menu:** *Implementation Guide (IMG) → Financial Accounting → General Ledger Accounting → Business Transactions → Prepare Cross-Company Code Transactions*

  Or

- **mySAP ERP IMG Menu:** *Implementation Guide (IMG) → Financial Accounting (New) → General Ledger Accounting (New) → Business Transactions → Prepare Cross-Company Code Transactions*

■ These clearing accounts can be set up as either a G/L account or as a subsidiary ledger. In both cases you need to configure in transaction code OBYA with different posting keys.

■ Figure 2.25 depicts the cross-company code configuration between company codes 1,000 and 2,000. In this case company code 1,000 clearing account 194,002 for company code 2,000 is set up as a G/L account. Similarly, in company code 2,000, clearing account 194,001 for company code 1,000 is set up as a clearing account. Company code 1,000 initiates Dr. entry with company code 2,000. The system creates receivables by debiting G/L account 194,002 in company code 1,000 and payable in company code 2,000 by crediting 194,002.

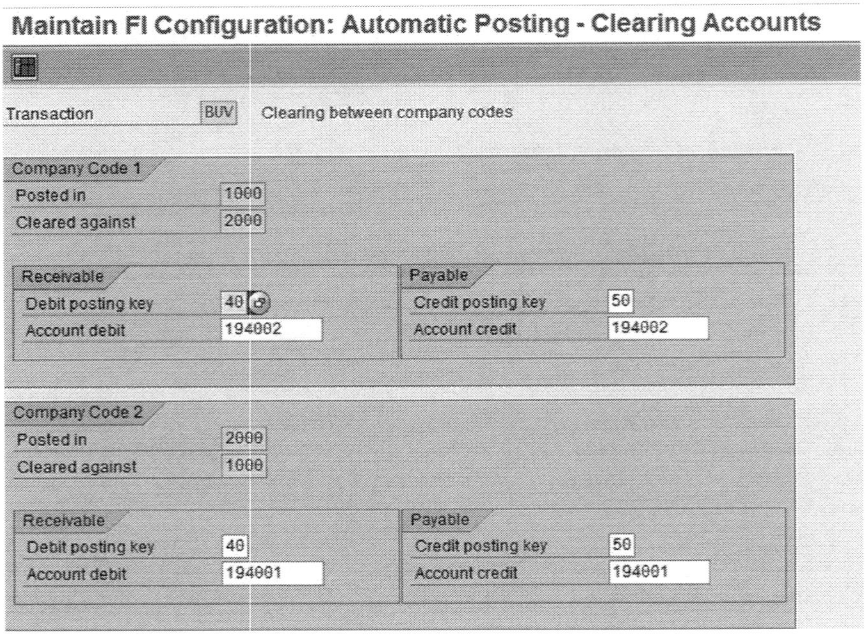
Maintain FI Configuration: Automatic Posting - Clearing Accounts
Transaction
BUV
Clearing between company codes
Company Code 1
Posted in
1000
Cleared against
2000
Receivable
Debit posting key
40
Account debit
194002
Payable
Credit posting key
50
Account credit
194002
Company Code 2
Posted in
2000
Cleared against
1000
Receivable
Debit posting key
40
Account debit
194001
Payable
Credit posting key
50
Account credit
194001

FIGURE 2.25 T.Code: OBYA cross-company configuration.

- When the system posts cross-company code transactions, it generates a cross company code document. The cross-company code document is the combination of the document number of originated company code + company code + fiscal year.
- Figure 2.26 depicts a cross-company code document. You can see there are three document numbers: cross-company code document number, document number for company code 1,000, and document number for company code 3,000.

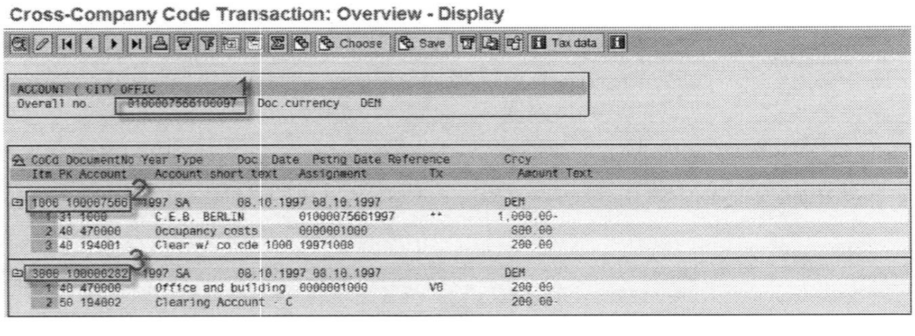
Cross-Company Code Transaction: Overview - Display
Choose
Save
Tax data
Doc.currency DEM
C.E.B. BERLIN
Occupancy costs
Office and building
Clearing Account - C
1
2
3

FIGURE 2.26 Cross-company code document.

Question — 22

You can post financial transactions to

A. *Multiple company codes*

B. *Multiple business areas*

C. *Multiple cost centers*

D. *All of the above*

2.3.18 Foreign Exchange

- An exchange rate difference occurs during the following circumstances:

  - When you clear open items

  - When you valuate open items for your financial statements

- When you clear open items, the system runs through the foreign exchange valuation process and post exchange loss or gain to pre-configured accounts.

- Occasionally, you maintain a certain account in something other than local currency. In these circumstances, you need to reevaluate the account for your financial statement, because financial statements must be prepared on local currency.

- In the foreign exchange reevaluation process, the system generates two types of foreign exchange differences: realized loss or gain and unrealized loss or gain.

- Realized gain or loss arises when you are clearing open items. This normally occurs in either of the following circumstances:

  - When you are clearing open items in a G/L account or between G/L accounts, such as offsetting Dr. entries with Cr. entries

  - When you post an incoming payment against a customer invoice

  - When you post an outgoing payment to clear vendor invoices

- In these circumstances, the system posts the foreign exchange difference, if any, to realized gain or loss, because these are final settlements of open items.

▪ Unrealized foreign gain or loss arises when you are revaluating your foreign currency open items or foreign currency G/L accounts for financial statement. Foreign exchange differences that arise in this process are posted to unrealized account to minimize foreign exchange exposure, while the final settlement of the transaction presents a true and fair presentation of the financial statement.

▪ While making the final settlement of foreign currency open items or foreign currency G/L accounts, the system corrects the balance sheet adjustment account post foreign exchanges difference, if any occurs.

▪ As the system posts realized, unrealized gains or losses to pre-configured set of G/L account automatically, the system expects that you have configured the SAP application. You can configure the SAP application through either:

- **Transaction Code**: OB09

  Or

- **R/3 IMG Menu:** Implementation Guide (IMG) → Financial Accounting → General Ledger Accounting → Business Transactions → Open Item Clearing → Define Accounts for Exchange Rate Differences

  Or

- **mySAP ERP IMG Menu:** Implementation Guide (IMG) → Financial Accounting (New) → General Ledger Accounting (New) → Business Transactions → Open Item Clearing → Define Accounts for Exchange Rate Differences

▪ This configuration is client specific rather than company code specific. You can assign different sets of accounts based on the G/L account, currency, and currency type. If you keep the currency and currency type field blank, the system assumes that this configuration is applicable for all currencies and currency types.

▪ Figure 2.27 shows account determination of foreign exchange losses and gains. It consists of four parts:

1. **Header**: Consists of G/L account, currency, and currency type for which you are making account determination.

Display View "Acct Determination For OI Exch.Rate Differences": Detail

Chart of Accounts	INT	Sample chart of accounts
G/L Account	140000	
Currency		
Currency type		

Exchange rate difference realized

Loss	230000
Gain	280000

Valuation

Val.loss 1	230010
Val.gain 1	280010
Bal.sheet adj.1	140099

Translation

Loss	230020
Bal.sheet adj.loss	230030
Gain	280020
Bal.sheet adj.gain	280030

FIGURE 2.27 T.Code OB09 foreign currency configuration.

2. **Exchange rate difference realized**: Here you assign income statement G/L accounts to the system, which will then post foreign exchange realized gains and losses.

3. **Valuation**: When you valuate open items or foreign currency G/L accounts, the system posts the G/L account maintained in this section.

4. **Translation**: The G/L accounts maintained in this section are posted with foreign exchanges losses or gains that arise during valuation, when your group currency is different than the operating currency.

▪ You can run foreign exchange valuation for G/L, AP, or AR through either:

- *Transaction Code*: F.05

  Or

- **SAP Menu:** *SAP menu → Accounting → General Ledger → Periodic Processing → Closing → Valuate → Foreign Currency Valuation.*

▪ You must maintain the account determination for foreign currency realized, as well as unrealized losses and gains, G/L accounts for all reconciliation accounts, and open item managed accounts.

2.3.19 Holding/Parking a Document

▪ You can save a document in a two different ways: hold a document or park a document. Holding and parking a document is applicable in a similar way to all sub-modules of FI, such as general ledger accounting, accounts receivable, accounts payable, and assets accounting.

▪ *Hold Document*: Hold document is used to save entered data temporally into the system memory, which can be completed at a later period. In case of hold document:

- System does not assign a document number to saved document

- System does not update the G/L account balance

- System does not consider entered data for evaluation

- Hold document is named by the user

- The document does not need to be a balanced document

▪ *Park Document*: Similar to hold document, you can temporarily park an incomplete document and complete and post it at a later date. In case of park document:

- System assigns a document number

- System does not update the G/L account balance

- Park document data is available for real time evaluation

- System doesn't balance transactions

- System does not carry out substitute functionality for parked document

▪ You may choose to park a document for many reasons. A few reasons are:

- *Separation of Duties*: Parking functionality helps to follow the principle of dual control, where the data enterer is not allowed to post data.

- *Non-availability of information*: While entering a transaction, you may not have enough data to complete the document.

- A parked document can be completed, changed, and posted at a later point in time by the person who entered the document, or someone else, to convert the parked document into a financial document.

- A park document is largely used in order to enforce dual control, authorization, and the implementation of workflow.

- In the case of a cross-company code document, the system creates one park document. When you post the parked document, the system creates cross-company code documents and company code documents.

- A parked document can be edited and completed all at once or step by step. The system logs all changes in the parked document. You can view these changes before or after posting a parked document. You may post individual or multiple parked document through either:

  - **Transaction Code**: *FBV0*

    Or

  - **SAP Menu:** *SAP menu → Accounting → General Ledger → Document → Closing → Parked Documents → Post/Delete.*

- You can't edit or change the following objects in a parked document:

  - Document currency

  - Document type and document number

  - Company in the document header

- You can edit or change an individual document or several documents through work list. If you are posting several parked documents through selection list, the system provides a list that indicates the document posting status. The system provides a list of documents that could not be processed due to missing objects.

- When you post a parked document, the system performs the following functions:

  - Creates an account document, which updates the G/L, AP, AR, and AA balances, if applicable

  - Logs a document change log

  - Deletes parked document information

  - Carries validation or substitution, if applicable

Question – 23

When a document is parked

A. System assigns a document number but doesn't update the general ledger, customer balance, or vendor balance

B. System assigns a temporary document number and doesn't update the general ledger, customer balance, or vendor balance

C. The document is posted with the actual document number

D. The document is posted with a temporary account number

Question – 24

You can _____.

A. Modify

B. Delete

C. Post

D. All of the above

Question – 25

The document header reference field is controlled through

A. Document Type

B. Field status group assigned to general ledger accounts

C. Posting key

D. All of the above

Question – 26

A financial document should have at least two line items, however, you can't have more than 999 line items.

A. True

B. False

Question – 27

To see line items in the general ledger, you need to activate the line item management in the general ledger master record.

A. True

B. False

Question – 28

Every company code must have a(n) _____ chart of account.

A. Operating

B. Group

C. Country

2.4 Accounts Payable (SAP® FI-AP)

- In day to day business, an enterprise purchases various products and services from its business partner called the vendor. Depending on which SAP modules you are using, account payable modules interact with other modules. Most account payable modules get their data from material management (MM) modules.

- Accounts payable is a sub-module of SAP FI modules and treated as a sub-ledger of general ledger. In the following section we'll discuss various concepts, configurations, and use of the accounts payable module.

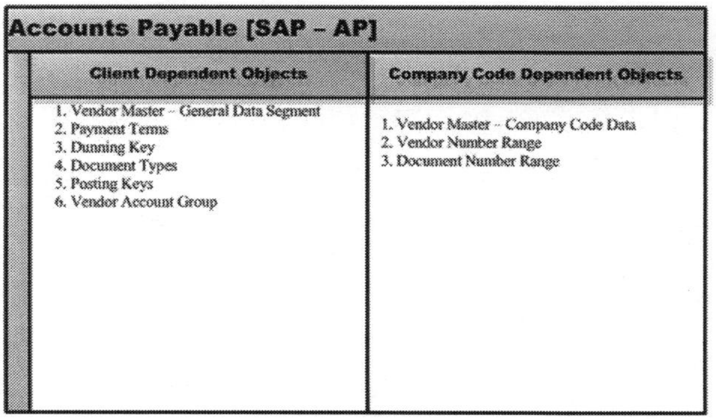

Accounts Payable [SAP – AP]	
Client Dependent Objects	**Company Code Dependent Objects**
1. Vendor Master – General Data Segment 2. Payment Terms 3. Dunning Key 4. Document Types 5. Posting Keys 6. Vendor Account Group	1. Vendor Master – Company Code Data 2. Vendor Number Range 3. Document Number Range

FIGURE 2.28 Accounts payable objects. © Copyright 2012. SAP AG. All rights reserved.

■ Figure 2.28 depicts various client dependent and company code dependent objects of account payable. You can use a client dependent object in more than one company code, while company code dependent objects are specific to company code. You can't share company code dependent objects with more than one company code.

2.4.1 Vendor Account Group

■ You should group together vendors with similar attributes under one group. This allows you to maintain vendor master in a similar way. You base the groupings on geography, trade practice, and business segments. For example, you can group vendors as government vendors and normal vendors.

■ Vendor grouping is called an account group. Vendor group determines:

- *Vendor number range*: In SAP, it is identified with an unique number within a client. You assign a number rage ID to a vendor group.

- *One time vendor*: Whether or not the vendor belongs to a one-time vendor.

- *Fields for input*: The vendor master consists of numerous fields. A field may be relevant for one vendor but not relevant to another. Based on vendor groups, you can control which fields are relevant for the vendor master.

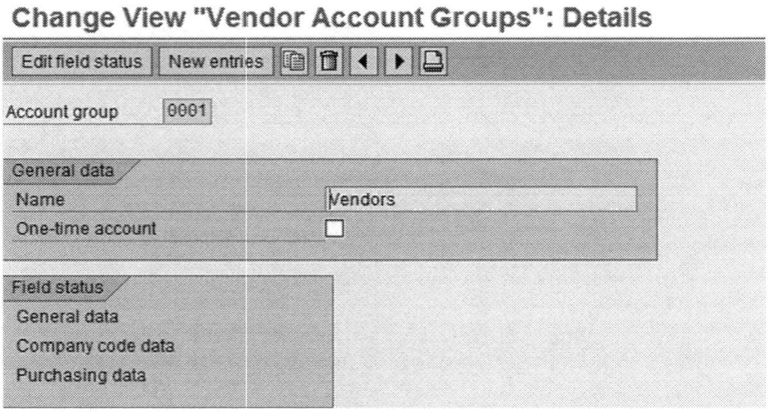

FIGURE 2.29 T. Code OBD3 vendor account group.

■ Figure 2.29 depicts the vendor group 0001. By checking and not checking you can determine whether the vendor is a one time vendor or not. You can also maintain field status of the vendor master record by double clicking on general data, company code data, or purchasing data of vendor master records.

2.4.2 Vendor Number Ranges

▪ As a vendor master is created at the client level, the vendor number is same for all company codes within a client.

▪ The vendor numbers can external or internal.

▪ In the case of an *internal number range*, while saving, the vendor master record system assigns the next available number from the assigned number range. The internal number rage will always be numerical.

▪ In the case of an *external number rage*, the user needs to key in the vendor number while creating vendor master record. With the external number range, the vendor number can be alpha numeric. The external number range is suitable in a situation where an application other than SAP controls the vendor master data.

▪ You can create or manage the vendor number range through either:

- ***Transaction Code****: XKN1*

  Or

- ***R/3 IMG Menu****: Implementation Guide (IMG) → Financial Accounting → Accounts Receivable and Accounts Payable → Vendor Accounts → Master Data → Preparations for Creating Vendor Master Data → Create Number Ranges for Vendor Accounts*

  Or

- ***mySAP ERP IMG Menu:*** *Implementation Guide (IMG) → Financial Accounting (New) → Accounts Receivable and Accounts Payable → Vendor Accounts → Master Data → Preparations for Creating Vendor Master Data → Create Number Ranges for Vendor Accounts.*

▪ Figure 2.30 shows the vendor number range maintenance screen. In this screen, you need to assign the number range to an ID. The external column appears in the last column controls, whether or not the number range is internal or external. If the check mark is active that means the number range is external. If the number range is external, the current number will be always blank. In the case of an internal number range, the current number column will display the next available number.

Maintain Number Range Intervals

NR Object   Vendor

Intervals

No.	From number	To number	Current number	Ext
01	0000000001	0000099999		☑

FIGURE 2.30 T. Code: XKN1 create vendor number range.

- After the creation of the vendor number range, you need to assign the number range to a vendor group. You can assign one number range to multiple vendor groups. In this case, the assigned number range will be shared with multiple vendor groups.

- You can assign a number range through either:

  • **Transaction Code**: OBAS

    Or

  • **R/3 IMG Menu**: *Implementation Guide (IMG) → Financial Accounting → Accounts Receivable and Accounts Payable → Vendor Accounts → Master Data → Preparations for Creating Vendor Master Data → Assign Number Ranges to Customer Account Groups*

    Or

  • **mySAP ERP IMG Menu:** *Implementation Guide (IMG) → Financial Accounting (New) → Accounts Receivable and Accounts Payable → Vendor Accounts → Master Data → Preparations for Creating Vendor Master Data → Assign Number Ranges to Customer Account Groups.*

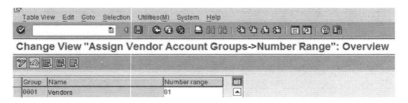

Table View   Edit   Goto   Selection   Utilities(M)   System   Help

Change View "Assign Vendor Account Groups->Number Range": Overview

Group	Name	Number range	
0001	Vendors	01	

FIGURE 2.31 T.Code: OBAS vendor number range assignment.

- Figure 2.31 depicts, number range 01 assigned to vendor group 0001.

2.4.3 Normal Vendor vs. One Time Vendor

▪ In SAP there are two types of vendors: a normal vendor and a one time vendor. All vendors other than one time vendors are considered normal vendors. One time vendors are vendors with whom you do rarely business.

▪ The vendor account group determines whether the vendor master record is a normal vendor or one time vendor.

▪ Normal vendor master records hold information specific to a vendor, while a one-time vendor master does not contain any specific information relating to a vendor.

▪ While posting to a normal vendor, the system copies vendor related information to transactions, but in the case of a one time vendor, you need to key in the vendor related information at the transaction level.

Question – 29

When you post to a one-time vendor or customer you enter details such as vendor name and address, at the line item level.

A. True

B. False

2.4.4 Vendor Master Records

▪ Like G/L master record views, a vendor master record has three views. A complete vendor master record has the following three views:

• General data segment

• Company code segment

• Purchasing organization segment

▪ *General data segment*: General segment data are maintained at the client level. This data are shared by other company codes if they use the same vendor master data.

▪ *Company code segment*: Company code segment contains data that are relevant for a company code. These data are not shared by other company codes. Different company codes will give a different set of data for one vendor.

▪ *Purchase organization data*: Purchase organization segments contain data specific to that purchase organization.

▪ While creating the vendor master, you need key in the vendor account group. The vendor account group controls:

   • Vendor number range assignment

   • Field status of vendor master record

   • Whether the vendor is a normal vendor or one time vendor

▪ Vendor master record fields are controlled at three levels: account group specific control, transaction specific control, and company code specific control.

▪ *Account group specific control*: Using the transaction code OBD3, you can see that there is field status control group. You can control vendor master layout at the account group level, which means all vendors falling under one group have similar screens and fields.

▪ *Transaction specific control*: To maintain vendor master data, you are performing three types of activities: create, change, and display. Through transaction specific control you can control the field status vendor master record. For example, you can set one field as display through transaction specific control. While creating the vendor master, the system will not allow entering or editing in that particular field.

▪ You can perform a transaction specific control through either:

   • **Transaction Code**: *OB23*

     Or

   • **R/3 IMG Menu**: *Implementation Guide (IMG) → Financial Accounting → Accounts Receivable and Accounts Payable → Vendor Accounts → Master Data → Preparations for Creating Vendor Master Data → Define Screen Layout per Activity (Vendors).*

     Or

   • **mySAP ERP IMG Menu:** *Implementation Guide (IMG) → Financial Accounting (New) → Accounts Receivable and Accounts Payable → Vendor Accounts → Master Data → Preparations for Creating Vendor Master Data → Define Screen Layout per Activity (Vendors).*

▪ *Company Code specific control*: Through company code specific control, you can control the field status of the company code segment.

- You can perform a company code specific control through either:

  - **Transaction Code**: OB23

    Or

  - **R/3 IMG Menu**: Implementation Guide (IMG) → Financial Accounting → Accounts Receivable and Accounts Payable → Vendor Accounts → Master Data → Preparations for Creating Vendor Master Data → Define Screen Layout per Company Code (Vendors).

    Or

  - **mySAP ERP IMG Menu:** Implementation Guide (IMG) → Financial Accounting (New) → Accounts Receivable and Accounts Payable → Vendor Accounts → Master Data → Preparations for Creating Vendor Master Data → Define Screen Layout per Company Code (Vendors)

- Once the vendor master is created and saved, it is not possible to change the vendor group assignment.

- If you use both FI-AP and MM modules it is better to maintain the vendor master data centrally, so you can minimize the risk of missing information.

- You can run transaction code: S_ALR_87010052 to find out the missing vendor master record.

- To restrain the user from creating duplicate vendor master records, you can use match code and/or activate the duplicate check indicator in the vendor master.

- In order to have good control over the vendor master record management, you can configure some fields, such as a bank account of a vendor, as critical or sensitive. If anyone makes changes to these fields, the system expects that another person is responsible for confirming these changes. This principle in SAP called in *dual control principle*.

- In case of dual control principle, if changes are made to a specified field, the vendor will be blocked for payment until the time of confirmation.

- In order to configure the dual control principle follow either:

  - **Transaction Code: SPRO**

Or

- **R/3 IMG Menu:** *Implementation Guide (IMG) Financial Accounting → Accounts Payable Accounts Receivable → Vendor Accounts → Master Data → Preparations for Creating Vendor Master Data → Define Sensitive Fields for Dual Control (Vendors)*

- You can confirm these changes either individually or collectively through the list function. To confirm individually follow either:

  - **Transaction Code**: *FK08*

    Or

  - **R/3 IMG Menu**: *Accounting → Financial Accounting → Accounts Payable → Master Records → Confirmation of Change → Single*

    Or

  - **mySAP ERP IMG Menu:**

- To confirm multiple vendors follow either:

  - **Transaction Code**: *FK09*

    Or

  - **R/3 IMG Menu**: *Accounting → Financial Accounting → Accounts Payable → Master Records → Confirmation of Change → List*

    Or

  - **mySAP ERP IMG Menu**

- Now you will come to know some of important fields and functions of vendor masters.

Question – 30

The vendor master contains following views at

A. *General data*

B. *Company code data*

C. *Purchasing organization data*

D. *All of the above*

Question – 31

You can create a vendor master

A. Centrally.

B. In the MM module only

C. In the FI module only

D. All of the above

2.4.5 The Vendor is Also a Customer

■ A business partner who is supplying material and services is called the vendor. A business partner who is procuring goods and services is called the customer. In a given situation, a vendor may also be procuring goods and services from the entity to which it is supplying material. In SAP, the FI module vendor and customer are treated separately and you need to maintain separate master records: a vendor master record and a customer master record for the same business partner.

■ It is obvious that you will give or receive payment to or from your business partner after taking into consideration what you are paying to the vendor and your business partner is paying you.

■ In order to clear vendor's open item against a customer, or a customer's open item with a vendor, you need to carry out following additional steps:

• Enter customer number in vendor master and vice versa

• Select the field "clearing with vendor" in the vendor account or the corresponding field in the customer account

Change Vendor: Control

Tax categories

| Vendor | 600010 | BR01 Vendor 2 |

Account control
| Customer | 700201 | Authorization | |
| Trading Partner | | Corporate Group | |

FIGURE 2.32 T.Code: FK02 vendor and customer.

■ Figure 2.32 depicts a vendor master record control tab page of company segment data, where you can assign a customer number. If you are not seeing this field in the vendor master record, check your configuration in T.CodeOBD3, OB24, OB25.

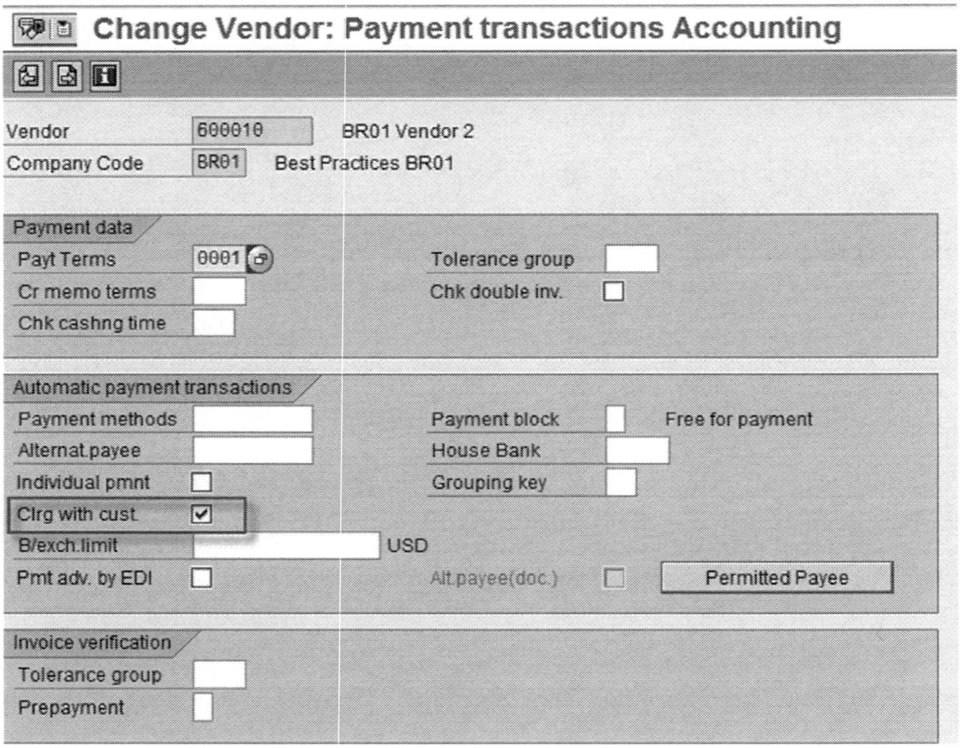

FIGURE 2.33 Vendor master record control tab page of company segment data.

■ To know this partner relationship executes the Transaction Code S_ALR_87101120. This report depicts vendor and customer relationship.

2.4.6 Alternative Payee

■ *Alternative payee* is a business partner to whom you are directed to pay on behalf of others. This type of situation arises in the following situations:

• When your supplier or service provider directs you to pay another business partner on behalf of the supplier.

- When your business partner's business or property is subject to court attachment. In this case, you need to pay to the court instead of the supplier.

- SAP offers the following options with regards to alternative payee:

  - Alternative payee

  - Alternative payee in document

  - Permitted payee

- Alternative Payee: In the vendor master record you will find the alternative payee field on the general data-payment transaction screen and the company code data-specific payment screen. Alternative payee in the company code segment has priority over the general data segment. Figure 2.34 depicts the alternative payee field of the vender master.

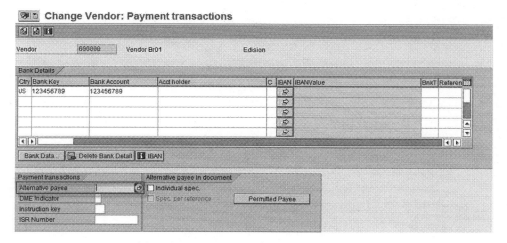

FIGURE 2.34 XK02-General data-alternative payee.

- In this option, you need to first create an alternative payee master as vendor and in the subsequent step you assign an alternative payee vendor master to the vendor master.

- Alternative payee in document: This option is general data – payment transaction as shown in Figure 2.35. If you choose this option, the system allows you to enter alternative payee information while entering

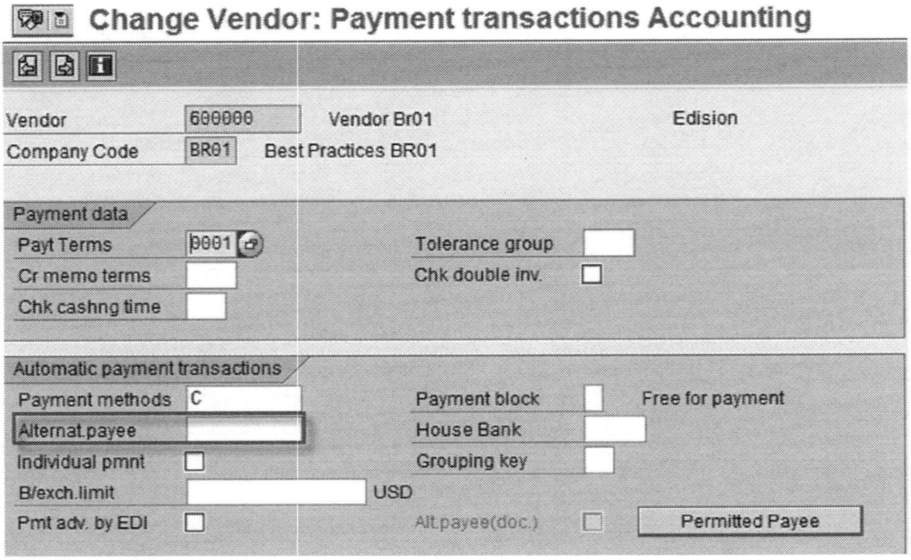

FIGURE 2.35 XK02 Company code segment-alternative payee.

the transaction. This option is similar to entering vendor master information, such as a one-time vendor.

- In order to avail this functionality, you need to check the "individual spec" check box in the vendor master. Once "individual spec" is checked, you will find an additional check box "individual payee" while entering transaction. In order to enter alternative payee information, you need to check the "individual payee" box. Once it is checked, the system will come up with an "address and bank data" pop-up window, where you can enter the alternate payee information.

- *Permitted payee*: In this option, you can assign multiple permitted payees to a vendor. First, create all permitted payee as vendors and then assign these alternative payees to vendor master. This option allows the assignment of multiple permitted payees to the same vendor.

- If you assign multiple alternative payees to vendor master, the system allows you to choose a payee from the permitted list while entering a transaction.

- Figure 2.37 depicts the vendor master where you can assign multiple permitted payees.

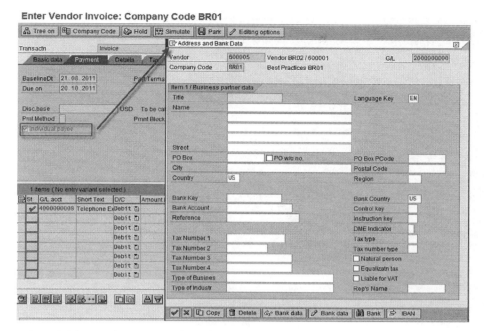

FIGURE 2.36 FB60-Alternate payee document.

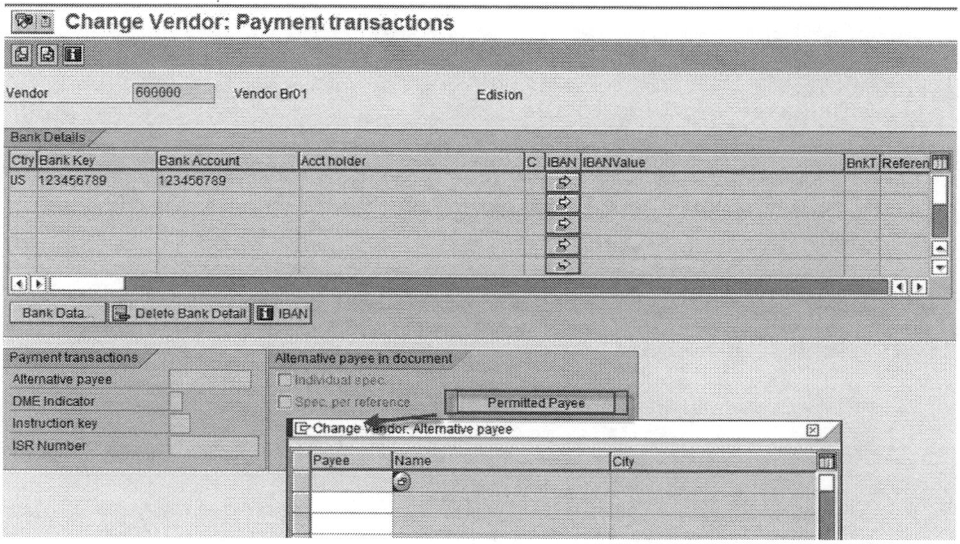

FIGURE 2.37 XK02-Permitted payee at general data.

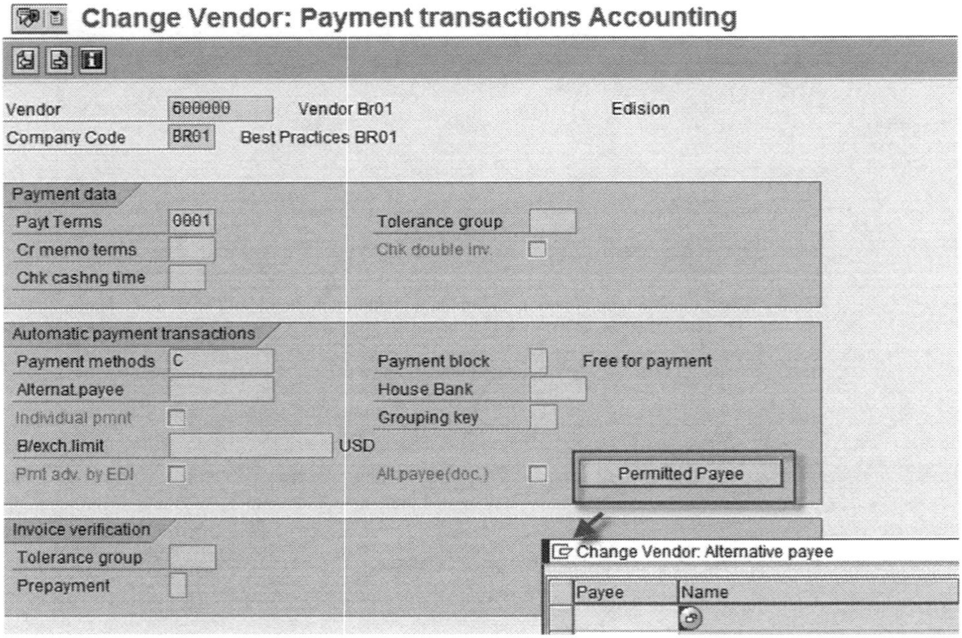

FIGURE 2.38 XK02-Permitted payee at company code data.

- You can see vendor and alternative relations through the following options and choose "Payment Data" in the selection screen.

  - ***Transaction Code***: S_ALR_87012086

    Or

  - **SAP Menu**: *SAP menu → Information Systems → Accounting → Financial Accounting → Accounts Payable → Reports for Accounts Payable Accounting → Master Data → Vendor List*

    Or

  - ***mySAP ERP IMG Menu***

- The effect of alternative payee is that payment will be remitted to the alternative payee by clearing open items of the vendors.

2.4.7 Head Office and Branch Accounts

- You may encounter a situation where your supplier has multiple branches responsible for supplying materials or services, and the head

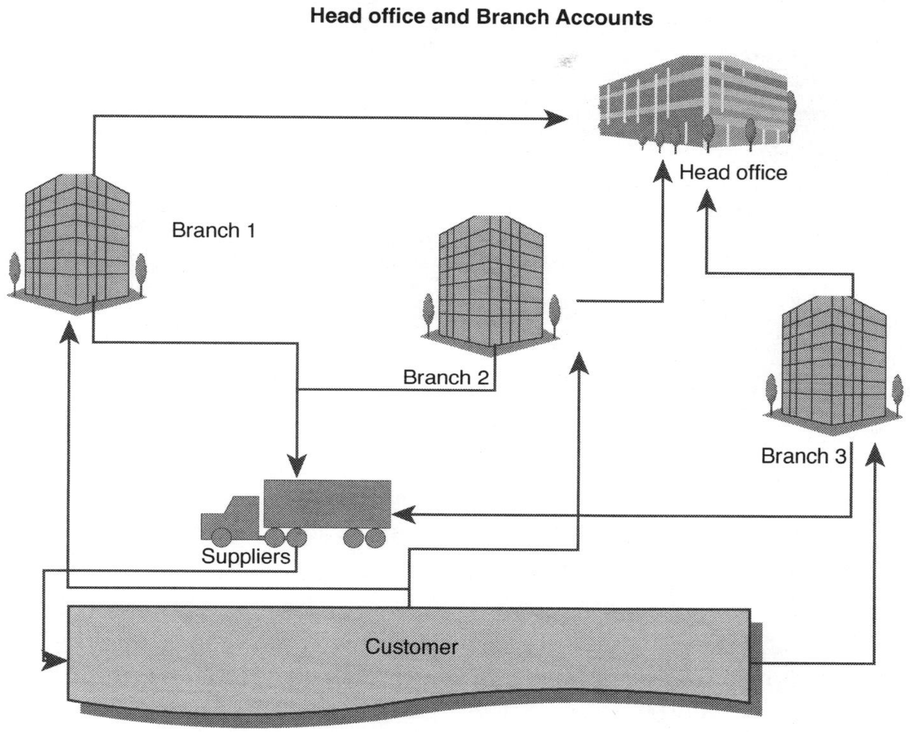

Head office and Branch Accounts

FIGURE 2.39 Head office and branch account.

office is responsible for all other activities. This situation also arises when your supplier has a shared service concept.

- In this situation, you need to create two vendor masters: one for the branch that supplies materials or services and another for the head office vendor. In the subsequent step, you need to link the head office account by entering the head office vendor number in the branch master record.

- Figure 2.40 depicts the head office field in the company code data and the accounting information account tab pages of the vendor master.

- Once you assign the head office vendor account to the branch office vendor master, all items posted to the branch account are automatically transferred to the head office account.

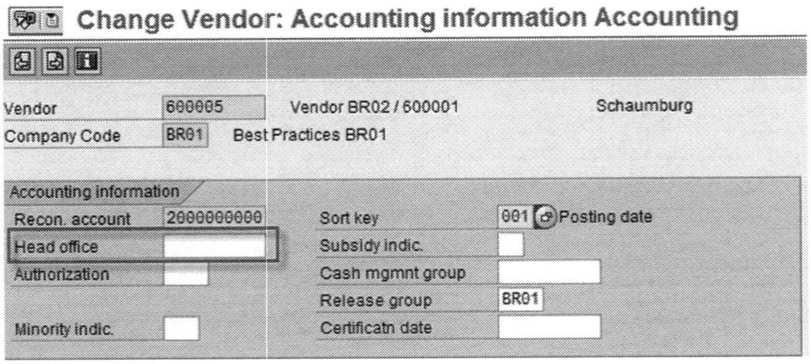

FIGURE 2.40 XK02-company code data-head office account.

- Invoke either of the following options and choose "additional selections" to display the branch and head office relation:

  - *Transaction Code*: S_ALR_87012086

    Or

  - *SAP Menu*: SAP menu → Information Systems → Accounting → Financial Accounting → Accounts Payable → Reports for Accounts Payable Accounting → Master Data → Vendor List

2.4.8 Terms of Payment

- Payment term represents an agreement between business partners for payment of invoices and related cash discount terms.

- In payment term configurations you define:

  - The reference date (base line date) from which date the system starts counting the due date

  - Calculation of due date

  - What would be the cash discount percentage if the customer makes remittance before due date

- SAP system comes with few pre-delivered payment terms, however, you can define your own through either:

  - *Transaction Code*: OBB8

    Or

- **R/3 IMG Menu**: *Implementation Guide (IMG) → Financial Accounting → Accounts Receivable and Accounts Payable → Business Transactions → Incoming Invoices/Credit Memos → Maintain Terms of Payment*

  Or

- **mySAP ERP IMG Menu:** *Implementation Guide (IMG) → Financial Accounting (New) → Accounts Receivable and Accounts Payable → Business Transactions → Incoming Invoices/Credit Memos → Maintain Terms of Payment*

- If you want the system to propose a payment term, then you need to assign payment terms in the customer master, however, you can override the system's proposed payment terms. In SAP, the application system provides functionality to enter payment terms in the company code segment, as well as the sales area segment.

- It is not necessary that both terms of payment should be same. The system proposes payment terms depending on the transaction's orgins.

- If the transaction is originated from the sales and distribution module, then the system defaults the sales areas payment term in FI document.

- If transaction originated in FI, then the system proposes FI payment terms.

- System only proposes payment terms from the master records for invoice entries not credit or debit notes. You can broadly classify credit/debit notes as follows:

  - Credit/debit note related to customer invoice

  - Credit/debit notes not related to customer invoice

- In case of credit/debit notes related to a customer invoice, then you naturally expect that the credit note should be linked to the original invoice. You can link a credit/debit note to the original invoice by entering the original invoice number in the invoice reference field during the credit/debit note entry.

- In the case of a non-invoice related credit/debit note, enter "V" in the "invoice reference" in order to activate payment terms.

- Payment terms are created at the client level and can be used by any company code. Depending on the business requirement you can use same payment term for both customer and vendor, or you can create a one payment term for the vendor and another for the customer through account type maintenance in the payment term screen.

■ In order to calculate payment due to date, you need a reference date, which is called base line date in SAP. SAP provides four possible options that you need to choose while maintaining payment terms:

- No default
- Document date
- Posting date
- Entry date

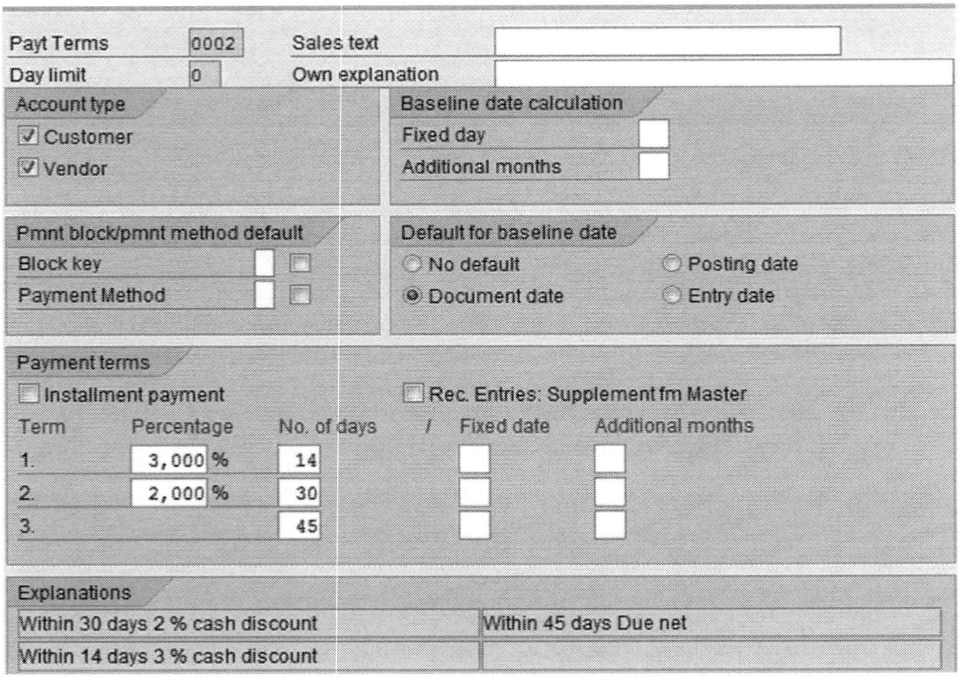

Payt Terms	0002	Sales text	
Day limit	0	Own explanation	

Account type	Baseline date calculation	
☑ Customer	Fixed day	
☑ Vendor	Additional months	

Pmnt block/pmnt method default	Default for baseline date	
Block key	○ No default	○ Posting date
Payment Method	◉ Document date	○ Entry date

Payment terms

☐ Installment payment   ☐ Rec. Entries: Supplement fm Master

Term	Percentage	No. of days	/	Fixed date	Additional months
1.	3,000 %	14			
2.	2,000 %	30			
3.		45			

Explanations	
Within 30 days 2 % cash discount	Within 45 days Due net
Within 14 days 3 % cash discount	

FIGURE 2.41 OBB8 payment terms.

■ Figure 2.41 shows a pre-delivered payment term "0002." As both customer and vendor check boxes are checked, you can use this payment term for customer as well as vendor. The document date has been selected as a base line date. If you use this payment term, the due date will be the document date plus 45 days. If the customer pays within 14 days of the document date, the system will allow three percent as a cash discount. However, if the customer pays 14 days after the document date and within 30 days of the document date, the system allow two percent as a discount.

■ Through payment terms, you can also control the payment block and the default payment method.

■ The SAP application provides functionality for installment payment of an invoice. In the case of installment payment, an invoice will be divided over a period of time with different payment terms.

■ The configuration of an installment payment term consists of two steps:

• Step 1: define the main payment terms and the installment payment terms

• Step 2: define installment for main payment terms and assign an installment payment terms

You can define the main payment terms as well as the installment payment terms through transaction code OBB8, while you can perform Step 2 through either:

• **Transaction Code**: *OBB9*

   Or

• **R/3 IMG Menu**: *Implementation Guide (IMG) → Financial Accounting → Accounts Receivable and Accounts Payable → Business Transactions → Incoming Invoices/Credit Memos → Define Terms of Payment for Installment Payments*

   Or

• **mySAP ERP IMG Menu:** *Implementation Guide (IMG) → Financial Accounting (New) → Accounts Receivable and Accounts Payable → Business Transactions → Incoming Invoices/Credit Memos → Define Terms of Payment for Installment Payments*

■ The following few figures depict configuration of installment payment terms. Here the business requirement is that you are allowed to pay supplier invoices in three installments, as follows:

- Installment 1: 30% of invoice amount due within 15 days of the base line date

- Installment 2: 40% of invoice amount due within 30 days of the base line date

- Installment 3: 3% of invoice amount due within 45 days of the base line date

Payt Terms	0017	Sales text	
Day limit	0	Own explanation	

Account type
- ☑ Customer
- ☑ Vendor

Baseline date calculation
- Fixed day
- Additional months

Pmnt block/pmnt method default
- Block key ☐
- Payment Method ☐

Default for baseline date
- ⦿ No default
- ○ Document date
- ○ Posting date
- ○ Entry date

Payment terms
- ☑ Installment payment
- ☐ Rec. Entries: Supplement fm Master

Term	Percentage	No. of days	/	Fixed date	Additional months
1.	%				
2.	%				
3.					

Explanations

Payable in 3 partial amounts	1 installment: 30,000 % with payment ter
2 installment: 40,000 % with payment ter	3 installment: 30,000 % with payment ter

FIGURE 2.42 OBB8 installment payment terms.

- As Figure 2.42 shows, you have created a payment term for the installment payment. In this payment term you have selected only an installment payment, so there is no need to set up other attributes of payment terms like cash discount or a cash discount period. You enter this payment term in the vendor master records.

- Figures 2.43, 2.44, and 2.45 all show that you have created an additional three payment terms for your three installments. In these three payment terms, you need to maintain the baseline date, cash discount period, and the percentage if there is any.

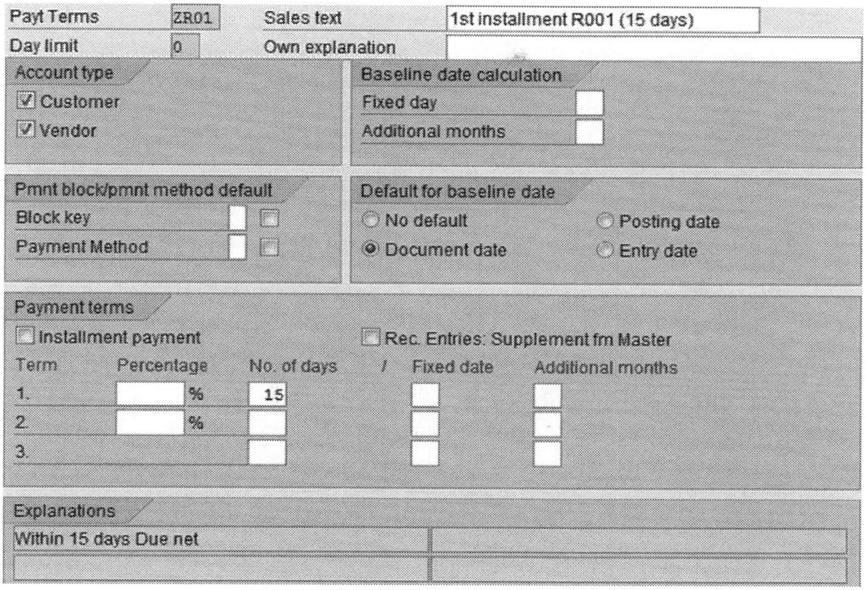

| Payt Terms | ZR01 | Sales text | 1st installment R001 (15 days) |
| Day limit | 0 | Own explanation | |

Account type
- ☑ Customer
- ☑ Vendor

Baseline date calculation
- Fixed day
- Additional months

Pmnt block/pmnt method default
- Block key ☐
- Payment Method ☐

Default for baseline date
- ○ No default   ○ Posting date
- ◉ Document date   ○ Entry date

Payment terms
☐ Installment payment   ☐ Rec. Entries: Supplement fm Master

Term	Percentage	No. of days	/	Fixed date	Additional months
1.	%	15			
2.	%				
3.					

Explanations

Within 15 days Due net

FIGURE 2.43 OBB8 Installment one payment term.

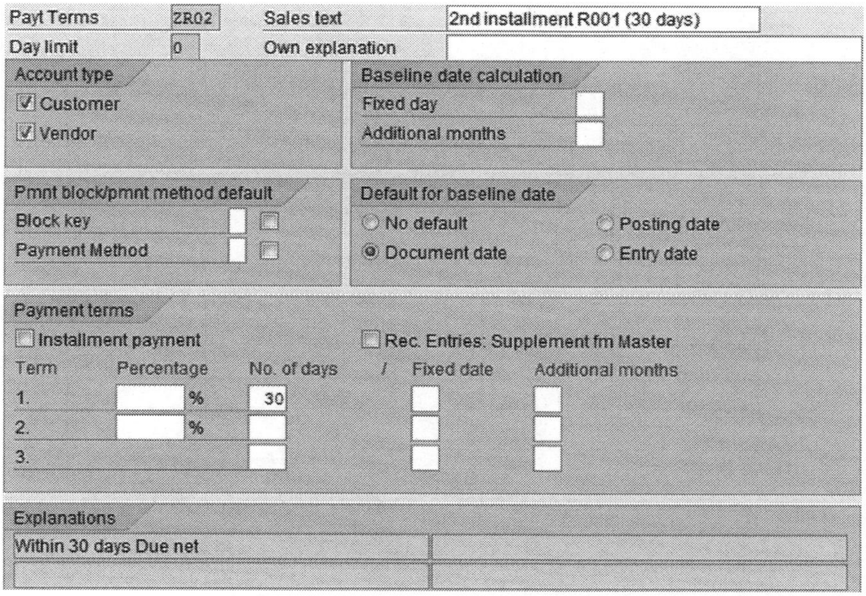

| Payt Terms | ZR02 | Sales text | 2nd installment R001 (30 days) |
| Day limit | 0 | Own explanation | |

Account type
- ☑ Customer
- ☑ Vendor

Baseline date calculation
- Fixed day
- Additional months

Pmnt block/pmnt method default
- Block key ☐
- Payment Method ☐

Default for baseline date
- ○ No default   ○ Posting date
- ◉ Document date   ○ Entry date

Payment terms
☐ Installment payment   ☐ Rec. Entries: Supplement fm Master

Term	Percentage	No. of days	/	Fixed date	Additional months
1.	%	30			
2.	%				
3.					

Explanations

Within 30 days Due net

FIGURE 2.44 Installment two payment terms.

- In Figure 2.43, you have configured the first installment payment terms with the document date as the baseline date. The amount due is within 15 days of the document date.

- In Figure 2.44, you have configured the second installment payment terms with the document date as the baseline date. The amount is due within 30 days from the document date.

- In Figure 2.45, you have configured the third installment payment terms with the document date as the baseline date. The amount due is due within 45 days from the document date

- As Figure 2.46 depicts, you have assigned installment payment terms i.e. ZR01, ZR02, ZR03 to R001, and also defined what would be the installment percentage.

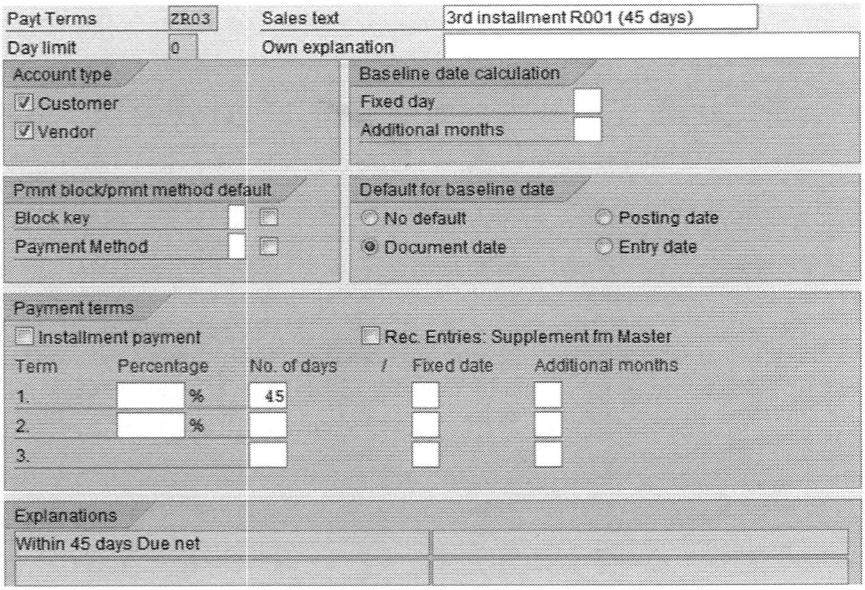

| Payt Terms | ZR03 | Sales text | 3rd installment R001 (45 days) |
| Day limit | 0 | Own explanation | |

Account type		Baseline date calculation	
☑ Customer		Fixed day	
☑ Vendor		Additional months	

Pmnt block/pmnt method default		Default for baseline date	
Block key	☐	○ No default	○ Posting date
Payment Method	☐	◉ Document date	○ Entry date

Payment terms
☐ Installment payment   ☐ Rec. Entries: Supplement frm Master

Term	Percentage	No. of days	/	Fixed date	Additional months
1.	%	45		☐	☐
2.	%			☐	☐
3.				☐	☐

Explanations
Within 45 days Due net

FIGURE 2.45 Installment three payment terms.

Terms of Paymen	Inst	Percent	Pmnt term	
0017	1	30,000	0001	▢
0017	2	40,000	0001	
0017	3	30,000	0001	

FIGURE 2.46 OBB9 installment definition.

- When you post a vendor invoice with payment term R001, then system creates three line items for every installment, with relevant payment terms i.e. ZR01, ZR02, and ZR03.

2.4.9 Reconciliation Accounts

- A reconciliation account represents a G/L account that contains summary information for sub-ledgers. In the SAP application, the following FI sub-modules are treated as sub-ledgers to FI general ledger accounting (FI-GL) sub-modules:

  - Accounts Receivables (FI-AR)

  - Accounts Payable (FI-AP)

  - Assets Accounting (FI-AA)

- Since reconciliation accounts are meant to hold only summary information, transactions are not posted directly.

- You assign reconciliation account to the customer and vendor master in the accounting information tab company code segment. In other words, reconciliation account maintenance is specific to company code.

- While creating a G/L account master record, you need to determine what type of reconciliation it is by selecting from the available options in the reconciliation field of control tab of chart of the account segment.

- Figure 2.47 depicts a G/L master record chart of account control data tab pages. In order to make a G/L master record a reconciliation account, choose a relevant account type from the available options.

- When you post the vendor invoice and debit note, you need to post to the vendor and the reconciliation account at the same time as the transactions. In the SAP application, you may come across another kind of reconciliation account called an alternative reconciliation account, which will be discussed later in this section.

2.4.10 Special G/L Transactions

- The term special G/L transactions is often confused with special ledger in the SAP application. In this section, you will learn special G/L transactions.

- Special G/L transactions are transactions that carry special treatment in the financial statement. Normally, you deal with special G/L transactions

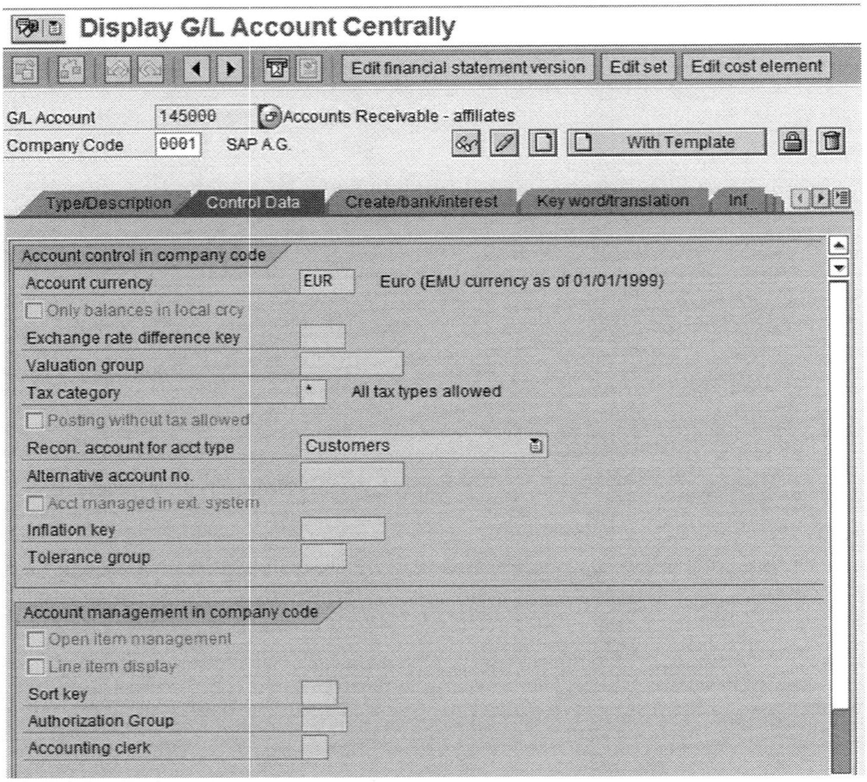

FIGURE 2.47 T.Code: FS00 G/L account master records.

in the account receivable and payable shown separately in the financial statement, such as, vendor down payments, letter of credit, bills of exchange, and guarantee money.

- When you post a transaction to a vendor with a special G/L transaction indicator, the document is posted to an alternative reconciliation account instead of a normal reconciliation account.

- The SAP application comes with the following pre-configured special G/L indicator, however, you can create your own special G/L indicator in customization.

  - A: down payment on current assets

  - B: financial assets down payment

- F: down payment request

- I: intangible asset down payment

- M: tangible asset down payment

- O: amortization down payment

▪ To meet your business needs, you can create new special G/L indicators through either:

- **Transaction Code**: OBYR

    Or

- **R/3 IMG Menu**: *Implementation Guide (IMG) → Financial Accounting → Accounts Receivable and Accounts Payable → Business Transactions → Down Payment Made → Define Alternative Reconciliation Account for Down Payments*

    Or

- **mySAP ERP IMG Menu:** *Implementation Guide (IMG) → Financial Accounting (New) → Accounts Receivable and Accounts Payable → Business Transactions → Down Payment Made → Define Alternative Reconciliation Account for Down Payments*

▪ In the above configuration steps, you assign an alternative reconciliation account to a normal reconciliation account based on special G/L indicator. This relation between alternative reconciliation account and normal reconciliation account determines which alternative reconciliation account will be posted (Figure 2.47).

Maintain Accounting Configuration : Special G/L - Accounts

Properties

Chart of Accounts	BR01	chart of account BR01
Account Type	K	Vendor
Special G/L ind.	A	Down payment on current assets

Account assignment

Recon. acct	Special G/L account	Planning level	Input tax clearing
2000000000	1000000003		

FIGURE 2.48 Alternative reconciliation account assignment.

▪ Due to the special nature of business processes and different screen layouts, special G/L transactions are categorized into three categories: down payment related transactions, transactions related to bills of exchange, and others transactions.

▪ In special G/L transactions, you can see three types of transactions: automatic offsetting entries, noted items, and free offsetting entries.

▪ *Automatic offsetting entries*: We use this function to attain a balanced financial statement. Examples of these types of transactions are bank guarantees and bills of exchange. These types of entries are used for statistical purposes and used in financial statement as a note to financial statement. You can configure automatic offsetting entries through either:

  • ***Transaction Code***: *OBX3*

    Or

  • ***R/3 IMG Menu***: *Implementation Guide (IMG) → Financial Accounting → Accounts Receivable and Accounts Payable → Business Transactions → Postings with Alternative Reconciliation Account → Other Special G/L Transactions → Define Accounts for Automatic Offsetting Entry*

    Or

  • ***mySAP ERP IMG Menu:*** *Implementation Guide (IMG) → Financial Accounting (New) → Accounts Receivable and Accounts Payable → Business Transactions → Postings with Alternative Reconciliation Account → Other Special G/L Transactions → Define Accounts for Automatic Offsetting Entry*

▪ *Noted items*: Noted items are generally used to remind the user community of expected transactions. These are single line documents that do not post to G/L accounts. In other words the G/L balance doesn't get affected by this type of transaction. In the case of noted items, the system doesn't validate a zero balance check, such as own payment requests and bills of exchange requests.

▪ If you want to pay down a payment through an automatic payment program, then it is a pre-requisite that you need to have a down payment request. You will learn more about the down payment business process in Chapter 5.

- *Free offsetting entries*: Special G/L transactions are free of setting entries, other than statistical and noted item nature. Through configuration, you can determine your alternative reconciliation account, such as a down payment made or payment received.

Question – 32

When you post special general transaction system updates in

A. Sub-ledger and reconciliation ledger

B. Sub-ledger and alternative reconciliation ledger

C. Reconciliation accounts only

D. None of the above

Question – 33

A down payment request makes

A. A noted item posting in the vendor or customer accounts

B. An actual entry in the customer accounts

C. An actual entry in the vendor accounts

D. An actual entry in the vendor and customer accounts

2.4.11 Dual Control Principle

- You can implement dual control principle to control vendor customer master changes. Dual control principle works in a similar way in both account payable and account receivable.

- In order to implement dual principle, you need to configure the fields relevant for dual principle in IMG. You can configure through either:

  - *Transaction Code*: SPRO

    Or

  - *R/3 IMG Menu*: Implementation Guide (IMG) → Financial Accounting → Accounts Receivable and Accounts Payable → Vendor

Accounts → Master Data → Preparations for Creating Vendor Master Data → Define Sensitive Fields for Dual Control (Vendors)

Or

- **mySAP ERP IMG Menu:** *Implementation Guide (IMG) → Financial Accounting (New) → Accounts Receivable and Accounts Payable → Vendor Accounts → Master Data → Preparations for Creating Vendor Master Data → Define Sensitive Fields for Dual Control (Vendors)*

■ You can confirm the changes for a single vendor or a list of vendors. You can choose either of the options to SAP application provides:

- **Transaction Code:** *S_ALR_87012090*

  Or

- **SAP Menu**: *SAP Menu → Information Systems → Accounting → Financial Accounting → Accounts Payable → Reports for Accounts Payable Accounting → Master Data → Display/Confirm Critical Vendor Changes*

Question – 34

Non-integrated vendor invoices can be entered in

A. Financial Accounting – Accounts payable module only

B. Material management module only

C. FI-AP and MM modules

D. FI-AR, MM, and SD modules

Question – 35

The automatic payment program

A. Generates payment orders only

B. Generates payment orders and accounting transactions

C. Generates accounting transactions only

D. None of the above

Question – 36

The system updates vendor reconciliation and alternative reconciliation periodically.

A. *False*

B. *True*

2.5 Accounts Receivable (SAP FI-AR)

- Due to today's complex business environment, proper maintenance and tracking of accounts receivable is critical.

- Accounts receivable represents money owed by the customer on the sale of product and services. The accounts receivable component records and administers accounting transactions with your customer. This sub-component is an integral part of mySAP ERP Financials and interacts with other modules or sub-components of mySAP ERP Financials, such as sales and distribution module, assets accounting, and general ledger.

- In the accounts receivable module you will see different types of SAP objects. Before preceding further it is important to know what are they and what is their nature (Figure 2.49).

Accounts Receivable [SAP FI-AR]	
Client Dependent Objects	**Company Code Dependent Objects**
1. Customer Master – General Data 2. Payment Terms 3. Dunning Key 4. Posting Keys 5. Document Types 6. Customer Account Groups	1. Vendor Master – Company Code Data 2. Vendor Number Range 3. Document Number Ranges

FIGURE 2.49 Accounts receivable.

2.5.1 Customer Group

▪ You use customer group to classify customers depending on geographical area, business segment, and product. Customer groups control:

- Customer number range

- Customer master field layout

- Whether the customer is a onetime customer or not

▪ You can create or maintain a customer group through either:

- *Transaction Code*: SPRO

    Or

- *R/3 IMG Menu*: *Implementation Guide (IMG)* → *Financial Accounting* → *Accounts Receivable and Accounts Payable* → *Customer Accounts* → *Master Data* → *Preparations for Creating Customer Master Data* → *Define Account Groups with Screen Layout (Customers)*

    Or

- *mySAP ERP IMG Menu:* *Implementation Guide (IMG)* → *Financial Accounting (New)* → *Accounts Receivable and Accounts Payable* → *Customer Accounts* → *Master Data* → *Preparations for Creating Customer Master Data* → *Define Account Groups with Screen Layout (Customers)*

▪ The SAP application has a number of fields to capture information relating to a customer. Some of the information may be needed or dependent on geography or the product. Based on your requirements, you can create a number of customer groups. Through these customer groups you can control customer master data fields.

▪ Customer master fields are controlled through account group specific field status, transaction specific field status, and company code specific field status.

▪ *Account group specific field status*: Through the customer account group, you can decide whether the field can be suppressed, required entry, optional, or display. All customers falling under one group will have the same field status.

▪ *Transaction based field status*: Depending on which transaction code you are using, the fields can be editable or display. Transaction-based control further controls what could be a field status, when the user changes, or display mode.

- *Company code specific field status*: Since the customer master is a client dependent master, the SAP application provides functionality through which you can control which fields are editable, displayed, or hidden, depending on the company code.

- The system checks account group specific field status, transaction specific field status, and company code specific field status, which means the field status has highest priority.

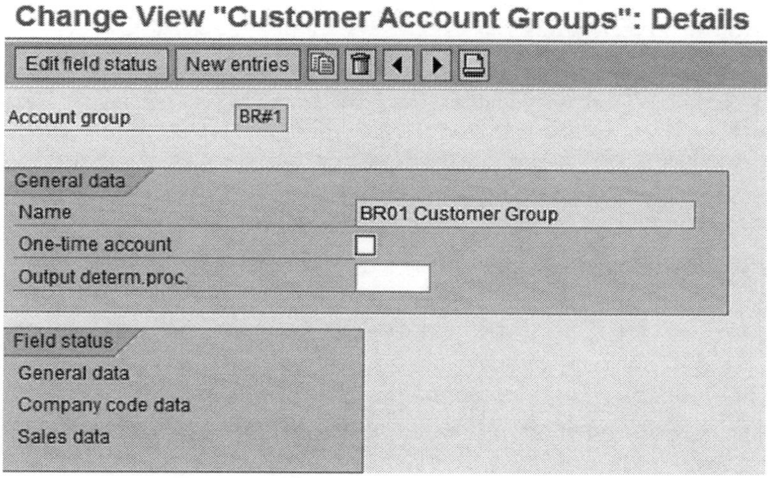

Change View "Customer Account Groups": Details

| Edit field status | New entries |

Account group   BR#1

General data

Name	BR01 Customer Group
One-time account	☐
Output determ.proc.	

Field status

General data

Company code data

Sales data

FIGURE 2.50 SPRO-customer group.

- Figure 2.50 depicts "change view" and "customer account groups." On the details screen, if you want to create a new account group, choose "new entries." To manage the account group field specific field status, select any field status group such as "general data" and then choose "edit field status."

2.5.2 Customer Number Range

- In SAP, the customer is identified by an ID called customer number. The customer number is unique to each the client so you cannot have the same ID for two different customers. The customer number is controlled through the customer number range.

▪ Like vendor number range, the customer number can be internal or external.

  • *Internal Number Range:* In the case of an internal number range system, assign the next available number while saving the customer master data. An internal number range always in numeric format.

  • *External Number Range:* External number ranges can be alpha numeric. The system does not assign customer numbers while creating the customer master system and expects the user to key in the customer number.

▪ You can create and maintain a customer number range through either:

  • **Transaction Code***: XDN1*

    Or

  • **R/3 IMG Menu**: *Implementation Guide (IMG) → Financial Accounting → Accounts Receivable and Accounts Payable → Customer Accounts → Master Data → Preparations for Creating Customer Master Data → Create Number Ranges for Customer Accounts*

    Or

  • **mySAP ERP IMG Menu:** *Implementation Guide (IMG) → Financial Accounting (New) → Accounts Receivable and Accounts Payable → Customer Accounts → Master Data → Preparations for Creating Customer Master Data → Create Number Ranges for Customer Accounts*

▪ By activating the "Ext" field against number range, you can determine whether the number range is external or internal.

▪ In Figure 2.51 number ranges 04 and 05 are an external number range, while all other number ranges are internal. In the case of internal number ranges, the system updates the current number field, which shows the current number in use.

▪ Number ranges are assigned to a customer group. One number range can be assigned to more than one customer groups. In that case, the customer groups shares number range.

2.5.3 Customer Master Records

▪ In order to post a transaction to a customer, the system expects that you already have the business partner's master data. Master data contains

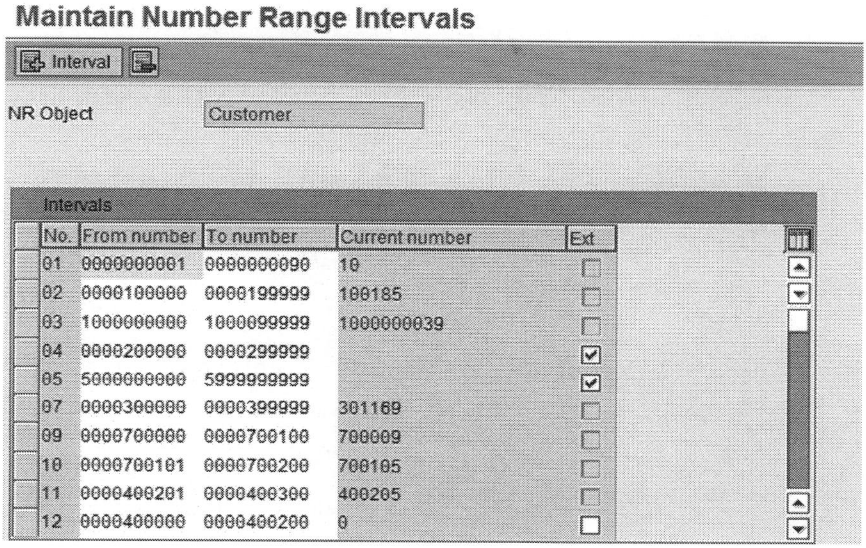

Maintain Number Range Intervals

No.	From number	To number	Current number	Ext
01	0000000001	0000000090	10	☐
02	0000100000	0000199999	100185	☐
03	1000000000	1000099999	1000000039	☐
04	0000200000	0000299999		☑
05	5000000000	5999999999		☑
07	0000300000	0000399999	301169	☐
09	0000700000	0000700100	700009	☐
10	0000700101	0000700200	700105	☐
11	0000400201	0000400300	400205	☐
12	0000400000	0000400200	0	☐

NR Object: Customer

FIGURE 2.51 XDN1-customer number range.

information relating to your business partner's name, addresses, and bank account. You need to create a customer master record before any transaction takes place.

- A customer master is created at the client level and the customer number is unique for each client because the customer master is used by accounting, sales, and distribution modules. Every company code creates its own master data, just as every sales area creates an item won data set.

- A complete customer master record consists of the following three segments:

  - *General Data*: Contains information that is specific to the client. These data are accessible in every company code residing in the same client.

  - *Company Code Data*: Company code view contains a set of data relevant to the company code. These data can't be shared with other company codes. If a company code wants to use an existing company code, it needs to extend the customer master data.

  - *Sales Area Data*: Similar to company code data, sales area data or view contains information that is relevant from a sales point of

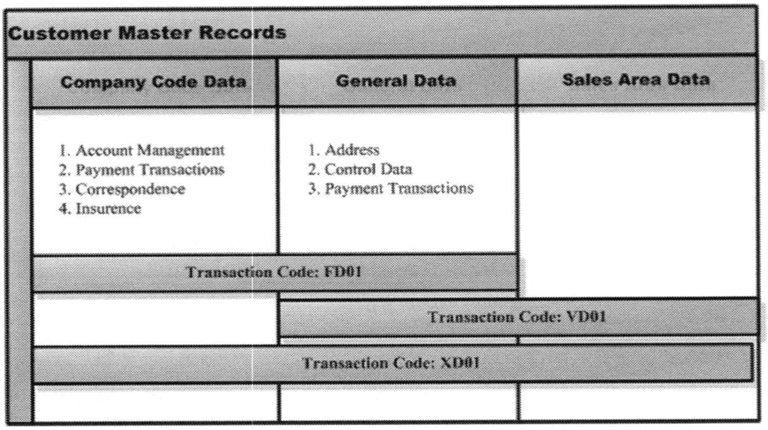

FIGURE 2.52 Customer master data. © Copyright 2012. SAP AG. All rights reserved.

view. These data are specific to a sales organization. Every sales organization will have its own set of data.

- You can create customer master data centrally through either:

  - **Transaction Code**: XD01

    Or

  - **SAP Menu**: SAP Menu → Accounting → Financial Accounting → Accounts Receivable → Master Records → Maintain Centrally → Create

- You can check the completeness of the customer master through either:

  - **Transaction Code**: S_ALR_87009973

    Or

  - **SAP Menu**: SAP Menu → Accounting → Financial Accounting → Accounts Receivable → Master Records → Maintain Centrally → Create

- In SAP ERP Financials, offer two types of customer master (1) Normal Customer Master and (2) One-time Customer.

2.5.4 Normal Customer vs. One-Time Customer

- *One-Time Customer*: One-time customers are those customers with whom you rarely do business. A one-time customer master record doesn't contain any specific information to that customer. You enter customer specific information while entering transactional data.

- *Normal Customer Master*: Customer masters other than one time customer master records are called normal customer records. In the case of a normal customer record, you maintain all the required information specific to that customer.

- Later in this section, you will learn about more important attributes and functionality of customer masters.

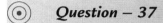

Question — 37

When posting to a one-time vendor or customer

A. *System adopts master data information from the customer or vendor master records*

B. *You need not to capture customer/vendor master information*

C. *You enter customer/vendor information in line items*

D. *None of the above*

2.5.5 Alternative Payer

- Like vendor master, you will find alternative payer in the customer master in general data and company code data. Alternative payer works the same way as alternative payee works. The only difference is that you receive money through alternative payer to pay money to alternative payee. Refer to the alternative payee section of account payable for more information.

2.5.6 Head Office and Branch Account

- The head office and branch concept has already been covered in accounts payable. The only difference is that in the account payable section you learn about head office and branch payable functionality, and in account receivable you will deal with the head office and branch customer. To learn more about the branch and head office concept, refer to the head office and branch section of accounts payable section.

2.5.7 Terms of Payment

In the account payable section, you learned that the payment term can be used by both accounts payable and account receivable. Configuration, concept, and usage of payment term is similar in both accounts payable and accounts receivable.

■ Refer to section 1.3.8 of account payable to learn more about payment terms and its usage.

2.5.8 Reconciliation Account

■ Like accounts payable, account receivable is also a subsidiary ledger. The concept of a reconciliation account applies the same way as it applies to accounts payable. Refer to section 1.3.9 to learn more about reconciliation account and its applicability in SAP application.

2.5.9 Special G/L Transactions

■ As discussed in the account payable sections, the SAP application offers various kinds of special G/L transactions. The concept and definition of customer special G/L transactions is similar to accounts payable.

■ You can configure special G/L transaction through either:

- *Transaction Code*: OBXR

  Or

- *R/3 IMG Menu*: Implementation Guide (IMG) → Financial Accounting → Accounts Receivable and Accounts Payable → Business Transactions → Down Payment Received → Define Alternative Reconciliation Account for Down Payments.

  Or

- *mySAP ERP IMG Menu:* Implementation Guide (IMG) → Financial Accounting (New) → Accounts Receivable and Accounts Payable → Business Transactions → Down Payment Received → Define Alternative Reconciliation Account for Down Payments

Question – 38

Through a down payment request you create

A. *A noted item with customer or vendor*

B. *A down payment request that updates customer balance*

C. *Down payment request that updates alternative reconciliation account*

2.5.10 Dunning

- Dunning refers to sending reminders to customers or vendors as a reminder for outstanding payment. It is sometimes called as a payment reminder or dunning notice.

- In order to enable dunning functionality, you need to carry out a number of configuration steps. Out of these steps in the configuration of dunning procedure is one of the most important tasks to activate the dunning functionality and is called the dunning procedure. You can reach the configuration steps by following the menu path given below:

  - ***Transaction Code****:FBMP*

    Or

  - ***R/3 IMG Menu****: Implementation Guide (IMG) → Financial Accounting → Accounts Receivable and Accounts Payable → Business Transactions → Dunning → Dunning Procedure → Define Dunning Procedures*

    Or,

  - ***mySAP ERP IMG Menu:*** *Implementation Guide (IMG) → Financial Accounting (New) → Accounts Receivable and Accounts Payable → Business Transactions → Dunning → Dunning Procedure → Define Dunning Procedures*

- Dunning program selects overdue open items of the business partners and determines the dunning level. Based on the dunning level, the system determines a dunning letter that could be sent out.

- In the dunning functionality you use the following new objects or terminologies:

  - *Dunning procedures*: Dunning procedure contains a set of control parameters to choose open items of business partners and determines the dunning level, the test (dunning letter), and the threshold limit for dunning functionality. You can configure dunning procedure through transaction code FBMP. You need to assign dunning procedure to the customer master. Figure 2.53 depicts the standard dunning procedure delivered by SAP. In the figure, the title bar shows multiple options for configuration of different functionalities or attributes of the dunning procedure. For example:

- How often you want to send dunning letters? The number of days that you enter in the dunning interval determines how often you want to dun your business partner.

- How many times do you want to send dunning letters? The number of dunning levels determines how many times you send dunning letters.

- If you choose "Dunning Texts" you can assign a dunning letter script based on the dunning levels.

- If you choose "Minimum Amount" you can configure the threshhold limit for sending a dunning notice.

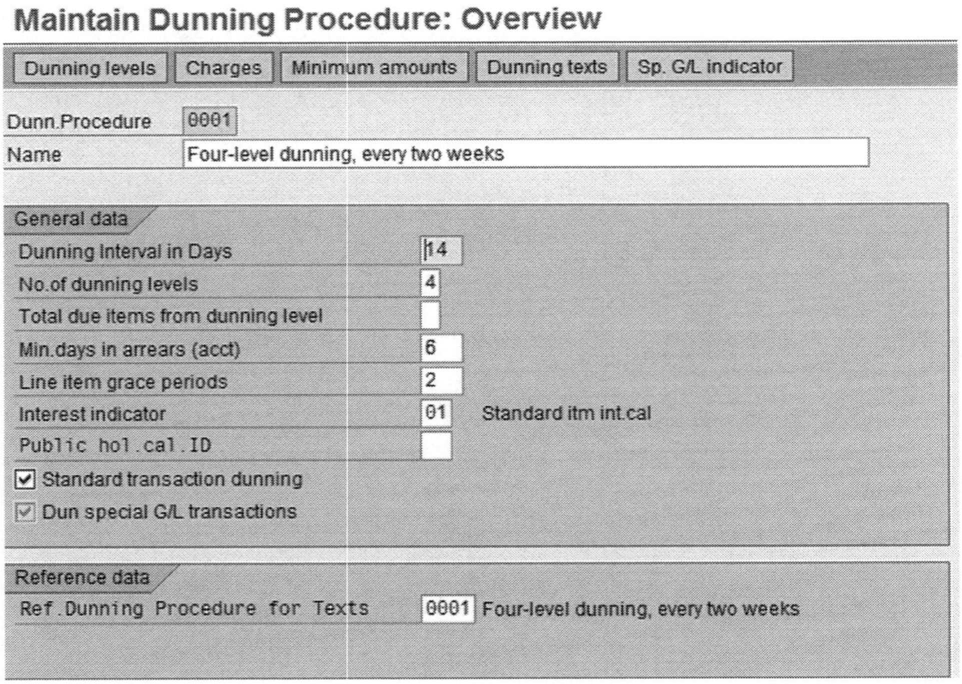

Maintain Dunning Procedure: Overview

Dunning levels	Charges	Minimum amounts	Dunning texts	Sp. G/L indicator

Dunn.Procedure   0001
Name   Four-level dunning, every two weeks

General data

Dunning Interval in Days	14
No.of dunning levels	4
Total due items from dunning level	
Min.days in arrears (acct)	6
Line item grace periods	2
Interest indicator	01 Standard itm int.cal
Public hol.cal.ID	
☑ Standard transaction dunning	
☑ Dun special G/L transactions	

Reference data

Ref.Dunning Procedure for Texts   0001 Four-level dunning, every two weeks

FIGURE 2.53 Dunning procedure.

- *Dunning levels*: The dunning level determines how many times you want send dunning letters. Based on the dunning interval, the system calculates the due date for sending out dunning letters.

- *Dunning areas*: The dunning area is an organizational unit within a company code. You assign a dunning area to your business partner. You can assign a dunning area to multiple customers but a customer can have only one dunning area in a given point of time.

- Figure 2.54 depicts the correspondence tab of customer master data. You can see the field for dunning procedure assignment. If you choose the dunning area button, you can assign the dunning area.

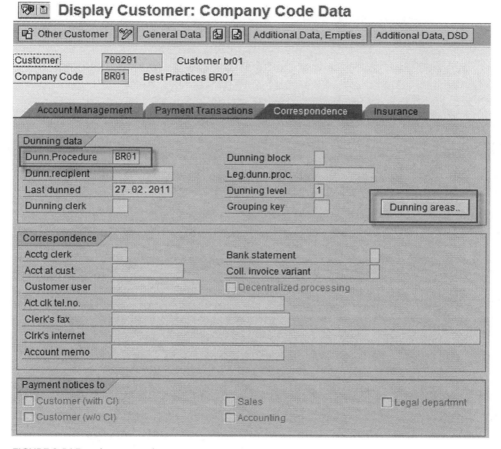

FIGURE 2.54 Dunning area assignment to customer master.

- You can run the dunning program through either the batch process or manually. You can manually run a dunning program by using the following menu path:

- *Transaction Code*: F150

  Or

- *R/3 SAP Menu*: *Accounting → Accounts Receivable → Periodic Processing → F150 – Dunning*

◼ When you run a dunning program, the system creates a dunning proposal. Once the system creates the dunning proposal you can:

- Set a dunning block

- Reset a dunning block

- Change dunning level

◼ Once the dunning notice is printed, the system updates the business partner's master data with the dunning date and dunning levels.

 Question – 39

When you execute the dunning program, the system generates

A. *Dunning letters only*

B. *Dunning letters as well as system updates general ledgers balances*

C. *System post interest and expenses that you have configured in dunning procedures*

D. *None of the above*

2.5.11 Dual Control Principle

◼ In order to prevent unauthorized changes, you can implement the dual control principle provided by the SAP application. In dual control principle, you can configure certain fields in the customer master as sensitive. If changes are made to these fields, someone other than the person who made changes needs to confirm the change. Dual principle is equally applicable to vendor master.

◼ In order to implement dual principle, you need to configure fields relevant for dual principle in IMG. You can configure through either:

- *Transaction Code*: SPRO

  Or

- **R/3 IMG Menu**: *Implementation Guide (IMG) → Financial Accounting → Accounts Receivable and Accounts Payable → Customer Accounts → Master Data → Preparations for Creating Customer Master Data → Define Sensitive Fields for Dual Control (Customers)*

   Or

- **mySAP ERP IMG Menu:** *Implementation Guide (IMG) → Financial Accounting (New) → Accounts Receivable and Accounts Payable → Customer Accounts → Master Data → Preparations for Creating Customer Master Data → Define Sensitive Fields for Dual Control (Customers)*

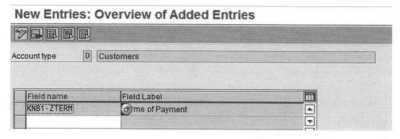

FIGURE 2.55 SPRO-dual control configuration.

- Figure 2.55 depicts the configuration screen of dual control principle. In this case, you have defined the payment term as a sensitive field. The SAP application provides number fields to those that can be defined for dual control principle.

- If you change the sensitive fields, the customer master is blocked for payment. The system removes the payment block once the changes are confirmed by someone other than the person who made the changes.

- You can confirm the changes for a single customer or a list of customers. You can choose either of the options the SAP application provides:

   - **Transaction Code:** *S_ALR_87012183*

      Or

   - **SAP Menu**: *SAP Menu → Information Systems → Accounting → Financial Accounting → Accounts Receivable → Reports for Accounts Receivable Accounting → Master Data → Display/Confirm Critical Customer Changes*

2.5.12 Over Payment/Under Payment

■ Payment differences generally arises while clearing if a customer has made an under payment or overpayment.

■ Normally underpayment arises under the following circumstances:

• The customer has made an unauthorized deduction for cash discount

• The customer has some concern over the quality of the material

• Shipment got delayed

■ While processing incoming payments or clearing customer open items, the system checks tolerance groups assigned to user concerns (employee tolerance) and customer tolerance groups.

■ You can categorize customer underpayment into two categories: authorized deduction and unauthorized deduction.

■ Authorized deductions are those deductions that are within the customer tolerance limit. Based on the customer tolerance group configuration, the system either determines an allowable cash discount and posts a cash discount to a G/L account or posts to an overpayment/under payment account to charge as revue or expenses.

■ Unauthorized deductions are deductions that have not been agreed upon. Unauthorized deductions may be either a material amount or immaterial amount.

■ If the unauthorized deduction is immaterial, then it can be processed automatically by adjusting the cash discount amount. However, these cash discounts should be within the permitted limit of employee tolerances.

■ Material unauthorized deductions can be treated in either of the following ways:

• As a partial payment

• As a residual payment

■ *Partial Payment*: A material unauthorized deduction may be posted to a customer account as a partial payment. A partial payment doesn't clear any open customer items, including incoming payments on all open items. These open items can be cleared by an other incoming payment or credit note.

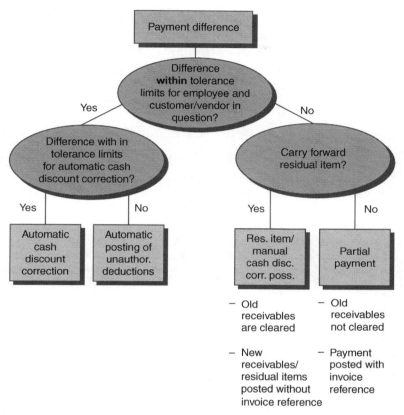

FIGURE 2.56 Outgoing payment difference.

■ *Residual Payment*: A residual payment clears customer open items and creates a new open item under paid amount. A new open item inherit the payment terms and line item attributes from the original line item.

2.5.13 The Customer is also a Vendor

■ In your day to day business, you may be dealing with an entity who is purchasing product from you as well as selling product to you. As the SAP application has a demarcation between vendor and customer master records, you need to create two separate master data: one for the customer and another for vendor master records.

■ Transactions posted to customers are recorded in customer ledgers in the same way transactions posted to vendors are recorded in the vendor ledger. Now you must be looking for functionality when you offset the vendor balance with the customer and vice versa.

■ To offset customer balance with the vendor you need to meet following two requirements:

● Assign vendor master in the customer master record in the control tab of general data

● Activate "clearing with vendor" in the company code data and payment transaction tab pages

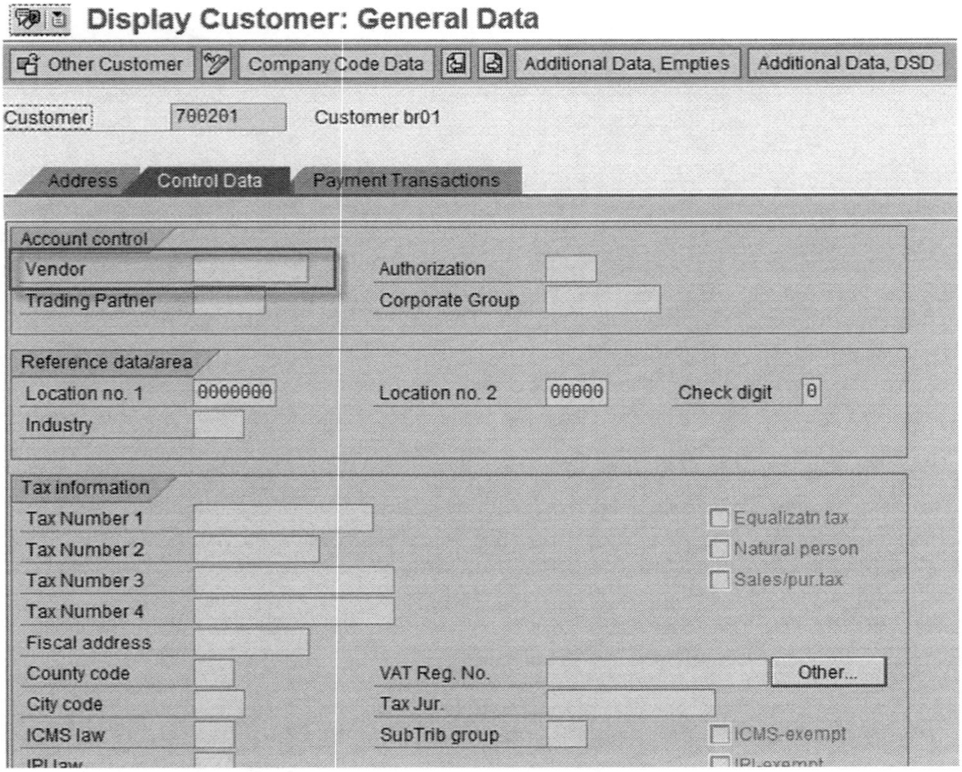

FIGURE 2.57 FD03-customer master control data.

■ Like the vendor master, in the customer master you need to key in the vendor number in the company code data and control tab of the customer master record as shown in Figure 2.57. In the company code data – payment transaction tab check the box "clearing with vendor," as seen in Figure 2.58.

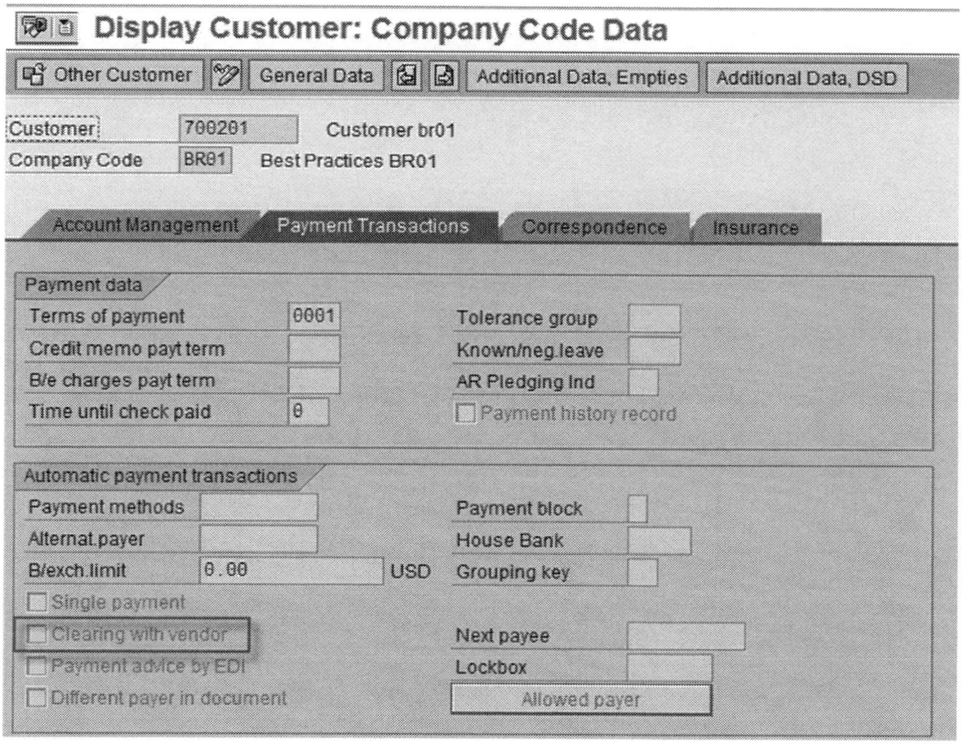

FIGURE 2.58 Customer master-company code data.

⊙ **Question – 40**

Base line date should always one of the following: document date, posting date and entry date.

A. *True*

B. *False*

2.6 Assets Management (SAP® FI-AM)

- Assets accounting is used for managing and supervising fixed assets. Assets accounting is sometimes called assets management and is part of the SAP's core financial accounting module. Similar to the accounts payable and accounts receivable modules, assets accounting module is treated as a subsidiary ledger in financial accounting.

- Due to SAP's integrated approach, assets accounting modules talk to accounts payable, the accounts receivable component of financial accounting, and material management.

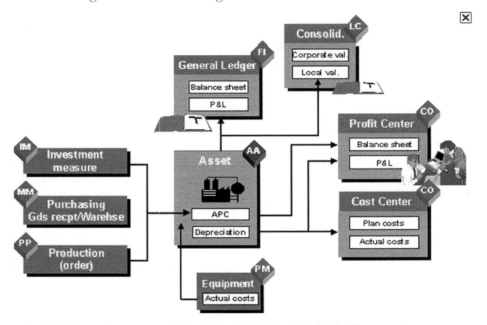

FIGURE 2.59 Assets Management in SAP © Copyright 2012. SAP AG. All rights reserved.

- The assets accounting module takes care of the entire life cycle of an asset starting with acquisition of an asset, its wear and tear, improvements, a retirement assets, scrap, and transfers.

- With the assets accounting module you can also manage assets under contraction and lease assets.

- The assets accounting component of SAP ERP financials uses various new objects to manage assets. In the following section, you will come to know these new objects.

2.6.1 Chart of Depreciation

- *Chart of depreciation* is the index of the depreciation area. In order to comply with various legal and statutory requirements, you need to manage your assets in different ways, such as providing deprecation and valuation.

- SAP has provided country specific template chart of depreciation for most countries. All company codes within a country can use the same chart of depreciation. Chart of deprecation is not company code specific.

- In a chart of deprecation, you define depreciation areas for both internal and external reporting. In a chart of depreciation, you can create and maintain up to 99 depreciation areas.

- You can't use the SAP provided chart of deprecation as it is. To use these templates you need to copy it into a different name.

- You can reach the chart of depreciation configuration screen by navigating the following menu path:

  - **SAP IMG Menu**: *Financial Accounting → Asset Accounting → Organizational Structures → Copy Reference Chart of Depreciation/ Depreciation Areas → Copy Reference Chart of Depreciation*

- Figure 2.60 shows the SAP provided chart of depreciation template 1US for the United States of America. In the case of book depreciation areas 1, option 1 is selected, which means this depreciation area posts to the general ledger account. In the column "Target Group," you can assign the ledger group (in case of the SAP general ledger).

- After copying from the SAP given template, you can add and delete depreciation areas. Once your chart of depreciation is ready, you need to assign your chart of depreciation to your company code. You can assign your newly created chart of depreciation to company code by using the following menu path:

  - **SAP IMG Menu**: *Financial Accounting → Asset Accounting → Organizational Structures → Copy Reference Chart of Depreciation/ Depreciation Areas → Assign Chart of Depreciation to Company Code*

- You can assign a chart of depreciation to N number of company codes, while a company code can have only one chart of depreciation.

Change View "Define Depreciation Areas": Overview

Chart of dep.   1US   Sample chart of depreciation: USA

Define Depreciation Areas

Ar.	Name of depreciation area	Real	G/L	Trgt Group
1	Book depreciation	☑	1	
2	Book depreciation	☑	0	
3	Book depreciation	☑	0	
10	Federal Tax ACRS/MACRS	☑	0	
11	Alternative Minimum Tax	☑	0	
12	Adjusted Current Earnings	☑	0	
13	Corporate Earnings & Profits	☑	0	
17	Fed Tax MACRS (for states not allowing bonus depr)	☑	0	
30	Consolidated balance sheet in local currency	☑	0	
31	Consolidated balance sheet in group currency	☑	0	
32	Book depreciation in group currency	☑	0	
40	State modified ACRS	☑	0	
50	Derived area	☐	0	

FIGURE 2.60 Chart of depreciation 1US template.

Assignment of CoA is independent from the assignment of the chart of depreciation. For example, while company code A and company code B are using the same CoA, they can use two separate charts of depreciation.

2.6.2 Assets Master Data

- You can organize your fixed assets in various levels based on your reporting requirements. You can group together various components of assets under main assets. For example, keyboard, mouse, and PC can be grouped under "desktop" as main assets, and individually recognized as sub-assets. Furthermore, all desktops can be grouped under an assets class called workstations. Workstations and laptops can be grouped as computers for the balance sheet. Mainly, assets are structured under assets level, such as group assets, main assets, and sub–assets; account determination level such as building, plant and machinery, and furniture fixture; and general ledger level, keeping in mind the reporting requirement.

▪ Like customer master records and vendor master records, you use assets master record to track asset-related transactions.

▪ When you create an assets master record, you select the assets class. Assets class determines various important default values and field layout of the assets master record.

▪ You can create an assets master record through either of the following navigation options:

• **SAP Menu:** *Accounting → Financial Accounting → Organizational Structures → Fixed Assets → Asset → Create → Asset*

• **Transaction Code:** *AS01*

▪ You assign controlling objects in the assets master. When you post transactions and run period end activities, the system determines the controlling objects to be posted with the transactions based on cost object assignment in the assets master records.

2.6.3 Assets Classes

▪ You can group assets with similar attributes under an assets class. In mySAP ERP Financials you can create as many assets classes as you want. Asset classes are client specific, which means any company codes within a client can use asset class. SAP comes with a few pre-delivered assets classes. If you need more asset classes, you can create them by navigating the following menu path:

• **SAP IMG Menu:** *Financial Accounting → Asset Accounting → Organizational Structures → Asset Classes → Define Asset Classes*

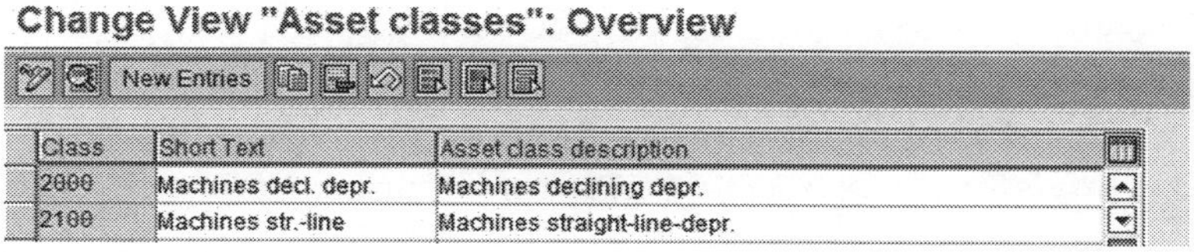

FIGURE 2.61 Assets class.

▪ Once you double click on the any of the assets class, the system will bring up the following screen where you can set up the attributes.

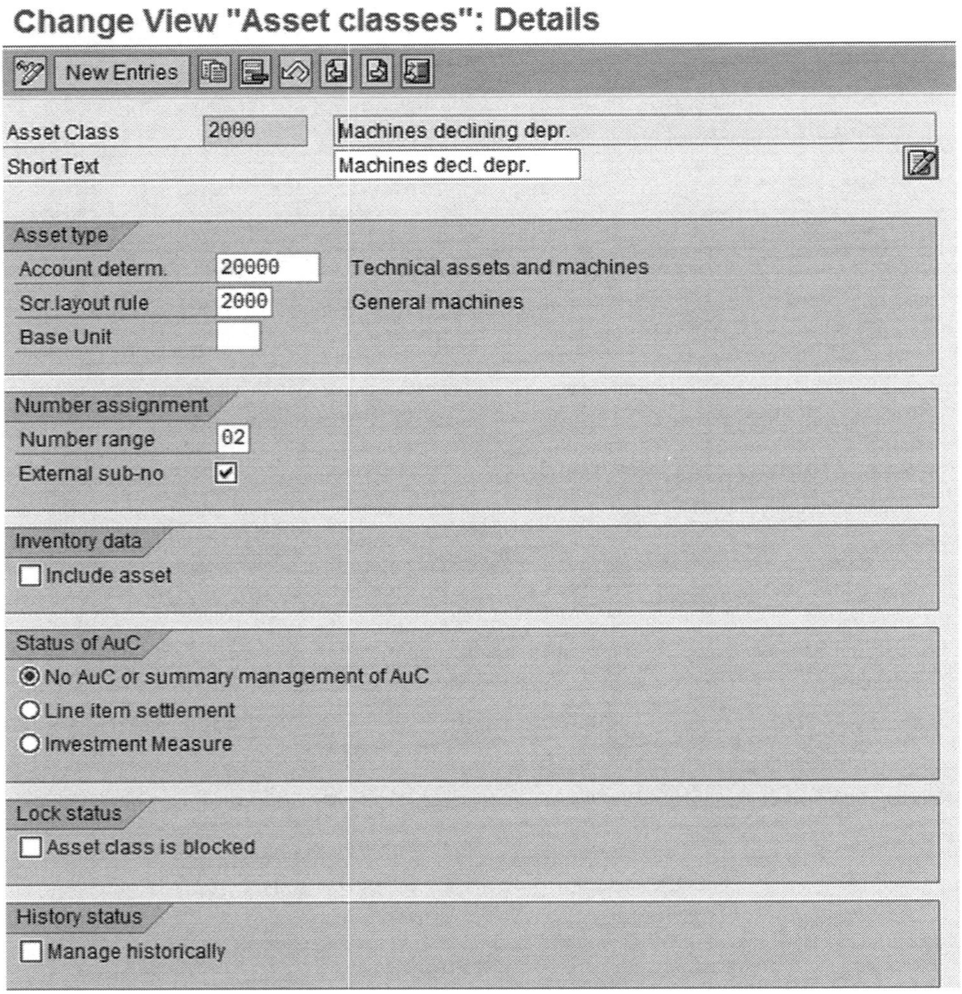

Change View "Asset classes": Details

| [✎] New Entries | 🗎 🗒 📝 🗃 🗃 📑 |

| Asset Class | 2000 | Machines declining depr. |
| Short Text | | Machines decl. depr. | [📝] |

Asset type
Account determ.	20000	Technical assets and machines
Scr.layout rule	2000	General machines
Base Unit		

Number assignment
| Number range | 02 |
| External sub-no | ☑ |

Inventory data
☐ Include asset

Status of AuC
◉ No AuC or summary management of AuC
○ Line item settlement
○ Investment Measure

Lock status
☐ Asset class is blocked

History status
☐ Manage historically

FIGURE 2.62 Attributes of assets class.

- Figure 2.62 depicts attributes of assets class where you can assign the account determination key and the assets number range.
- If you want to structure your assets class based on general ledger, you need to use the following menu path:
  - **SAP IMG Menu:** *Financial Accounting → Asset Accounting → Organizational Structures → Asset Classes → Generate Asset Classes from G/L Accounts (1 to 1)*

- Assets class controls the following attributes of an assets master: screen layout of assets master records, number range of assets, master data maintenance level, account determination for transactions, and valuation areas at chart of depreciation level.

- Asset SAP allows you to copy assets class attributes to assets and sub-assets, it is best practice maintain any default values in the assets class so that you can reduce data maintenance at the assets and sub-assets level.

- When you create an asset, you always need to select an asset class in the initial screen.

2.6.4 Assets Number Range

- In assets class you assign *assets number range* ID. Assets number ranges works in the same way as the other number ranges you have studied so far. Asset number ranges can be internal or external. In the case of internal number range, the system assigns an asset number from the number range assigned to assets class, while external number range system expects that the user will key a number out of an assigned number range. See Figure 2.58.

- Assets number ranges are company code specific. You can create and maintain asset number ranges by using the following menu path:

  - **SAP IMG Menu:** *Financial Accounting → Asset Accounting → Organizational Structures → Asset Classes → Define Number Range Interval*

Display Number Range Intervals

NR Object	Asset Number
Subobject	1000

Intervals

No.	From number	To number	Current number	Ext	
01	000000001000	000000001999	1147	☐	▲
02	000000002000	000000002999	2304	☐	▼
03	000000003000	000000003999	3405	☐	
04	000000004000	000000004999	4182	☐	
05	000000005000	000000005999	5008	☐	
06	000000006000	000000006999	0	☐	
09	000000900000	000000999999	0	☐	

FIGURE 2.63 Assets number range.

- Sub-assets master uses an additional suffix number to the main asset. In the standard functionality you do not need to create the *sub assets number range*. If you have not checked the "External sub-no" check box in the asset class (Figure 2.57), the system assigns a two character number after the main asset number. If you have checked the "External sub-no" check box, the system expect that you will add a two character numeric number.

2.6.5 Group Assets

- Normally assets and sub-assets are evaluated and depreciated individually within assets management, but in some cases, to comply with legal or statutory requirements, you need to depreciate assets as a group. In these circumstances, you create another new SAP object called asset group. Like assets master record, you need to create a group asset master and design its layout through screen layout control. You can create group asset master record by using the following navigation options:

  - **SAP Menu:** *Accounting → Fixed Assets → Asset → Create → Group Asset*

  - **Transaction Code:** *AS21*

- A group asset can have up to 9,999 sub-numbers. While creating group assets, you need to select an assets class.

- You assign an asset master data to group assets by keying in the group assets master ID in the depreciation areas of the asset master data.

- You cannot post a transaction directly to group assets. When you post to an asset, the system duplicates transactional data for group asset.

2.6.6 Low Value Assets (LVA)

- Low value assets are special types of assets and need special configuration. Normally low value assets are those assets whose money value of these assets is very nominal. Determination of low values depends on business practice and legal requirement. Low value assets are generally depreciated in the year of purchase. In order to have special treatment, you need to configure special assets class, threshold limit for LVA, and a deprecation key. SAP has provided deprecation key "GWG" which depreciate assets fully in the year of acquisition. You can configure the thresh hold limit by navigating the following menu path:

- **SAP IMG Menu:** *Financial Accounting → Asset Accounting → Valuation → Amount Specifications (Company Code/Depreciation Area) → Specify Amount for Low Value Assets*

Change View "Amount for low-value assets": Overview

Ar	Name of depreciation area	LVA amount	MaxLVA pur	Crcy
01	Book depreciation	410.00	423.00	EUR
02	Book depreciation	410.00	423.00	EUR
03	Book depreciation	495.30	511.00	USD
20	Cost-accounting depreciation	410.00	423.00	EUR
51	Investment support posted to liabilities	410.00	423.00	EUR
60	Book depreciation	410.00	423.00	EUR
61	Special tax depreciation for APC in fin.s	410.00	423.00	EUR

Company Code 1000 IDES AG

Dialog Structure
▽ ☐ Company code selection
　　☐ Amount for low-value assets

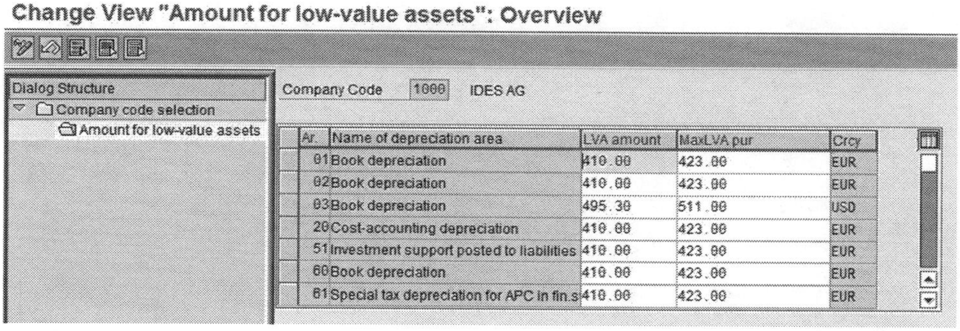

FIGURE 2.64 Amount for low value assets.

- Figure 2.64 depicts a low value threshold limit. This configuration is company code dependent and in this screen you can see low value threshold limit per deprecation areas.

- At assets class level you configure how the system will determine the low value. SAP has provided two type checks: individual check and quantity check. In the case of *individual check* while posting, the APC systems compares the APC cost with the LVA threshold limit. In the case of *quantity check*, the system divides the total APC value with number of assets and compares the result with the LVA thresh hold limit. You can configure the value check determination by navigating the following menu path:

  - **SAP IMG Menu:** *Financial Accounting → Asset Accounting → Valuation → Amount Specifications (Company Code/Depreciation Area) → Specify LVA Asset Classes*

- Figure 2.65 depicts a low value check at assets class level and the available options. This check is at chart of deprecation and assets class level is not specific to any company code.

2.6.7 Assets Under Construction (AUC)

- *Assets under construction* are another kind of special assets class. From a business practice and legal point of view you show AUC separately

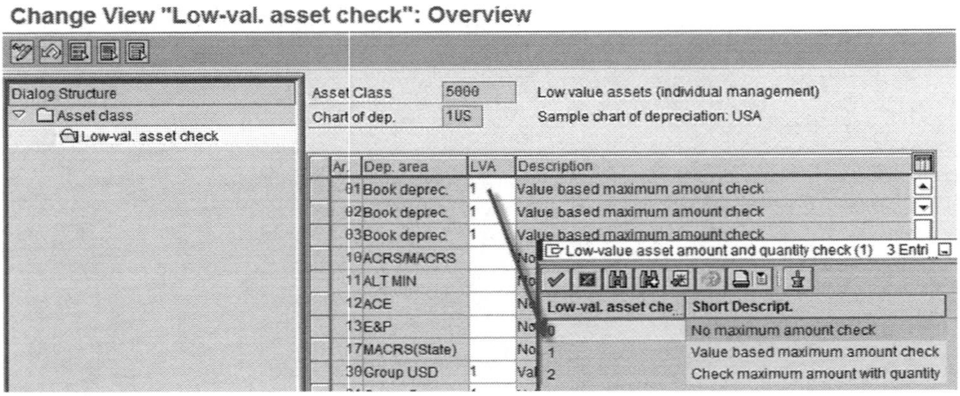

Change View "Low-val. asset check": Overview

FIGURE 2.65 Low value check at assets class level.

in our financial statement. Due to the special treatment, you normally create a special assets class and account determination for assets under construction. SAP facilitates the capture of the AUC value in two ways: individual management and collective management. Under *individual management* you create separate master data for each AUC and collect relevant cost. In case of *collective management*, you create a single master data for AUCs and during settlement you distribute these collective costs based on certain allocation methods. Normally, you don't provide deprecation on AUC. SAP has provided a depreciation key 000 which doesn't depreciate assets.

2.6.8 Leased Assets

- Lease assets are another kind of special assets. Depending on the lease terms, assets either remains property of the lessor or manufacturer and are treated differently in your financial statement. From an accounting point of view, a lease can be classified into two categories: operating lease, and financial lease. In the case of a *financial lease* you capitalize assets after excluding interest portion, while in the case of an *operating lease* you don't capitalize assets, and instead show lease installment as a finance charge.

2.6.9 Account Determination

- *Account determination* is a key that forms a bridge between assets class and assets general ledger account. In assets class, you assign an account determination key. In account determination you assign a general ledger to the account determination key.

■ You can assign multiple assets class to a single account determination key and a single general ledger to one or more account determination keys.

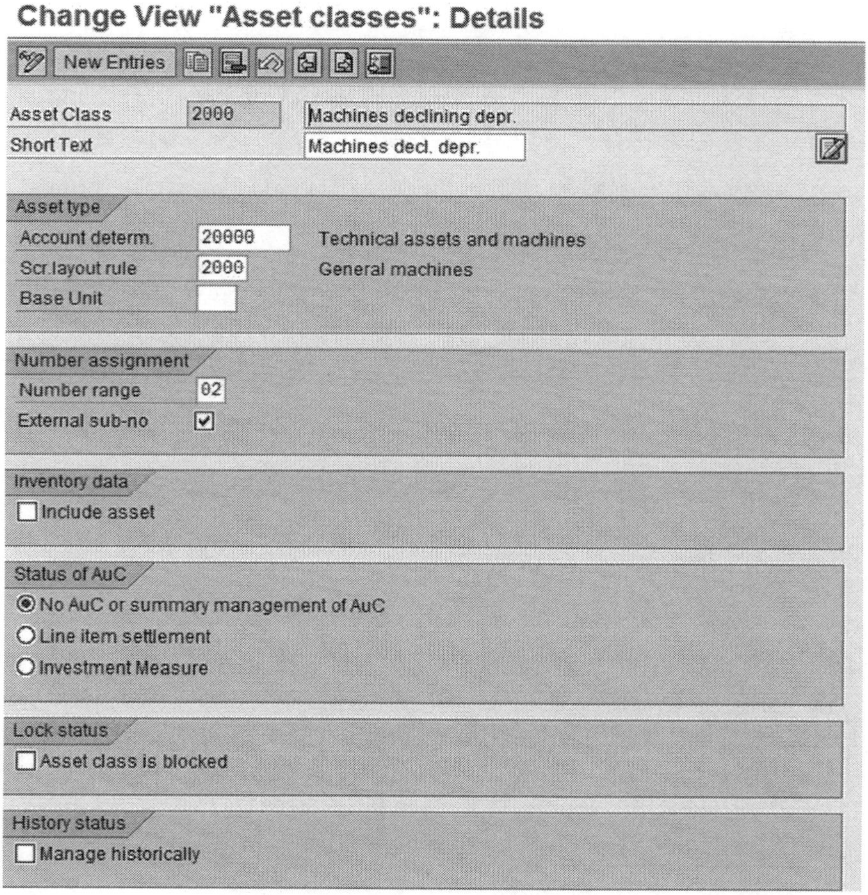

Change View "Asset classes": Details

🖉 New Entries	🗈 🖫 🙇 🖅 🖹 🖅

Asset Class	2000	Machines declining depr.	
Short Text		Machines decl. depr.	🗷

Asset type

Account determ.	20000	Technical assets and machines
Scr.layout rule	2000	General machines
Base Unit		

Number assignment

Number range	02
External sub-no	☑

Inventory data

☐ Include asset

Status of AuC

◉ No AuC or summary management of AuC
○ Line item settlement
○ Investment Measure

Lock status

☐ Asset class is blocked

History status

☐ Manage historically

FIGURE 2.66 Assignment of account determination key to assets master.

■ When you do acquisition, retirement, and depreciation posting, the system determines a correct general ledger account based on account determination configuration. In real-time, the system updates one depreciation area, while through period end activity (deprecation posting run) you can update other depreciation areas.

■ The system determines the correct general account based on following objects. You assign general ledger account based on chart of account, chart of deprecation, account determination key, and depreciation areas:

- *Company code*: When you are entering transactions you are entering company code

- *Chart of depreciation*: Once the company code is determined by the system, the system derives an associated chart of depreciation assigned to the company code

- *Chart of account*: You assign a chart of account to a company code based on company code information and the system-derived assigned chart of account.

- *Account determination key*: When you create assets, you create it under an assets class. The system derives account determination that you have assigned to assets class.

- *Depreciation area*: You create depreciation areas in the chart of depreciation, based on chart of depreciation, while the system determines which depreciations are relevant for posting.

- You can reach account determination configuration screen by using the following menu path:

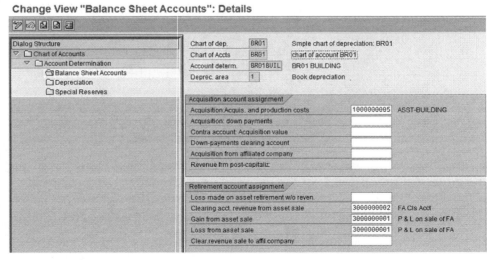

FIGURE 2.67 Balance sheet account determination.

- **SAP IMG Menu:** *Financial Accounting → Asset Accounting → Integration with the General Ledger → Assign G/L Accounts*

- Figure 2.67 depicts balance sheet account determination. In the top of the screen, you can see a chart of deprecation, chart of account, account determination key, and deprecation area. The system looks for a unique combination of these objects. Once it finds this combination, based on transaction type, the system determines what general ledger account with which it will be posted.

- Assets accounting uses *transaction type* for classification of business transaction. Transaction types help in the account determination process to identify appropriate G/L accounts.

2.6.10 Depreciation Areas

- Chart of depreciation contains list of *depreciations areas* that you are going to use in one or more assets. Different depreciation areas hold different parameter keys for the calculation of depreciation. For example, one is used for tax purpose, and another used for book purposes.

- After production start of the system, you can add new depreciation areas and add existing assets to new depreciation area; however, SAP recommends that you create all depreciation areas before putting the system into production.

- You can create and delete depreciation areas by using the following menu path:

  - **SAP IMG Menu:** *Financial Accounting → Asset Accounting → Valuation → Depreciation Areas → Define Depreciation Areas*

- In a chart of depreciation, you can manage up to 99 different depreciation areas. In asset class or in asset master, you maintain depreciation-area specific parameters. You can also activate or deactivate any specific depreciation area at assets class or assets level. You can reach this configuration screen by using the following menu path:

  - **SAP IMG Menu:** *Financial Accounting → Asset Accounting → Valuation → Determine Depreciation Areas in the Asset Class*

- Figure 2.68 depicts deprecation area 01 specific values in assets class 1,000. In this screen, you can also maintain the default values such as minimum life of the assets, maximum life of the assets, and depreciation

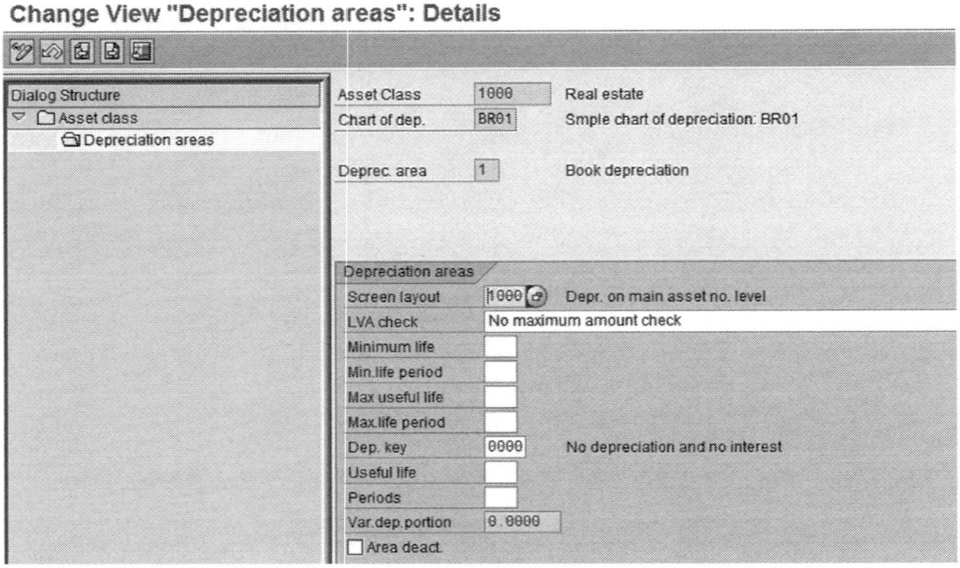

Change View "Depreciation areas": Details

FIGURE 2.68 Depreciation area specific default values.

keys. The Area check box indicates whether the deprecation area is active or not. If it is checked, it indicates depreciation areas to activate in assets class level.

■ In this configuration, step you also assign depreciation areas specific screen layout. Deprecation areas screen layout controls what fields are allowed for input and maintenance level of deprecation areas specific values.

■ The values of assets are determined in depreciation areas. While posting a transaction, sometimes you need to calculate a new value based on determined value. You can do so through *derived depreciation*.

■ In the case of derived depreciation areas, the system applies a mathematical formula on the determined value of other depreciation areas (maximum four depreciation areas) to determine a new value.

■ The depreciation area which posts to the general ledger is normally called book depreciation area, which generally carries values for preparation of the financial statement. Book depreciation has some special significances compared to other depreciation areas:

- Book deprecation area updates general ledger in real-time

- It doesn't adopt values from other depreciation areas, but is used as reference for other depreciation areas

- The currency book depreciation area should always be the same as the company code currency

- You must have account determination configuration for book depreciation area

- You can't delete this depreciation area

■ If you are working in a multi-currency environment, you may come across a situation when different company codes operate under different currencies. In those circumstances, you use group currency for smoother consolidation, and in assets accounting you need have an additional depreciation area called *group depreciation area*. To maintain group depreciation area ingroup currency, you need to assign a group currency key to depreciation area.

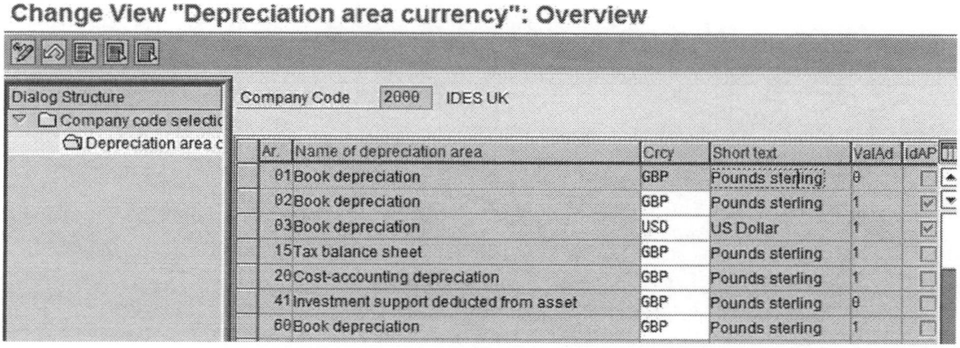

Change View "Depreciation area currency": Overview

Company Code	2000	IDES UK				

Ar.	Name of depreciation area	Crcy	Short text	ValAd	IdAP
01	Book depreciation	GBP	Pounds sterling	0	☐
02	Book depreciation	GBP	Pounds sterling	1	☑
03	Book depreciation	USD	US Dollar	1	☑
15	Tax balance sheet	GBP	Pounds sterling	1	☐
20	Cost-accounting depreciation	GBP	Pounds sterling	1	☐
41	Investment support deducted from asset	GBP	Pounds sterling	0	☐
60	Book depreciation	GBP	Pounds sterling	1	☐

Dialog Structure
▽ ☐ Company code selectio
    🗁 Depreciation area c

FIGURE 2.69 Determination of deprectaion areas other than company code currency.

■ Figure 2.69 depicts deprecation areas of company code 2,000. Company code currency of a company code is GBP. For consolidation purposes, the company code has created an additional deprecation area in USD. You can reach this configuration screen by using the following menu path:

- **SAP IMG Menu:** *Financial Accounting → Asset Accounting → Valuation Currencies → Define Depreciation Areas for Foreign Currencies*

2.6.11 Depreciation Key

- *Depreciation key* contains five *depreciation methods* that control the calculation of depreciation and imputed interest amount for deprecation areas. These calculation methods are: base method, declining balance method, maximum amount method, multi-level method, and period control method. You can create a deprecation key by using the following navigation path:

  - **SAP IMG Menu:** *Financial Accounting → Asset Accounting → Depreciation → Valuation Methods → Depreciation Key Maintain → Depreciation Key*

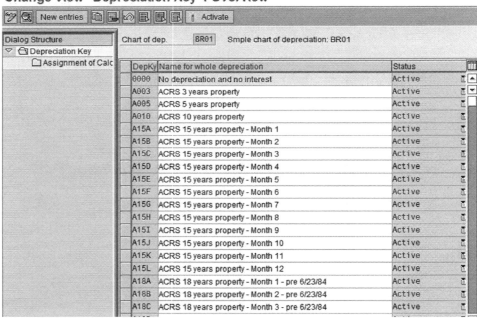

FIGURE 2.70 Deprectaion keys.

- If you double click any of the deprecation key, the system will come up with the screen shown in Figure 2.71. It relates to attributes of deprecation key LINR. In short, deprecation key LINR is used for storing line deprecation, or deprecation amount = (APC cost – scrap value)/ number of useful year.

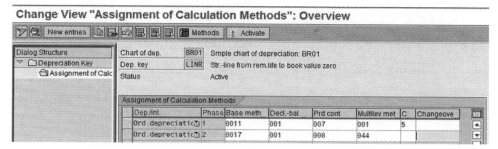

FIGURE 2.71 Deprectaion key attributes.

- Figure 2.71 shows two phase of deprecation calculations. The first row or phase is valid for the first five years (refer to column named "C"); while the second row is valid from sixth year onwards.

- Beside calculation method, deprecation keys contain what would be the scrap value of assets after the useful life of the assets, whether or not the depreciation rate will remain constant or changes during the life of the assets.

2.6.12 Depreciation Methods

- *Depreciation methods* provide a base for the calculation of deprecation. First, you need to maintain each calculation method separately and then assign all five calculation methods to a deprecation key. Base method is a chart of deprecation independent object and other calculation methods are charts of deprecation dependents. You can assign one calculation method to each different deprecation key.

- SAP comes with few default calculation methods, but if a default calculation method does not fit your requirement you can create your own calculation methods by copying from the standard one.

- *Base Method*: Base method contains general control-following parameters required for the calculation of deprecation. Base method is a client-dependent calculation method and can be used by more than one chart of deprecation. Base method controls or determines:

  - Type of deprecation

  - Deprecation calculation methods;

  - Treatment of the end of deprecation

- You can reach configuration screen by using the following menu path:

  - **SAP IMG Menu:** *Financial Accounting → Asset Accounting → Depreciation → Valuation Methods → Depreciation Key → Calculation Methods → Define Base Methods*

- *Declining Balance Method*: Diminishing deprecation includes both the declining balance method and the sum of the year digits method. In declining balance method, the system calculates depreciation by multiplying factor with the rate of deprecation derived from useful life of assets. You can reach the configuration screen by using the following menu path:

  - **SAP IMG Menu:** *Financial Accounting → Asset Accounting → Depreciation → Valuation Methods → Depreciation Key → Calculation Methods → Define Declining-Balance Methods*

- *Maximum Amount Method***:** In the maximum method you specify the maximum amount the system should calculate up to until a certain calendar date. You can reach the configuration screen by using the following menu path:

  - **SAP IMG Menu:** *Financial Accounting → Asset Accounting → Depreciation → Valuation Methods → Depreciation Key → Calculation Methods → Define Maximum Amount Methods*

- *Multi-Level Method*: You use multi-level method to provide deprecation based on percentage. Here you can specify rates of deprecation in percentage based on time, by defining the validity date. You can reach configuration screen by using the following menu path:

  - **SAP IMG Menu:** *Financial Accounting → Asset Accounting → Depreciation → Valuation Methods → Depreciation Key → Calculation Methods → Define Multi-Level Methods*

- *Period Control Method*: Period control method determines what the deprecation would be in the initial year of assets acquisition, addition, improvement, and what would be deprecation on the end date of assets transactions. You can reach the configuration screen by using the following menu path:

  - **SAP IMG Menu:** *Financial Accounting → Asset Accounting → Depreciation → Valuation Methods → Depreciation Key → Calculation Methods → Maintain Period Control Methods*

2.6.13 Transactional Data

- In configuration, you will determine which depreciation area will update general ledger account in real time and which depreciation areas will be updated periodically (Figure 2.72). In real-time, the system only updates one depreciation area. In addition to real-time posting, you can also configure whether you want to post APC (Acquisition Production Cost) only, depreciation value only, or both for other deprecation areas. You can reach the configuration screen by using the following menu path:

  - **SAP IMG Menu:** *Financial Accounting → Asset Accounting → Integration with the General Ledger → Define How Depreciation Areas Post to General Ledger*

Change View "Define Depreciation Areas": Overview

Chart of dep.	1US	Sample chart of depreciation: USA

Define Depreciation Areas

Ar.	Name of depreciation area	Real	G/L	Trgt Group	
1	Book depreciation	☑	1		
2	Book depreciation	☑	0		
3	Book depreciation	☑	0		
10	Federal Tax ACRS/MACRS	☑	0		
11	Alternative Minimum Tax	☑	0		
12	Adjusted Current Earnings	☑	0		
13	Corporate Earnings & Profits	☑	0		
17	Fed Tax MACRS (for states not allowing bonus depr)	☑	0		
30	Consolidated balance sheet in local currency	☑	0		
31	Consolidated balance sheet in group currency	☑	0		
32	Book depreciation in group currency	☑	0		
40	State modified ACRS	☑	0		
50	Derived area	☐	0		

FIGURE 2.72 Depreciation posting rule.

- Through configuration you can also determine how the system will determine the APC and depreciation value. SAP has provided functionality through which you can determine the value for other deprecation areas. You can reach the configuration screen by using the following menu path:

  - **SAP IMG Menu:** *Financial Accounting → Asset Accounting → Valuation → Depreciation Areas → Specify Transfer of APC Values*

  - **SAP IMG Menu:** *Financial Accounting → Asset Accounting → Valuation → Depreciation Areas → Specify Transfer of Depreciation Terms*

Change View "Depreciation areas: Rules for value takeover": Overview

Chart of dep.   1US   Sample chart of depreciation: USA

Ar.	Name of depreciation area	ValAd	Ide	
01	Book depreciation	00	☐	
02	Book depreciation	01	☑	
03	Book depreciation	01	☑	
10	Federal Tax ACRS/MACRS	01	☑	
11	Alternative Minimum Tax	01	☑	
12	Adjusted Current Earnings	01	☑	
13	Corporate Earnings & Profits	01	☑	
17	Fed Tax MACRS (for states not allowing bonus depr)	01	☑	
30	Consolidated balance sheet in local currency	01	☐	
31	Consolidated balance sheet in group currency	30	☑	
32	Book depreciation in group currency	01	☑	
40	State modified ACRS	01	☐	

FIGURE 2.73 APC transfer rule.

- Figure 2.73 depicts the APC transfer rule for other deprecation areas. The figure depicts the configured deprecation area for all deprecation, except 01 and 31 will derive value from deprecation area 01. As the book depreciation area receives real-time posting, the system doesn't allow any configuration.

- Figure 2.74 depicts the deprecation transfer rule for a deprecation area from other deprecation areas. In some of the deprecation areas, you have configured to transferred deprecation terms from 01, while with others you left the transfer rule blank where you felt that deprecation was not applicable.

Change View "Depreciation areas: Rules for takeover of deprec. terms":

Chart of dep.   1US   Sample chart of depreciation: USA

Ar.	Name of depreciation area	TTr	Identical	
01	Book depreciation	00	☐	
02	Book depreciation	01	☑	
03	Book depreciation	01	☑	
10	Federal Tax ACRS/MACRS		☐	
11	Alternative Minimum Tax		☐	
12	Adjusted Current Earnings		☐	
13	Corporate Earnings & Profits		☐	
17	Fed Tax MACRS (for states not allowing bonus depr)		☐	
30	Consolidated balance sheet in local currency	01	☐	
31	Consolidated balance sheet in group currency	30	☑	
32	Book depreciation in group currency	01	☑	
40	State modified ACRS	01	☐	

FIGURE 2.74 Depreciation transfer rule.

- Assets account receives its posting from different components of SAP application, including: material management, accounts receivable, account payable, plan maintenance, and controlling.

- You can use the material management module for procurement cycle of an assets starting from creation of purchase requisition, goods receipts, and invoice verification.

- During the preceding material management transactions, the system checks the existence of master data, whether assets is a valuated assets or not, and determines assets capitalization date.

- *Assets Acquisition*: After creation of assets master the first transaction in assets accounting is capitalization/purchase of an asset. You can capitalize/purchase an asset in a varieties of ways, including:

  - *External acquisition* (Not integrated with material management): In the case of external acquisition, you are purchasing assets from your business partner. You can carry out this transaction in different ways: integrated acquisition with accounts payable or not an integrated purchase. In the case of integrated purchase you update accounts payable and assets management at the same time. While in case of not integrated purchases you perform assets acquisition in two steps. You can perform external acquisitions by navigating the following options:

    - SAP Menu (Integrated with AP): *Accounting → Financial Accounting → Fixed Assets → Posting → Acquisition → External Acquisition → With Vendor (Transaction Code – F-90)*

    - SAP Menu (Integrated with AP): *Accounting → Financial Accounting → Fixed Assets → Posting → Acquisition → External Acquisition → ABZON – Acquis. w/Autom. Offsetting Entry Vendor (Transaction Code – ABZON)*

  - *External acquisition* (Integrated with material management): You can purchase an asset through a material management module. In the case of integrated purchase with MM, like other material purchase processes, you generally follow the creation of purchase requisition (Transaction code: ME51N) > creation of purchase order (Transaction code: ME211N) > posting goods receipts (Transaction code: MEGO) > posting invoice receipts (Transaction code: MIRO).

- *Capitalizing assets under construction*: Sometimes you create an asset by utilizing internal activities, such as supplying material from the warehouse, or by procuring a material which is used in construction process (refer assets under construction). SAP has provided various options to capture the costs relevant to bring the assets in question. Once the assets are completed, you can capitalize AUCs by distributing and settling to assets. You can reach the settlement or distribution functionalities by using the following navigation options:

  – SAP Menu (Distribution): *Accounting → Financial Accounting → Fixed Assets → Posting → Capitalize Asset u. Const. → Distribute [Transaction Code – AIAB]*.

  – SAP Menu (Distribution): *Accounting → Financial Accounting → Fixed Assets → Posting → Capitalize Asset u. Const. → Settle [Transaction Code – AIBU]*.

- *Subsequent purchase*: Subsequent purchase represents the cost of improvement to an existing asset or cost of an add on. Subsequent purchases can be treated in following ways, depending on nature of addition:

  – Posting to a existing asset

  – Posting to a sub asset

▪ Based on acquisition, improvement cost, and deprecation key parameters, the system determines planned deprecation expenses for the future period. If your controlling area is active, you can transfer controlling planned deprecation expenses to determine planned overhead cost or planned product cost.

▪ *Deprecation*: Periodically you depreciate assets toward wear and tear of assets. Depreciation can be further categorized by planned deprecation and unplanned deprecation. Planned deprecation can be further divided into ordinary deprecation and special deprecation. *Ordinary deprecation* represents planned deduction for normal wear and tear of an asset. *Special deprecation* represents a reduction of an asset's value towards wear and tear for tax purpose. Depreciation, other than ordinary deprecation, is treated as unplanned deprecation, which arises in various circumstances, such as damage, loss, or outdated technology.

▪ Sometimes, a situation warrants distributing depreciation expenses to more than one cost object. As assets master data doesn't facilitate assignment to multiple cost objects in the assets master, you collect deprecation expenses in a shared service cost center (a distribution cost center) and then apply controlling allocation process to distribute depreciation and interest expenses to other cost objects.

▪ In the period end activities, one of the most important activities in assets accounting is "running depreciation run." To carry out a depreciation run you need the following configure assets accounting components:

- Document type for deprecation posting

- Depreciation areas to be posted

- Rules for deprecation posting

- Posting process

▪ *Document Type*: SAP system comes with pre-delivered document types. When you execute deprecation posting system creates financial posting using document type that you have configured. For depreciation posting, the system expects you to assign a document type in the configuration steps. SAP has delivered document type "AF" for depreciation posting, which is assigned to a country template. When you create your own chart of deprecation with reference to a country template, the system automatically copies the document type assignment. If you want to assign different document type, you can do so through configuration by using the following menu path:

- **SAP IMG Menu:** *Financial Accounting → Asset Accounting → Valuation Post APC Values Periodically to the General Ledger → Specify Document Type for Periodic Posting of Asset Values*

▪ The system expects the document type assigned for deprecation posting should have the following attributes:

- Assets and general ledger account types should be allowed for posting with this document type

- The number range of deprecation document should be an external number range

▪ In configuration, you decide which deprecation areas will create financial posting. While generating the financial posting, the system checks whether the chart of account and chart of deprecation are assigned to a company code or not. Whether or not you have assigned a deprecation document type to a company, you can reach the configuration screen to control financial posting by using the following navigation path:

- **SAP IMG Menu:** *Financial Accounting → Asset Accounting → Valuation → Valuation → Depreciation Areas → Define Depreciation Areas → Define Depreciation Areas*

▪ Standard SAP comes with the following control indicator for *posting control*. You need to assign one control indicator to each depreciation area:

Posting to G/L	Short Description
0	Area does not post
1	Area posts in real-time
2	Area posts APC and depreciation on periodic basis
3	Area posts depreciation only
4	Area posts APC directly and depreciation
5	Area posts APC only
6	Area posts only APC directly

▪ As the preceding configuration is client specific, the assignment of posting rules applies to all company code that use the chart of depreciation.

▪ *Posting Rules*: In posting rule configuration you determine how often you want to run a depreciation posting run. SAP has provided the following depreciation posting run rules:

- Monthly posting

- Bi-monthly posting

- Quarterly posting

- Semi-annual posting

- Annual posting

▪ Whatever options you have selected, the system expects to plan deprecation as per your selection. However, you can always run unplanned deprecation to accommodate any special circumstances. You can provide deprecation and imputed cost by running a deprecation run. You can reach deprecation run functionality by choosing either of the following menu options:

- **SAP Menu:** *Accounting → Fixed Assets → Periodic Processing →*
  Depreciation Run → Execute

- **Transaction Code:** *AFAB*

■ Every transaction in assets accounts updates forecasted deprecation
in assets management, but the system only updates the general ledger,
controlling when you run periodic deprecation run.

■ In special circumstances, you need to revise your forecasted deprecation
for an assets or group of assets. For example, initially while capitalizing
a desk top you have considered you will deprecate it at 20% per year.
After one year of using the desktop, you realized that due to rapid
changes in technology, the desktop will be replaced within another two
years. In this circumstance, the depreciated value of the desktop should
be 33% at the end of the second year, which means in the second year
you will provide 46% deprecation [33% (new revised depreciation rate)
+ 13% for the last year], which may not be reasonable from a second
financial statement point of view.

■ To cope with this type of circumstance, SAP has provided two methods
to spread extra past deprecation: catch-up method and smoothing.

■ *Catch-up method*: In this method, the system determined the
deprecation amount as the difference between the planned deprecation
up to this period – and the depreciation posted up to this period.

■ *Smoothing*: In smoothing method, the system distributes the difference
between the forecasted deprecation and deprecation already provided
to the remaining posting periods.

2.6.14 Information System

■ SAP has provided a series of standard reports. You can enhance these
reports and build new reports to meet your reporting requirement.
You can reach the assets account information system by navigating the
following menu path:

- **SAP Menu**: *Accounting → Fixed Assets → Information System →*
  Various

- **SAP Menu**: *Information Systems → Accounting → Financial*
  Accounting → Fixed Assets → Various

■ *Assets history sheet* is one of the most important reports for the year-end
and financial statement points of view.

- SAP has provided a few country-specific assets history sheets. Since the structure of assets history sheet varies from country to country and is detected by law, if SAP-provided reports don't fit your requirement you can build your own assets history sheet.

- Creation of assets history sheet is a two-step process: create assets history sheet version and then create asset history sheet structure. You can reach assets history sheet version creation screen by using the following menu path:

  - **SAP IMG Menu**: *Financial Accounting → Asset Accounting → Information System → Asset History Sheet → Define History Sheet Versions*

- Once you have created assets history sheet version, you create layout structure by defining rows and columns by choosing the detail "icon." In assets history sheet, the system uses history sheet group and transaction type to plot assets opening balance, transactions, deprecations, retirements, and closing balance.

- *Asset explorer* is one of the most important display reports in assets accounting. This report display all related objects and transactions in one screen. Assets explorer consists of:

  - Header used as selection parameter, where you enter asset number, company code, and fiscal year

  - Deprecation areas overview tree displays all applicable deprecation areas relevant to asset

  - Objects overview tree displays assets related objects, such as vendor, purchase order number, and cost centers

  - Tab pages displays planned and posted deprecation, allows for comparison between different deprecation areas and fiscal year

Question – 41

The system updates APC cost in real-time for all deprecation areas, while when you do periodic processing system updates deprecation expenses.

A. True

B. False

Question – 42

You can post transactions to a group asset.

A. True

B. False

Question – 43

Deprecation posting reduces assets balance by crediting assets.

A. True

B. False

2.7 CO Enterprise Structure (SAP® CO)

- Controlling module is a core application component of SAP application, now called **management accounting,** helps management for analysis of financial data and to make informed decisions.

- You use financial accounting to generate financial statement (i.e., balance sheet, income statement, and cash flow statement) for external accounting. Financial statements are prepared to comply with various legal requirements, business needs, and accounting standards.

- On the other side, management needs various control reports such as cost analysis report and cost center reports for effective control of an organization. You use management accounting to comply with the reporting requirements of management.

- Management accounting consists of different application component, such as:

  - Cost element accounting

  - Cost center accounting

  - Internal order

  - Product cost planning

  - Profitability analysis

  - Profit center accounting

You will learn more about these components later in this chapter.

- Controlling areas is the basic and highest organizational unit in a management account. All the activities in cost element accounting, cost center accounting, and internal order are happening within the controlling area. Figure 2.75 depicts the organizational hierarchy of the controlling area.

MANAGEMENT ACCOUNTING

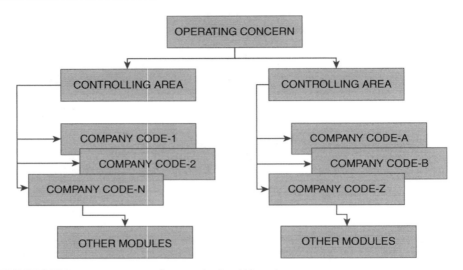

FIGURE 2.75 Manegement accounting organizational hierarchy.

- Within a client you can have an infinite number of controlling areas. You can create a controlling area by using the following menu path:

  - **SAP IMG Menu**: *Controlling → General Controlling → Organization → Maintain Controlling Area*

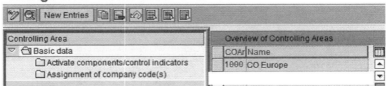

FIGURE 2.76 Controlling area creation.

- In order to use components of controlling areas, you need to activate these components for your controlling area. In Figure 2.76, if you select controlling area and double click on "Activate components/control indicator" the system will take component activation screen as shown in Figure 2.77.

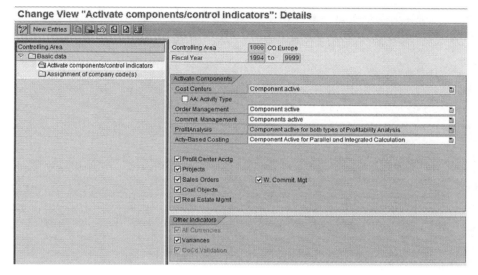

FIGURE 2.77 Controlling area components activation.

- In Figure 2.77, you can see that SAP has provided a central place for the activation of various components of controlling. Before stepping forward in controlling, you need to ensure that you have activated the required components.

- You can assign an infinite number of company codes to a controlling area. To assign company codes to a controlling area, double click on "assignment of company code(s)." Figure 2.78 shows company code assignment to the controlling area 1,000.

- You can assign company codes to one controlling area if they fulfill the following conditions:

  - All company codes should be using the same chart of account

  - The number of normal posting periods should be the same for all those company codes

- Every transaction that is relevant for controlling creates a separate document for the controlling area. Like financial accounting, a controlling

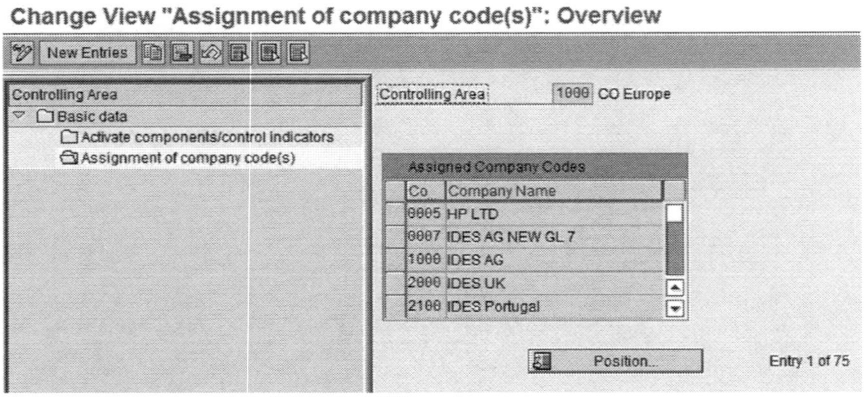

FIGURE 2.78 Company code assignment to controlling area.

area document is unique within a controlling area, which is definable through a controlling area document number (Transaction Code: KSB5). The system assigns controlling document numbers based on your configuration. You can reach the configuration screen for maintenance of the controlling area document by using the following menu path:

- **SAP IMG Menu:** *Controlling → General Controlling → Organization → Maintain Number Ranges for Controlling Documents*

■ In controlling, you use version as a data container. You can create and maintain different versions for different planning scenarios. The SAP application comes with pre-delivered version 0. Version 0 always holds actual data, in addition to planning data. You can reach the configuration screen of controlling by using the following menu path:

- **SAP IMG Menu:** *Controlling → General Controlling → Organization → Maintain Versions*

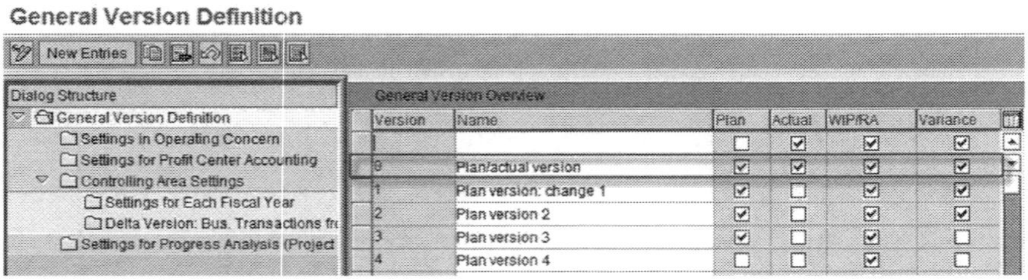

FIGURE 2.79 Controlling area version management client specific.

Change View "Settings for Each Fiscal Year": Overview

New Entries	Copy Method

Dialog Structure	Controlling Area	1000	CO Europe
▽ ☐ General Version Definition	Version	0	Plan/actual version
☐ Settings in Operating Concern			
☐ Settings for Profit Center Accounting			
▽ ☐ Controlling Area Settings			
☐ Settings for Each Fiscal Year			
☐ Delta Version: Bus. Transactions fr			
☐ Settings for Progress Analysis (Project			

Version Settings for Each Fiscal Year

Year	Version Locked	Integrated Planning	Copying Allowed
2012	☐	☑	☑
2013	☐	☑	☑
2014	☐	☑	☑
2015	☐	☑	☑

FIGURE 2.80 Controlling area version management controlling area specific.

- In order to post data to a planning version, you need to activate a respective control indicator. As shown in Figure 2.79, you activated actual and planning data and in Figure 2.58 you can maintain parameter specific to a controlling area.

- By activating the lock indicator, you can control whether posting is allowed in the version or not.

- In management accounting, you can track and record transactions in three currencies: company code currency, controlling area currency, and the currency of the cost object.

Question – 44

Company codes assigned to controlling areas should have same

A. *Operating chart of account*

B. *Country chart of account*

C. *Group chart of account*

2.8 Cost Element Accounting (SAP® CO-CEL)

- As a carrier of cost, you use the cost element accounting in controlling. All expenses and incomes that are relevant for management accounting are posted in management accounting using the primary cost element.

- In the SAP application, all high level cost elements are divided into two types: primary cost element or secondary cost element.

- *Primary Cost Elements*: Primary cost elements are those cost elements for which you have corresponding general ledger master records. You can create a primary cost element manually or through automated process. Before posting a transaction in financial accounting into SAP, the system expects that you have created the necessary primary cost element. Depending of the usage of primary cost elements, primary cost elements are categorized as:

  - 01: Primary costs/cost reducing revenues

  - 03: Accrual calculation using the percentage method

  - 04: Accrual calculation using the target=actual method

  - 11: Revenues

  - 12: Sales deductions

  - 22: External settlement

  - 90: Cost elements for balance sheet accounts in FI

- *Secondary cost elements:* Secondary cost elements are those cost elements that are used within management accounting for assessment and settlement. A secondary cost element has a corresponding general ledger master records. Secondary cost elements are categorized as:

  - 21: Internal settlement

  - 31: Order/project results analysis

  - 41: Overhead

  - 42: Assessment

  - 43: Internal activity allocation

  - 50: Incoming orders: sales revenue

  - 51: Incoming orders: other revenues

  - 52: Incoming orders: costs

  - 61: Earned value

- You can create a primary cost element by using the following navigation options:

- **SAP Menu**: *Accounting → Controlling → Cost Element Accounting → Master Data Cost Element → Individual Processing → Create Primary*

- **Transaction Code**: *KA01*

▪ When you create a primary cost element system, the checks whether a general ledger account exists in financial account. If the system doesn't find a corresponding general ledger account, a message pops up. From the cost element screen you can create a general ledger master record and vice versa.

▪ You can create secondary cost elements by following the following navigation options:

- **SAP Menu**: *Accounting → Controlling → Cost Element Accounting → Master Data Cost Element → Individual Processing → Create Secondary*

- **Transaction Code**: *KA06*

▪ You can group cost elements with similar attributes into a *cost element group*. Cost element groups facilitate: easy reporting, instead of keying individual cost element, you can use the cost element group; distribution; and assessment.

▪ When you create a cost element, it falls under a cost element category. The cost element category determines those for which you can use a cost element.

2.9 Cost Center Accounting (SAP® CO-CCA)

▪ *Cost center accounting* is part of the overhead cost-controlling component of management account. In overhead cost controlling, you use cost centers, internal order, activity types, and statistical key figures to collect overhead relevant costs. The term overhead refers to those costs that are not relevant, or you can't assign directly to any services or products.

▪ Cost center accounting collects all costs on the basis of the source of such cost, and helps management for further analysis of the occurrence of such cost.

- In order to use cost center accounting, you need to activate the cost center accounting component in controlling. You can reach the configuration screen by using the following menu path:

- **SAP IMG Menu:** *Controlling → Cost Center Accounting → Activate Cost Center Accounting in Controlling Area*

2.9.1 Cost Center Group

- When you create a controlling area, you need to name the cost center standard hierarchy. Creation of the standard hierarchy is one the pre-requisites for the creation of the cost center master. Cost center standard hierarchy is the upper most node in the cost center hierarchy. You can build branches under the standard hierarchy by creating a node or sub-node under it.

- You can group together cost centers with similar attributes under a *cost center group*. You can create a cost center group by using the following navigation options:

  - **SAP Menu:** *Accounting → Controlling → Cost Center Accounting → Master Data Cost Center Group → Create*

  - **Transaction Codes:** *KSH1*

- You can move, change, or delete cost center groups by using the following menu path:

  - **SAP Menu:** *Accounting → Controlling → Cost Center Accounting → Master Data Cost Center Group → Create*

  - **Transaction Codes:** *KSH2*

2.9.2 Cost Center Master Data

- When you create a cost center, you assign cost center to a *cost center category* and a cost center group. The cost center category controls the following parameters of the cost centers:

  - Certain default values for cost centers such as lock, record quantity

  - Allowed activity types for cost centers. You assign activity types to cost center categories

  - Used for functional area assignment, reporting, and cost center evaluation

- A few examples of a cost center category are a production cost center, Service cost center, and administration cost center.

- You can create your own categories by using the following menu path:

  - **SAP Menu:** *Accounting → Controlling → Cost Center Accounting → Master Data → Cost Center → Define Cost Center Categories*

  - **Transaction Codes:** *OKA2*

- You can organize your cost centers based on geography, products, responsibility, functions, or any combination of the above.

- You can create a cost center by using the following navigation options:

  - **SAP Menu:** *Accounting → Controlling → Cost Center Accounting → Master Data Cost Center Cost Center → Individual Processing → Create*

  - **Transaction Codes:** *KS01*

- Some of the important attributes of cost center master data include:

  - Cost center master data are time dependent, which means over the period of the time you will have multiple data set represented by different time interval

  - Cost center master data is company code specific. Even though you can assign multiple company codes to a controlling, cost centers always represent one company code

  - You can record transactions in cost center currency, which is different from company code

- Figure 2.81 represents a cost center 1,000 of controlling area 1,000. You can integrate cost center accounting by assigning various SAP objects in the cost center master data. If you navigate the control tab (Figure 2.82) of the cost center master data, you can see various control indicators, where you can control what data are allowed for the cost center at that particular point of time.

- By navigating Environment → Where used list (Figure 2.83), you can see the usage of the cost center master data in various functionalities.

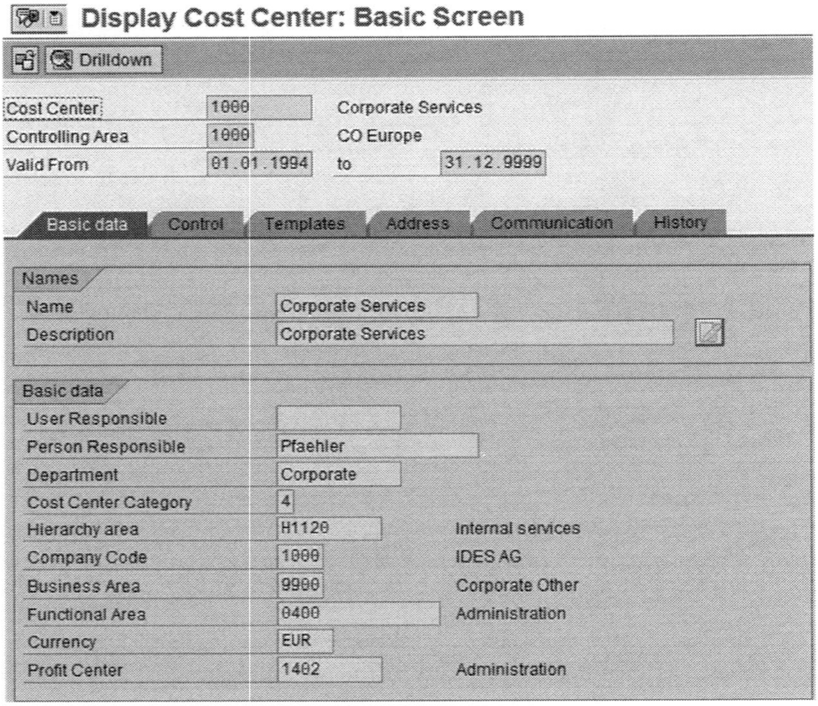

Display Cost Center: Basic Screen

Drilldown

Cost Center	1000	Corporate Services	
Controlling Area	1000	CO Europe	
Valid From	01.01.1994	to	31.12.9999

Basic data | Control | Templates | Address | Communication | History

Names
Name	Corporate Services
Description	Corporate Services

Basic data
User Responsible		
Person Responsible	Pfaehler	
Department	Corporate	
Cost Center Category	4	
Hierarchy area	H1120	Internal services
Company Code	1000	IDES AG
Business Area	9900	Corporate Other
Functional Area	0400	Administration
Currency	EUR	
Profit Center	1402	Administration

FIGURE 2.81 Cost center master data.

Display Cost Center: Indicators

Drilldown

Cost Center	1000	Corporate Services	
Controlling Area	1000	CO Europe	
Valid From	01.01.1994	to	31.12.9999

Basic data | **Control** | Templates | Address | Communication | History

☐ Record Quantity

Lock
☐ Actual primary costs	☐ Act. secondary costs	☐ Actual revenues
☐ Plan primary costs	☐ Plan secondary costs	☐ Plan revenues

☐ Commitment update

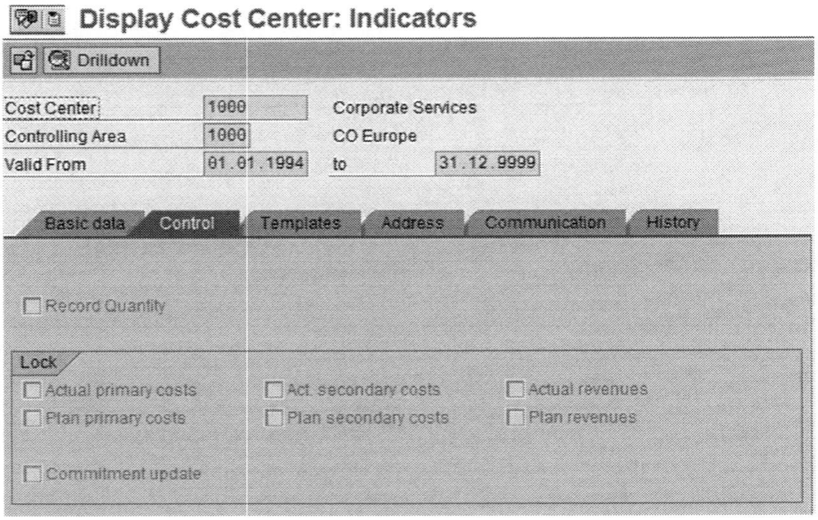

FIGURE 2.82 Control tab cost center master data.

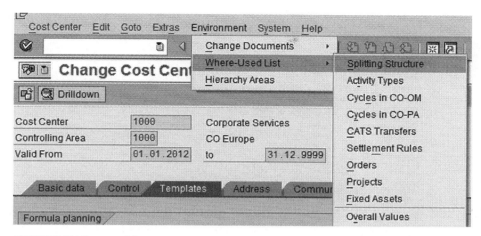

FIGURE 2.83 Where used list.

2.9.3 Statistical Key Figures (SKF)

- *Statistical Key Figures* (SKF) are used as an allocation basis while assessment, distribution, and reposting. They are the statistical data such as number of employees, area in square meters, etc., and have no financial impact. You use SKF generally where you didn't find any other easy way to measure cost. A few examples of SKFs are number employees to allocation cost like cafeteria cost and square footage of office space to divide cost energy consumed.

- You can create SKF by using the following navigation options:

  - **SAP Menu**: *Create Accounting → Controlling → Cost Center Accounting → Master Data → Statistical Key Figures → Individual Processing → Create*

  - **Transaction Code**: *KK01*

- Figure 2.84 depicts a statistical key figure master data of the controlling area 1,000. SKFs are controlling area specific. The main attributes of SKF master are unit of measurement and SKF category.

- SKFs are divided into two categories such as total value SKF and fixed value SKF.

- *Total Value SKFs* are those SKFs whose value could be changed from one period to the next. When you post SKF values, these values are valid for the posting period only, and the system doesn't carry these values to future periods.

Display Statistical Key Figure: Master Data

| Stat. key figure | 4510 | |
| Controlling area | 1000 | CO Europe |

| Basic data | | |
| Name | Power usage, drying process | |

| Stat. key fig. UnM. | KWH | Kilowatt hours |

| Key fig. cat. | ○ Fxd val. | |
| | ◉ Tot. values | |

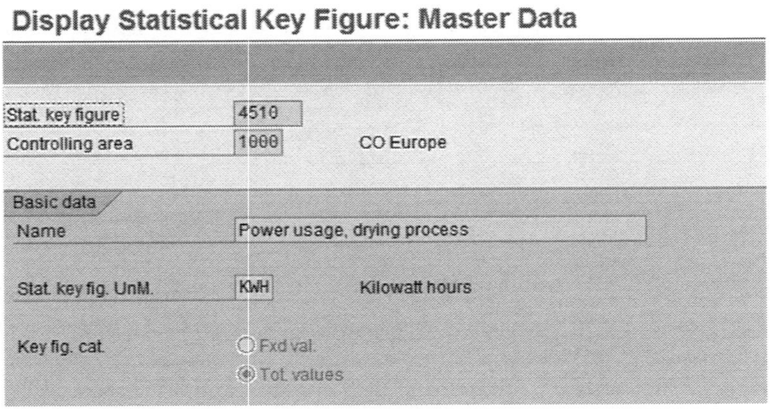

FIGURE 2.84 Stastistical key figure.

- *Fixed value SKFs* are those SKFs whose value doesn't change, or changes very rarely, such as office space in square feet. When you post fixed value SKFs, the system carries these values to future periods until the end of the fiscal year. However, you can overwrite these values by posting SKF values.

2.9.4 Activity Types

- Activity types represent an activity or service provided by one cost object to other objects. You use activity types to track services between cost centers. You use activity types to allocate costs to or from one cost centers to one or more cost centers. In the allocation process, sending cost centers are credited with activity rate X with the amount of activity provided, while receiving cost centers are debited with activity rate X amount of activity.

- You can create an activity type by using the following navigation options:

  - *SAP Menu*: Create Accounting → Controlling → Cost Center Accounting → Master Data → Activity Type → Individual Processing → Create

  - *Transaction Code: KL01*

Display Activity Type: Basic Screen

Activity Type	1000	Internal Transport
Controlling Area	1000	CO Europe
Valid From	01.01.1994	to	31.12.9999

Basic data | Indicators | Output | History

Names

| Name | Internal Transport |
| Description | Internal Transport |

Basic data

| Activity Unit | D | Days |
| CCtr categories | * |

Allocation default values

ATyp category	1	Manual entry, manual allocation
Allocation cost elem	614000	DAA Intern. Transp.
Price indicator	

☐ Actual qty set   ☐ Average price

☐ Plan quantity set   ☐ PreDistribFixedCosts

Variance Values for Actual Allocation

| Actl Acty Type Cat. | | As in planning |
| Act. price indicator | |

FIGURE 2.85 Activity type master data.

- Figure 2.85 shows activity type 1,000 master data. Activity types are controlling area specific and valid for specific periods. While creating activity types, you assign the number of SAP objects to activity type masters:

  - Allowable cost center category

  - Allocation cost element

  - Activity type category

- *Allocation cost element* is a secondary cost element used within controlling and assigned to an activity type. While posting an activity type you use allocation cost elements for debit/credit confirmation.

- By assigning cost center categories you can restrict the usage of activity types for a limited number of cost centers.

- When you create an activity type, the system expects that you need to assign an activity type category. SAP has provided four types of activity categories: manual entry and manual allocation, indirect calculation and indirect allocation, manual entryand indirect allocation, and manual entry and no allocation.

2.9.5 Periodic Allocation

- During closing, you carry out a lot of activities to prepare management reports. Cost center account is not an exception. In this section, you will learn about the following important closing activities:

  - Periodic allocation

  - Actual reposting

- *Periodic allocation*: During the normal business process you collect in cost centers. In the closing process, you allocate these costs right to the cost centers. To carry out the allocation process, SAP has provided two types of allocation processes: distribution and assessment.

- You allocate cost to one cost center or a group of cost centers through user defined keys: percentage rate, amounts, and statistical key figures.

- *Distribution*: Distribution is used to allocate primary costs from one or more cost centers to one or more other cost centers. In the distribution process, costs are debited or credited using the original cost elements.

- *Assessment*: Assessment works the same was as distribution works, the only difference being that in assessment process you use assessment cost element (a secondary cost element). Costs which are to be assessed are grouped together and debited and credited under the assessment cost element.

- *Reposting:* Reposting is a posting aid, used frequently to correct posting within a management account without affecting financial accounting. There are two type of reporting: transaction based reposting and periodic reposting. Distribution reposting is used to transfer primary cost from one or more objects to one or more objects. The main difference between reposting and distribution is in the case of distribution the amount appears on the credit side of sending objects and the debit side of receiving objects, while in reposting, the transaction will simply be moved from the debit side of the sending object to the debit side of the receiving objects.

- Transaction-based reposting is normally used to correct incorrect posting, while periodic reposting is used like the distribution process to allocate period end cost.

- To run either distribution or assessment or periodic reposting, you need to configure application components using the following steps:

  - Define a cycle: a cycle is a collection of segments. Within a cycle you can create up to 999 segments. For performance reasons, SAP recommends that you create multiple cycles with a small number of segments.

  - Define a segment for cycle: segment refers to the grouping of sending objects (cost centers), receiving objects (cost centers or internal orders), and division criteria (fixed amount, percentage, SKFs).

  - Determines senders and receivers: in this segment, you define which are costs centers will send cost and receiving objects.

  - Determine allocation methods: in this segment, you maintain how the system will distribute sending cost centers costs to receiving cost centers.

- To create allocation cycles and segments, use the following menu paths:

  - ***Distribution***

    - ***SAP IMG Menu***: *Controlling → Cost Center Accounting → Actual Postings → Period-End Closing → Distribution → Define Distribution*

  - ***Assessment***

    - ***SAP IMG Menu***: *Controlling → Cost Center Accounting → Actual Postings → Period-End Closing → Assessment → Maintain Assessment*

  - ***Periodic Reposting***

    - ***SAP IMG Menu***: *Controlling → Cost Center Accounting → Actual Postings → Period-End Closing → Periodic Reposting → Define Periodic Repostings*

Question – 45

When you post an expense, the system expects .... has to be assigned.

A. Cost object

B. A cost and revenue object assignment

C. Revenue object assignment

D. None of the above

Question – 46

In the distribution process, SAP groups together primary cost elements and secondary cost elements for distribution.

A. False

B. True

Question – 47

What is the integration point between Financial Accounting (FI) and Management Account (CO)? In the distribution process, SAP groups together primary cost elements and secondary cost elements for distribution.

A. False

B. True

Question – 48

During month end closing when we run transaction code KALC (reconciliation posting) the system groups together cross entity posting and creates a summarized posting in financial posting.

A. False

B. True

Question – 49

What is the relation between cost center(s) and company code?

A. 1 (Cost Center) : 1 (Company Code)

B. N (Cost Center) : 1 (Company Code)

C. 1 (Cost Center) : N (Company Code)

D. N (Cost Center) : N (Company Code)

Question – 50

In cost center assessment, which of the following objects can you use as receiver of the cost.

A. Cost center(s)

B. Internal order(s)

C. Activity type(s)

D. Statistical key figure(s)

Question – 51

For allocating primary cost and secondary cost you use _____ for allocation.

A. Assessment

B. Reposting

C. Distribution

D. Settlement

2.10 Internal Order (SAP® CO-IO)

- Internal order is a flexible tool in management accounting, used for varieties of purposes. Depending on the usage of internal order, it can be split into four categories: overhead cost orders, investment orders, accrual orders, and orders with revenue.

2.10.1 Internal Order Types

- *Overhead Orders*: These types of orders are used to monitor overhead costs that you are incurring for specific purposes.

- *Investment Orders*: You use investment orders to track costs that you have been incurring for an investment projects, such as assets under constructions.

- *Accrual Order*: Accrual orders are used to accrue costs to offset the impact of uneven occurrences of cost in financial accounting, such as bonus payment for employees.

- *Orders with revenue*: You use these types of orders to track cost and revenue for an order.

- In order to use internal order components in a management account you need to activate the internal order component in specific controlling area. If you have not activated this component during the creation of the controlling area, you can activate it now by navigating the following menu path:

  - **SAP IMG Menu:** *Controlling → Internal Orders → Activate Order Management in Controlling Area*

- Figure 2.86 shows activation of internal order components for controlling area 1,000.

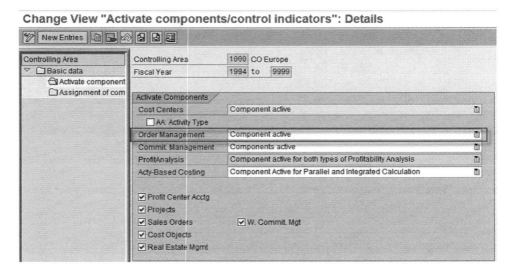

FIGURE 2.86 Activation of internal order in controlling area.

- While creating the internal order master, you need to create internal order under internal order type. *Internal order types* control and hold large amount of internal order master data attributes. Some examples are internal order number range, settlement profile, or order status management.

- You can create internal order types by using the following menu path:

  - **SAP IMG Menu:** *Controlling → Internal Orders → Order Master Data → Define Order Types*

- Figure 2.87 features a SAP delivered and attributed internal order type 0100. You can see that the various attributes required for internal order are assigned to inter order type. You can compare an internal order type with G/L account group and vendor/customer account groups.

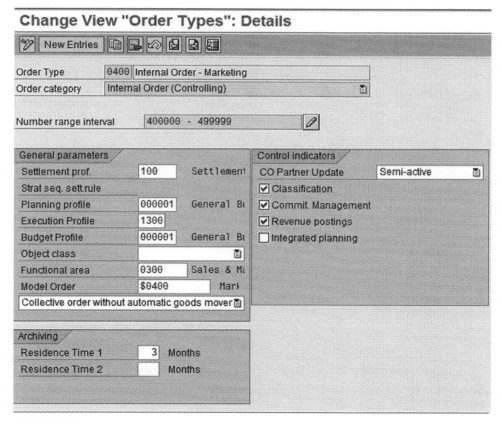

FIGURE 2.87 Internal order type.

2.10.2 Internal Order Category

▪ When you create an internal order type, you need to create it under an *internal order category*. Internal order categories control technical characteristics of an internal order type, i.e., purpose of internal order, structure and function of an order, and the transactions you use to process. SAP comes with the following pre-delivered order categories:

- 01 Internal order (controlling)
- 02 Accrual calculation order (controlling)
- 03 Model order (controlling)
- 04 CO production order
- 05 Product cost collector
- 06 QM order
- 10 PP production order
- 20 Network
- 30 Maintenance order
- 40 Process order
- 50 Inspection lot
- 60 Personnel order
- 70 Shipping deadlines

▪ An internal order is uniquely identified within controlling through a number called an *internal order number*. The numbering concept on an internal order is the same as other components of SAP, i.e., internal number range or external number range. You can create an internal order number range by using the following menu path:

- **SAP IMG Menu:** *Controlling → Internal Orders → Order Master Data → Define Order Types*

▪ Figure 2.88 depicts an internal order number range. This number range screen is similar to other number ranges you have studied so far. Internal order number ranges are not specific to any internal order type, year, or controlling area. Once you have created an internal order number range, you need to assign an internal order number range to an internal order type.

■ In internal order, you use *status management*. Internal order status management controls business transactions that are allowed at a particular point of time. From inception of internal order, depending on phase of internal, you need to change the internal order status. SAP comes with pre-delivered general status management by following the order status.

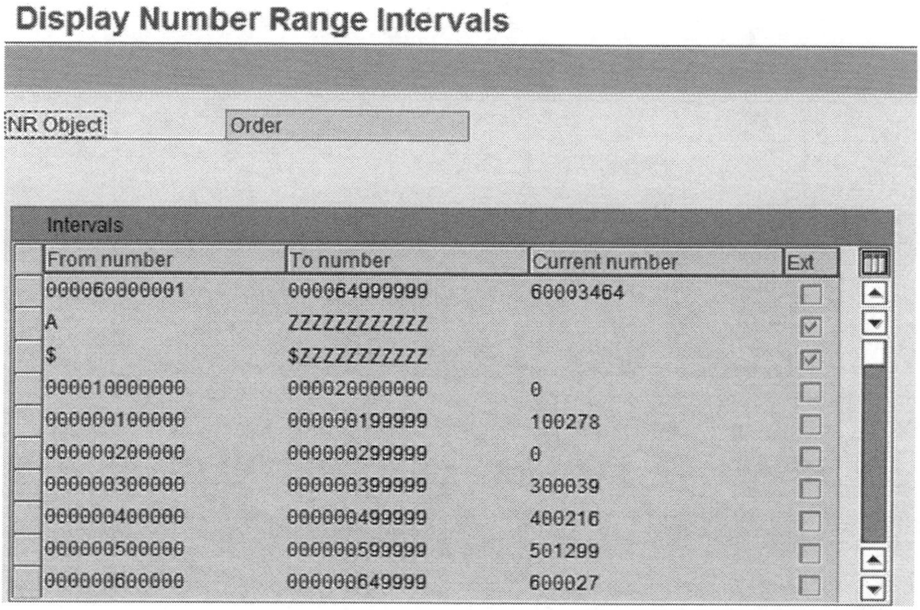

Display Number Range Intervals

NR Object		Order			

Intervals

From number	To number	Current number	Ext	
000060000001	000064999999	60003464	☐	
A	ZZZZZZZZZZZZ		☑	
$	$ZZZZZZZZZZZ		☑	
000010000000	000020000000	0	☐	
000000100000	000000199999	100278	☐	
000000200000	000000299999	0	☐	
000000300000	000000399999	300039	☐	
000000400000	000000499999	400216	☐	
000000500000	000000599999	501299	☐	
000000600000	000000649999	600027	☐	

FIGURE 2.88 Internal order number range.

■ Figure 2.89 depicts the internal order 0400-Internal Order-Marketing, which comes pre delivered in the SAP system. Internal order type 0400 uses general status management. Figure 2.90 depicts the general status management attributes and business transactions allowed on each status.

■ If general status management is not suitable for you, you can create your own status profile and assign it to an internal order type.

■ *Status Profile*: You can create user status profiles and arrange the desired status profile. While creating user status profiles you need to give status numbers. By using the LOWEST and HIGHEST fields for a status you can determine what the lowest status that can be returned to or the highest status that can be attained from that status. You can create a status profile by using the following navigation options:

- **SAP IMG Menu:** *Controlling → Internal Orders → Order Master Data → Status Management → Define Status Profiles*

Change View "Order Types": Details

| New Entries | | | | | | |

General parameters

Settlement prof.	100	Settlement
Strat seq. sett.rule		
Planning profile	000001	General Bu
Execution Profile	1300	
Budget Profile	000001	General Bu
Object class		
Functional area	0300	Sales & Ma
Model Order	$0400	Marl
Collective order without automatic goods mover		

Control indicators

CO Partner Update	Semi-active
☑ Classification	
☑ Commit. Management	
☑ Revenue postings	
☐ Integrated planning	

Archiving

Residence Time 1	3	Months
Residence Time 2		Months

Master data display

Order layout	
Print form	
✎ Field selection	

Status management

⦿ General status management	○ Order status management
Status profile	
☑ Release immediately	Order status (processed)
☐ Status dependent field select.	

FIGURE 2.89 Internal order type.

Display the Field Selection: Overview of the Order Status

Field selection

Order Type | 0400 | Internal Order - Marketing

Order Status

S	Order Status	Lo	Hi	Created	Released	Comp	Closed	Trans.	Pla	D	
10	Planning	10	20	●	○	○	○	PLAN	☐	●	▲
20	Setup costs	10	30	○	●	○	○	RECH	☑	○	▼
25	Follow-up costs	20	30	○	○	●	○	RECH	☐	○	
30	Running costs	20	50	○	●	○	○	ALL	☐	○	
40	Follow-up costs	30	50	○	○	●	○	RECH	☐	○	
50	Settlement	40	60	○	○	●	○	ABSL	☐	○	
60	Closed	60	60	○	○	○	●		☐	○	

FIGURE 2.90 General status manegement.

2.10.3 Internal Order Master Data

■ You use internal order master data to define attributes and assign various attributes, which you then use while posting transactions and period end activities.

■ When creating an internal order master data, you select an internal order types. Some of the fields of internal order master are populated with internal order type attributes and you fill in other fields.

■ You can create an internal order master data by using the following navigation options:

• **SAP Menu:** Accounting → Controlling → Internal Orders → Master Data → Special Functions → Order → KO01 – Create

• **Transaction Code:** KO01

■ Figure 2.91 depicts internal order number 40,000 master data. Internal order master data are divided into the following various tab pages:

• Assignment tab: holds various default assignments of the internal orders

Display Internal Order: Master data

📄 | Settlement Rule

Order	400000		Order type	0400	Internal Order - Marl
Description	Marketing Campaign: Motorcycles TV OLD	📄		

Assignments | Control data | Prd-end closing | General data | Investments

Assignments

Company Code	1000	IDES AG
Business Area	1000	Business Area for 1000
Plant		
Functional Area	0300	Sales & Marketing
Object Class	Overhead	📄
Profit Center	1000	Motorcycles
Responsible CCtr	3200	Marketing
User Responsible		
WBS element		
Requesting CCtr		
Requesting Co.Code		
Requesting order		
Sales Order	0	
External order no.		

FIGURE 2.91 Internal order master data.

- Control tab page: controls internal status profile, at different stages of the life cycle of internal order. The system accepts different sets of business transactions. One other important attribute you maintain here is the statistical internal order indicator, which you will learn more about later in this chapter. Refer to Figure 2.92.

- Period-end closing: in the period end closing tab pages you are assigning a costing sheet, interest profile, and overhead key to transfer cost to different objects.

- General Data: this tab page holds historical information for information purpose.

- Investments: tab pages contain information for investment measures.

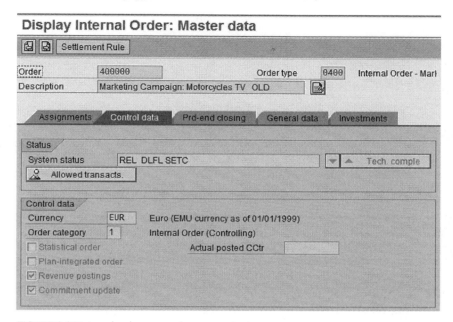

FIGURE 2.92 Internal order master data: control tab.

- From the allocation point of view, the overhead internal orders can be divided into two types: real internal orders and statistical internal orders.

- *Statistical internal orders* are internal orders that are used to track cost. In the case of statistical internal orders, you can allocate cost from internal orders to any cost center or internal order. While posting, if you are selecting a statistical internal order, the system expects a real cost object. By checking and unchecking the "statistical order" check box in the Figure 2.92, you can treat an internal as statically or real.

- Internal orders that are not statistical internal orders are real orders.

- When you post transactions to an internal order and the internal order is a statistical internal order, other cost objects get real posting. If the internal order is a real internal order, internal order gets real posting and other cost objects get statistical posting.

- You can group together several internal orders with the same attributes in a hierarchical structure. You can build internal order hierarchy up to as many levels as you want. You can use master data groups for analysis, planning, and allocations. You can also create internal order groups by using the following navigation option:

- **SAP Menu:** *Accounting* → *Controlling* → *Internal Orders* → *Master Data* → *Order Group* → *Order* → *KO01 – Create*

- **Transaction Code:** *KO01*

2.10.4 Transactional Data

■ Like other cost objects, internal orders get transactional data either from direct posting or internal allocation process. When you are posting financial data that are relevant for controlling, the system expects a cost object. The cost objects can either be internal order, cost center, or WBS elements. You can key these cost objects or the system can derive these cost objects based on the configurations.

■ You can assign cost objects (in this case, internal order) by:

- Assigning internal order in the cost element master data. This assignment is company code independent

- Assigning internal order to cost elements through transaction code: OKB9, this assignment is company code dependent

■ You can reach default assignment screen by using the following menu path:

- **SAP IMG Menu:** *Controlling* → *Internal Orders* → *Actual Postings* → *Settlement* → *Maintain Automatic Account Assignment*

Change View "Default account assignment": Overview

Co..	Cost Elem.	B..	Cost Ctr	Order	Prt.	Profit Ctr	Acct assignm
1000	232000				✓		
1000	232500				✓		
1000	261100			9AEUDE_STAFA			
1000	261200			9AEUDE_STAFA			
1000	282000				✓		
1000	282500				✓		
1000	417000		9030				
1000	800000		1000				
1000	801000					1000	
1000	880000					9990	
1000	880099				✓	9990	
2200	606100		1100				
2200	624200		FR-LOG				
3000	417000		9010				
3000	474231		3200				
5500	400000						
5500	410000		SC-1				
5500	415000		SC-1				
5500	417000		SC-1				
5500	893020		SC-1				
5500	894020		SC-1				

FIGURE 2.93 Default account assignments.

■ Figure 2.93, shows a default account assignment for company code 1,000. In the figure screen you can assign cost center, internal order, or profit centers to cost elements by company codes.

■ Sometimes business requires cost objects to be determined or derived from the assigned profit center. In order to accomplish this business requirement you can assign cost objects to profit centers by navigating "details per profit center" in the dialog structure as shown in Figure 2.94.

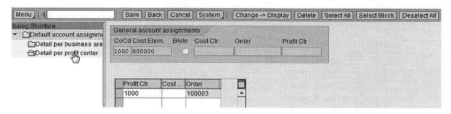

FIGURE 2.94 Derivation of cost objects from profit centers.

2.10.5 Internal Order Settlement

■ Within overhead management, cost is posted to cost centers, internal orders, or WBS elements. During the closing activities, you allocate these costs from cost centers to internal order, or cost centers through assessment or distribution. Similarly, after completion of purpose of the internal order you settle (called *internal order settlement*) internal order costs to other internal orders, cost centers, or WBS element.

■ In the settlement profile, you enter a range of control parameters for an internal order settlement. You assign settlement profile either to internal order type or you can reference an internal order or model order. You can create a settlement profile by navigating the following menu path:

• **SAP IMG Menu:** *Controlling → Internal Orders → Actual Postings → Settlement → Maintain Settlement Profile*

■ Figure 2.95 shows an SAP-delivered settlement profile, what is assigned to an order type, shown in Figure 2.89. In a settlement profile you are determining:

• What are allowed settlement receivers for the inter order

• Whether settlement is allowed or not, and if allowed, what portion can be settled

• Document type used for settlement

• Document resident time

Settlement profile	100	Settlement of marketing orders	

Actual Costs/Cost of Sales		Valid Receivers	
◉ To Be Settled in Full		G/L account	Settlement Not Allowed
◯ Can Be Settled		Cost center	Settlement Optional
◯ Not for Settlement		Order	Settlement Not Allowed
		WBS element	Settlement Optional
Default Values		Fixed asset	Settlement Not Allowed
Allocation structure	A1 CO Allocation st	Material	Settlement Not Allowed
Source structure		Network	Settlement Not Allowed
PA transfer str.	10 PA settlement, m	Profit. Segment	Settlement Optional
Default object type	PSG Profitability se	Sales order	Settlement Not Allowed
		Cost objects	Settlement Not Allowed
Indicators		Order Item	Settlement Not Allowed
☑ 100%-validation		Business proc.	Settlement Not Allowed
☑ %-Settlement		Real Est. Object	Settlement Not Allowed
☐ Equivalence numbers			
☐ Amount settlement		**Other Parameters**	
☐ Variances to Costing-Based PA		Document type	SA G/L account document
		Max.no.dist.rls	100
		Residence time	3 Months

FIGURE 2.95 Settlement profile.

- When an internal order is settled to general ledger accounts or fixed assets, the settlement is called *external settlement*. The system creates an FI document during the settlement process, otherwise internal order settlements are called *internal settlements*.

- In order to settle an internal order, you need to create a settlement rule for the internal order. Settlement rules contain:settlement receivers (for example, cost centers or internal orders), settlement share (for example 10%, 20%, or 100%), and settlement types (for example, PER–periodic settlement). The settlement profile holds some of the important parameters of settlement rule; you can't create a settlement rule without assigning a settlement profile.

- Settlement rule is valid for a specific period, i.e., you can have different settlement rules for different periods of time. You can control a settlement rule validity period by entering a valid date in the field of settlement rule.

- In the internal order settlement process, you use either original cost elements or settlement cost elements as a carrier of the cost. When you use original cost elements the cost is debited and credited under the original cost element. If you have decided to use the settlement cost element, all sending cost will be grouped under the settlement cost element while debiting and crediting.

- The system creates a settlement document while in the settlement process, and uses unique settlement document number ranges. You can create a settlement document number ranges by using the following menu path:
  - **SAP IMG Menu:** Controlling → Internal Orders → Actual Postings → Settlement → Maintain Number Ranges for Settlement Documents
- You can initiate internal order settle process by using the following navigation options:
  - **SAP Menu:** Accounting → Controlling → Internal Orders → Period-End Closing → Single Functions → Settlement → Individual Processing
  - **Transaction Code:** KO88

Question – 52

While making a financial posting, if a transaction is relevant to expenses, you are assigning a controlling objects. Which of the following are cost objects?

A. Cost center accounting

B. Internal order

C. WBS elements

D. Profit centers

Question – 53

You can settle an internal order to which of the following objects.

A. Internal orders

B. Cost centers

C. General ledger

D. Assets

E. All of the above

F. Non of the above

Question – 54

While posting a financial transaction you assigned a cost center and an internal (real) order. Which object will get real postin?

A. *Internal order*

B. *Cost center*

C. *Internal order and cost center*

D. *All of the above*

E. *Non of the above*

In the next section, you will learn about classic profit center accounting. Later on, you will learn how classic profit center accounting is different than SAP general ledger profit center accounting.

2.11 Profit Center Accounting (SAP® CO-PCA)

- Profit center accounts help you to analyze internal profit and loss in different areas or units within your company, called profit centers. You can structure profit centers based on products, geographic regions, function, or markets.

- Profit centers derive data that are relevant for cost and profits from different profit relevant objects materials, cost centers, orders, projects, sales orders, assets, cost objects, and profitability segments through assignment of profit centers to the relevant master data.

- In addition to flow of goods and services, you transfer selected balance sheet line items like receivable, material, and assets to treat profit centers as an investment center. This way, you can calculate the statistics such as return on investment.

- Profit center accounts takes data from other components and represent its own way in a profit centric view. Due to SAP's integrated solution profit center, relevant data are automatically transferred to relevant profit centers and create additional line items for profit center account point of view.

- In order to use a profit center account, you need to go through certain configuration steps.

- The first step towards configuration of profit center accounting is setting up or activating the profit center components in controlling. You can reach the configuration screen by using the following the navigation options:

  - **Transaction Code**: 0KE5

    Or

  - **R/3 IMG Menu:** *Controlling → Profit Center Accounting → Basic Settings → Controlling Area Settings → Maintain Controlling Area Settings*

Change View "EC-PCA: Controlling Area Settings": Overview

Controlling Area	1000	CO Europe

Controlling Area Settings

Dummy Profit Center	9999	Dummy profit center
Standard Hierarchy	H1	PrCtr Hierarchy CO area 1000
Elim. of Int. Business Vol.	☑	
PCtr Local Currency Type	30	Group currency
Profit Center Local Currency	EUR	
Store Transaction Currency	☑	
Valuation View	Legal Valuation	
ALE Distribution Method	No distribution to other systems	

Control Indicators

From Yr	Active Indicator
1994	☑

Position...   Entry 1 of 1

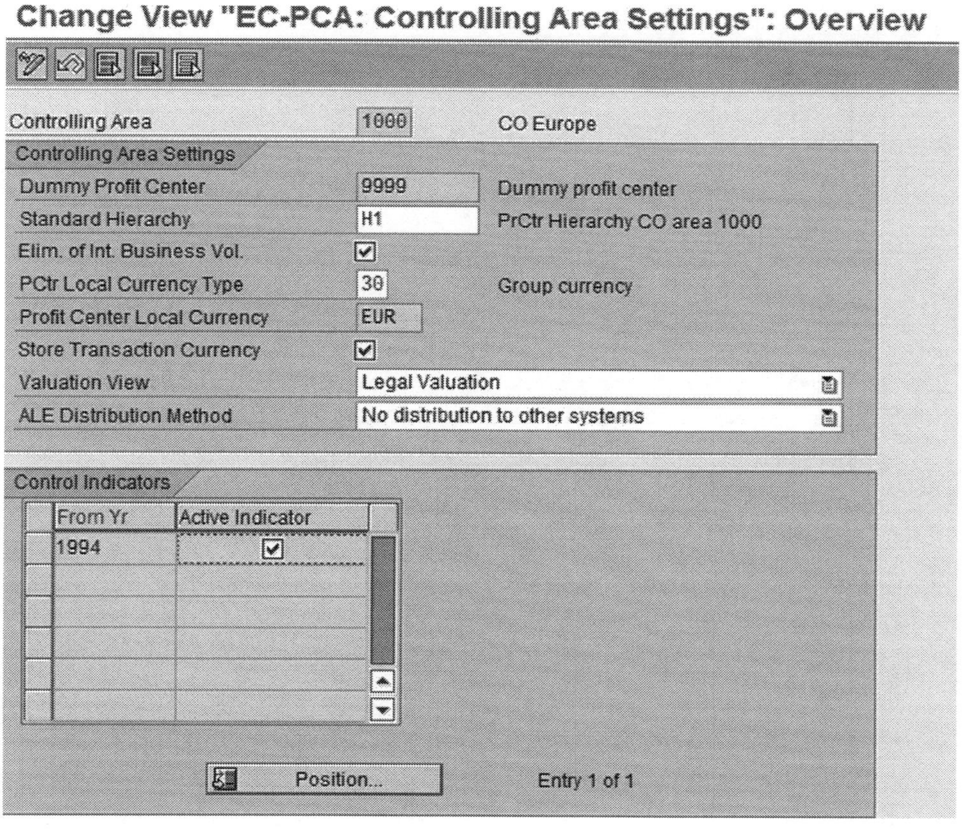

FIGURE 2.96 Profit center accounting setting.

- Figure 2.96 shows the configuration of profit center accounts at the controlling area setting. In the screen, you can see two different profit center accounting objects: standard hierarchy and dummy profit center.

▪ *Standard hierarchy* represents the top most nodes in the profit centers hierarchy. In Figure 2.96, you are just naming the standard hierarchy, but in the later step you can describe and create organizational hierarchy by creating profit center groups and profit centers.

▪ *Dummy profit center* is a unique profit center master data that receives all postings that were made to objects not assigned to a specific profit center.

▪ By checking the "elim. of internal business" box, you can prevent the system from updating objects of the same type, which are assigned to the same profit center, such as assessment cost centers that were assigned to same profit centers.

▪ In profit center accounting, you can record transactions in controlling area currency, group currency, or profit center currency. If you are selecting the last option, you need to define currency and key in the profit center local currency field.

▪ The system automatically stores transactions under company code currency and profit center reporting currency, however, if you want to capture a transaction in transaction currency then you need to check the "store transaction check" box.

▪ The valuation dropdown box provides the options of legal view, group view, and profit center valuation to select the transfer pricing options available to be used to value material and goods movement between profit centers.

▪ *Legal View*: This valuation method is used to value the transfer of material and services among profit centers using the method used for company codes.

▪ *Group View*: In this method, materials and services are valued by using the group valuation approach, which is an already agreed upon amount affiliated entities.

▪ *Profit Center Valuation*: This method is used when you are using a true profit center concept. Normally, profit centers transfer goods and services among themselves as if they are doing transaction with a external entity.

- Before creating a profit center, you need to define the structure of profit centers by creating profit center groups and sub-groups under the standard hierarchy that was discussed earlier.

- When you create a profit center master data, you need to assign a profit center group, ensuring you are created or defined in a tree structure.

- In addition to *profit center standard hierarchy*, you can define two more profit center hierarchies called alternative profit center hierarchy for reposting purposes.

- If your cost center structures are the same as profit center structure, you can create profit center hierarchy with reference to cost center hierarchy.

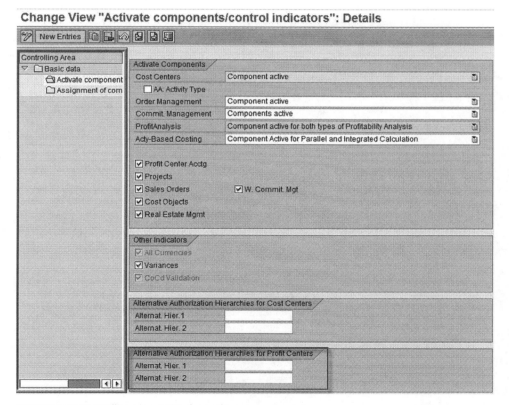

FIGURE 2.97 Controlling area setting for profit center account.

- Figure 2.97 shows controlling area configuration for profit center accounting. In this configuration, you are performing the following steps:

- Activating profit center component

- Assigning company codes to controlling area

- Defining alternative hierarchies for cost center accounting and profit center accounting

▪ You can reach the configuration screen by using the following menu path:

- **R/3 IMG Menu:** *Controlling → General Controlling → Organization → Maintain Controlling Area*

2.11.1 Profit Center Master Data

▪ When you create a profit center master data you create it under a controlling area. While creating a master data, you define profit center number, profit center description, validity period, lock indicator, and assign a profit center group.

▪ You can create a profit center by using the following navigation options:

- **SAP Menu:** *Accounting → Controlling → Profit Center Accounting → Master Data → Profit Center → Individual Processing → Create*

- **Transaction Code: KE51**

▪ As the profit center has a validity period, you can create multiple sets of masters with respect to different validity periods.

▪ By locking and unlocking you can control whether the profit center is allowed for posting or not. If the profit center is locked for posting, when you try to post, the system comes up with error message.

▪ You can assign more than one company code to a controlling area. When you create a profit center master data by default, the system will assign profit center to all company codes. However, you can restrict profit center assignments by unchecking the check box against company code as shown in Figure 2.98.

▪ Every change in the profit center master data is documented by the system. You can see these changes by clicking the "change docs for master data" button in the history tab of the profit center master data, seen in Figure 2.99.

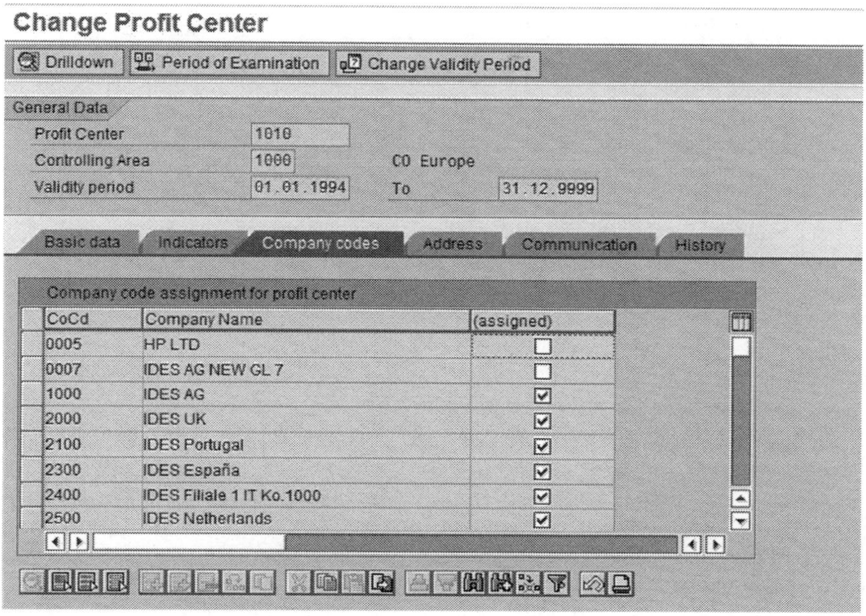

Change Profit Center

Drilldown	Period of Examination	Change Validity Period

General Data

Profit Center	1010	
Controlling Area	1000	CO Europe
Validity period	01.01.1994	To	31.12.9999

Basic data	Indicators	Company codes	Address	Communication	History

Company code assignment for profit center

CoCd	Company Name	(assigned)	
0005	HP LTD	☐	
0007	IDES AG NEW GL 7	☐	
1000	IDES AG	☑	
2000	IDES UK	☑	
2100	IDES Portugal	☑	
2300	IDES España	☑	
2400	IDES Filiale 1 IT Ko.1000	☑	
2500	IDES Netherlands	☑	

FIGURE 2.98 Profit center assignment.

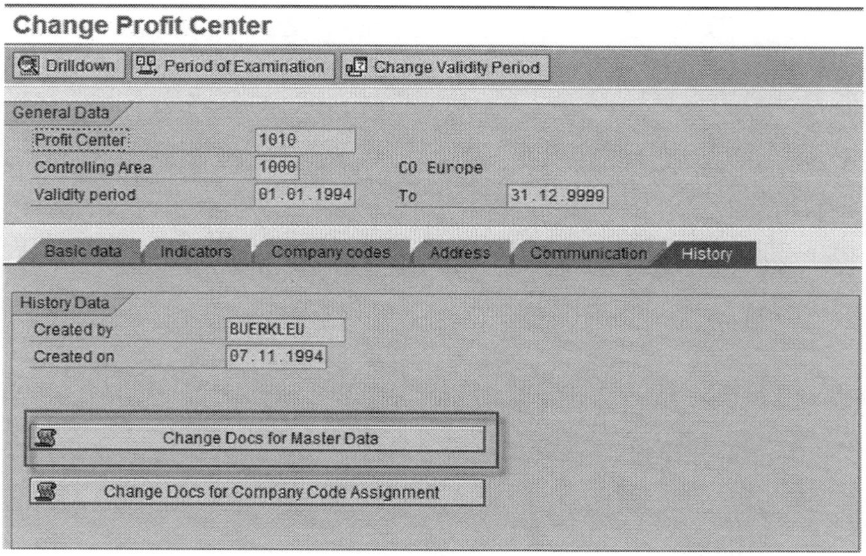

Change Profit Center

Drilldown	Period of Examination	Change Validity Period

General Data

Profit Center	1010	
Controlling Area	1000	CO Europe
Validity period	01.01.1994	To	31.12.9999

Basic data	Indicators	Company codes	Address	Communication	History

History Data

Created by	BUERKLEU
Created on	07.11.1994

Change Docs for Master Data

Change Docs for Company Code Assignment

FIGURE 2.99 Profit center master data change document.

- Technically, profit centers are divided into two types of profit centers: normal profit centers and dummy profit center. In profit center structure, you can have an infinite number of normal profit centers and only one dummy profit center.

- For your profit center standard hierarchy, you need to create dummy profit center master data through a special transaction code provided by SAP through IMG. You can reach this special function through either of the following options:

  - **SAP IMG Menu:** *Controlling → Profit Center Accounting → Master Data → Profit Center → Create Dummy Profit Center*

  - **Transaction Code: KE59**

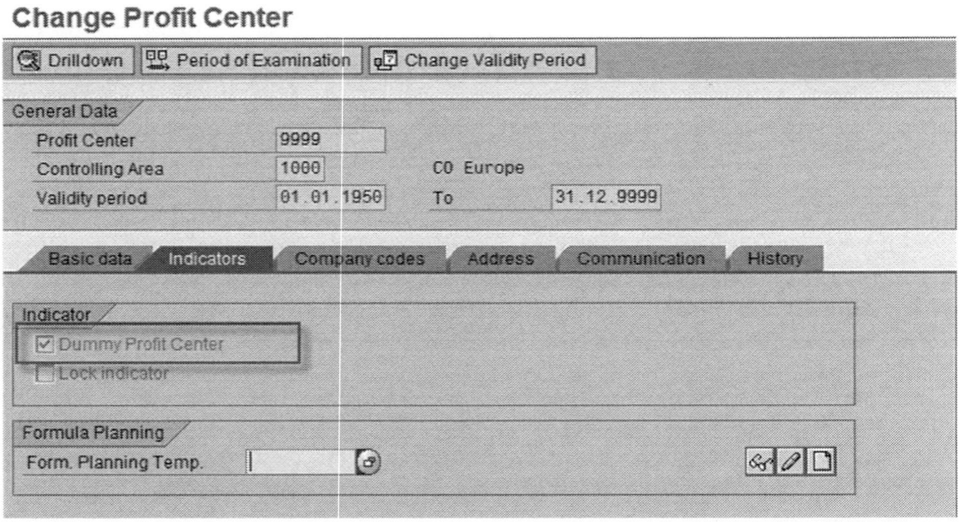

Change Profit Center

| ☒ Drilldown | 🔲 Period of Examination | 🔲 Change Validity Period |

General Data

Profit Center	9999		
Controlling Area	1000	CO Europe	
Validity period	01.01.1950	To	31.12.9999

| Basic data | Indicators | Company codes | Address | Communication | History |

Indicator
- ☑ Dummy Profit Center
- ☐ Lock indicator

Formula Planning
Form. Planning Temp. | | 🔘 | 🖉 📄

FIGURE 2.100 Dummy profit center.

- Figure 2.100 depicts the dummy profit center of controlling area 1,000. The only difference in the dummy profit center master is that the indicator dummy profit center is checked. If you are creating a profit center though other transaction codes, you will see that this check box is grayed out and not allowed for input.

- The system automatically posts to dummy profit center when you post cost or sales to an object that is not assigned to a profit center, such as if you are posting to a cost center and the cost center is not assigned to any profit center.

▪ This way, the system ensures that financial accounting is reconciled with controlling. Later on through the allocation process you can correct the dummy profit center posting by transferring posting to a correct profit center.

▪ The differences between a normal profit center and a dummy profit center are:

- You create a dummy profit center through a *special transaction* available in customizing. You can't create a dummy profit center through a normal profit center create transaction code.

- In the case of a normal profit center, you need to specify a *validity period*, while in case of the dummy center you do not specify a validity period. It is automatically valid for the maximum validity period.

- You cannot *copy* the dummy profit center from an existing profit center.

- A *switch* identifying it as the dummy profit center is automatically set.

▪ SAP has provided functionality for mass maintenance of profit center master data. Generally, you use this functionality to realign profit center master data with your organization structure. You can reach the mass maintenance functionality by using following navigation options:

- ***SAP Menu: Accounting*** → *Controlling* → *Profit Center Accounting* → *Master Data* → *Profit Center* → *Collective Processing* → *KE55 – Master Data*

- ***Transaction Code: KE55***

2.11.2 Profit Center Groups

▪ In profit center accounting, you use *profit center groups* to use as a node in the standard hierarchy or to create an alternative hierarchy. Profit center groups provide the following advantages:

- Used for information systems to display reports for certain groups

- Used for allocation process to allocate dollars

- Used for your planning process

- Used to build two more alternative hierarchies for your controlling area. See Figure 2.100.

▪ You can create an infinite number of hierarchical profit center structures for information systems, allocation processes, and for planning. You can create profit center groups by using the following navigation path:

- **SAP Menu: Accounting** → *Controlling* → *Profit Center Accounting* → *Master Data* → *Profit Center Group* → *KCH1 – Create*

- **Transaction Code: KCH1**

2.11.3 Transactional Data

▪ Profit centers get their data through indirect and direct posting. Almost all cost and revenue data flows to the profit center accounting through indirect posting, such as when you post to a cost center and the profit center assigned to that cost center master data is populated with transactional data.

▪ Sometimes to prepare a balance sheet based on profit center, you post transactional data only to the posting center, described here as direct posting. Direct posting are very minimal in profit center accounting. You can create profit center posting only through the following navigation options:

- **SAP Menu:** *Accounting* → *Controlling* → *Profit Center Accounting* → *Actual Postings* → *Profit Center Document* → *Enter*

- **Transaction Code: 9KE0**

▪ In overhead accounting you use cost center, internal order, and projects to collect costs relevant to these objects. To flow these data to profit center accounting, you need to assign profit centers to the master data of cost center, internal order, or projects. This assignment ensures that data captured in these components will flow to profit center accounting.

▪ In cost center master data, seen in Figure 2.101, SAP provides profit center fields to assign profit center. You can assign multiple cost centers to a profit center, but only one profit center can be assigned to a cost center. This is called a default assignment, which can be overwritten by keying a new profit center while entering a transaction.

Display Cost Center: Basic Screen

Drilldown

Cost Center	1000	Corporate Services	
Controlling Area	1000	CO Europe	
Valid From	01.01.1994	to	31.12.9999

Basic data | Control | Templates | Address | Communication | History

Names

Name	Corporate Services
Description	Corporate Services

Basic data

User Responsible		
Person Responsible	Pfaehler	
Department	Corporate	
Cost Center Category	4	Administration
Hierarchy area	H1120	Internal services
Company Code	1000	IDES AG
Business Area	9900	Corporate Other
Functional Area	0400	Administration
Currency	EUR	
Profit Center	1402	Administration

FIGURE 2.101 Profit center assignment to cost center.

- While making the previous assignment, the system ensures that the controlling area of the cost center is same as the profit centers.

- You use internal order to collect cost for specific projects and events. Like cost centers in internal order, you have to assign a profit center, as seen in Figure 2.102, in the same way you assign a profit center to a plant maintenance order.

- In product costing, you use the cost objects to collect costs that can't be assigned to a cost center or internal order. In order to reconcile controlling with financial accounting, you need to assign profit centers to cost objects. In the cost object master data, you need to assign a profit center, seen in Figure 2.103.

Display Internal Order: Master data

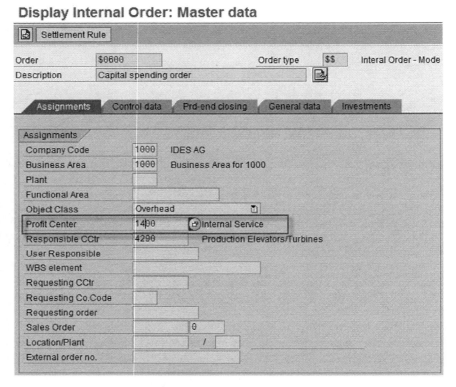

FIGURE 2.102 Profit center assignment to internal order.

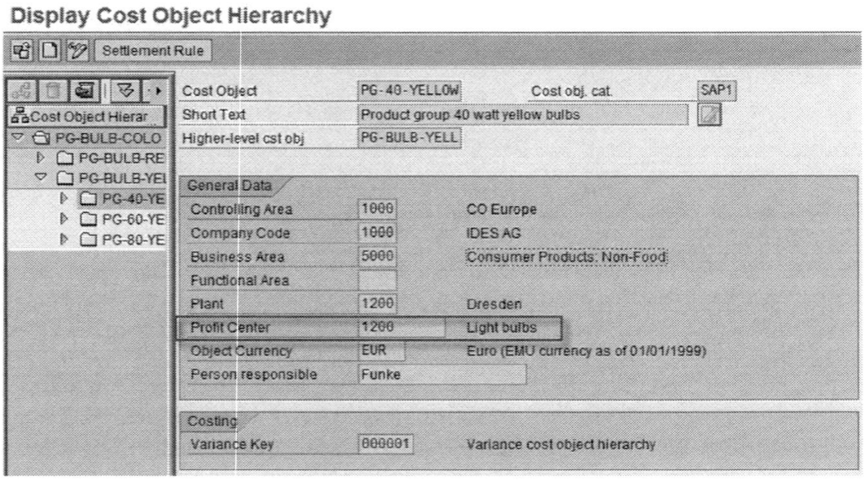

FIGURE 2.103 Profit center assignment to cost object.

- In profitability management, you use characteristics and value fields to determine the result of a profitability segment. You use characteristics to determine profitability segment such as materials, customers, and plant and distribution channels. One of these characteristics will always be a profit center.

- You use a project for a complex task that involves multiple cost centers or internal orders, and a project involves multiple activities grouped under a node. In order to have better tracking, you assign a profit center not to the project definition, but to project sub-components called work breakdown structure, network header, and network.

- When you assign a profit center to a project definition, the profit center assigned to project definition is defaulted unless a specific profit center is assigned to WBS element.

- To move internal goods for sales and production orders, you use material master. Material master forms the basis for derivation of profit center. In material master, you assign a profit center.

- Depending on the material and business scenarios, you assign profit centers in different views of material. SAP has provided profit center assignment fields in different views of material master, such as storage two views, general plant view, and sales view. Even though you can assign a profit center in different views you will always assign the same profit center.

- In the allocation tab of PP (Production Planning) production orders and process orders, SAP has provided a field to assign a profit center. Depending on order, the system proposes the profit center, which reduces manual intervention needed to assign profit centers. In the case of PP, the production order system assigns a profit center from the material master general plant view of the material to be produced. In the case of process orders, the system proposes a profit center from the main product.

- When you allocate costs to a production order or process order, the system-assigned profit center gets posted from the production order or process order.

- While settling the production order or process order, the system gives credit to the assigned profit center.

- In the case of sales orders, the system gets profit center from the material master of the order item.

- Some the default profit center assignments don't suit the business requirements. In those cases you can opt for assignment of profit center through substitution.

- To know the profit center assignment and derivation, SAP has provided a very useful tool called *assignment monitor*. Assignment monitor is a central point where you can see the profit center assignments of various objects. Through assignment monitor you can change and/or make a new assignment. You can reach the assignment monitor screen by using either of the menu paths:

  - **SAP Menu:** *Accounting* → *Enterprise Controlling* → *Profit Center Accounting* → *Master Data* → *Assignment Monitor*

  - **Transaction Code: 1KE4**

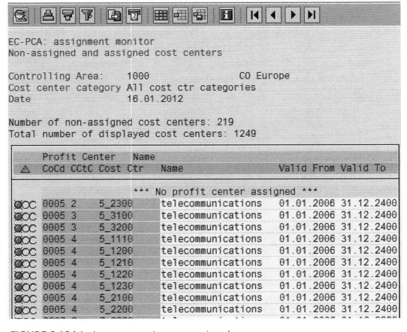

FIGURE 2.104 Assignment monitor: not assigned cost centers.

- Figure 2.104 depicts the assignment monitor for cost centers that are not assigned to profit centers.

- From assignment monitor you can call up the cost center list, internal order list, or material list to see profit center assignment. If any corrections are required, you can quickly navigate to change mode and make the necessary assignment.

- Normally, you post profit center accounting using the following data:

  - All postings affecting primary cost elements and secondary cost elements

  - Other income statement accounts directly assigned to profit center through the automatic account assignment, transactions related to material management, and sales and distribution modules.

  - Balance sheet items that were transferred

- In financial accounts, when you post to an income statement account for which a primary cost element exists, the system expects to assign a cost object. The cost object here can be either a cost center, internal order, or WBS element. Normally, you assign profit center to all of these cost objects so the profit center gets its profit when you post to these cost object. If there is no such default, the system expects to enter profit center while making financial transactions.

- In material management, you move material for different purposes. In some cases, these transactions cross profit centers associated with the material concerned. These types of transactions are tracked in the general ledger through the account determination process.

- In the case of goods receipts and invoice receipts based on account assignment, the system creates a profit center posting.

- In the production process, you use the production order to capture the cost of a product. All materials issued in the production process are captured in the production order and profit center associated with the final, or main product. After completion of the production process, you settle the costs collected in the production order to the final product. In the settlement process, the system credits the profit center associated to the production order by debiting the profit center associated with the final product.

- You assign sales orders to a profit center, thus the profit center associated with sales passes the delivery note subsequently to the billing document. Thus, revenue associated with the billing document is posted to the profit center account.

- You post directly to the profit center in the case of not-integrated revenue, such as income from investment.

- By transferring balance sheet items as part of month-end activities, you can treat the profit center as the investment center. In this case, the person in in charge of the profit center is not only responsible for the generation of income, but also for the return on investment.

- When you transfer balance sheet items to a profit center, the system determines the profit center by:

  - **Material**: In case of inventory value, the system determines profit center based on the profit center assignment to the material master

  - **Assets**: In case of assets you are assigning to the cost center or internal order orders, the system derives the appropriate profit center.

  - **Valuated sales order stock**: The system derives the profit center from the respective profit center.

  - **Account Receivable**: When you transfer account receivable balances, the system distributes the receivables between profit centers based on profit and center assigned revenue line items.

  - **Accounts Payable**: Accounts receivable are distributed among profit centers based on the profit center assignment to the material that has been procured through the purchase order.

  - **Down Payments**: Customer or vendor down payments are not always specific to a purchase order or sales order. In the absence of a proper relation, the system cannot determine the appropriate profit center. In these circumstances, the system allows you to manually assign the correct profit centers.

- To transfer a balance sheet item, you need to configure the SAP application so that you can initiate the transfer of balance sheets items to profit center accounting manually or through batch processing. In the configuration steps, you need to determine which balance sheet accounts you want to transfer to which profit centers. You can reach the configuration screen by using the following menu path:

  - **SAP IMG Menu:** *Controlling → Profit Center Accounting → Actual Postings → Choose Additional Balance Sheet and P&L Accounts → Choose Accounts*

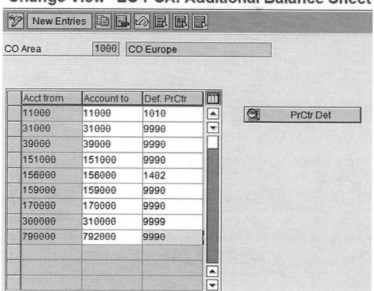

FIGURE 2.105 Balance sheet accounts.

■ In addition to the system's derivation rule, you can build your own rule to derive a profit center based on a certain field value. You can reach the configuration screen by using the following menu path:

• **SAP IMG Menu:** *Controlling → Profit Center Accounting → Actual Postings → Choose Additional Balance Sheet and P&L Accounts → Derivation Rules for Finding the Profit Center*

Default assignment to a profit center: Display Rule Values

Derivation rule
No value filter active

Account Number	Account Number Name	to Account Num	to Account Number	Company Code	Company Code Name	Busine	Business Ar	As	Profit Cent	Profit Center Name
790000	Unfinished products	792000	Unfinished products	1000	IDES AG	9800	Accessories	=	1010	Sales accessories I

FIGURE 2.106 Profit center derivation rule.

■ Once you have determined the balance sheet G/L account to be transferred and have set the derivation rules, you can transfer the opening balance of balance sheet items to profit center accounting. This is a one time activity. You can reach the opening balance transfer functionality by using the following navigating menu path:

- **SAP IMG Menu:** *Controlling → Profit Center Accounting → Actual Postings → Transferring Selected Balance Sheet Items →*

  .... *Generate Opening Balance for Material Stocks*

  .... *Generate Opening Balance for Work in Process*

  .... *Generate Opening Balance for Assets*

  .... *Generate Opening Balance for Payables and Receivables*

  .... *Perform Account Control for Valuation Differences*

- Periodically, the system updates profit center accounting with financial data once you have updated the profit center accounting with the open figure. The system performs a delta or incremental data load on each update.

- You can manually transfer financial data to profit center accounting, but be sure to make note of it. Per the SAP design, the system will first delete data that were already transferred to a profit center account and then load manual data.

- During the year-end activities, you need to carry forward profit center accounting balances to the next year. You can perform balance carry forward by using the following navigating menu paths:

  - **SAP Menu:** *Accounting → Controlling → Profit Center Accounting → Actual Postings → Period-End Closing → Balance Carry Forward*

  - **Transaction Code:** *2KES*

- In controlling, you use the allocation process to move balances between cost objects. During the allocation process, the system creates transactions, which are posted to profit centers based on the profit centers assignment to the cost objects, such as cost centers, internal orders, or WBS elements. The system uses the primary cost element or the secondary cost elements to capture these data.

- Like cost center accounting and internal order, in profit center accounting you can perform the allocation process. Normally, you adopt the allocation process in the profit center account where you initially collected. In some circumstances, transactions in one profit center need to be distributed among various profit centers:

- When you are maintaining profit centers as service profit centers

- Transferred assets or material that, due to account assignment, are posted to one profit center and need to be distributed among other profit centers.

▪ Profit center accounting doesn't support reporting. In the allocation process, you use profit center distribution or assessment. Profit center distribution or assessment follows the same processes as cost center accounting.

▪ Like cost center accounting, in profit center accounting you can assess or distribute profit center data based on either percentage, specific amount, or Statistical Key Figure (SKF).

▪ If you are planning to use statistical key figures that you are using in a cost center accounting, you can transfer those key figures into profit center accounting.

▪ Profit center accounting also facilitates entering external data that are not available in SAP application. You can profit center document entry functionality by using the following menu path:

- **SAP Menu:** *Accounting → Controlling → Profit Center Accounting → Actual Postings → Profit Center Document → Enter*

- **Transaction Code:** *9KE0*

▪ In profit center accounting, all data that are transferred from external system or created in real-time are stored in average balance ledger 8Z. Typically, balance ledger amounts are stored based on their average periodical weight. If the translations are updated in profit center account periodically, the system stores the end balance but not the day to day transactions.

2.11.4 Planning in Profit Center Accounting

▪ Profit center planning normally starts once overhead accounting planning data is complete.

▪ SAP has provided tools to plan profit center accounts by adopting different methods. These tools include: cop existing plan and/or actual data to a new set of plan data, post plan by transactions, manually plan profit centers, and distribute and assess profit centers.

- The data container of planning data is versions. You can maintain different versions for different sets of planning data.

- In SAP, plan version is valid for all CO modules, but the usage of plan version in specific applications requires maintenance of additional parameters.

- SAP has provided a different set of reports, through which you can compare different planning versions and/or actual data.

- Due to the integrated approach of the ERP application, you can transfer planning data of other components of SAP application to profit center accounting. To transfer data from other components, you need to maintain necessary control parameters for profit center accounting.

- In order to protect plan data from further unintended modification, you can lock the planning version by setting the lock indicator.

- In a profit center account, you can transfer profit center planning data either in real-time or through a batch process. If you want to transfer data in real-time, then you need to set the online data transfer indicator as active, otherwise you need to transfer planning data fiscal year.

- To enter manual planning data, you use planning layout. To enter data, you can use the SAP-provided planning layout or you can create your own layout. You can reach the planning layout configuration screen by using the following menu path:

  - **SAP IMG Menu:** *Controlling → Profit Center Accounting → Planning → Manual Planning → Planning Layout*

    .... *Maintain Planning Layout for Costs/Revenues*

    .... *Maintain Planning Layout for Balance Sheet Accounts*

    .... *Maintain Planning Layout for Statistical Key Figures*

- Planning layout helps in many ways, such as:

  - You can plan in any currency

  - You can create a formula to derive a figure for specific rows or columns

  - You can plan for more than one column

  - You can plan for any period dimensions, like monthly, quarterly, half yearly, or yearly

- Like the actual allocation process, you can allocate plan data in profit center accounting. Once you have completed planning in the profit center, you can use the allocation process (plan distribution and plan assessment) in profit center accounting to transfer data from one or more profit centers to one or more profit centers.

2.11.5 Information System

- In profit center accounting, SAP has provided many of box reports you can use for your analysis purposes. In addition to standard reports, you can build reports as per your requirements with report painter/report writer and drilldown.

- For profit center accounting, SAP comes with libraries 8A2, 8A3, and 8A4. You can find all standard reports and report groups under these standard libraries. You can reach these standard reports by navigating the following menu path:

  - **SAP Menu:** *Accounting → Controlling → Profit Center Accounting → Information System .... (various reports)*

- When you call up line item reports, the system accesses line items from the total table GLPCA. Similarly, profit center planning reports can access planning data from GLPCP.

Question – 55

In classic profit center accounting, every posting to profit center accounting is a statistical posting.

A. False

B. True

Question – 56

SAP has provided _____ to see assignments of profit centers to various SAP objects.

Like profit center accounts, SAP has provided another profitability measurement tool called profitability analysis (CO-PA). In the next section, you will come to understand various aspect of profitability management. CO-PA is a very useful tool in the hands of management to measure the performance of a segment.

2.12 Profitability Analysis (SAP® CO-PA)

Today's business is not concentrated in any one region, country, or continent. Due to competition and such large accessibility to markets, management always needs a good analysis tool for better control and for margin analysis.

To stay top on of the market, sales departments make every effort to concentrate on product, geography, and customer. This can be done if the sales department is equipped with updated and reliable data.

All this requires a good and flexible tool that gives timely reports to facilitate decision making. SAP controlling profitability analysis provides all the information to make an informed decision.

There are a number of things that all companies want to use profitability analysis for, such as to generate a report by products, customers, and geography called a segment. Some of the segments come with pre-delivered mySAP ERP Financials, while others can be customized as per your business requirement.

In this section, you will come across key concepts such as of profitability analysis andconfiguration guidance, as well as questions and answers.

- *Profitability analysis* is tool that helps to evaluate a market segment. You can classify market segments by product, geography, customer, or any combination of a strategic business unit. The main objective of CO-PA is to provide information to marketing, sales, and corporate planners for decision making.

- The results of profitability analysis can be analyzed with a multi-dimensional reporting tool, which provides slice and dice functionality.

- The SAP application provides two forms of profitability analysis: costing-based profitability analysis and account-based profitability analysis.

- *Costing-based profitability analysis*: In costing-based profitability analysis, costs and revenues are grouped together based on sale of product and services. This form of profitability analysis emphasizes matching revenues generated from sale of product and services with the expenses incurred to generate these revenues.

- *Account-based profitability analysis*: Account-based profitability analysis system captures data according to the account posted. In this

TABLE 2.3 Costing-Based COPA vs Account-Based COPA

Costing Based CO-PA	Account Based CO-PA
Currencies: You can store transactions	
– Company code currency	– Transaction currency
– Operating Currency	– Company code currency
	– Controlling area currency
– Transactions are stored in COPA special table, and thus does not burden CO tables	– Transactions are posted into CO tables and systems creates separate line items for COPA postings (COEP, COEJ, COSP, COSS)
– Need reconciliation to reconcile COPA with financial data at particular point of time	– COPA is reconciled with financial accounting.
– Quantity and amount are stored in value field with reference a characteristics	– Amounts are stored in general ledgers.

form of profitability analysis, the system summarizes situation changes over the period of time.

■ Table 2.3 describes the differences between cost-based CO-PA and account-based CO-PA.

2.12.1 Operating Concern

■ The operating concern is the highest reporting level in COPA. An operating concern consists of at least one controlling area, however, you can assign more than one controlling area to an operating concern.

■ You can create an operating concern through either:

- *mySAP ERP IMG Menu: Implementation Guide (IMG) → Controlling → Profitability Analysis → Structures → Define Operating Concern → Maintain Operating Concern*

2.12.2 Characteristics

■ In CO-PA, *characteristics* are used for analysis dimension such as customer, product, and sales organization. In CO-PA, you will come across two types of characteristics: fixed characteristics and non-fixed characteristics.

■ *Fixed characteristics* are pre-delivered characteristics and available for use by all operating concerns in a client.

▪ *Non-fixed characteristics* are user-defined characteristics. We can classify these non-fixed characteristics based on how they are created. Characteristics are used both in costing-based CO-PA and account-based CO-PA

- *Created with reference to reference tables*: You can create characteristics with reference to customer master records, material master records, and sales documents.

- *Created from scratch*: These types of characteristics are used especially in CO-PA and are customer specific. For example, you can create characteristics like continents.

- *Predefined characteristics*: In addition to fixed characteristics, SAP comes with a few pre-delivered characteristics.

▪ You need to add all non-fixed characteristics to the field catalog before you use them in the operating concern. In order to carry characteristic values, each characteristic uses a check table.

▪ To create or maintain characteristics fields follow either:

- ***mySAP ERP IMG Menu:*** *Implementation Guide (IMG) → Controlling → Profitability Analysis → Structures → Define Operating Concern → Maintain Characteristics*

2.12.3 Value Fields

▪ In costing-based CO-PA, value fields store the quantities and amounts for analysis. The value fields can be either highly summarized or highly detailed.

▪ Like non-fixed characteristics, you need to add value fields to the fields catalog before you use them in an operating concern. You can access value fields from the fields catalog from any client in a system.

▪ SAP provides a few suggested value fields in the field catalog that can be used in the new operating concern. You can also add custom value fields to the field catalogue. As per SAP's best practice, you can create custom value fields starting with VV and they should be five characters long.

▪ You use value fields to retain various posted values, not the calculated values. While executing CO-PA reports, the system calculates fields like net sales, gross sales, and profit margins.

- To create or maintain value fields follow either:

  - ***mySAP ERP IMG Menu:*** *Implementation Guide (IMG) →*
    Controlling → Profitability Analysis → Structures → Define
    Operating Concern → Maintain Value Fields

- In account-based CO-PA, all values are updated to accounts and
  transactions are recorded in up to three currencies under fixed basic key
  figures. You use fixed basic key figures for reporting purpose.

- In order to get started with CO-PA configuration, you need to structure
  the operating concern. Structuring an operating concern involves
  following steps:

  - Select characteristics to be used. You can select only those
    characteristics that are available in fields catalog.

  - Select value fields to be used. You can select only those value fields
    that are available in fields catalog.

  - Select attributes of the operating concern. Attributes of an operating
    concern consist of the definition of currency type, fiscal year variant,
    and types of CO-PA. (Figure 2.108)

- *Currency Types*: mySAP ERP Financials allows you to capture
  transactional data: in case of costing based CO-PA (the system always
  updates in operating concern currency and you can store data in
  company code currency) and in an account-based CO-PA where you
  can store data in three currencies (transaction, company code, and
  controlling area).

- Capturing data in company code currency makes sense when your
  operating concern consists of multiple company codes using different
  local currency.

- While structuring the operating concern, you need to assign fiscal year.
  The *fiscal year* you assign to the operating concern must agree with
  the controlling area and company code in respect to normal posting
  periods.

- *Account-based CO-PA and costing-based CO-PA*: Both of these
  methods have their advantages and disadvantages. While structuring
  an operating concern, you need to decide what your options would be.
  However, you can choose both options if you want.

- Once you have decided your operating concern structure, you need to generate an operating concern environment. The operating concern generation program builds operating concern tables, programs, and data dictionary.

- Costing-based CO-PA stores transaction data in its own separate table. When you generate an operating concern, the system generates these tables. Due to the separate sets of tables, costing-based CO-PA doesn't overload other standard tables and gives faster execution speeds of CO-PA reports.

- Figure 2.107 and Figure 2.108 depict operating concern attributes of operating concern IDEA. Figure 2.107 shows types of COPA activated for operating concern IDEA, while Figure 2.108 depicts attributes of operating concern IDEA.

- Costing-based CO-PA uses the following specific CO-PA tables:

  - CE1XXXX Actual line items, where XXXX is operating concern ID

  - CE2XXXX Plan line items

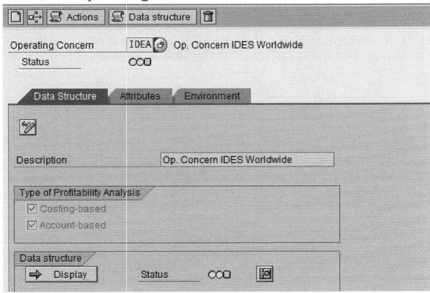

FIGURE 2.107 Operating concern: activation of type of COPA.

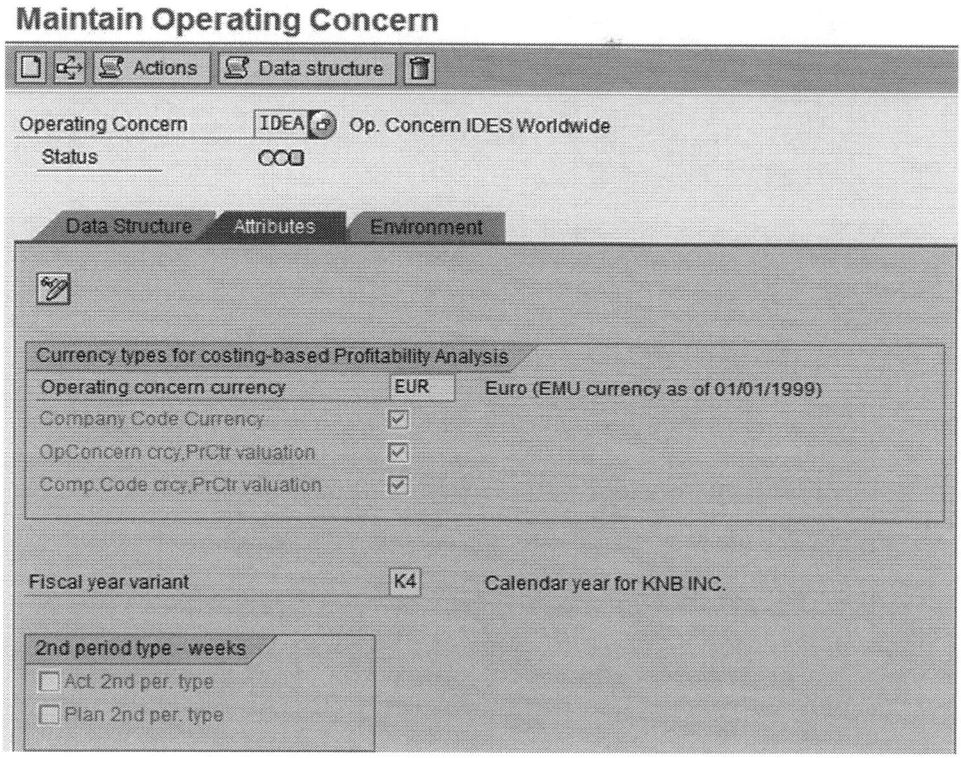

Maintain Operating Concern

FIGURE 2.108 Operating concern attributes.

- CE3XXX Summary records by profitability segments
- CE4XXXX Profitability segment definition
- In account-based CO-PA, transaction data are stored in the controlling overhead tables. As overhead tables are being shared by overhead accounting and by profitability analysis, it affects the execution speed of reports.
- While generating operating concern, the system generates CE4XXXX tables for account-based profitability analysis.
- Account-based profitability analysis uses the following tables:
  - COEJ Actual line items
  - COEP Plan line items

- COSS / COSP Summary records by profitability segments
- CE4XXXX Profitability segment definition
- Both costing-based profitability analysis and account-based profitability analysis uses the same CE4XXXX segment definition table while posting transaction data.
- CE3XXXX table store summarized transactional data. While executing the profitability report, the system access CE3XXXX and CE4XXXX tables.

2.12.4 Transactional Data

- Not all transactional data are posted to profitability analysis. Only relevant data are posted to profitability analysis, which is determined through automatic and manual mapping, and through derivation and valuation configuration.
- Automatic derivation happens when automatic data transfer happens from other modules, such as:
  - Billing document
  - Transfer of overhead
  - External data transfer
- The other type of derivation is manual derivation. These types of data generally generate in FICO modules. For example:
  - Settling orders and projects
  - Direct posting from FI
  - Manually created COPA line items;
  - Manually entry of planning data
- In contrast to automatic and manual derivation, another frequently used type of derivation is called derivation strategy. Derivation strategy is generally used for user-defined characteristics.

2.12.5 Characteristic Derivation

- Characteristic derivation consists of *derivation steps* (derivation strategy). The purpose of characteristic derivation is to derive characteristic from the profitability analysis related transactions.

- When you generate an operating concern, the system generates standard derivation rules. The standard derivation rules include:

  - Steps for deriving fixed characteristics

  - Steps for deriving the characteristics you selected from SAP tables

  - Steps for determining units of measures for the quantity fields assigned in the sales and distribution application, or in planning

- If you have created user-defined characteristics, you need to define your own derivation logic.

- Each derivation consists of the definition of the logical inter relationship between the known source characteristics and characteristics to be derived. Through the derivation process, one or more characteristic values are derived from one or more source fields.

- To locate characteristic values for all profitability analysis, the system goes through a number of derivation steps. This sequential derivation step is called derivation strategy.

- In customization, you define the sequence of derivation steps, through which the system locates characteristics values. In each derivation steps, you configure:

  - Under what circumstances the steps should be executed

  - Whether initial values are allowed for source fields in a step

  - Whether the step should be overwrite an existing characteristics value

  - Whether an error message should generate if the step is unsuccessful

2.12.6 Derivation Type

- While generating an operating concern, the system also generates standard derivation steps to derive characteristic values of all known characteristics and dependencies.

- You can change the system generated derivation steps and add your own derivation steps in a logical way to make chains of derivation steps. However, derivation of controlling area, product, company code, and customer are non-modifiable.

- SAP ERP Financials provides different derivation type to derive characteristics in a different way depending on dependencies, sources, and target fields.

- There are: derivation rule, table lookups, moves, customer hierarchy, and customer enhancement.

- *Derivation rule*: Derivation rules are used to derive characteristic values through user defined logic. A derivation rule determines which source characteristics or combination of characteristic values results target characteristic values. The rule is used mostly to derive characteristic values for user-defined characteristics. You can configure derivation rules for a specific time period.

- *Table lookup*: Table lookup is another method through which you can derive characteristics from other known characteristics. You need to evaluate sales performance by country, so by using table lookup to the customer can derive country where the sales have occurred.

- When you are generating an operating concern system, the system builds a few table lookups. However, you can change them and create your own table lookups.

- *Move and Clear*: This derivation type helps move whole or part of a characteristic, as well as clear one or more characteristics from the transactions.

- You can reach the configuration screen to create derivation rule by navigating the following menu paths:

  - *mySAP ERP IMG Menu: Implementation Guide (IMG) → Controlling → Profitability Analysis → Master Data → Define Characteristic Derivation*

2.12.7 Data Feed to COPA

- Data flow to COPA depending on the type of COPA you are using and the modules you are using. In this section, you will come to know how and from where COPA gets its data to generate segmental reports.

- *Data Feed from Sales and Distribution Module*: Quantities, revenue, discounts, and the cost of goods sold are transferred to COPA, where you generate billing document in SD module in the case of a costing-based COPA. In the case of an account-based COPA, the system updates COPA with the cost of goods sold information when you create outbound delivery, revenue, and discounts when you create billing documents.

- *Data Feed from Overhead Accounting*: Overhead cost not relevant to production collected in cost centers is allocated to profitability segments through assessment. In the assessment process, sending cost centers are created with cost that are being sent and debited to receiving cost centers. The cost center assessment to COPA works in the same way as it works within overhead accounting. You need to define the cycle and segment to assess cost centers to COPA.

- In overhead accounting, you use internal order, sales orders, and plant maintenance order, to collect cost for specific purposes. After completion of a project you can settle these costs either to another cost objects or directly to COPA profitability segments.

- In account-based COPA, the costs are settled through the settlement cost element specified in settlement structure.

- In costing-based COPA, the costs are settled using the original cost elements to value field specified in transfer structure.

- In COPA, you use allocation structure and PA transfer structure for the settlement of internal orders and assessment of cost centers.

- *Allocation structure* consists of one or more settlement assignments. A allocation structure consists of the type of cost (cost elements or groups of cost element) that needs to be allocated with which received type (cost centers and COPA segments).

  - *mySAP ERP IMG Menu: Implementation Guide (IMG) → Controlling → Cost Center Accounting → Actual Postings → Period-End Closing → Assessment Define → Allocation Structures*

- A *PA transfer structure* consists of assignments of costs and revenues to the value fields in costing-based COPA. You use a PA transfer structure in order settlement, FI direct posting, and internal activity allocation in CO. You can create a PA transfer structure by using the following navigation path:

  - *mySAP ERP IMG Menu: Implementation Guide (IMG) → Controlling → Profitability Analysis → Flows of Actual Values → Order and Project Settlement → Define PA Transfer Structure for Settlement*

- *Data feed from FI*: Expanses and incomes that are not related to overhead, material management, sales, and distribution can be posted directly to COPA from financial accounting. A couple of examples of these types of costs are advertisement and insurance fees.

- While making a financial accounting transaction in a costing-based COPA, you can directly assign transaction to characteristics by calling a special screen layout. In the case of an account-based COPA, data are posted to the same cost and revenue elements.

- *Production variances*: When you are receiving material from the production process, if any price variances arise, these price variances are settled to profitability segments.

- *Data-feed through valuations*: Some expenses, such as freight expenses and sales-sensitive elements, will not be available until they have incurred. In order to determine fair profitability segmental result, SAP has provided functionality called valuation. Through valuation, you can calculate tentative figures for supplemental expenses.

- You can calculate supplemental expenses by using one or more of the following techniques:

  - With the help of costing sheet

  - By mapping the product cost component technique to value fields

  - By using an existing user

- With the help of a costing sheet, you can calculate supplemental costs that can't be determined right away. A cost sheet is a structural presentation of calculation and uses SAP's famous condition technique to calculate supplemental figure.

- You can reach the configuration of a costing sheet by using the following navigation path:

  - ***mySAP ERP IMG Menu***: *Implementation Guide (IMG)* → *Controlling* → *Profitability Analysis* → *Master Data* → *Valuation* → *Create Condition Types and Costing Sheet*

- A costing sheet consists of sets of condition types. Each condition type has access to either a value or calculation. In COPA, each condition type mapped to value field.

- A product costing module is used to estimate the cost of a material. You can view cost estimates in different views like by item, cost element, or cost component.

- Through configuration, you are assigning cost components to value fields. When you do valuation, the system transfers cost estimation information to COPA through cost components.

- With the help of value field analysis you can find out how transactional data flows to SAP COPA. You can reach value field analysis functionalities by navigating the following menu path:

  - ***mySAP Menu:*** *Accounting → Controlling → Profitability Analysis → Tools → Analyze Value Flows → .... Various*

- Value field analysis depicts the value flows:

  - Transfer of billing documents and sales order from sales and distribution module

  - Direct posting from financial accounting

  - Direct posting from material management module

  - Settlement of internal orders and projects

  - Overhead assessment from cost center accounting

  - External data transfer

2.12.8 Information System

- SAP has provided an interactive reporting functionality for COPA called drilldown reporting. In drilldown reporting, you can generate reports for a reporting characteristic or group of characteristics.

- The functions of drilldown reporting is divided into three levels based on functionalities:

  - *Level 1*: Contains basic functions of drilldown reporting. Report allows you to send output through SAPmail.

  - *Level 2*: Contains the rest of the features of drill down reporting, allows the user to download data, and displays reports in graph.

  - *Level 3*: All level offers all functionalities of drilldown reporting

- COPA drilldown reports are either basic reports or form reports.

- *Basic Reports*: Basic reports are designed and built based on a predefined basic structure.

- You can build a basis report either from the IMG menu or from the application menu. While creating basic reports, the system expects you to key the "from" and "to" dates, in case of costing based COPA record types, versions, plan, or actual indicator.

- If you have created characteristic hierarchies, you can use them in the basic reports.

- *Form Reports*: These types are more complex and designed for specific-user requirements.

- In form reports, form determines content and structure of the report. The content of the form is generally fixed but you can change form in special circumstances.

- Basic reports and form reports are valid for one type of COPA. For example, if report X is designed for costing based COPA, it can't be used for account based COPA.

Question – 57

In COPA, SAP comes with pre-delivered characteristics, company code, purchase organization, sales organization, and materials, and pre-defined automatically for every operating concern. These are known as

_____.

Question – 58

When you post data to a costing-based COPA, the system updates transactional in special COPA tables.

A. True

B. False

Question – 59

Like other modules, in controlling profitability analysis, system uses _____ as highest-level entity.

A. Operating concern

B. Plant

C. Controlling area

D. Company code

Question – 60

In account-based profitability analysis, the system updates and stores the actual transactions in the company code currency.

A. True

B. False

Question – 61

In account-based profitability analysis, _____ store the amounts for reporting.

Question – 62

A derivation strategy consists of a number of derivation steps, which derive different _____.

Answer Key

Question No.	Answers	Question No.	Answers
1	A, B	32	B
2	True	33	A
3	True	34	A
4	A	35	B
5	B	36	A
6	False	37	C
7	A	38	A
8	B	39	A
9	False	40	B
10	A, B, C	41	B
11	C	42	B
12	B	43	B
13	C	44	A
14	D	45	A
15	C	46	A
16	A	47	A
17	D	48	B
18	A	49	B
19	D	50	A, B
20	D	51	A
21	B	52	A
22	D	53	E
23	A	54	A
24	D	55	B
25	A	56	assignment monitor
26	A	57	fixed characteristics
27	A	58	True
28	A	59	operating concern
29	True	60	True
30	D	61	accounts
31	D	62	characteristics

CHAPTER **3**

SAP® GENERAL LEDGER

In This Chapter

3.1 Introduction

- Prior to mySAP® ERP Financials 2004, customers of SAP need to install and configure different components of SAP to meet different financial reporting needs of an enterprise. This situation becomes very complicated when various external stockholders are demanding financial statements based on different criteria.

- Due to the globalization of business, financial statement readers demand adoption of unified accounts polices and principles, so that everyone reads and interprets financial statement in the same way.

- mySAP® ERP Financials provides a unified solution by combining the cost of sales accounting, profit center accounting, special purpose ledgers, and profit center accounting.

- SAP general ledger (formally New G/L) has the following advantages over classic general ledger:

  - *Extended data structure*: Compared to classic G/L total tables, mySAP ERP Financials comes with new tables with additional field. You can also extend the total table, as per your requirements.

  - *Real-time document splitting*: Due to the document splitting functionality, you can prepare balance sheets and profit & loss accounts at the profit center level or segment level.

  - *Real-time reconciliation between FI & CO*: In classic G/L, you can run transaction code KALC to periodically post a summarized reconciliation. For example, any cross company code allocation in controlling generates financial transactions when you run reconciliation postings at the end of the month. Thus, there is no need to run separate reconciliation postings to reconcile the FI and CO modules.

  - *Multiple ledgers*: SAP general ledger comes with multiple ledger functionality so that you can create multiple ledgers for parallel reporting.

  - *Interfaces*: The way you are interfacing now remains unchanged in SAP G/L

  - *Upstream software*: Feeder systems of financial accounting like sales and distribution and material management work in the same as with classic G/L.

  - *Combination of components*: SAP G/L is a combination of classic G/L and special purpose ledger. If you are using classic G/Land special purpose ledger you can replace these two with SAP G/L. Users need to familiar with one application that is SAP G/L.

  - *New Dimension*: To accomplish segmental reporting, the new G/L includes a new reposting dimension called segment.

  - *Drilldown reporting*: In new G/L, SAP has improved the reporting functionality by providing drilldown-reporting options.

■ When you use classic G/L, the system stores data in different tables for the different components given below:

- G/LT0 – Classic FI: G/L total table

- G/LFUNCT – Cost-of-sales ledgers

- COFIT – Reconciliation ledger

- G/LPCT – EC-PCA / classic Profit Center Accounting

■ mySAP ERP G/L uses special purpose techniques to capture transactional data.

■ To portray more than just valuation view, in mySAP ERP you can create multiple ledgers.

■ mySAP ERP comes with one pre-delivered ledger called leading ledger. All company codes pertaining to a client are assigned to the leading ledger.

■ You can assign different characteristics (called scenarios) and fiscal years to ledgers to portray financial results.

■ The posting period checks are always performed for leading ledgers or representative ledgers.

■ If a ledger group does not contain the leading ledger, one of the ledgers in the group becomes the representative ledger. Otherwise, the leading ledger is considered as representative ledger. This approach means that postings are made only if the the leading or representative ledger allows.

■ mySAP ERP does not validate any other fiscal-year definitions that exist in other ledgers of the ledger group. The software updates the other ledgers in every case, which does not prevent completion of the posting.

■ In addition to entry view what you are seeing now in classic G/L, mySAP ERP Financials provides an additional display called general ledger view.

■ The general ledger view is specific to a ledger. You can view more than one general view depending on the number of ledgers you have configured and the data you have entered.

■ mySAP ERP Financials comes with a new total table FAGLELEXT, which contains additional data fields compared to a standard table.

Table **FAGLELEXT** updates with profit center, segment, cost of sales, and cost center. If the standard table doesn't suit you, you can create your own custom table by adopting **FAGLELEXT** as template.

■ mySAP ERP Financials comes with two new additional tables **FAGLFLEXA** (stores actual line items) and **FAGLFLEXP** (stores plan line items). Depending on the scenarios you are using and the data you are entering, the system updates these two tables.

■ One of the aims of SAP G/L is to generate financial statements based on multiple dimensions. To achieve this, SAP comes with a document splitting functionality.

■ For each financial posting, the system applies the document splitting functionality and inherits account assignment information from the assigned accounts to the non-assigned accounts.

■ The mySAP ERP Financials offers improvements integrating financial accounting with and assets management, controlling, and consolidation.

■ Financial accounting integration with controlling offers the transfer of cross entity controlling posting in real time, thus avoiding gaps between financial accounting and controlling, and helping to speed up closing.

■ Depreciation postings are made to the corresponding ledger group as complete postings for specific depreciation areas.

■ The transfer is possible because the standard delivery of the new G/L contains all the fields required for company consolidation or profit-center consolidation, including fields for partner company, partner profit center, and consolidation transaction type.

■ The use of mySAP ERP Financials G/L is optional for old customers, who need to activate the SAP G/L functionality in order to use it, while it is compulsory for new customers and comes standard.

■ If an existing customer is upgrading from the lower version to the higher version and wants to utilize SAP G/L functionality, he needs to activate first using transaction code: FAGL_ACTIVATION.

Note

While activating the SAP general functionality you may encounter an error saying "View/table V_FAGL_ACTIVEC can only be displayed and maintained with restrictions." This is because by default ECC 6.0 comes with new G/L.t. That's why you are getting this error. FAGL_ACTIVATION needs to be run only when you are migrating from another version to ECC 6.0.

- mySAP ERP Financials comes with a new set of menu paths for both "easy access" and IMG. You can activate and deactivate these menus through transaction code SE38 by running the following programs:

  - Activate/deactivate SAP general ledger easy access menus: RFAGL_SWAP_MENU_NEW

  - Activate/deactivate SAP general ledger easy IMG menus: RFAGL_SWAP_IMG_NEW

- Similarly you can activate/deactivate the old menu by running the following programs through transaction code: SE38:

  - Activate/Deactivate Old Menu: RFAGL_SWAP_MENU_OLD

  - Activate/Deactivate Old Implementation Guide: RFAGL_SWAP_IMG_OLD

Question – 1

Transaction code FAGL_ACTIVATION is used to call activation of SAP G/L functionality.

A. *True*

B. *False*

For a more detailed understanding, the rest of this chapter has been divided into small sections.

3.2 Master Data

3.2.1 Segments

- Various legal requirements like IFRS (International Financial Reporting Standard), IAS (International Account Standard) and GAAP (General Accepted Accounting Principles) require segment reporting. The *segment* can be a line to a business or geographical area, that means to need your financial statement below company code level.

- To bring this functionality to life, mySAP ERP comes up with a new entity called a segment. You can create and/or maintain segments by using the following the navigation option:

  - **ECC IMG Menu:** Enterprise Structure → Definition → Financial Accounting → Define Segment

- Segments are treated like other account assignment objects, such as cost centers and profit centers.

- Segments are assigned to a profit center's master through transaction code KE51 / KE52. Whatever data is posted to profit centers is also posted to the related segments.

- The purpose of segment definition is to meet the segment reporting requirement of IAS/IFRS/GAAP. Segments are available below the company code level and are used as account assignments in mySAP ERP Financials.

- Segment field derives its data from profit center and customer development. With profit center, a segment is assigned to profit center master data. When you post data to profit center, the segment field is automatically populated with values. With customer development, you can derive values through BAdl: **FAGL_DERIVE_SEGMENT**.

- Figure 3.1 shows assignment of a segment to profit center master data. A segment can be assigned to one or more profit centers, while a profit center can have only one segment.

- The assignment of a segment to a profit center means that if you assigned a segment to a profit center and saved the profit center master data, you can edit/change the segment field in the profit center.

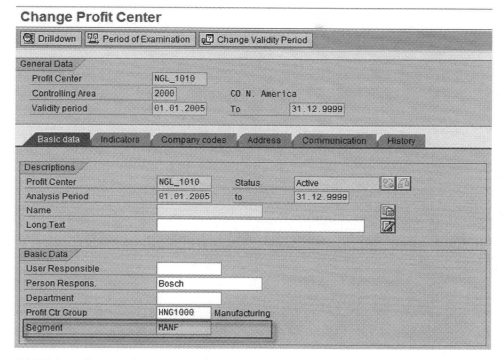

FIGURE 3.1 Assignment of segment to profit center.

* In order to use segment field, make sure that you have considered following points:

  • *Scenario definition*: You have defined scenarios

  • *Assignment of scenario*: You have assigned the segment scenario to the desired ledger

  • *Derivation*: In order to derive value to the segment, you need to assign segments to profit centers

  • *G/L field status*: Maintain field status group of field status variant, segment as optional

  • *Posting key field status*: Maintain field status for segment field of posting key as optional

  • *Display layout*: Display financial document by using correct layout

3.2.2 Profit Center Accounting

▪ Another key change in SAP G/L is profit center accounting, which is part of financial accounting. Previously in classic G/L, all profit center transactions were stored in a separate table called 8A table. In SAP G/L, if a profit center scenario is assigned to one or more ledgers, the system updates new SAP general tables with profit centers and partner profit centers.

▪ This eliminates the need for reconciliation between general ledger total table (G/LT0) and profit center total table (G/LPCT).

▪ With the integration of profit center accounting in SAP G/L, SAP G/L's splitting functionality and assignment of scenarios helps to generate financial statements based on additional dimensions, such as profit centers and segments.

▪ In SAP G/L profit center accounting, planning is possible with respect to an account. With this new functionality, secondary activity planning is not possible.

▪ You can do planning in SAP G/L accounting via the following SAP menu path:

- **ECC SAP Menu:** Accounting → Financial Accounting → General Ledger → Periodic Processing → Planning → Planned Values → Enter (New)

▪ Use of profit center planning requires certain configurations. Make sure that you have configured the following steps:

- Activate total table: The first step in planning configuration is to activate the total table for planning. You can find the configuration screen by using the following menu path:

  – **ECC IMG Menu:** Financial Accounting (New) → General Ledger Accounting (New) → Planning → Technical helps → Install Summary Table.

- *Import a planning layout*: To enter planning data, the system needs a layout template. SAP has provided templates in the source clients 000. You can import these templates by using the following the menu path:

  – **ECC IMG Menu:** Financial Accounting (New) → General Ledger Accounting (New) → Planning → Technical helps → Install Summary Table.

- *Create a planning document type*: Every transaction you enter in SAP application is stored electronically called a document. Like actual posting, planning posting also creates a planning document. In this activity you will assign a document type that will be used exclusively for planning posting. Use the following menu path to reach determination of planning document type:

  – **ECC IMG Menu:** Financial Accounting (New) → General Ledger Accounting (New) → Planning → Define document types for planning.

- *Define document number range*: A SAP document is identified by a document number. For profit center planning, you have created a document type. In this step, you will create a document number range. You can reach the configuration screen by using the following the menu path:

  – **ECC IMG Menu:** Financial Accounting (New) → General Ledger Accounting (New) → Planning → Define Document Number Ranges for plan Documents.

- *Defined a plan version*: Versions help create data sets for various scenarios. To store data, you need a version to be created in first place. Later on if you want to transfer data to controlling you can map profit center planning data by creating an identical planning version on controlling overhead management modules. If you want to transfer profit center planning data to controlling you need to do it manually.

- *Assign a plan version to a fiscal year*: Finally to use a planning version that we have created in our earlier step, you need to assign the planning version to a company code and fiscal year.

- Since profit center accounting is shifted to the financial accounting module, now you can perform allocation within a financial account to move costs and revenues from one profit center to another. Now in SAP G/L accounting, you can perform assessment and distribution within financial accounting, but you can't do reposting in G/L.

- In addition to CO allocation process, allocation process in financial accounting adds a new step in the closing process.

- The allocation process in controlling (if real time integration is active) and financial accounting generates a financial document. In classic profit center accounting, the allocation process doesn't create a financial document.

- The first step in starting the allocation process is the creation of a cycle. A cycle is the grouping of segments treated in a same way. A financial accounting cycle is always assigned to a version in financial accounting. In a segment, you are grouping together sending profit centers and receiving profit centers.

- In the allocation process, you use sender profit centers, receiving profit centers, and distribution methods with the cycle and segment concepts you are using in controlling now.

- *Sender profit center(s)*: Sender profit center(s) is/are profit center(s) from which you are transferring posting to one or more profit centers. In case of sending profit center, you can define what portion you want to transfer from the sending profit centers to the receiving profit center. The amount can be either a fixed amount or afixed percentage.

- *Receiving Profit Center(s)*: The profit center will absorb the posting from the sending profit center. The posting can be transferred to the receiving profit center(s) based on distribution methods. These distribution methods can be fixed amounts, fixed percentages, fixed shares, and variable shares. For variable shares you are using tracking factors.

- The allocation process previously mentioned consists of distribution and settlement.

- In the distribution allocation process, the system transfers postings from one or more profit centers to one or more profits center through the same G/L account. For example, if you are transferring X amount that is posted to general ledger account GL1 from profit center PC1 to profit center PC2, the system uses G/L account GL1 to credit PC1 and debit PC2.

- Financial accounting distribution generates an accounting document, which you can reverse and re-run through profit center distribution.

- The second method of allocation is assessment. Like overhead assessment, the system uses cycle and segment concepts. In assessment, the system uses an assessment G/L account to distribute posting from one or more sending profit centers to one or more receiving profit centers.

Question – 2

Segment master data is always company code dependent.

A. True

B. _False_

Question – 3

Choose the correct answer. The relationship between profit center and segment are

A. _One profit center: once segment_

B. One profit center: many segments

C. _Many Profit Centers: one segment_

Question – 4

In mySAP ERP Financials, SAP has provided the following allocation methods.

A. Distribution

B. Assessment

C. Reposting

D. All of the above

Question – 5

In mySAP ERP Financials, you can transfer planning data relating to primary cost elements as well as to secondary cost elements in integrated planning.

A. True

B. False

3.3 Ledger and Ledger Groups

- As discussed in the introduction section of this chapter, new G/L comes with a combination of the functionalities of classic G/L and special purpose ledger. It has all the functionality of classic G/L with an enhanced future of special purpose ledger.

- In classic G/L, you use different ledgers in different components to accomplish various reporting requirements. For example, general ledger 00 in classic G/L, ledger 8A in profit center accounting, and ledger 0F in cost of sales accounting. Maintaining different ledgers in different components poses a reconciliation problem for the SAP user community. This is alleviated in mySAP ERP Financials through the ledger concept.

3.3.1 Total Table

- The total table (**FAGLFLEXT**) of SAP G/L is updated with more entries as compared to the classic G/L table GLT0, such as, cost center, profit center, and segments. The system updates certain fields of the total table depending on the assignment of scenarios to the ledger. Later in this section, you will learn more about scenarios and their uses.

- The total table can be extended with customer fields, or you can create own table. Use the following menu path to add new customer field to total table:

  - **ECC IMG Menu:** Financial Accounting (New) → Financial Accounting Global Settings (New) → Ledgers → Fields → Customer → Include Fields in Totals Table

- If the standard tables do not fit your requirements, you can create your own custom table. When you create a custom table, the system creates a total table as well as actual line item tables. You can reach the configuration screen by navigating the following menu path:

  - **ECC IMG Menu:** Financial Accounting (New) → Financial Accounting Global Settings (New) → Ledgers → Fields → Customer → Include Fields in Totals Table → Extras → Create table group

- In the subsequent steps, you need to assign the custom table to a leading ledger and other non-leading ledgers.

3.3.2 Scenarios

- A *scenario* defines which fields are updated in the ledger when posting a transaction in financial accounting.

- mySAP ERP Financials comes with six scenarios and you can't create your own scenarios. However, if you have created a custom field, you can add these custom fields to one or more scenarios allowing the ledger to be updated with the new fields. These scenarios are showcased in Table 3.1.

TABLE 3.1

Scenarios	Scenarios Technical name	Fields to Update
Cost Center Update	FIN_CCA	Updates receiver and sender cost center field
Preparations for Consolidation	FIN_CONS	Updates consolidation transaction types and trading partner fields
Business Area	FIN_GSBER	Updates sender business area and receiver area fields
Profit Center Update	FIN_PCA	Updates profit center and partner profit center
Segmentation	FIN_SEGM	Updates segments and partner segments and profit center fields
Cost of Sales Accounting	FIN_UKV	Updates the sender functional area and receiver functional area fields

- To update the desired field you need to assign one or more scenarios to a ledger or ledgers. You can reach the scenarios assignment configuration screen by using the following navigation path:

  - **ECC IMG Menu:** Financial Accounting (New) → Financial Accounting Global Settings (New) → Ledgers → Ledger → Assign Scenarios and Customer Fields to Ledgers

3.3.3 Leading Ledgers

- In each client you will have exactly one *leading ledger*. In mySAP ERP, the leading ledger comes with ledger ID "0L".

- Leading ledger is the only ledger that is integrated with controlling, which means that if you are posting a transaction to a non-leading ledger, the transaction doesn't flow to controlling.

- The general question that arises in every implementation project is which accounting principle will be portrayed for the leading ledger.

- The answer to this question is tricky and requires careful consideration. The following are a few points to be considered while taking decision in this respect:

- *Future requirement*: A few countries have already adopted the IFRS accounting principle, and a few countries are planning in the future to adopt IFRS. Adoption of the accounting principle influences the choice of a leading or a non-leading ledger.

- *Controlling*: As you are aware, only the leading ledger is integrated with controlling. This is another factor that drives the selection of a leading or non-leading ledger for accounting principle.

- *IS Solution*: All IS solutions are not compactable with the ledger concept of SAP G/L. For example, FERC account (part of IS utility) gets its data from controlling objects and the G/L. As FERC accounting is based on US GAAP, you need to adopt US GAAP accounting principle for leading ledger.

- *Approaches*: For parallel accounting, the SAP customer can adopt an account solution or ledger solution based on business requirements, which you will learn more about in the parallel accounting section. If the account solution is adopted, then you have no choice other than leading ledger.

▪ Leading ledger gets most of its attributes, such as currency, fiscal year, and period posting variant, from the company code.

3.3.4 Non-leading Ledgers

▪ To portray financial statements in different accounting principles, you can create one or more non-leading ledgers. In mySAP ERP, you can have at best 99 ledgers, including leading ledgers.

▪ Like leading ledger, a non-leading ledger does not come in delivered SAP application. To use one or more non-leading ledgers, you need to create a non-ledger. You can reach the configuration screen by navigating the following menu path:

- **ECC IMG Menu**: Financial Accounting (New) → Financial Accounting Global Settings (New) → Ledgers → Ledger → Define and Activate Non-Leading Ledgers

Change View "Settings for Non-Leading Ledgers in General Ledger": Over

New Entries

Ledger   C1

Settings for Non-Leading Ledgers in General Ledger									
Co	Company Name	C1	Crcy 1	C2	Crcy 2	C3	Crcy 3	FV	Var.
C201	Best Pratice-Subsidiary-2	10	INR					C2	

FIGURE 3.2 Definition non-leading ledger.

■ Figure 3.2 depicts the definition of a non-leading ledger. As you can see, now you can assign different fiscal years and posting period variants to a non-leading ledger. This way you can use ledgers with different fiscal years.

3.3.5 Activation of Leading and Non-Leading Ledger

■ For data flow, you need to assign total tables to leading and non-leading ledgers. You can reach the configuration menu through the following menu path:

- **ECC IMG Menu:** Financial Accounting (New) → Financial Accounting Global Settings (New) → Ledgers → Ledger → Define Ledgers for General Ledger Accounting

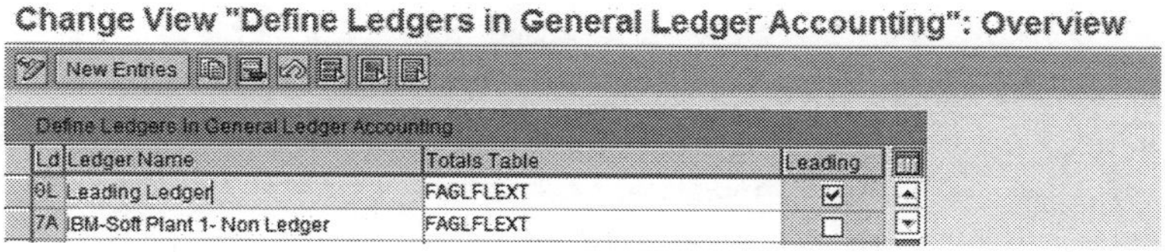

FIGURE 3.3 Ledger definition and total table assignment.

■ As you can see in Figure 3.3, ledger "0L" is marked as the leading ledger. This is a client level configuration and every client needs to have one leading ledger. If you have created a customer-defined total table you can assign customer-defined tables to ledgers.

3.3.6 Ledger Group

■ A *ledger group* is a combination of one or more ledgers. This facilitates the application of functions and interfaces in the uniform way to all ledger forms that are part of the ledger groups. When you create a ledger, the system creates a ledger group for that individual ledger automatically.

■ In addition to these automatically created groups, you can create additional groups to apply functions uniformly to set up ledgers.

■ You define your ledger groups in Customizing for Financial Accounting by using the following the navigation option:

- **ECC IMG Menu:** Financial Accounting (New) → Financial Accounting Global Settings (New) → Ledgers → Ledgers → Define Ledger Group.

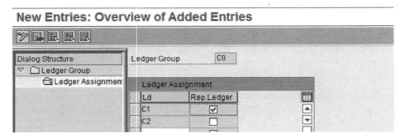

FIGURE 3.4 Ledger groups.

- In Figure 3.4 you can see that you have grouped together ledger C1 and C2 under ledger group C0. Now, when you choose ledger group C0 while posting, the system automatically posts the transaction to both C1 and C2 ledgers.

- A document is always posted to all ledgers unless you have selected a ledger group. mySAP ERP Financials provides two brands of new transaction codes (transaction codes are FB01L, FB50L) to post transactions to one or more ledgers or ledger groups. In this way, you can restrict your financial postings to specific ledgers.

Question – 6

mySAP ERP Financials comes with pre-delivered leading ledgers and non-leading ledgers.

A. *True*

B. *False*

Question – 7

You can assign a different fiscal year variant to a leading ledger (other than fiscal year variants assigned to a company code).

A. *True*

B. *False*

Question – 8

mySAP ERP Financials comes with pre-delivered total tables, however, you can also create your own total table. Identify the pre-delivered total tables name that comes with the standard SAP application.

A. *FAGLFLEXC*

B. *FAGLFLEXA*

C. *FAGLFLEXP*

D. *FAGLFLEXT*

Question – 9

Scenarios assigned to ledgers are mutually exclusive, meaning that if one scenario is assigned to one ledger, you can't assign that scenario to another ledger.

A. *True*

B. *False*

3.3.7 Fiscal Year Varient (FYV)

▪ You can create and assign fiscal year variants by using either of the following navigation options:

- **ECC IMG Menu**: Financial Accounting (New) → Financial Accounting Global Settings (New) → Ledgers → Fiscal Year and Posting Periods →

  ....Maintain Fiscal Year Variant (Maintain Shortened Fisc. Year)

  ....Assign Company Code to a Fiscal Year Variant

  Transaction Code:

  ....Maintain Fiscal Year Variant (Maintain Shortened Fisc. Year) – OB29

  ....Assign Company Code to a Fiscal Year Variant – OB37

3.3.8 Period Posting Variant (PPV)

- Through posting period variant you can control the opening and closing of the posting period. You can create, maintain, and assign posting period variants by using either of the following navigation options:

  - **ECC IMG Menu** → Financial Accounting (New) → Financial Accounting Global Settings (New) → Ledgers → Fiscal Year and Posting Periods → Posting Periods →

    .... Define Variants for Open Posting Periods

    ....Open and Close Posting Periods

    ....Assign Variants to Company Code

  - **Transaction Code**:

    .... Define Variants for Open Posting Periods

    ...... Define Variants for Open Posting Periods

    ....Open and Close Posting Periods

    ......Assign Variants to Company Code

- We have already covered the usage and configuration of fiscal years and posting period variants in our previous chapter. In this chapter, discussions will explore the new functionalities of mySAP ERP Financials.

- In addition to previously mentioned classic G/L functionality for posting period control, SAP G/L (mySAP ERP Financials with enhancement package 4) comes with a third interval of from and to period columns. This provides additional control for the postings coming from CO as a part of real-time FI/CO reconciliation. Refer to 356483 for the current setting.

- You can use this new functionality, by using either of the following navigation options:

  - **ECC Menu:** Accounting → Financial Accounting → General Ledger → Environment → Current Settings → Open and Close Posting Periods.

  - **Transaction Code**: FAGL_EHP4_T001B_COFI

▪ In this new functionality, you can see that SAP has provided three intervals. These three period intervals provide flexibility for posting control under:

- First period interval: Any user assigned to the authorization group can post to the first period interval.

- Second period interval: All users can only post in period two.

- Third period interval: The interval three is used for real-time FI/CO integration postings. Even though the first period and second period for FI posting is closed, if the third period is opened, the system posts CO to the FI reconciliation posting.

▪ With mySAP ERP Financials 2005 with enhance package 4, you can control posting by account assignment objects, such as cost centers and profit centers.

▪ You can reach this new functionality by using either of the following navigation options:

- **ECC IMG Menu:** Financial Accounting (New) → Financial Accounting Global Settings (New) → Ledgers → Fiscal Year and Posting Periods → Posting Periods → Open and Close Posting Periods According to G/L Account Assignment Objects

- **Transaction Code**: FMGL_PERIOD_CONTROL

▪ This navigation option brings you to Figure 3.5, where you can select your account assignment object by how you want to control your posting. In this case, we have selected cost center.

▪ To maintain the allowed posting period, select the posting period variant row and double click on *permitted period*. The system will bring up the screen shown in Figure 3.6.

▪ In Figure 3.6 you can see that, like transaction code OB52, it has two posting period intervals. The only difference is that in OB52 we have an account number range and here we have an account assignment number range.

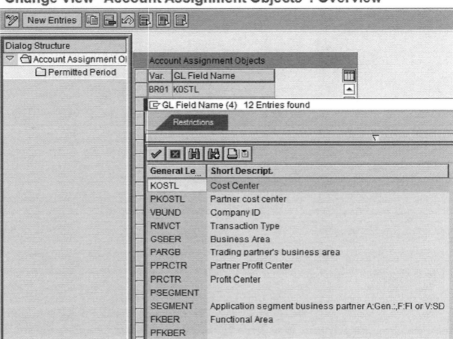

FIGURE 3.5 Period control by account assignment objects –1.

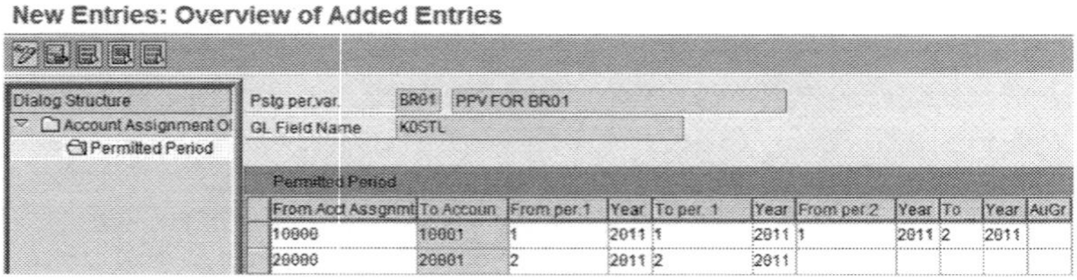

FIGURE 3.6 Period control by account assignment objects –2.

3.4 Document Splitting

- Once you activate SAP G/L (new general ledger), you can see financial documents in two views: entry view and general ledger view.

- *Entry View*: This view contains FI document lines originally entered or transferred through the interface. This is the same as what you are seeing in the classic G/L FI document view. Figure 3.7 shows the entry view of an FI document that has been posted to company code 0006.

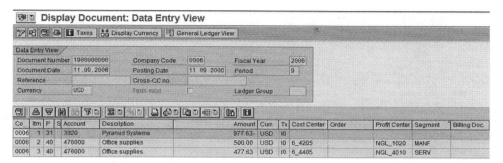

FIGURE 3.7 FI document entry view.

- *General Ledger View*: The general ledger view displays an FI document that contains line items originally entered or transferred, split line items generated by document splitting, or additionally generated clearing items. Documents in the G/L view always apply to a specific ledger. In Figure 3.8 you can see that the system has generated the G/L view of the FI document number "1900000000." This view has three windows: entry view, ledger view, and ledger line items.

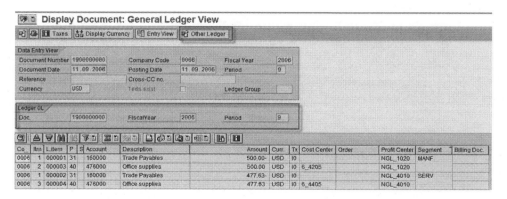

FIGURE 3.8 FI document G/L view.

- In ledger view, you can see two FI document numbers: the document entry view number when you use classic general ledge G/L, and the ledger view document number relevant to a particular ledger.

- You can switch between ledgers to see FI documents from the view of other ledgers. Figure 3.9 shows ledger selection options in transaction code: FB03.

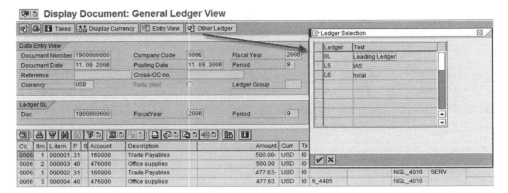

FIGURE 3.9 FI document: Ledger selection.

▪ From release mySAP ERP Financials 2005, SAP provides functionality to simulate the G/L entry view in addition to the entry view. This increases the early detection of posting errors and helps prevent incorrect transaction from being entered.

▪ The document split functionality ensures that line items are split and balanced, as per desired dimensions, so that you can prepare a complete financial statement for the selected dimensions. In order to activate the document split function, you need to go through a set of configuration menu items to define the splitting rules, which will be covered later in this section.

▪ Let us first study the various types of document splitting functionalities. There are three types of document splitting: passive document splitting, active document splitting, and zero balance.

▪ mySAP ERP Financials split is a financial document prepared in the sequence mentioned previously.

▪ *Passive document splitting*: In passive splitting, the system transfers the splitting dimensions from the reference document and splits the subsequent document. This is best suited for when you are performing an outgoing payment by clearing one or more vendor open items.

▪ *Active document splitting*: Active splitting consists of the document splitting by itself based splitting configurations. The best example of this is when you are posting a vendor document and the vendor line items are split based on expense line items. In configuration, you are defining what needs to split based on what line items.

- *Zero Balance*: To generate a financial statement based on certain dimensions, you need line items to be balanced with respect to those dimensions. When you perform document splitting using zero balancing in the new G/L, the system posts additional zero-balancing clearing items so that the document is balanced for these characteristics. The system uses zero balancing concepts to balance financial transitions, which uses multiple dimensions, such as when you are reposting an expense from one G/L, where both G/Ls post to different profit centers or segments, or when you are making a correction profit center posting by reposting transactions from one profit center to another. You can also use it when you are reposting from one segment to one or more segments.

- When designing the document splitting process, the following assumptions have been taken into account:

  - *Document entry*: The document splitting process doesn't disturb the document entry process, which means that the way the user enters a transaction in classic G/L is the same way the user will enter a transaction in SAP G/L. Say, for example, you are booking a vendor invoice for certain expenses that are distributed between two cost centers. In classic G/L, the account payable user creates two line items when entering transactions: one for expenses and one for the vendor line item. In this example, SAP G/L is expecting two line items for the vendor. To facilitate the user interface, the SAP G/L user will enter data the way he is entering transactions in classic G/L.

  - *Account Display*: Even though SAP G/L creates multiple lines for vendors, when the user displays vendor line items, the system will display them the way you are seeing vendor line items.

- In order to a split document, you need to define the splitting characteristics. You can define document spitting characteristics by using the following navigation:

  - **ECC IMG Menu:** Financial Accounting (New) → General Ledger Accounting (New) → Business Transactions → Document Splitting → Define Document Splitting Characteristics for General Ledger Accounting

Change View "Document Splitting Characteristic for General Ledgers": O

Field		Zero balance	Partner field		Mandatory Field	
Business Area		☐	PARGB		☐	
Profit Center		☑	PPRCTR		☑	
Segment		☑	PSEGMENT		☐	
Business partner		☐			☐	

FIGURE 3.10 Document splitting characteristics.

- In Figure 3.10, you can see that business areas, profit center, segment, and business partners are defined as document splitting characteristics.

- If you are planning to prepare a financial statement based on any characteristic(s), you need to set the Zero balance indicator of that characteristic(s). In Figure 3.10, you can see that the Zero balance characteristic is flagged for the profit center and segment.

- Activation of document splitting is a client-level activity, however, you can deactivate the document splitting functionality by deselecting document splitting functionality for a company code by visiting the following configuration menu path:

  - **ECC IMG Menu:** New General Ledger Accounting under Financial Accounting (New) → General Ledger Accounting (New) → Business Transactions → Document Splitting → Activate Document Splitting

FIGURE 3.11 Activation of document splitting.

- Figure 3.11 shows the activation of the document splitting functionality at the client level. When you activate the document splitting functionality, you need to tell the system which document splitting method the system will adhere to.

- In Figure 3.12, you can see that against some of the company codes the inactive check mark is active. This means that the document splitting functionality is inactive for those company codes.

Change View "Deactivation per Company Code": Overview

| | New Entries | | | | | | |

Dialog Structure	Deactivation per Company Code		
☐ Activate Document Splitting			
☐ Deactivation per Company Code	**Company Code**	**Company Name**	**Inactive**
	0000	⊘gent Solutions	☑
	0001	SAP A.G.	☑
	0002	SAP A.G.	☑
	0003	voice connect	☐
	0004	MET NJ 02	☐
	0005	HP LTD	☐
	0006	IDES US INC New GL	☐
	0007	IDES AG NEW GL 7	☐
	0008	IDES US INC New GL 8	☐

FIGURE 3.12 Deactivation of document splitting at company code level.

- In mySAP ERP Financials, the system splits the document (active split) based on the splitting method, business transactions, business transaction variants, and the item category. We will study all these components in detail.

- *Splitting Method*: The splitting method consists of a set of rules. In the rules, you can define how and under what circumstances the system will perform splitting. mySAP ERP Financials comes with certain splitting methods, however, you can create your own splitting methods if the pre-determined splitting methods don't suit you.

- You can reach the configuration screen through the following menu path:
  - **ECC IMG Menu:** Financial Accounting (New) → General Ledger Accounting (New) → Business Transactions → Document Splitting → Extended Document Splitting → Define Document Splitting Method

Change View "Splitting method": Overview

| | New Entries | | | | | | |

Method	Text
0000000001	Splitting: Customer, Vendor, Tax
0000000002	Splitting: Customer, Vendor, Tax, Money, Co.Code Clearing
0000000012	Splitting: Same as 0000000002 (Follow-Up Costs Online)
0000000101	Splitting for US Fund Accounting
0000000111	Splitting for US Fund Accounting (Follow-Up Costs Online)
BZ00000013	Splitting: Same as 0000000002 (Follow-Up Costs Online) Brazi

FIGURE 3.13 Pre-delivered splitting method.

▪ Figure 3.13 depicts pre-delivered document splitting methods.

▪ *Business Transactions*: Business transactions represent the logical division of business events. A business transaction is always linked with a business transaction variant. Business transactions, along with the business transaction variant, determine item categories. mySAP ERP Financials comes with the following pre-delivered business transactions:

- 0000   Unspecified posting
- 0100   Transfer posting from P&L to B/S account
- 0200   Customer invoice
- 0300   Vendor invoice
- 0400   Bank account statement
- 0500   Advance tax return (regular tax burden)
- 0600   Goods receipt for purchase order
- 1000   Payments
- 1010   Clearing transactions (account maintenance)
- 1020   Resetting cleared items

▪ You can create new business transactions by using the following navigation option:

- **ECC IMG Menu:** Financial Accounting (New) → General Ledger Accounting (New) → Business Transactions → Document Splitting → Extended Document Splitting → Define Business Transaction Variants

Change View "Business transaction": Overview

New Entries				

Dialog Structure	Transactn.	Description
▽ 🗁 Business transaction	0000	Unspecified posting
▽ 🗁 Accounting transaction variant	0100	Transfer posting from P&L to B/S account
🗁 Assigned item categories	0200	Customer invoice
	0300	Vendor invoice
	0400	Bank account statement
	0500	Advance tax return (regular tax burden)
	0600	Goods Receipt for Purchase Order
	1000	Payments
	1010	Clearing transactions (account maint.)
	1020	Resetting cleared items

FIGURE 3.14 Business transactions.

- Figure 3.14 depicts pre-delivered business transactions. You assign business transaction variants to the business transactions. Item categories are assigned to each business transaction variant.

- *Business Transaction Variant*: Business transaction variants help business transactions by linking together the business transactions and item categories. You can use a business transactions variant to define rules to split documents. For example, a vendor invoice is a business transaction and is based on a certain category of vendor invoice you want to split in different ways. To accomplish this, you can create two variants for the business transactions vendor invoice, and based on business transaction variant, you can assign item categories.

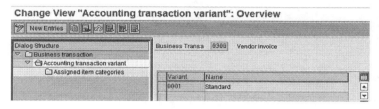

FIGURE 3.15 Business transaction variants.

- Figure 3.15 depict the business transaction variant of business transaction "Vendor invoice." You can add a business transaction variant to a business transaction vendor invoice by selecting the "new entries" button.

- *Item Category*: Item category is the further classification of business transactions within a financial document.

Change View "Assigned item categories": Overview

New Entries

Dialog Structure
▽ ☐ Business transaction
▽ ☐ Accounting transaction variant
☐ Assigned item categories

Business Transa   0300   Vendor invoice
Transaction Var   0001   Standard

Cat.	Description	Forbidd.	Required	Only once
01000	Balance Sheet Account	☐	☐	☐
01100	Company Code Clearing	☐	☐	☐
01300	Cash Discount Clearing	☐	☐	☐
03000	Vendor	☐	☑	☐
03100	Vendor: Special G/L Transaction	☐	☐	☐
05100	Taxes on Sales/Purchases	☐	☐	☐
05200	Withholding Tax	☐	☐	☐
06000	Material	☐	☐	☐
07000	Asset	☐	☐	☐
20000	Expense	☐	☐	☐
30000	Revenue	☐	☐	☐
40200	Exchange Rate Difference	☐	☐	☐
80000	Customer-Specific Item Category	☐	☐	☐

FIGURE 3.16 Item categories.

■ Figure 3.16 depicts the assignment of item categories to a business transaction and business transactions variant. In a later stage, you assign the G/L accounts to item categories.

You can display the content of the document splitting method by using the following navigation options:

- **ECC IMG Menu:** Financial Accounting (New) → General Ledger Accounting (New) → Business Transactions → Document Splitting → Extended Document Splitting → Define Document Splitting Rule

- **Transaction Code:** GSP_RD

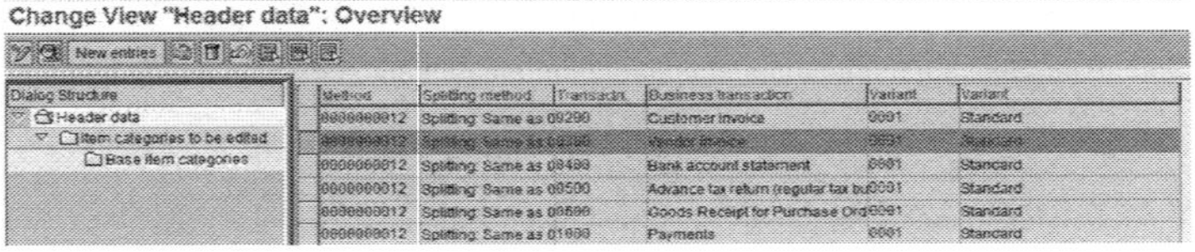

FIGURE 3.17 Document splitting rule.

■ Once you have created item categories, you need to assign the item categories to a G/L or range of G/Ls. Figure 3.18 depicts the assignment of item categories to G/L accounts. The assignment of item categories to a G/L helps to determine how the individual document items are to be handled. The following accounts are assigned to item categories:

- Revenue account

- Expense account

- Bank account/cash account

- Balance sheet account

■ Other accounts are already internally coded inside the system, so you do not need not to assign them to item categories.

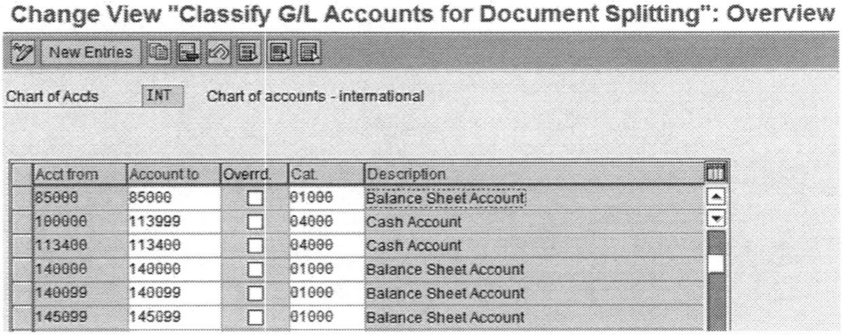

FIGURE 3.18 Assignment item categories to G/L accounts.

- You can use the configuration screen to assign item categories to G/L accounts by navigating the following menu path:

  - **ECC IMG Menu:** Financial Accounting (NEW) → General Ledger Accounting (New) → Business Transactions → Document Splitting → Classify G/L Accounts for Document Splitting

Error

When posting, you may come across the error message "There is no item category assigned to account XXXXX", where XXXXX is your G/L account.

This is a document splitting error for SAP G/L. The system will pop up this message when you have not assigned the concerned G/L to an item category. To fix this error message you need to assign the G/L account to an item category. Navigate to **ECC IMG Menu** Financial Accounting (New) → General Ledger Accounting (New) → Document Splitting → Classify G/L Accounts for Document Splitting to assign general ledger account.

- Now you know how the system is spiting accounting documents on document type and G/L accounts for active splitting. The second type of splitting is passive splitting or splitting for follow up process. This splitting process applies to the clearing process generally used for incoming payment, outgoing payment, or the clearing of open items. In the active splitting process, the vendor line item is split based on expense line items. Now that the vendor line item has all the splitting attributes, the system split payment line item based on vendor line item when you pay vendor line items.

- The third type of splitting is ZERO balance. This situation arises when you need to re-class a certain posting, for example, if the user has entered the wrong profit center. In this case, the system creates additional line items to balance dimensions by posting a clearing account. You need to assign a clearing G/L account by navigating the following menu path:

  - **ECC IMG Menu:** Financial Accounting (NEW) → General ledger accounting (NEW) → Business transactions → Document splitting → Define Zero-Balance Clearing Account

- To split a financial transaction while posting, the system determines which splitting rule system will apply by looking into the document type you are using. To enforce the splitting rule you need to assign a business transaction variant to the document type. The business transaction variant determines which item categories are allowed to split line items. By navigating the following menu path, you can assign a business transaction variant to a document type:

- **ECC IMG Menu:** Financial Accounting (NEW) → General Ledger Accounting (New) → Business Transactions → Document Splitting → Classify Document Types for Document Splitting

■ Sometimes the system can't determine account assignments, without which the system can't split line items, which will lead to unbalanced accounting entries. To avoid this type of situation you can set up *default account assignment objects*. You can reach the configuration screen by navigating the following menu path:

- **ECC IMG Menu:** Financial Accounting (New) → General Ledger Accounting (New) → Business Transactions → Document Splitting → Edit Constants for Non-assigned Processes

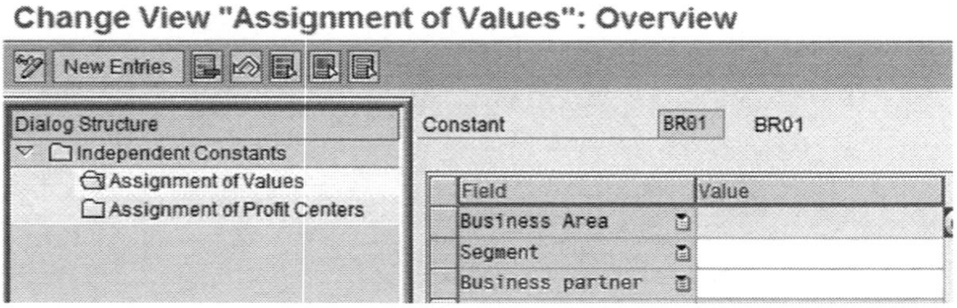

FIGURE 3.19 Default account assignment.

■ In Figure 3.19 you can see that you first created a constant variant. Under that variant you have assigned default account assignment objects.

Question – 10

When you post a transaction, the system always creates ZERO balancing line items to balance entities without any addition configuration.

A. True

B. False

Question – 11

Activation of document splitting is at the company code level.

A. True

B. False

Question – 12

Choose the correct answer. In mySAP ERP, the financial document splitting functionality works in the following order:

A. Active splitting, Passive splitting, Zero balance

B. Passive splitting, Active splitting, Zero balance

C. Zero balance, Passive splitting, Active splitting,

Question – 13

You need to activate the "Zero balance" indicator for a dimension in order to correctly work the document splitting functionality in mySAP ERP Financials.

A. True

B. False

3.4.1 Parallel Accounting

- Parallel accounting means presenting and preparing financial statements based on different accounting principles. For example, a financial statement can be based on the US GAAP principle and another set of financial statements can be based on the IFRS accounting principles.

- To portray the financial statements in different valuation approaches, mySAP ERP Financials comes with leading ledger and non-leading concepts. You can create as many as 98 non-leading ledgers in mySAP ERP Financials.

- In SAP G/L with the ledger concept, you now have two solutions to portray parallel accounting: account solution and ledger solution.

- In account solution, you use one ledger with multiple accounts to portray financial statements.

- In ledger solution, you use more than one ledger, which represents one accounting principle. SAP comes with pre-delivered 0L ledger, called the leading ledger. You can have only one leading ledger per client. Depending on the requirements, you can create custom ledgers called non-leading ledgers.

- In the later stages, you assign scenarios to ledgers. Assignment of scenarios decides which fields will be updated in which ledgers.

- In some cases you want to prepare a financial statement that start at a different period. In SAP G/L, you can assign a fiscal year variant that is different than what you have assigned to the company code. For example, one accounting principle fiscal year is a calendar year, while another accounting principle's fiscal year may start at April. In these circumstances, you assign calendar fiscal year to the company code, which will be used as the leading ledger, and the fiscal year that starts in April as the non-leading ledger.

- To accommodate various valuation principles, SAP has updated its foreign currency valuation programs. Now you can create valuation areas based on accounting principles, and later you need to assign valuation areas to accounting principles and accounting principles to ledgers. In this way, you can post different foreign currency valuations to various ledgers. Refer to foreign exchange valuations.

- If document splitting is active, the system inherits document-splitting characteristics from open items to foreign exchange valuation postings.

- SAP has improved the standard interface/manual transaction code FB01, FB50 through new transaction codes FB01L, FB50L. You can now post transactions to one ledger or ledger group.

3.5 Integration with Other Modules

3.5.1 SAP G/L Integration with Accounts Payable

- Account assignments for the object of expense accounts are inherited from vendor and tax line items. If the expenses line items belong to different account assignments, the system splits the vendor line items as per the account assignment of expenses line items.

- Even though the system splits vendor line items, if you call up a vendor line item display report, you can see only one line item, as you would see in classic G/L.

When you pay a vendor, the system inherits account assignment objects to payment line items and splits payment line items.

3.5.2 SAP G/L Integration with Accounts Receivable

- Like accounts payable, when you post receivable line items you assign account assignment objects to revenue line items. Based on the account assignment object of revenue line items, the system transgers the account assignment objects from customer line items to revenue line items.

■ When you post an incoming customer payment, the system transfers the account assignment from the customer line items to the incoming payment line items.

3.5.3 SAP G/L Integration with Assets Management

■ You can configure an assets account module to post as many as 99 depreciation areas to accommodate various valuation approaches.

■ In assets accounting, the system posts in real time to one depreciation area and when you perform periodic processing, the system post to other depreciation areas.

■ In mySAP ERP Financials, you can now configure which depreciation areas posting posts to which ledger group. In this way, you can portray financial statements in different valuation approaches by posting by depreciation areas to different ledger groups. You can reach this configuration screen by navigating:

- **ECC IMG Menu:** Financial Accounting (New) → Asset Accounting → Business Transactions → Integration with the General Ledger → Define How Depreciation Areas Post to General Ledger

Change View "Define Depreciation Areas": Overview

Chart of dep.   1US   Sample chart of depreciation: USA

Ar.	Name of depreciation area	Real	G	Trgt Group
1	Book depreciation	☑	1	
2	Book depreciation	☑	0	
3	Book depreciation	☑	0	
10	Federal Tax ACRS/MACRS	☑	0	
11	Alternative Minimum Tax	☑	0	
12	Adjusted Current Earnings	☑	0	
13	Corporate Earnings & Profits	☑	0	
17	Fed Tax MACRS (for states not allowing bonus depr)	☑	0	
30	Consolidated balance sheet in local currency	☑	0	
31	Consolidated balance sheet in group currency	☑	0	
32	Book depreciation in group currency	☑	0	
40	State modified ACRS	☑	0	
50	Derived area	☐	0	

FIGURE 3.20 Depreciation area assignment to ledger group.

- Figure 3.20 depicts a SAP delivered chart of depreciation. You can see that SAP has provided the "Trgt Group" field. In the target group field, you can assign the desired ledger group. If the target ledger group field is blank, then the system will post to all ledgers of the relevant company code.

- In SAP version SAP R/3 enterprise and later SAP programs use RAPOST2000, which is a successor of the old program RABUCH00. The old program RABUCH00 posts depreciation postings in batch processing, while the new program RAPOST2000 uses real time posting.

- When you post assets acquisition postings with different account assignment objects, the system transfers account assignment objects of assets line items to vendor line items.

- In classic G/L, you run program SAPF181 to post cash discounts that you have received in a post-capitalization period. In SAP G/L, you can avoid running program SAPF181 if you have already configured the post cash discount functionality before posting the assets acquisition. The system posts cash discounts you have received to assets accounts instead of cash discount accounts. You can reach the configuration screen to activate this functionality by navigating the following menu path:

  - **ECC IMG Menu** Financial Accounting (New) → General Ledger Accounting (New) → Business Transactions → Document Splitting → Define Post-Capitalization of Cash Discount to Assets

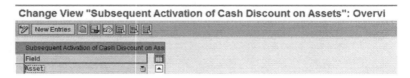

FIGURE 3.21 Post capitalization cash discount.

3.5.4 SAP G/L Integration with Controlling

- mySAP ERP Financials alleviates one the most awaited integration processes: i.e. CO to FI real-time posting . Since SAP released R/2, SAP is providing a real-time integration between FI to CO, which means when you are posting FI transaction, the system also creates a controlling document and vice versa. This functionality is not available for SAP released prior to mySAP ERP.

- Prior to the release of mySAP ERP Financials, you had to run transaction code KALC to post cross-controlling objects posting to FI in a summarized form, which happens at the end of the month. This means throughout the month you will see that there are differences between FI and CO.

- In mySAP ERP Financials, you can eliminate the running of reconciliation postings by activating real-time integration variant control. You can reach the configuration screen of real time variant control integration screen by using either of the navigation options:

  - **ECC IMG Menu:** Financial Accounting (New) → Financial Accounting Global Settings (New) → Ledgers → Real-Time Integration of Controlling Cross-company code with Financial Accounting → Define Variants for Real-Time Integration.

Change View "Variants for Real-Time Integration CO->FI": Details

New Entries

Var. for R-T Integ.　　　0001

Variants for Real-Time Integration CO->FI

☑ R.-Time Integ:Active　　Key Date:Active from　　18.08.2011

☑ Acct Deter.: Active

Document Type　　　SA

Ledger Group (FI)　　0L

Text　　　Statndard Variant for intergration

Selection of Document Lines for Real-Time Integration CO->FI

	☑ Cross-Company-Code	☑ Cross-Profit-Center	
◉ Use Checkboxes	☑ Cross-Business-Area	☑ Cross-Segment	
	☑ Cross-Functionl-Area	☑ Cross-Fund	☑ Cross-Grant
○ Use BAdI			
○ Use Rule	Rule		
○ Update All CO LIs			

Technical Settings

☑ Trace Active

☐ Do Not Summarize Documents

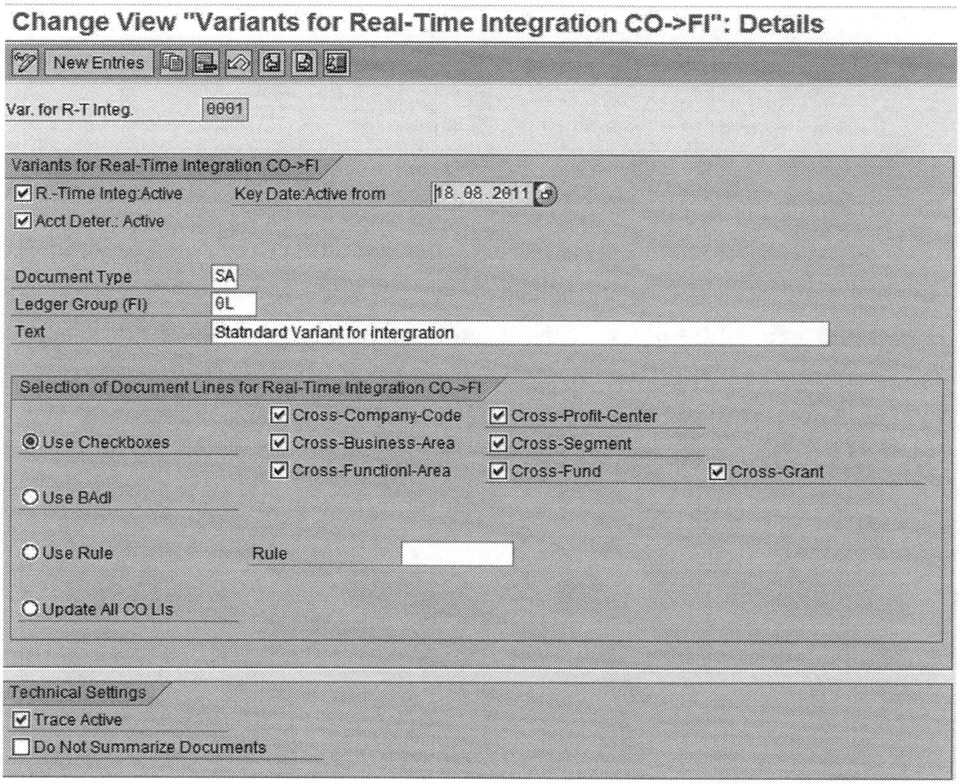

FIGURE 3.22 Variant for real-time integration.

▪ You can set up this CO to FI integration variant based on objects such as cross company code, cross profit center, and cross functional area.

▪ After defining the variant you need to assign the variant to your company code. You can navigate to the assignment screen by using either of the following paths:

- **ECC IMG Menu:** Financial Accounting (New) → Financial Accounting Basic Settings (New) → Ledgers → Real-Time Integration of Controlling Cross-company code with Financial Accounting → Assign Variants for Real-Time Integration to company codes.

▪ These reconciliation postings are posted to primary or secondary cost elements based on your configuration. You can reach the account determination configuration screen by using the following navigation option:

- **ECC IMG Menu:** Financial Accounting (New) → Financial Accounting Basic Settings (New) → Ledgers → Real-Time Integration of Controlling with Financial Accounting → Account Determination for Real-Time Integration.

▪ You can determine the G/L account based on CO transaction for secondary cost elements. Once again, it depends on how much detail you want to capture in financial accounting for CO to FI posting.

▪ You can see that in CO to FI integration variant posting, there is an activation date, and the system posts only real time posting after the defined date. If you want to transfer CO to FI posting before the activation date, you can transfer by using the following the menu path:

- **ECC IMG Menu:** Financial Accounting (New) → Financial Accounting Basic Settings (New) → Ledgers → Real-Time Integration of Controlling with Financial Accounting → Account Determination for Real-Time Integration → Transfer CO Documents Retrospectively.

▪ You can navigate from CO document to FI reconciliation and vice versa. This ensures that the reconciliation posting is traceable. This is possible due to real time posting of CO to FI for each and every activity. In classic G/L this is not possible because you run reconciliation posting as a period end activity, which creates a summary posting.

Error

When you execute transaction code: KALC to run the Reconciliation program, system will come up with following error message:

General Ledger Accounting is active. See long text

Message no. FAGL_COFI008

Diagnosis

You want to perform a reconciliation posting of Controlling with Financial Accounting.

System Response

New General Ledger Accounting is activated. In this way, the real-time integration of Controlling with Financial Accounting is implemented for reconciliation.

Procedure

Check whether you can use real-time integration as an alternative to a CO → FI reconciliation posting.

Procedure for System Administration

You can suppress this message if you do not want to use real-time integration. You can continue to use the reconciliation posting in that case.

This error message is applicable to mySAP ERP Financials version 5.0 and above. Once you activated New GL Functionality, the transaction code KALC became inactive because In NEW G/L the CO to FI posting is a real-time posting.

■ SAP G/L integration with material management:

Question – 14

The system creates financial a posting for all cross-dimensional posting.

A. *True*

B. *False*

Question – 15

Once you have activated real-time integration between CO and FI, the system creates financial postings retrospectively from the origination of transactions.

A. *True*

B. *False*

Question – 16

In mySAP ERP Financials, you can navigate to a CO document from a FI document and vice versa.

A. *True*

B. *False*

3.6 Reporting

3.6.1 Report Tables

▪ After the activation of SAP G/L, by default all the reports read only SAP G/L tables.

▪ Even if you have activated the new G/L, the system continues to post to GLT0 in addition to posting to FAGLFLEXT. As a part of the new G/L implementation project, you need to deactivate updating GLT0 to avoid the dual update of the totals table. You can reach the configuration screen by navigating the following menu path:

• **ECC IMG Menu:** Financial Accounting (New) → Financial Accounting Global Settings (New) → Tools → Deactivate Update of Classic General Ledger

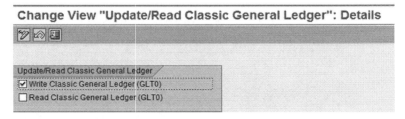

FIGURE 3.23 Read and write to classic total table.

▪ If you have developed a few custom reports in the later version, by default these custom reports read the classic G/L table, i.e. GLT0. In order to read the new SAP G/L tables you need to change these customer programs/reports.

▪ MySAP ERP Financials comes with functionality of ledger comparison. Now you can compare one or more ledgers. You can reach this functionality through the following menu path:

- **ECC IMG Menu:** Financial Accounting (New) → Financial Accounting Global Settings (New) → Tools → Compare Ledgers

- A new financial accounting drill down report is available for financial statements, as compared to the classic G/L report RFBILA00. The new report is much more flexible compared to the classic G/L report. With the help of the new report you can generate financial statements based on profit centers, segments, and you can also select the ledger. You can reach the new SAP G/L drill down report by navigating the following menu path:

  - **SAP Menu:** Accounting → Financial Accounting → General Ledger → Information System → General Ledger Reports (New) → Financial Statement / Cash Flow → General → Actual/Actual Comparisons → Financial Statement: Actual/Actual Comparison

  - **Transaction Code**: S_PL0_86000028

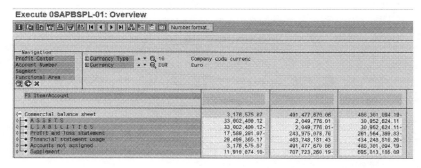

FIGURE 3.24 SAP G/L drill down report.

- Figure 3.24 depicts the SAP G/Ls' drill down functionality. Now it is very easy to turn the company code financial statement into the profit center financial statement by just using the navigation options.

- By executing transaction code FGI0, you can reach a set of reports of SAP G/L with drill down functionality.

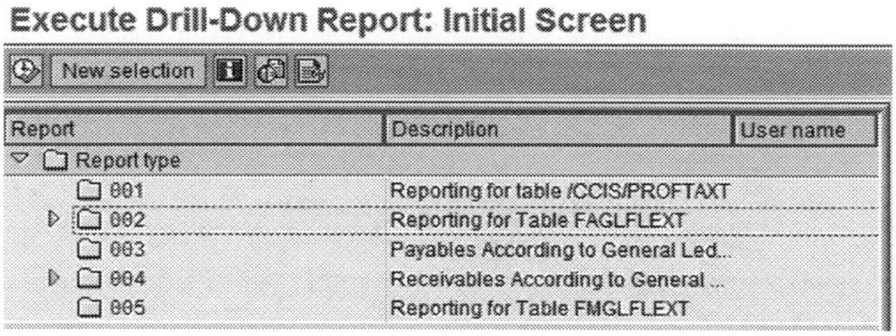

FIGURE 3.25 SAP G/L drilldown reports.

3.6.2 New Display

▪ With SAP G/L functionality you can display G/L balances as per your desired characteristics. To accomplish this functionality, SAP G/L provides new general balance display reports. You reach the new reports by using the following navigation options:

- **SAP Menu:** Accounting → Financial Accounting → General Ledger → Account → Display Balances (New)

- **Transaction Code**: FAGLB03.

▪ With the new reporting functionality you can select your desired ledger and characteristics that you have configured. You can add your desired characteristics in the report selection screen through configuration. You can reach the configuration screen by navigating the following menu path:

- **ECC IMG Menu :** Financial Accounting (New) → General Ledger Accounting (New) → Information System → Define Balance Display

▪ As you aware in SAP G/L, you can display a financial document in entry view and G/L view. Now with new reporting functionalities you can display G/L line items in entry view and G/L view. You can navigate either of the following options to reach the new reports:

- **SAP Menu:** Accounting → Financial Accounting → General Ledger → Account → Display Balances (New)

- **Transaction Code**: FAGLL03.

▪ In mySAP ERP Financials, SAP has provided a new set of open item display reports for accounts payable and receivable. With the help of new reports, you can see accounts payable and receivable open items by profit centers and segments. You can reach these new set of reports by navigating the following menu path:

- **SAP Menu:** Accounting → Financial Accounting → General Ledger → Information System → General Ledger Reports (New) → Line Items → Open Items →

  .... S_AC0_52000887 – Receivables: Profit Center

  ....S_AC0_52000888 – Payables: Profit Center

................S_PCO_36000218 – Receivables: Segment

................S_PCO_36000219 – Payables: Segment

3.6.3 Classic G/L vs. SAP G/L

- Up to SAP 4.7 EE, SAP customers didn't have any options other than the implementation of the classic general component of financial accounting module. If the SAP customer had different reporting requirements, they had to implement the special ledger component of the SAP application. From mySAP ERP Financials 5.0 and onwards, SAP has improved a lot financial accounting components by introducing SAP G/L (formally known as new G/L).

- Implementation of SAP G/L is optional for existing customers, but it is mandatory for new customers.

- In order to avoid implementation of multiple components of classic G/L such as special purpose ledger or profit center account, SAP G/L has combined all these functionalities and packaged it into SAP G/L.

- In the introduction section of this chapter, you learned about the advantages of the SAP G/L. Now it is imperative to learn the big differences between SAP G/L and classic G/L.

- *Extended Data Structure provides flexibility*:

- In SAP 5.0 ECC and higher, SAP provides four new tables: **FAGLFLEXT** (total table), **FAGLFLEXA** (actual line item table), **FAGLFLEXP** (planning line item table) & **FAGLFLEXR** (reporting table). These new tables are fused with multiple total tables (GLT0, GLPCT, etc) in classic G/L. One table provides more flexibility, faster response times, and avoids data redundancy, thus the reporting becomes faster. Now you can enhance all of these new tables with customer fields.

- *Segment reporting to ensure Statutory Requirements*

  IAS 14 requires segment reporting for an entity. As per IAS 14 segments refer to business and geographical segments for which a majority of their revenue is earned from sales to external customers and for which:

  - **Revenue** from sales to external customers and from transactions with other segments is 10% or more of the total revenue, external and internal, of all segments; or

- **Segment result**, whether profit or loss, is 10% or more of the combined result of all segments in profit or the combined result of all segments in loss, whichever is greater in absolute amount; or

- **Assets** are 10% or more of the total assets of all segments.

To achieve this segment reporting mySAP ERP financials provides document splitting functionality. Based on reportable segment, the system splits a document posted into G/L that helps to draw financial statements based on dimension. In classic G/L, the SAP customer was using special a purpose ledger to generate segment reporting.

■ *Real-Time Integration between FI and CO:*

The Allocation process creates additional posting line items. In classic G/L, if these postings cross company codes, the system generates a summarized reconciliation posting when you run the reconciliation ledger, generally as a part of month end activities. That means during that month financial accounting is out of balance with controlling. In SAP G/L, real time integration enables the immediate transfer of all controlling documents to Financial Accounting. This means that Financial Accounting is always reconciled with Controlling in real-time.

■ *Parallel Accounting:*

My SAP ERP financial provides two types of solutions for parallel accounting: ledger solution and accounting solution. With the ledger solution, SAP G/L comes with leading ledger and non-leading functionalities. Leading ledger is delivered by SAP enabling you to create up to 98 non-leading ledgers to portray for parallel accounts based on different accounting principles. With account solution, you can also implement parallel accounting with the use of accounting solutions. The account solution functionality is not new to mySAP ERP Financials. This solution is also available in SAP 4.7 EE.

■ *Reporting Functionality:*

mySAP ERP comes with new drill down reporting functionality. This new functionality allows you to see financial reports based on various characteristics or dimensions. You can now easily navigate from one characteristic to another without closing the repost display screen. mySAP ERP has delivered a few drilldown reports as a part of standard packaged solution. However, you are able to build your own custom reports. In classic G/L, the drill down reporting functionality comes with controlling – profitability analysis component. Besides the new drill down functionality, mySAP ERP Financials has enhanced some of the standard display screens and reports, such as:

- **Transaction code FB03**: In classic G/L if you are displaying a financial accounting document through transaction code FB03, you can see the account document the way you entered that document. In mySAP ERP Financials this screen is designated as entry view. In addition to entry view, mySAP ERP Financials SAP has provided another display view called G/L view. G/L view of document display is specific to a particular ledger, and you can navigate to different ledgers. In G/L view, you can see how financial document line items are split into different line items based on scenarios and related configurations.

- *Transaction code FBL3N*: In classic G/L, you use transaction code FBL3N to display line items of a G/L. Subject to line item management attributes are active in that particular G/L. This traditional line item display report is replaced by new line item report transaction code FAGLL03 in SAP G/L. In the new report, you can see line items in G/L view even though the line item attribute is not active.

- *Transaction code FS10N*: Traditional G/L display report is replaced by new SAP G/L display report (transaction code FAGLB03). In this new SAP, G/L report, you can choose new dimensions like profit centers and segments to see G/L balance by dimension.

- *New drill down reports*: In addition to the previous reports, there are a few new drill down reports provided by SAP. A few of them are listed in the report section of this chapter.

▪ *Reduce TCO by Faster Period Close Activities:*

By implementing SAP G/L, you can reduce a few of the closing activities, saving you a few man hours of month-end activities. Because of the reduced activities, you can close your books much faster than with classic G/L. These reduced activities include:

- Reconciliation ledger is not required

- Balance sheet adjustments are not required

- Profit and loss adjustments are not required
- Activities related to special purpose ledger are not required
- Depreciation posting is online instead of a batch session

3.6.4 Profit Center Accounting vs. SAP G/L Profit Center Accounting

After learning about the SAP G/L functionalities, you are likely wondering, *"how is classic profit center accounting different from SAP G/L profit center accounting?"* SAP G/L profit center accounting is different from classic profit center accounting both technically and functionally.

- As you aware the use of SAP G/L is optional for old SAP customers, while it is mandatory for new customers. In the profit center accounting world, SAP existing customers can use both classic profit center accounting as well as SAP G/L profit center accounting, while SAP's new customers must go with SAP G/L profit center accounting. SAP has provided these options to mitigate customer difficulties. However, SAP does not recommend to use both classic profit center accounting and SAP G/L profit center accounting, for the following reasons:

  - **Increased data volume**: If classic profit center accounting is active, the system updates 8A ledger for profit center posting. In SAP G/L if profit center scenarios FIN_PCA are assigned to any ledger, the system updates SAP G/L tables with profit centers and partner profit centers. That means you have the same transactional data in SAP G/L(s) and classic profit center accounting tables.

  - **Update response**: If scenario FIN_PCA is assigned to one or more ledgers and document splitting is active, some of the functionalities of classic profit center are not available, such as balance sheet adjustment (reports SAPF180, SAPF180A) and classic profit center transfer posting (transaction code 9KE0)

- *Dimension updates:*

  In classic G/L, you use transfer posting transaction code 1KEK to transfer receivable and payables to profit center accounting either manually or through batch processing. In SAP G/L, if splitting and zero balance functionalities are active, the system splits transactions in real-time and you can generate financial statements in real-time, without waiting for batch updates.

- *Reporting:*

  In classic profit center accounting, report painter reports are built on libraries 8A2, 8A3, 8A4, and 8A5 and report writer reports are built on libraries 8A0 and 8A1. In addition to specific libraries, classic profit center accounting uses classic profit center total tables GLPCT. In mySAP ERP Financials, SAP provides two libraries: 0FL and 0FS and these libraries are based on tables FAGLFLEXT and FAGLFLEXR respectively.

- *Ledger Comparison:*

  In classic profit center accounting, you use transaction code KE5T to compare balances in profit center accounting and financial accounting. In transaction code KE5T ledgers to be compared are fixed. In SAP G/L accounting, SAP has provided transaction code GCAC to compare ledgers. With the help of transaction code GCAC, you can compare any ledgers, and unlike transaction code KE5T there are no fixed ledgers.

- *Closing Functionality:*

  Transfer posting: In classic G/L, you are performing from one profit center to another to correct the profit center posting error or transferring a balance from a dummy profit center to other profit centers through transaction code: 9KE0. These transfer postings do not create financial accounting entries in classic G/L. With the advent of SAP G/L, transaction code 9KE0 is no longer available for that type of posting because pre-requisite to this transaction code is activation of profit center account at controlling area. In SAP G/L, you are not activating profit center account at controlling area level, in fact you are assigning profit center scenarios to the desired ledger. In SAP G/L, if you want to correct an incorrect posting to the profit center you have following options: you can choose assessment and distribution functionality which is new in SAP G/L and works in the same way as overhead assessment and distribution, or post manual journal entries to financial accounting.

- *Profit Center Planning*

  In classic G/L, you have integrated the planning functionality with cost centers and internal orders. With the integrated planning functionality, you can transfer controlling planning data to classic profit center accounting.

In SAP G/L, profit center accounting became a part of financial accounting (FI) module. With the changed integrated planning functionality, you can achieve integrated planning data transfer from controlling to financial accounting, and not vice versa:

- Activating the integrated planning indicator in the plan version in FI

- Activate integrated planning indicator in planning version of CO

- Both FI and CO both uses same planning versions

However, planning data from controlling will flow only when you have the right profit center in the cost centers master data. Planning data from controlling that are based on secondary cost centers are not transferred to FI, because in FI, we need a G/L account.

Now we can transfer controlling profitability planning data to SAP G/L through batch processing only.

In SAP G/L planned line items are stored in FAGLFLEXP tables in addition to total table FAGLFLEXT

■ *Foreign Exchange Valuation*

With the introduction of SAP G/L with parallel accounting, the foreign currency valuation process has changed from its traditional approach in the following ways:

Once SAP G/L is activated you can't run the old program, SAPF100, for foreign currency valuations. SAP has provided a brand new transaction code: FAGL_FC_VAL (program FAGL_FC_VALUATION). You can define the new transaction code by navigating the following menu path:

- **ECC SAP Menu:** Accounting → Financial Accounting → General Ledger → Periodic Processing → Closing → Valuate → Foreign Currency Valuation (New)

- Transaction Code: FAGL_FC_VAL

The above foreign currency valuation program needs certain new configurations that are covered in following bullet points. Ensure that you have configured the following steps before the execution of new foreign currency valuation program:

- **Valuation Area**: New valuation transaction code needs a valuation area in the selection screen. You can configure new valuation areas by following the IMG menu path: **Financial Accounting (New) → General Ledger Accounting (New) → Periodic Processing → Valuate → Define Valuation Areas**

- **Valuation Methods**: Valuation methods determine the method with which a foreign currency valuation is to be performed for the closing process. SAP has provided various procedures. You need to choose one of the procedures, for example, of a valuation method in the lowest value principle. You can reach the configuration screen by using the following IMG menu path: **Financial Accounting (New) → General Ledger Accounting (New) → Periodic Processing → Valuate → Define Valuation Methods**

- **Assignment of Valuation Areas and Accounting Principles**: If you are running parallel accounting, you need to assign valuation areas to the accounting principle. You can reach the configuration screen by following the IMG menu path: **Financial Accounting (New) → General Ledger Accounting (New) → Periodic Processing → Valuate → Assign Valuation Areas and Accounting Principles.**

- **Assign accounting principles to ledger groups**: In the last step, you will assign accounting principles to ledger groups. You can reach the configuration screen by following IMG menu path: **Financial Accounting (New) → General Ledger Accounting (New) → Periodic Processing → Valuate → Assign Valuation Areas and Accounting Principles**

- **Account determination:** You need to define revenue and expense accounts that need to be posted while running account foreign currency valuation. While valuating open items, the system makes postings to a balance sheet adjustment account and to a foreign exchange unrealized gain/ loss account. You can set account determinations based on valuation areas. If want to use the same account for all valuation areas, leave the valuation area field blank. IMG menu path: **Financial Accounting (New) → General Ledger Accounting (New) → Periodic Processing → Valuate → Foreign Currency Valuation → Prepare Automatic Postings for Foreign Currency Valuation**

Question – 17

In mySAP ERP Financials, *SAP has provided functionality to valuate open items based on different accounting principles and which can be posted to different ledgers.*

A. *True*

B. *False*

Answer Key

Questions	Answers	Questions	Answers
1.	True	10.	False
2.	False	11.	False
3.	A, C	12.	B
4.	A, B	13.	False
5.	False	14.	False
6.	False	15.	False
7.	False	16.	False
8.	D	17.	True
9.	False		

FINANCIAL SUPPLY CHAIN MANAGEMENT (FSCM)

4.1 SAP® FSCM

SAP® FSCM refers to Financial Supply Chain Management, which is a mySAP ERP Financials component. Its main aim is to optimize cash flow with effective cash management. In this section, you will learn about the components of financial supply chain management, which are discussed in subsequent bullet points:

- Financial Supply Chain management (FSCM) helps businesses by providing integration, better visibility, and control over all cash-related business processes. In a nutshell, FSCM

  - Provides better predictability of cash flow

  - Helps reduction of working capital requirement

- Reduces operating expenses by providing preventative and automated process

- Reduces multiple point of data entry through an end-to-end integration of business processes

▪ MySAP Financials comes with following components of SAP FSCM:

- SAP Credit Management

- SAP Biller Direct

- SAP Collections Management

- SAP Dispute Management

- SAP In-House Cash

▪ In this section, only SAP collection management and dispute management components of financial supply chain management have been discussed.

▪ By implementing financial supply chain management, you can achieve return on investments through the following benefits:

- *Reduced pay-offs*

- *Reduced billing costs*: Through biller direct, you can publish customer invoices in a portal from where customers can obtain the necessary invoices.

- *Faster balancing of invoices*: By implementing biller direct you can invoice faster as compared to any other mode of invoice generation.

- *Improved payment processing*: Through biller direct your customer can pay outstanding invoices through a credit card instead of mailing remittances to your lockbox.

- *Improved exception processing*: In the case of a customer concern, it will be taken care through dispute management.

- *Efficient cash collection*: Through collection management preventive action, your collection process will be faster than the traditional approach.

- *Collaboration with business partners*: Through dispute management you are taking care of customer concerns, thus establishing better collaboration with customers.

- *Reduced transaction costs*: By implementing in-house cases you can reduce banking fees by consolidating banking activities.

4.2 Business Partner

- In SAP, new modules other than SAP core modules such as FICO, MM, SD, and SAP use the business partner concept. A business partner can be a customer, vendor, or banker. This helps to management business partners centrally through the creation of single master data with multiple views.

- You can use the same business partner for different business relationships by assigning different business roles. When a business partner starts to maintain a different business relationship, you can create a new business partner view by assigning different roles, thus reducing data maintenance activities and redundant data.

- From the legal entity perspective, business partners are categorized into three categories: persons, organization, and groups. When you create a business partner, you need to choose one of the categories. Based on the business partner category, you need to fill in certain fields. *(NOTE: It is not possible to create any other business partner categories.)*

- SAP has provided the navigation menu path in the relevant modules/ sub modules to create business partner master data. Business partner master can be obtained through various menu paths. Sometimes, the system creates business partner master data when you create customer master data, vendor master data, or employee data. You can create business partner master data by using the following navigation options:

  - **SAP menu:** Accounting → Financial Supply Chain Management → Collections Management → MasterData → Business Partner Master Data

  - **Transaction Code:** UDM_BP

- Based on the types of number range assignment the system either assigns a business partner number or a user key business partner number.

- Depending on the business partner role you choose, the system comes up with tab pages as depicted in the Figure 4.1. Since business partner "COL109" is assigned with business partner role UDM000, you can see a tab page collection profile.

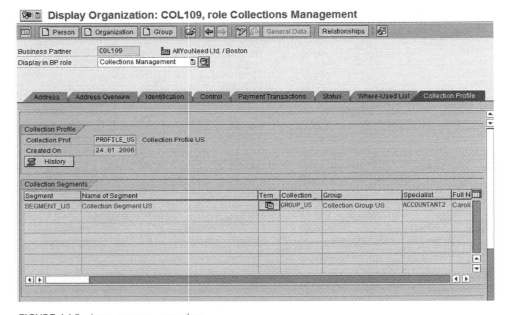

FIGURE 4.1 Business partner master data.

- We can now learn about the configuration steps of business partners.

4.2.1 Define Business Partner Roles

- The first configuration step of business partner master data configuration is the creation of the business partner role. The appearance of the business partner master data depends on the assignment of the business partner role. SAP comes with pre-delivered business partner roles. From these roles, you will use following roles for collection management:

  - UDM000 – Collections Management, used for collection management

  - FLCU00 – CVI: FI Customer, used for replication of customer master data in business partner

- You can reach the configuration screen by using the following menu path:

  - **SAP ECC IMG menu path:** Cross-Application Components → SAP Business Partner → Business Partner → Basic Settings → Business Partner Roles → Define BP Roles

- To the business partner role you need to assign a business partner view and the business partner category. Based on the business partner view, the system determines the business partner layout. Figure 4.2 depicts assignment BP view and BP category to business partner role FLCU00.

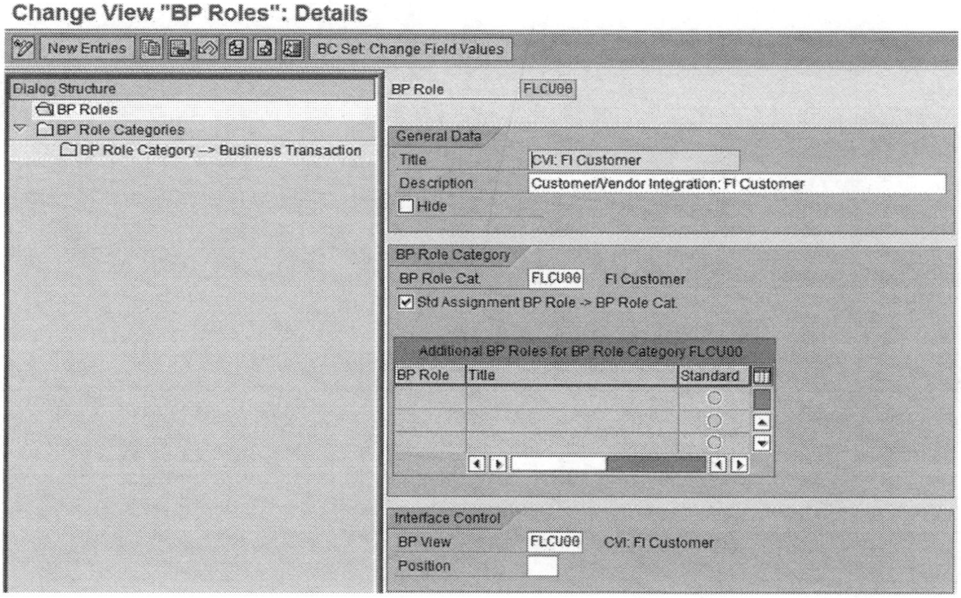

FIGURE 4.2 Assignment of business partner view and category to business partner role.

4.2.2 Define Number Ranges

- A business is represented through a unique business partner number. The business partner number can be either internal or external. Creation of the number range depends on how you are going to create the business partner. The customer will be created first and then the business partner, in which case you need to create an external number range with the same number range as the customer.

You can reach the configuration screen by using the following navigation path:

- **SAP ECC IMG menu path:** Cross-Application Components → SAP Business Partner → Business Partner → Basic Settings → Number Ranges and Groupings → Define Number Ranges

Display Number Range Intervals

NR Object	Business partner				

Intervals

	No.	From number	To number	Current number	Ext	
	02	A	ZZZZZZZZZ		☑	▲

FIGURE 4.3 Business partner number range.

- Figure 4.3 depicts the number range of business partner. In this case you have created external number range, later you will assign to business partner group.

4.2.3 Define Grouping and Assign Number Ranges

- Like customer groups and vendor groups, you can create business partner groups and later you will assign the business partner number range. You can reach the configuration screen by using the following navigation path.

  - **SAP ECC IMG menu path:** Cross-Application Components → SAP Business Partner → Business Partner → Basic Settings → Number Ranges and Groupings → Define Groupings and Assign Number Ranges

Change View "BP groupings": Overview

New Entries | BC Set: Change Field Values

Grouping	Short name	Description	Number ra	External	Int.Std.Grping	Ext.Std Grp
0001	Int.no.assgnmnt	Internal number assignment	01	☐	⦿	
0002	Ext.no.assgnmnt	External number assignment	02	☑		○
0003	Int.no.assgnmnt	Synchron. BP w Vendor	03	☐	○	

FIGURE 4.4 Business partner number range.

- Figure 4.4 depicts assignment of business partner number range 02 to business partner group 0002.

4.2.4 Activate Synchronization Options

■ In this configuration screen, you will activate synchronization direction option.

- **SAP ECC IMG menu path:** Cross-Application Components → Master Data Synchronization → Synchronization Control → Synchronization Control → Activate Synchronization Options

Source Object	Target Object	Act.Ind.
BP	CUSTOMER	☑
BP	VENDOR	☑
CUSTOMER	BP	☑
VENDOR	BP	☑

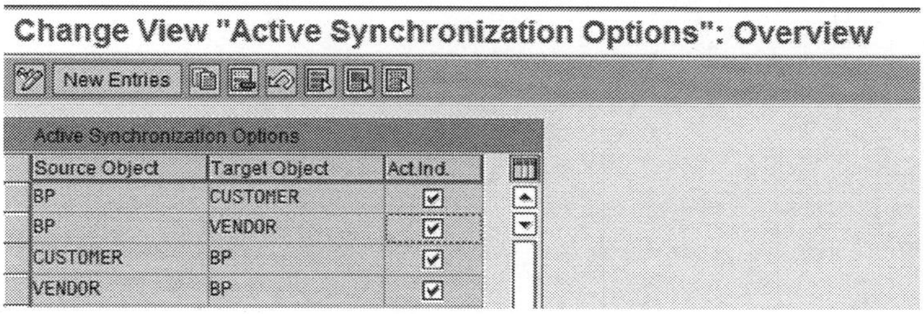

FIGURE 4.5 Synchronization options.

■ Figure 4.5 depicts the synchronization direction. In this example, you have activated it if you created a business partner, and the system will then create customer master data and vice versa.

4.2.5 Set Business Partner Role Category for Direction Business Partner to Customer

■ For customer integration you need to assign business partner role categories in the direction from the business partner to the customer. You can determine how the system creates a corresponding customer in Financial Accounting when you process a business partner. In the configuration steps, you will assign customer-based business partner role categories. Then the system will consider customer integration when you process the business partner. You can reach the configuration screen by using the following menu path:

- **SAP ECC IMG menu path:** Cross-Application Components → Master Data Synchronization → Customer/Vendor Integration → Business Partner Settings → Settings for Customer Integration → Set BP Role Category for Direction BP to Customer

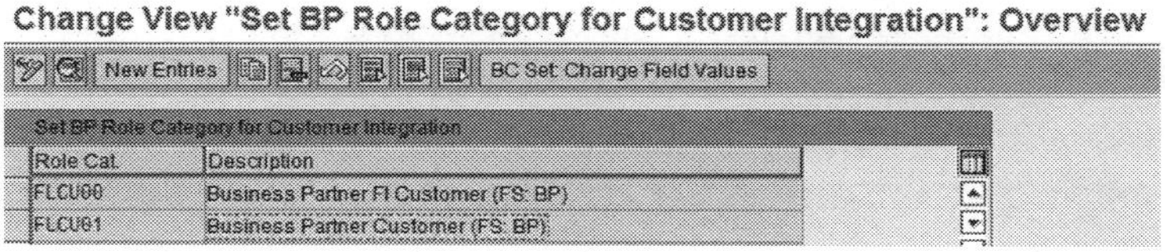

Role Cat.	Description
FLCU00	Business Partner FI Customer (FS: BP)
FLCU01	Business Partner Customer (FS: BP)

FIGURE 4.6 Business partner category assignment.

▪ Figure 4.6 depicts the business partner role assignment for customer integration. To see the customer integration selection double click on role category and the system will come up with screen shown in Figure 4.7.

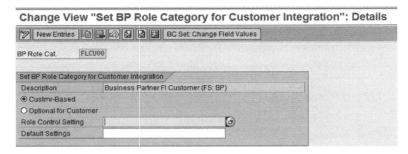

FIGURE 4.7 Business partner role category selection for customer integration.

4.2.6 Define Business Partner Role for Direction of Customer to Business Partner

▪ Now you will assign the business partner role to customer account group. Once the assignment is done when you create a customer master data system will create a business partner master data for the assigned role. You can reach the configuration screen by following the navigation given below.

- **SAP ECC IMG menu path:** Cross-Application Components → Master Data Synchronization → Customer/Vendor Integration → Business Partner Settings → Settings for Customer Integration → Define BP Role for Direction Customer to BP

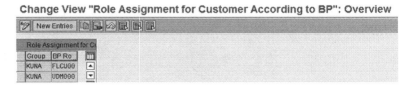

FIGURE 4.8 Assignment of Customer Group to BP Group.

4.2.7 Define Number Assignment for Direction Business Partner to Customer

▪ There is a configuration you need to use for business partner number synchronization with customer number. When you create/change a business partner, if the same number check mark is active, the system will look for a similar number for the customer master. If the business partner number range is not in sync with the customer number range, the system will come with an error message. You can reach the configuration screen by using the following menu path:

- **SAP ECC IMG menu path:** Cross-Application Components → Master Data Synchronization → Customer/Vendor Integration → Business Partner Settings → Settings for Customer Integration → Field Assignment for Customer Integration → Assign Keys → Define Number Assignment for Direction BP to Customer

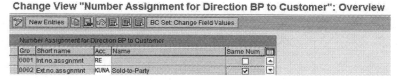

FIGURE 4.9 Number Assignment.

4.2.8 Define Number Assignment for Direction Customer to the Business Partner

- The configuration you need for the reverse direction of the above configuration by using the following menu path:

  - **SAP ECC IMG menu path:** Cross-Application Components → Master Data Synchronization → Customer/Vendor Integration → Business Partner Settings → Settings for Customer Integration → Field Assignment for Customer Integration → Assign Keys → Define Number Assignment for Direction Customer to BP

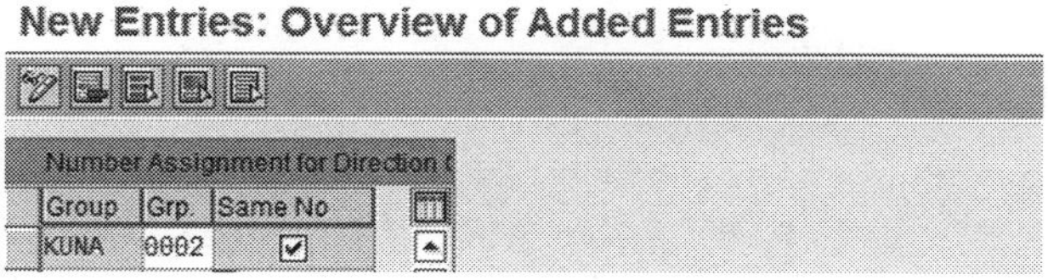

FIGURE 4.10 Overview of Added Entries.

4.2.9 Activate/Deactivate Standard Implementation for Mapping in FI-AR

- In this configuration screen, you can activate/deactivate the standard implementation of the Business Add-In Mapping: Business Partner-Customer/Contact Person without making any modifications. In order to activate your own implementation of this BadI, you can reach the configuration screen by following menu path given below.

- **SAP ECC IMG menu path:** Financial Supply Chain Management → Collections Management → Integration with Accounts Receivable Accounting → Master Data Distribution → Mapping of Master Data

▪ With the above configuration you can automate the creation of business partner master data. Naturally, some manual configuration is required to set up business partner master data from SAP collection management prospective. We will discuss configuration, the usage of collection management, and where you will use business partner instead of customers.

4.3 Collection Management

▪ The collection management application is part of the financial supply chain management. It helps with risk management and the customer relationship perspective for evaluation and prioritization of customer outstanding accounts.

▪ Through collection management, you can use preventive actions like sending payment reminders, making regular follow ups, and by getting new dates for outstanding payments through promise to pay. Collection management provides the following benefits:

  - *Increase efficiency* of the collection specialist and *decrease cost* of customer centric receivables management by generating an automated work list for prioritized customers based on predefined rules and by summarizing all relevant information and necessary activities for the collection of receivables in one application.

  - Ensure execution of company specific collection rules by establishing collection strategies.

▪ In SAP collection management, you can set up *collection strategies*. Collection strategy is a set of rules that enables you to select customer-opened items that can be expedited for collection processes.

▪ With the help of collection strategies you can generate an automated daily work list for collection representatives for collection follow-up.

▪ As a follow=up process, collection representatives:

  - Can create promise to pay agreement

  - Can create dispute cases

- Can create customer contact and document necessary information

- Can create an open item for re-submission

▪ The collection process will be overviewed by a collection manager. SAP collection management provides the following options to collection managers:

- Definition and adjustment of collection strategies

- Maintenance of collection groups

- Assigning work list entries and monitoring the processing of work lists

▪ In SAP collection management, you can create promise pay, a new SAP object. The collection representative creates a promise to pay when he establishes contact with the customer as a follow-up process based on the customer's statement. Later in this section you will learn the configuration steps of promise to pay and how to use it.

Configuration of collection management can be divided into two steps: configuration of collection management itself and configuration of integration point with accounts receivable. Next, we will discuss these configuration steps.

4.3.1 Activate Collection Management for Company Code

▪ The first step of SAP Collection Management configuration is activation. You can find the configuration screen by using the following menu path:

- **SAP ECC IMG menu path** : SAP Customizing Implementation Guide → Financial Supply Chain Management → Collections Management → Basic Settings for Collections Management → Basic Data → Define Company Codes for SAP Collections Management

FIGURE 4.11 Activation of company code for collection management.

- Figure 4.11 depicts the activation of company code 1000 for SAP collection management. You can activate another company code by clicking "new entries."

4.3.2 Define Basic Rules

▪ In order to prioritize a business partner for work list you need to define the conditions. Once the condition is fulfilled, the business partner priorities change and appear in the work list. SAP already provides a set of basic rules, however, you can also create your own. You can reach the configuration screen by navigating the following menu options:

- **SAP ECC IMG menu path**: SAP Customizing Implementation Guide → Financial Supply Chain Management → Collections Management → Basic Settings for Collections Management → Collection Strategies → Basic Rules → Define Basic Rules

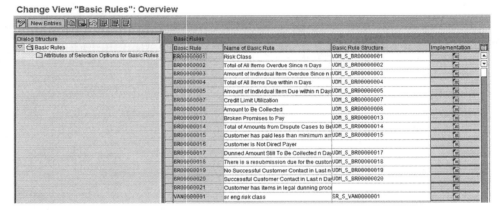

FIGURE 4.12 SAP-provided basic rules.

- The basic rules contain a set of selection conditions. Once all of these selection conditions are fulfilled, the business partners priorities changes and appears in the work list. You can create your own basic rules and add additional selection conditions to prioritize a business partner. Figure 4.13 depicts the inclusion of the field amount and the outstanding days for basic rule "BR00000002."

Change View "Attributes of Selection Options for Basic Rules": Overvie

Dialog Structure	Basic Rule	BR00000002	
▽ ☐ Basic Rules	Bas. Rule Stru.	UDM_S_BR00000002	
☐ Attributes of Selection Options for Basic Rules			
	Attributes of Selection Options for Basic Rules		
	Field Name	Single Field Option	No Multiple Selection
	AMOUNT	☐	☑
	NO_OF_DAYS	☑	☑

FIGURE 4.13 Selection conditions.

4.3.3 Define Collection Rules

- In the IMG activity you will first group together basic rules created or available in the last configuration step, and in the second step you will assign the collection of rules to the collection strategies.

  - **SAP ECC IMG menu path**: SAP Customizing Implementation Guide → Financial Supply Chain Management → Collections Management → Basic Settings for Collections Management → Collection Strategies → Collection Rules → Define Collection Rules

- When the system valuates a business partner for generation of the work list, the system checks the conditions of all basic rules, which are collected in the collection rule. In order to satisfy a collection rule all the basic rules assigned have to be satisfied.

4.3.4 Collection Strategy

- In SAP collection management, collection strategies are used to:

  - Determine business partners priorities in the work list

  - Determine currencies that the amounts will be displayed in the work list

  - Determine the time intervals for sorting business partner open payables

  - Determine integration with dunning in accounts receivable accounting

  - Determine of effect of the terms of payment on collections management

- You can reach the collection strategy configuration screen by using the following menu path:

  - **SAP ECC IMG menu path**: SAP Customizing Implementation Guide → Financial Supply Chain Management → Collections Management → Basic Settings for Collections Management → Collection Strategies → Collection Rules → Define Collection Rules

- Figure 4.14 depicts SAP delivered collection strategy, where you can see the assignment of collection rules and various other conditions that need to be fulfilled in order to make a business partner's open payable appear in the work list.

- You can create your own collection strategy by choosing the create icon in the initial screen of previous navigation path. You can also create a collection strategy through the following SAP menu:

  - **SAP menu:** Accounting → Financial Supply Chain Management → Collections Management → Current Settings → UDM_STRATEGY – Strategies

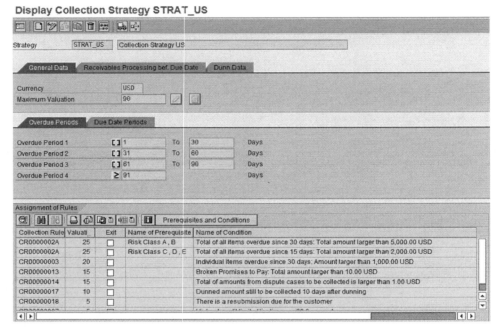

FIGURE 4.14 SAP delivered collection stratagy.

4.3.5 Collection Strategies

- Collection segments are used in SAP to group company codes, so that customer open items can be viewed collectively. All customer open items of relevant company codes are considered in a segment. A segment may consist of one or more company codes, while a company code can be assigned only one collection segment. You can reach the configuration screen by navigating the following menu path:

  - **SAP ECC IMG menu path**: SAP Customizing Implementation Guide → Financial Supply Chain Management → Collections Management → Basic Settings for Collections Management → Organizational Structure → Define Collection Segments

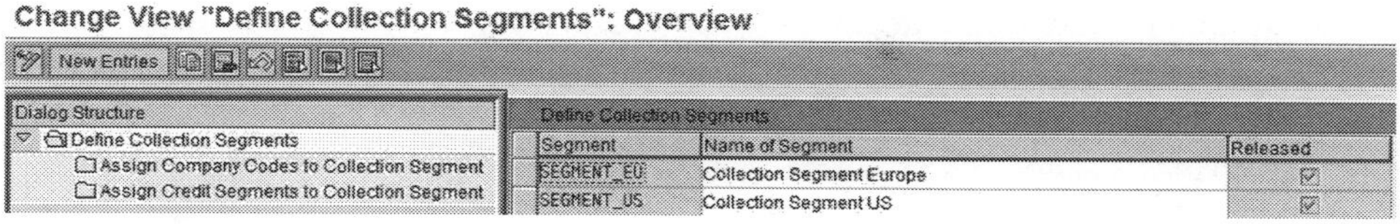

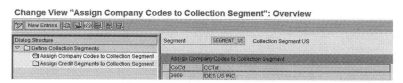

Change View "Define Collection Segments": Overview

FIGURE 4.15 SAP delivered collection segments.

▪ Figure 4.15 depicts SAP provided collection segment. You can see assigned company codes by selecting the segment row than choosing assign company codes as shown in Figure 4.16.

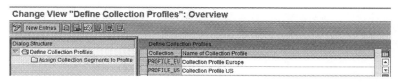

Change View "Assign Company Codes to Collection Segment": Overview

FIGURE 4.16 Company code assignment to collection segment.

• Once the collection segment is released (by checking the released check box in Figure 4.15), you cannot remove a company code.

Like company code, you can assign credit segments to collection segments by choosing the navigation option *"assign credit segments to collection segments"*

4.3.6 Collection Profile

▪ Collection profiles are a summary of collection statements. You can use collection profiles to divide company codes that participates in SAP collections management. You can reach the configuration screen of the collection profile by navigating the following menu path:

• **SAP ECC IMG menu path**: SAP Customizing Implementation Guide → Financial Supply Chain Management → Collections Management → Basic Settings for Collections Management → Organizational Structure → Define Collection Profiles.

Change View "Define Collection Profiles": Overview

FIGURE 4.17 SAP delivered collection profile.

▪ Figure 4.17 shows SAP delivered collection profiles. With collection profile you can group together collection segments.

■ You can assign collection segments by selecting collection profile and then choose assign collection segments to the profile as shown in Figure 4.18.

FIGURE 4.18 Assignment of segment to collection profile.

• You can review assignment segment and company code assignment (see Figure 4.19) by choosing assignment status of company codes in Figure 4.18.

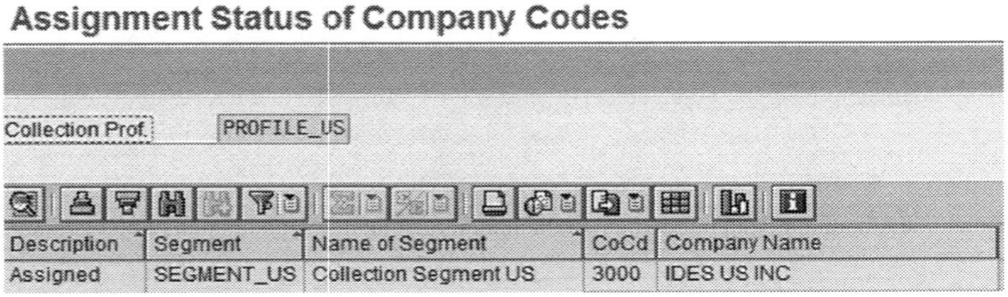

Assignment Status of Company Codes

Collection Prof.	PROFILE_US			

Description	Segment	Name of Segment	CoCd	Company Name
Assigned	SEGMENT_US	Collection Segment US	3000	IDES US INC

FIGURE 4.19 Assignment status.

Figure 4.20 depicts the not assigned company codes. You can assign a collection segment to a collection profile only when the company code belongs to a segment not assigned to any other segments.

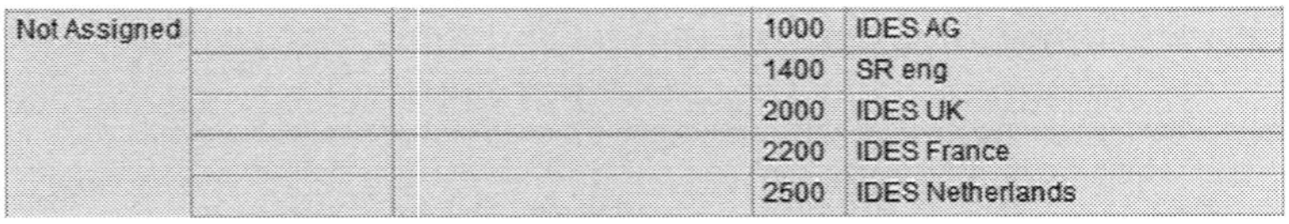

Not Assigned			1000	IDES AG
			1400	SR eng
			2000	IDES UK
			2200	IDES France
			2500	IDES Netherlands

FIGURE 4.20 Not assigned company codes.

4.3.7 Collection Groups

■ The next important configuration is the creation of a collection group. A collection group represents the grouping of a specialist who can establish contact with a customer. A collection specialist is assigned to a collection group, and each collection specialist will have one substitute specialist who can establish contact in the absence of the specialist. All collection specialists assigned to a group work under the same set up of rules. You can create collection group by using the following menu path:

- **SAP ECC IMG menu path:** SAP Customizing Implementation Guide → Financial Supply Chain Management → Collections Management → Basic Settings for Collections Management → Organizational Structure → Define Collection Groups

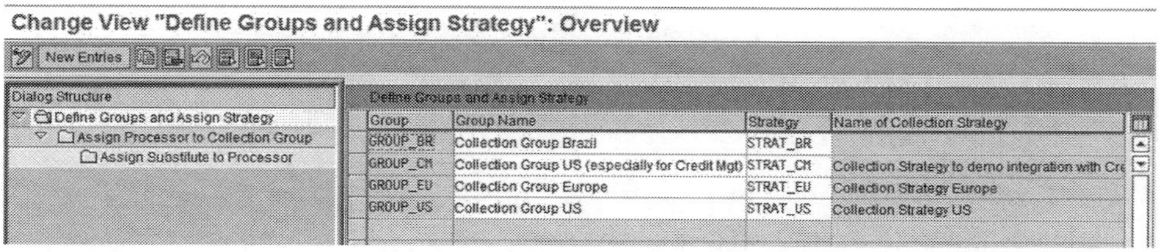

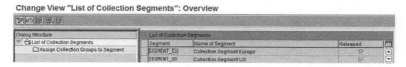

FIGURE 4.21 Collection group.

- Figure 4.21 depicts the pre-delivered collection group. You can see that you have to assign collection strategy to a collection group. By selecting a collection group row and navigating assign processor to a collection group, you can assign the collection specialist to a collection group.

4.3.8 Assign Collection Groups to Collection Segments

- Once the collection group and collection segments are created, you need to assign a collection group to a segment, ensuring that when you assign a collection profile to a business partner, the default collection segment is assigned to the business partner. You can reach the configuration screen by using the following menu path:

  - **SAP ECC IMG menu path:** SAP Customizing Implementation Guide → Financial Supply Chain Management → Collections Management → Basic Settings for Collections Management → Organizational Structure → Assign Collection Groups to Collection Segments

FIGURE 4.22 Collection segment.

- Figure 4.22 depicts the collection segments you have created earlier and you can assign the collection group by selecting a collection segment, and then select Assign Collection Groups to the segment in the left hand dialog box as shown in Figure 4.23 below.

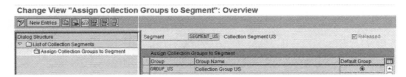

FIGURE 4.23 Assignment of collection group to collection segment.

- You can add a collection group to the collection segment by clicking the New Entries button.

4.3.9 Resubmission Reason

- The collection representative needs to assign a reason when she/he creates a *resubmission* a case in future dates. The collection specialist resubmits a case based on customer contact or when the customer is not reachable. You can reach the configuration screen by using the following menu path:

  - **SAP ECC IMG menu path**: SAP Customizing Implementation Guide → Financial Supply Chain Management → Collections Management → Basic Settings for Collections Management → Resubmit → Define Resubmission Reason

- Figure 4.24 shows SAP delivered resubmission reasons. You can create your own reason by choosing New Entries in the Change View "Maintenance of Resubmission Reason: Overview"

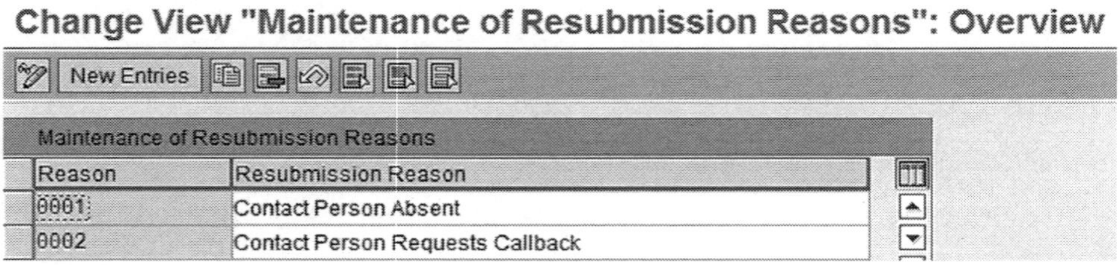

Change View "Maintenance of Resubmission Reasons": Overview

New Entries

Maintenance of Resubmission Reasons	
Reason	Resubmission Reason
0001	Contact Person Absent
0002	Contact Person Requests Callback

FIGURE 4.24 Resubmission reasons.

4.3.10 Case Types for Promise to Pay

- In collection management, SAP uses case records for promise to pay. Case records are a new SAP object and possess all information relating to promise to pay. You can create a case type configuration screen by navigating the following menu path:

  - **SAP ECC IMG menu path**: SAP Customizing Implementation Guide → Financial Supply Chain Management → Collections Management → Basic Settings for Collections Management → Promise to Pay → Define Case Types

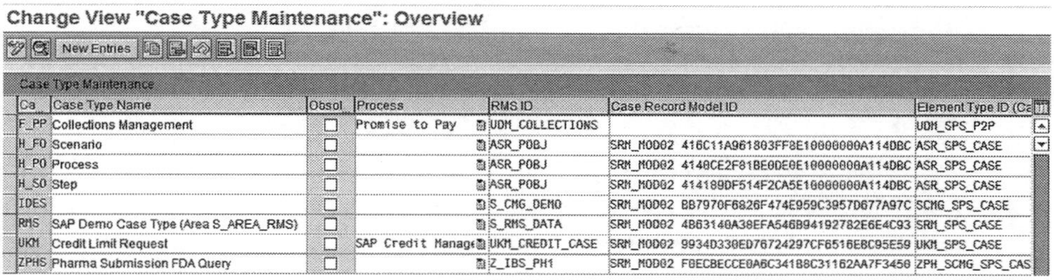

Change View "Case Type Maintenance": Overview

Ca	Case Type Name	Obsol	Process	RMS ID	Case Record Model ID	Element Type ID (Ca
F_PP	Collections Management	☐	Promise to Pay	UDM_COLLECTIONS		UDM_SPS_P2P
H_FO	Scenario	☐		ASR_POBJ	SRM_MOD02 416C11A961803FF8E10000000A114DBC	ASR_SPS_CASE
H_PO	Process	☐		ASR_POBJ	SRM_MOD02 4140CE2F81BE0DE0E10000000A114DBC	ASR_SPS_CASE
H_SO	Step	☐		ASR_POBJ	SRM_MOD02 414189DF514F2CA5E10000000A114DBC	ASR_SPS_CASE
IDES		☐		S_CMG_DEMO	SRM_MOD02 8B7970F6826F474E959C39570677A97C	SCMG_SPS_CASE
RMS	SAP Demo Case Type (Area S_AREA_RMS)	☐		S_RMS_DATA	SRM_MOD02 4B83140A38EFA546B94192782E6E4C93	SRM_SPS_CASE
UKM	Credit Limit Request	☐	SAP Credit Manage	UKM_CREDIT_CASE	SRM_MOD02 9934D330ED76724297CF6516EBC95E59	UKM_SPS_CASE
ZPHS	Pharma Submission FDA Query	☐		Z_IBS_PH1	SRM_MOD02 F8ECBECCE0A6C34188C31162AA7F3450	ZPH_SCMG_SPS_CAS

FIGURE 4.25 SAP delivered promise to pay case type.

- Figure 4.25 shows the SAP delivered promise to pay case type. Once you double click on the relevant promise to pay case type, you can see the attribute assignment to the case type, as shown in Figure 4.26.

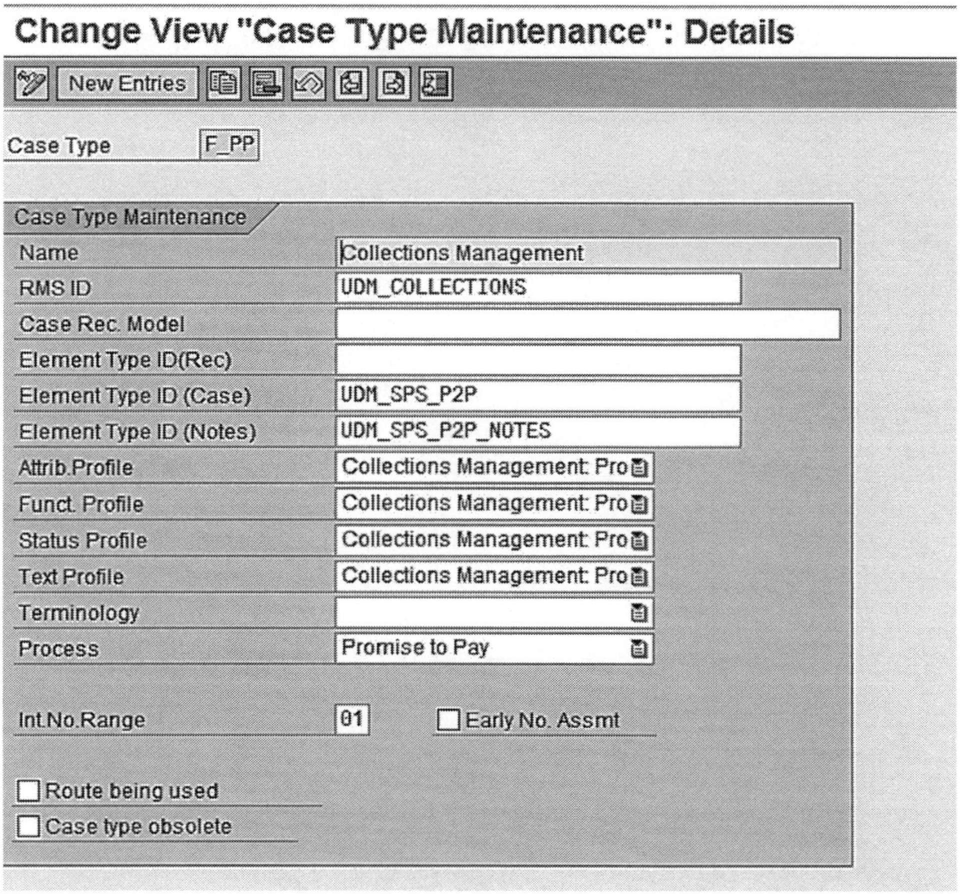

Change View "Case Type Maintenance": Details

Case Type   F_PP

Case Type Maintenance

Name	Collections Management
RMS ID	UDM_COLLECTIONS
Case Rec. Model	
Element Type ID(Rec)	
Element Type ID (Case)	UDM_SPS_P2P
Element Type ID (Notes)	UDM_SPS_P2P_NOTES
Attrib.Profile	Collections Management: Pro
Funct. Profile	Collections Management: Pro
Status Profile	Collections Management: Pro
Text Profile	Collections Management: Pro
Terminology	
Process	Promise to Pay

Int.No.Range   01   ☐ Early No. Assmt

☐ Route being used
☐ Case type obsolete

FIGURE 4.26 Promise to pay case type attributes.

- As Figure 4.26 shows, RMS ID, Element Type ID, Attribute Profile, Function Profile, Status Profile, Text profile, and number ranges are assigned to a case type. SAP comes with predefined template of these objects, however, you can also create your own from the scratch or by copying and changing the predefined objects. Purposes and configuration of these objects are described in dispute management section, and you may choose collection management from the menu path.

4.3.11 Activate SAP® Collections Management

- In order to use SAP® Collection Management you need to activate it first. This activation is a client level activation. You can reach the configuration screen by using the following menu path given below.

  - **SAP ECC IMG menu path**: SAP Customizing Implementation Guide → Financial Supply Chain Management → Collections Management → Integration with Accounts Receivable Accounting → Activate SAP Collections Management

Display View "BTE Application Indicator": Overview

Appl.	A	Text
FI-CM	☑	SAP Collections Management

FIGURE 4.27 Activation of SAP Collection Management.

- Figure 4.27 shows the activation of SAP Collection Management, which is a simple configuration by checking and unchecking the box in column A.

4.3.12 Default Case Type for Promise to Pay

- In your earlier steps you created a case type for promise to pay. In this configuration step, you will assign a case type to the company code so that the system will use this case type while creating a promise to pay case.

  - **SAP ECC IMG menu path**: SAP Customizing Implementation Guide → Financial Supply Chain Management → Collections Management → Integration with Accounts Receivable Accounting → Promise to Pay → Make Settings for Promise to Pay

Change View "Settings for Promise to Pay": Overview

New Entries

Settings for Promise to Pay

Co	Company Name	Case Type	Tolerance Days	Dunning Block
1000	IDES AG	Collections Managen		
2000	IDES UK	Collections Managen		
2200	IDES France	Collections Managen		
2500	IDES Netherlands	Collections Managen		
3000	IDES US INC	Collections Managen		
7001	IDES Brasil 7001	Collections Managen		

FIGURE 4.28 Case type assignment.

- Figure 4.28 shows the case type assignment to an individual company code. You can assign different case types to different company codes.

- After completion of all of the above configuration steps you can use SAP collection management in your business. Now it is time to know how to use SAP collection management.

4.3.13 Create Business Partner

- In SAP collection management you use the SAP business partner instead of the customer. A business partner can be a customer, vendor, or banker. The assignment of the business partner role determines which type of business partner it is. To replicate and/or automate the creation of a business partner with reference to the customer master you need to follow certain configuration steps, already covered in the first part of this chapter. You can also create a business partner master data with reference to a customer master data manually by using the following menu navigation options:

  - **SAP menu:** Accounting → Financial Supply Chain Management → Collections Management → Master Data → Business Partner Master Data

  - **Transaction Code:** UDM_BP

- Figure 4.29 shows business partner master data. Business master data consists of multiple views depending on the business partner role assignment. When you create a business partner master data, the system automatically assigns the "General Business Partner" partner role. The general business partner role consists of the general information relating to the business partner.

- In the case of business partner COL109, the business partner role collection management is assigned. Due to the assignment of collection management business partner role, you can see the collection profile tab.

- If you see the collection profile tab, you can see the collection segment assigned to the business partner. The system derives the collection group or collection specialist based on the segment assignment. See Figure 4.29.

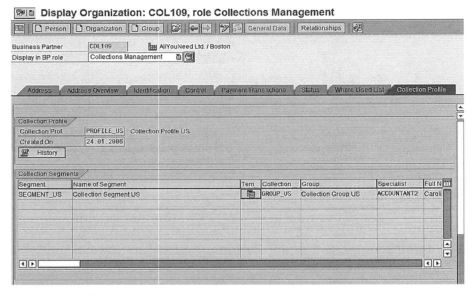

FIGURE 4.29 Business partner master data.

4.3.14 Distribution of Data to Collections Management

- Now the question becomes how the system will get customer open payables items into SAP collection management. In order to get requisite data into SAP collection management, you need to transfer data from your account receivable system. You can do so by using the following navigation option:

  - **SAP menu:** Accounting → Financial Supply Chain Management → Collections Management → Integration with Accounts Receivable Accounting → Periodic Processing → Distribution of Data to Collections Management

  - **Transaction Code :** FDM_COLL_SEND01

- If your account receivable system is in different landscape, you can transfer accounts receivable items through ALE.

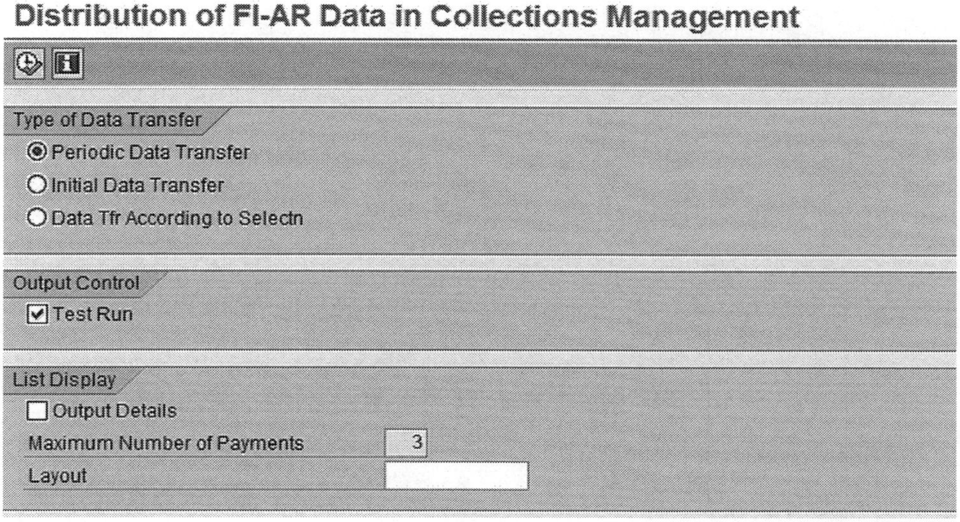

Distribution of FI-AR Data in Collections Management

FIGURE 4.30 Data transfer selection screen.

- Figure 4.30 shows the selection screen of accounts receivable data transfer screen. You can see that SAP has given three options of data transfer andyou can any one of the options based on your needs.

4.3.15 Generation of Work List

- Once the customer receivable line items are transferred, you can generate a work list for your collection specialist. You can reach the work list generation screen by using the following navigation options:

  - **SAP menu:** Accounting → Financial Supply Chain Management → Collections Management → Periodic Processing → Wordlists → Creation of Wordlists

  - **Transaction Code:** UDM_GENWL

- Figure 4.31 depicts the work list generation screen, where you can generate work lists based on collection segments. Once the work list is generated, the collection specialist can use work list.

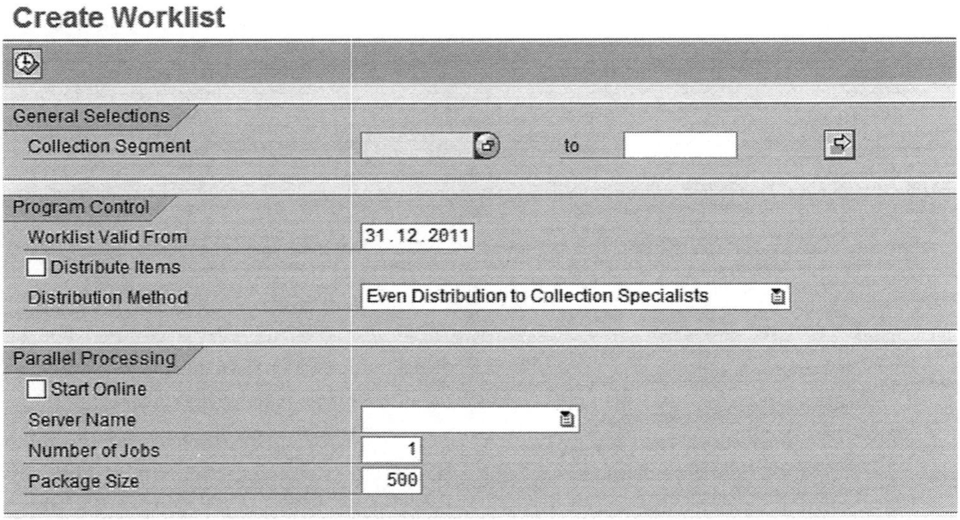

Create Worklist

FIGURE 4.31 Worklist generation screen.

4.3.16 Use of Work List

- Once a work list is generated, a collection specialist can access hisher work list by navigating either of the following options. Based on user assignment, the system will display work list items.

  - **SAP menu:** Accounting → Financial Supply Chain Management → Collections Management → Wordlists → My Work list

  - **Transaction Code:** UDM_SPECIALIST

- The collection supervisor can access the work list by navigation the following option:

  - **SAP menu:** Accounting → Financial Supply Chain Management → Collections Management → Wordlists → All Wordlists

  - **Transaction Code:** UDM_SUPERVISOR

- Figure 4.32 shows the supervisor's work list items. If you double click any of the line items, the system will come up with a new window as shown in Figure 4.33. In Figure 4.32, the system displays a summary of business partner line items that the collection specialist needs to establish contacts.

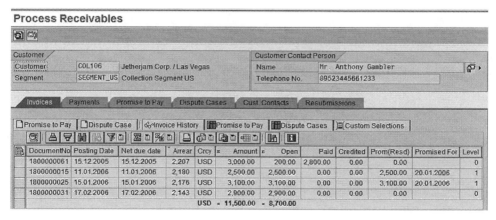

Worklist

Partner	Name of Business Partner	Priority	Currency	» Outstanding	» To Be Collected	» Promised	» Broken	» Disputed Amount	» Dunned	Highest Dun.Level	Last Dunning	L
COL106	Jetherjam Corp. / Las Vegas	Very High	USD	8,700.00	8,700.00	5,800.00	5,800.00	200.00	5,800.00	2	30.01.2006	1
COL101	Electronics Ltd. / Miami FL	Very High	USD	6,900.00	6,500.00	1,100.00	700.00	400.00	2,700.00	3	30.01.2006	1
COL103	Feelgood Products Ltd. / Philadelphia	Very High	USD	2,330.00	2,330.00	1,130.00	1,130.00	150.00	980.00	1	30.01.2006	2
COL109	AllYouNeed Ltd. / Boston	Very High	USD	7,400.00	5,900.00	6,000.00	6,000.00	1,500.00	6,000.00	2	30.01.2006	2
COL104	Pharmania Ltd. / Dallas	Very High	USD	4,700.00	4,700.00	2,400.00	2,400.00	0.00	2,400.00	1	20.01.2006	2
COL110	Jefferson's Electronics Ltd. / New York	Very High	USD	3,880.00	3,880.00	2,580.00	2,580.00	0.00	2,580.00	3	30.01.2006	0
COL111	Smith & Smithies Ltd. / San Francisco	High	USD	3,000.00	3,000.00	2,300.00	2,300.00	600.00	3,000.00	3	30.01.2006	0
COL107	BuyHere Ltd. / Los Angeles	High	USD	1,550.00	1,550.00	1,550.00	1,550.00	250.00	1,550.00	1	20.01.2006	3
COL102	More & More Ltd. / New York	High	USD	2,950.00	2,950.00	2,050.00	2,050.00	200.00	2,050.00	2	30.01.2006	1
COL112	Devonshire Best Products Corp / La Grange	High	USD	2,500.00	2,500.00	1,400.00	1,400.00	1,400.00	2,500.00	3	30.01.2006	1
COL105	ConsuMe Ltd. / Phenix	High	USD	4,000.00	4,000.00	2,900.00	2,900.00	0.00	2,900.00	2	30.01.2006	2
COL108	Better Than Good Corp. / Atlanta	Medium	USD	2,580.00	2,580.00	0.00	0.00	0.00	0.00			0
COL115	Harper & Harper Corp / San Diego	Medium	USD	2,000.00	2,000.00	0.00	0.00	0.00	400.00	1	20.01.2006	1
COL114	Black & White Corp / Colorado	Medium	USD	600.00	600.00	600.00	600.00	0.00	600.00	2	30.01.2006	2
			USD	53,090.00	51,190.00	29,610.00	29,210.00	4,700.00	33,460.00			

FIGURE 4.32 Supervisor worklist items.

- Figure 4.33 shows the business line items that were summed up in Figure 4.32. By navigating the different tabs, you can further analyze business partner's receivables like the line items for which dispute cases where created online items for which the customer has promised to pay. From this screen you can create a new promise to pay or dispute case by selecting a row and choosing the appropriate create icon.

Process Receivables

Customer				Customer Contact Person	
Customer:	COL106	Jetherjam Corp. / Las Vegas		Name	Mr. Anthony Gambler
Segment	SEGMENT_US	Collection Segment US		Telephone No.	89523445661233

Invoices / Payments / Promise to Pay / Dispute Cases / Cust. Contacts / Resubmissions

Promise to Pay | Dispute Case | Invoice History | Promise to Pay | Dispute Cases | Custom Selections

DocumentNo	Posting Date	Net due date	Arrear	Crcy	» Amount	» Open	Paid	Credited	Prom(Resd)	Promised For	Level
1800000061	15.12.2005	15.12.2005	2,207	USD	3,000.00	200.00	2,800.00	0.00	0.00		0
1800000015	11.01.2006	11.01.2006	2,180	USD	2,500.00	2,500.00	0.00	0.00	2,500.00	20.01.2006	1
1800000025	15.01.2006	15.01.2006	2,176	USD	3,100.00	3,100.00	0.00	0.00	3,100.00	20.01.2006	1
1800000031	17.02.2006	17.02.2006	2,143	USD	2,900.00	2,900.00	0.00	0.00	0.00		0
				USD	11,500.00	8,700.00					

FIGURE 4.33 Business partner line items.

4.3.17 Evaluation of Promise to Pay

- Based on customer contact and feedback, the collection specialist creates a promise to pay. Periodically, you can evaluate the promise to pay to review the status of promise to pay cases. Once you evaluate, the system selects all the promise to pay cases that are due and have a due date that has passed. If the business partner has not kept the promise to pay, the promise to pay cases are treated as broken. You can reach the promise to pay evaluation screen by using the following navigation options:

- **SAP menu:** Accounting → Financial Supply Chain Management → Collections Management → Integration with Accounts Receivable Accounting → Periodic processing → Evaluation of Promise to Pay

- **Transaction Code:** FDM_JUDGE

4.4 Dispute Management

- In order to improve the collection process and reduce outstanding payments, you need to resolve the customer's concern. The customer sometimes fails to pay an outstanding amount, or pays less than the expected amount, due to various reasons.

- Without the mySAP ERP Financials statement dispute, companies often use a manual process to resolve customer concerns.

- Manually processing dispute cases is time consuming and expensive, ties up significant organizational resources, and may also delay the resolution of the dispute cases.

- SAP dispute management fills the gap between customer billing and the collection process with its tight integration with other modules. SAP dispute management has the following features;

  - *Process streamline*: SAP dispute management controls and streamlines the processing of dispute cases.

  - *Organized information center*: SAP dispute management organizes and stores all information, objects, and soft documents centrally related to a dispute case.

  - *Center point for dispute resolution*: As a central component for handling dispute cases, SAP dispute management enables cross-department dispute case resolution.

  - *An integrated application*: SAP dispute management is integrated in financial and logistical processes.

  - *Reporting and tracking*: SAP dispute management offers reporting for: identifying quality problems, controlling the workload, and tracking the dispute process.

- In SAP dispute management you can structure the customer's complaints, which will help to track and resolve them, thereby optimizing the collection process and reducing the customer's outstanding payments by creating a dispute case.

- A dispute case is a business object that links to relevant transactions and business objects. It can be created using different options and can be processed by any department of an entity.

- A receivable becomes a dispute if the customer doesn't pay at all or paid an amount that is beyond the tolerance limit of clearing customer open items. Short payment or nonpayment arises due to varieties of reasons, some of which are justifiable and others are not. The justifiable reasons are:

  - Material are not good quality

  - Billed at price that is higher than the agreed price

  - Materials are not delivered on time

- You generally come to know a customer's complaint when:

  - The customer calls about his concern and notifies the sales organization

  - When you approach the customer for payment

  - When you receive a short payment

  - When you are processing bank statement through electronic bank statement

- Therefore, dispute cases can arise at various points of time after sales and before the collection of receivables.

- In dispute management, SAP has provided a functionality to create a dispute case at various processing steps after sale activities.

- In SAP dispute management, SAP uses case management to store all information and documentation relating to a dispute.

- SAP case management helps us to consolidate, manage, and process information about a complex problem or issue in a central collection point. Case management consists of cases, such as a dispute case.

- A *dispute case* is an electronic file for collecting relevant information, such as business partners, transactions, and documents, and displaying that information in a structured form.

- You can create a dispute case through either of the following:
  - From the financial document display [Transaction code: FB03]
  - While processing account statements [Transaction Code: FLB2]
  - From line list [Transaction code: FBL5N]
  - While clearing customer open items [Transaction Codes: F-32 & F-28]
  - Through the dispute management menu by adding open items to a dispute case [Transaction Code: UDM_DISPUTE]
  - Through automatic creation of dispute cases [Transaction Code : FDM_AUTO_CREATE]
- You can see previously created dispute cases by following any of the following options:
  - From financial document display screen [Transaction code: FB03]
  - Through line item display screen [Transaction Code: FBL5N]
  - While clearing customer open items [Transaction Code: F-32, F-28]
- You can close a dispute case in any of the following ways:
  - When you clear the customer open line items [Transaction Code: F-32, F-28]
  - When you reverse a customer's open item that is assigned to a dispute case [Transaction Code: FB08]
  - When you reset a cleared document that is assigned to a dispute case [Transaction code: FBRA]
  - When you update a dispute case with promises to pay
- In order to use SAP dispute management functionalities, you need to go through various configuration steps of account receivable components of financial accounting and dispute management components of financial supply chain management. It is very difficult to cover all of the configuration steps of dispute management. We will cover the required high-level configuration steps and the various objects around them.

4.4.1 RMS ID

- The first configuration step of dispute management is the creation of RMS ID. Here, RMS represents Records Management System. Record management system is the solution for electronically managing records. Record management system facilitates quick access to large volumes of information stored in the electronic form. In record management system you can create a hierarchical structure to groups and store information with similar attributes in one place.

- You can reach the configuration steps to create record management ID by following either of the following paths:

  - **SAP ECC IMG menu path:** Financial Supply Chain Management → Dispute Management → Dispute Case Processing → Create RMS ID.

  - **Transaction Code:** SRMREGEDITC

- In standard SAP, SAP has provided RMS ID:

  - UDM_DISPUTE: for application component Accounts Receivable Accounting

  - UDM_FICA_DISPUTE: for application component Contracts Accounts Receivable and payable (FI – CA)

- Figure 4.34 depicts the standard delivered RMS ID for dispute management. If this ID doesn't fit your requirements, you can create your own ID by right clicking on the RMS_ID node shown in the figure.

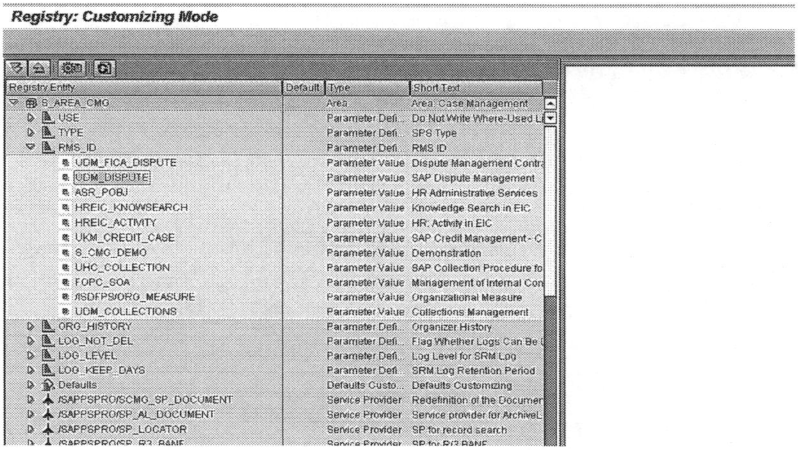

FIGURE 4.34 RMS ID for SAP dispute management.

4.4.2 Element Type

- Element type consists of a set of elements for a service provider. A service provider may have more than one element type, while an element type can have only one service provider. SAP has provided standard element type UDM_SPS_CASE_RECORD for Accounts Receivable Accounting and UDM_FICA_SPS_CASE_RECORD for contract Accounts Receivable and Payable of financial accounting. You can reach the configuration screen to create element type by using the following navigation options:

  - **SAP ECC IMG menu path:** Financial Supply Chain Management → Dispute Management → Dispute Case Processing → Element Types and Case Record Model → Create Element Type

  - **Transaction Code**: SRMREGEDITC

4.4.3 Record Model

- The case record model identifies the types of objects that can be related to a case, such as financial documents and customer or vendor master data. It also gives a logical structure that groups the objects. SAP recommends copying the standard SAP-delivered model and then changing it to meet customer needs instead of creating a case model from scratch.

  - **SAP ECC IMG menu path:** Financial Supply Chain Management → Dispute Management → Dispute Case Processing → Element Types and Case Record Model → Create and Process Case Record Model

  - **Transaction Code:** SRMREGEDITC

- Figure 4.35 depicts a standard case model UDM_DISPUTE provided by SAP. In this figure, you can see that various objects are grouped together in accordance to relevancy.

4.4.4 Attribute Profile

- The attribute profile defines the display and maintenance properties of each attribute. The attribute profile controls which case record fields will be displayed when a case is created from A/R, and the case search screen. You can compare the attribute profile with the field status configuration in financial accounting.

  - **SAP ECC IMG menu path:** Financial Supply Chain Management → Dispute Management → Dispute Case Processing → Attribute Profile → Create Attribute Profile

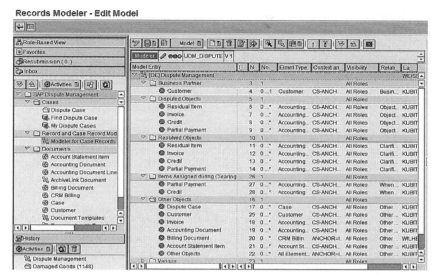

FIGURE 4.35 Standard case model provided by SAP.

- In pre-delivered SAP application, SAP has provided attribute profile FIN_DISP as a standard template for the attribute profile. You can create your attribute profile by copying from the standard delivered template and then edit it to fit your requirements.

Change View "Assign Attributes": Overview

Attrib.Profile FIN_DISP

Assign Attributes

Case Attrib.	Group	Row	Column	Required	Invisible	Dropdown	Checkbox
CASE_TITLE	1		1	☐	☐	☐	☐
CASE_TYPE	1	3	1	☐	☐	☐	☐
CATEGORY	1	4	1	☐	☐	☑	☐
CHANGED_BY	1	15	1	☐	☐	☐	☐
CHANGE_TIME	1	15	2	☐	☐	☐	☐
CLOSED_BY	1	16	1	☐	☐	☐	☐
CLOSING_TIME	1	16	2	☐	☐	☐	☐
CREATED_BY	1	14	1	☐	☐	☐	☐
CREATE_TIME	1	14	2	☐	☐	☐	☐
ESCAL_REASON	1	8	2	☐	☐	☑	☐
EXT_KEY	1	1	2	☐	☐	☐	☐
EXT_REF	1	3	2	☐	☐	☐	☐
FIN_BUKRS	1	2	2	☐	☐	☐	☐
FIN_CONTACT_FAX	1	19	2	☐	☐	☐	☐
FIN_CONTACT_FAXC	1	20	2	☐	☐	☐	☐
FIN_CONTACT_MAIL	1	19	1	☐	☐	☐	☐
FIN_CONTACT_NAME	1	18	1	☐	☐	☐	☐
FIN_CONTACT_TEL	1	18	2	☐	☐	☐	☐
FIN_COORDINATOR	1	7	1	☐	☐	☐	☐
FIN_CREDITED_AMT	1	11	1	☐	☐	☐	☐

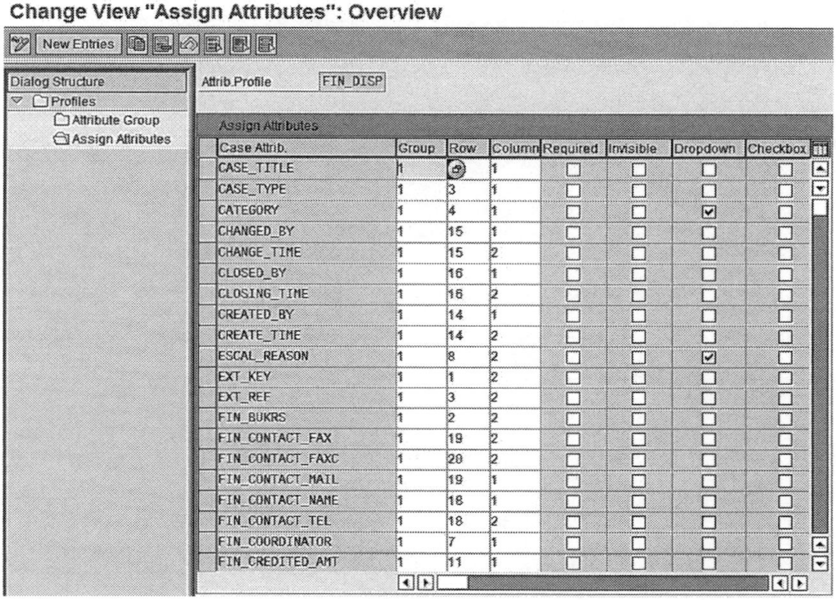

FIGURE 4.36 Attribute profile FIN_DISP.

■ In Figure 4.36, you can see the standard delivered attribute profile, where various fields of the dispute management case are listed along with its position, group, and maintenance level.

4.4.5 Function Profile

■ In function profile you define which functions are allowed for a case type. In the later stage you will assign function profile to case type. SAP comes with pre-delivered functional profile FIN_DISP. You can use the pre-delivered functional profile or you can create your own function profile if the pre-delivered function profile doesn't meet your requirements. You can reach the configuration screen of function profile by navigating the following menu path:

- **SAP ECC IMG menu path:** Financial Supply Chain Management → Dispute Management → Dispute Case Processing → Function Profile → Create Function Profile

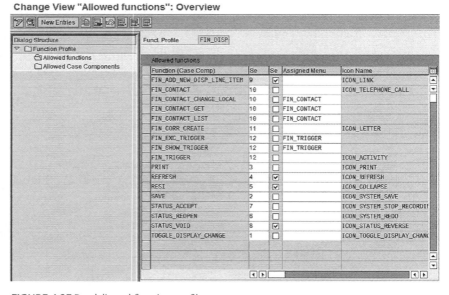

FIGURE 4.37 Pre-delivered function profile.

■ Figure 4.37 depicts the attributes of a pre-delivered function profile. You can see that you can decide which functions are allowed for this function profile. Once the function profile is assigned to the case type, the function profile detects the allowable functionality of a case.

4.4.6 Text Profile

▪ In dispute management cases you use text to store various notes. These notes are stored under a text ID. You need to create a text profile and later on you will assign the text profile to a case type. You can reach the configuration screen of text profile by using the following navigation path:

- **SAP ECC IMG menu path:** Financial Supply Chain Management → Dispute Management → Dispute Case Processing → Text Profile → Create Text Profile

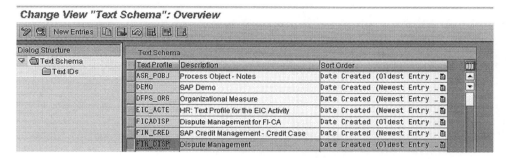

FIGURE 4.38 Stanadrd test profile.

▪ SAP comes with pre-delivered text profile FIN_DISP, shown in Figure 4.38. Under a text profile, text ID's are grouped as seen in Figure 4.39. You can decide the appearance of the sequence of text ID's.

Change View "Text IDs": Overview

ID	Meaning	Sequence	Invisible Ext
0001	Description	1	☐
0002	Internal Note	2	☑
0003	Concluding Remark	4	☐
0004	Reply	3	☐
F001	Customer Description	5	☐
F002	Customer Answer	6	☐

Text Profile: FIN_DISP

FIGURE 4.39 Text ID's within text profile.

4.4.7 Status Profile

- During the life cycle of a dispute case, attributes of the case will change depending on the progress of the case. In status profile, you can configure different statuses of the case that will be assigned by the system during the progression of case.

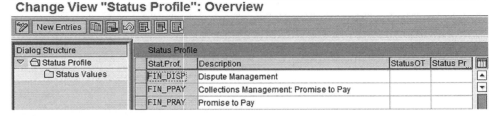

FIGURE 4.40 Standard status profile.

- Figure 4.40 depicts the standard status profile FIN_DISP provided by SAP. Once you select a status profile and choose status values, you can see various case statuses configured/provided by SAP, shown in Figure 4.41.

Change View "Status Values": Overview

Status	Status Description	SystmStat.	System Status Descr.
10	New	001	Open/New
20	Being Processed	002	In Process
21	To Be Collected	002	In Process
30	Closed	007	Closed
40	Confirmed	008	Confirmed
50	Voided	009	Voided/Deleted/Canceled

Status Profile: FIN_DISP

FIGURE 4.41 Case statuses.

- During the life of the case, a case will be either one of the statuses at any particular point in time. You can create your own status profile by copying the SAP provided status profile and then making the necessary changes to it. Configure SAP dispute management status profile by navigating the following menu path:

  - **SAP ECC IMG menu path:** Financial Supply Chain Management → Dispute Management → Dispute Case Processing → Status Management → Create Status Profile

4.4.8 Case Number Range

- Like other SAP objects, a case in SAP is identified by a case number. A case number can be an internal or external number range. You can create a case number range with number range ID and later you assign the number range ID to the case type. When you create a dispute case, the system assigns a case number and an internal number range from the assigned number rage. Figure 4.42 depicts the number range configuration of a dispute management.

Display Number Range Intervals

NR Object   Case Key

Intervals

No.	From number	To number	Current number	Ext	
01	000000000001	099999999999	1750	☐	▲
02	100000000000	199999999999	100000000009	☐	▼
35	350000000000	359999999999	0	☐	
77	200000000000	299999999999	0	☐	

FIGURE 4.42 Dispute case number range.

- Dispute case number range can be an internal or external number range. By choosing the EXT check box against the number range, you can make a number an external. You can reach the case number configuration screen by navigating:

  - **SAP ECC IMG menu path:** Financial Supply Chain Management → Dispute Management → Dispute Case Processing → Define Number Range Interval for Case

4.4.9 Dispute Case Type

- Disputes over case type are the central objects of dispute management. It controls the structure and properties of the dispute cases.

- All objects discussed and configured previously are assigned to a dispute case type.

- In this IMG activity, you can define the case types for SAP dispute management. The case type is the central property of a dispute case.

It groups the various customizing settings, such as attribute profile and status profile. When you create a case, you first have to specify a case type.

Change View "Case Type Maintenance": Overview

Ca	Case Type Name	Ob	Case Record Model ID	
FICA		☐	SRM_MOD02 D948297354E7F741BE4	▲
FIN	Receivables related disputes	☐	SRM_MOD02 0B3CD35E3C344F4397D	▼
F_DM	Dispute Management	☐	SRM_MOD02 0B3CD35E3C344F4397D	
F_PP	Collections Management	☐		
H_FO	Scenario	☐	SRM_MOD02 416C11A961803FF8E10	
H_PO	Process	☐	SRM_MOD02 4140CE2F81BE0DE0E10	
H_SO	Step	☐	SRM_MOD02 414189DF514F2CA5E10	
IDES		☐	SRM_MOD02 BB7970F6826F474E959	
RMS	SAP Demo Case Type (Area S_AREA_RMS)	☐	SRM_MOD02 4B63140A38EFA546B94	
UKM	Credit Limit Request	☐	SRM_MOD02 9934D330ED76724297C	
ZPHS	Pharma Submission FDA Query	☐	SRM_MOD02 F0ECBECCE0A6C341B8C	

FIGURE 4.43 SAP delivered dispute case type.

- Figure 4.43 depicts, an SAP delivered case type F_DM as a template, and you can use it as it is or create your own case type.

- To see all assigned attribute case types, double click on the case type row, you will navigated to Figure 4.44, where you can see all the assigned attributes of the case type.

- When you create a dispute case, it will be created under a case type. The dispute case type controls the attributes of a dispute case, such as dispute case number range, dispute case field status, and status profile.

- In dispute management, when you create a dispute case in dispute case processing, you need to select a dispute case type.

- If you have assigned a dispute case type to a company code in configuration (Figure 4.45), the system automatically selects the dispute case type when you are creating a dispute case from accounts receivable. You can reach the configuration screen via:

- **SAP ECC IMG menu path**: via Implementation Guide → Financial Supply Chain Management → SAP Dispute Management Process Integration → Define Default Values for Creating Dispute Cases

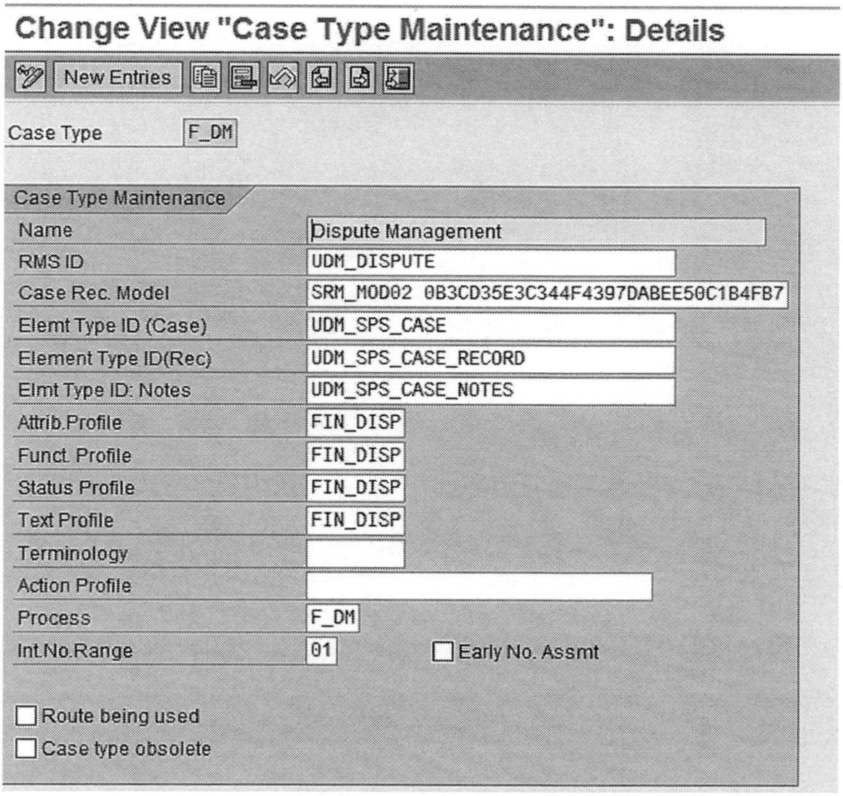

Change View "Case Type Maintenance": Details

New Entries

Case Type	F_DM

Case Type Maintenance

Name	Dispute Management
RMS ID	UDM_DISPUTE
Case Rec. Model	SRM_MOD02 0B3CD35E3C344F4397DABEE50C1B4FB7
Elemt Type ID (Case)	UDM_SPS_CASE
Element Type ID(Rec)	UDM_SPS_CASE_RECORD
Elmt Type ID: Notes	UDM_SPS_CASE_NOTES
Attrib.Profile	FIN_DISP
Funct. Profile	FIN_DISP
Status Profile	FIN_DISP
Text Profile	FIN_DISP
Terminology	
Action Profile	
Process	F_DM
Int.No.Range	01 ☐ Early No. Assmt

☐ Route being used
☐ Case type obsolete

FIGURE 4.44 Dispute case type attributes.

- Figure 4.44 depicts the attributes of SAP delivered case type. As we learned earlier in this section you have created all of these objects.

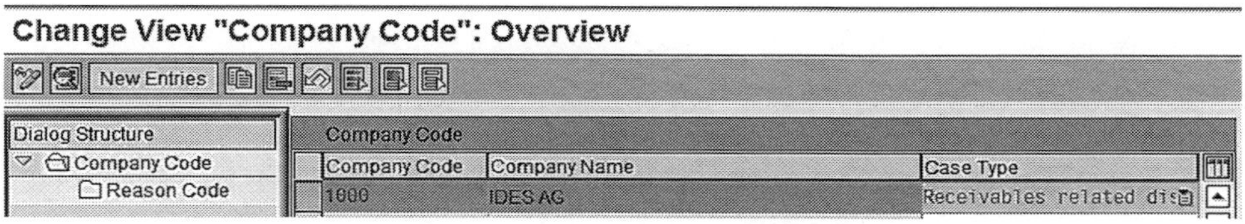

Change View "Company Code": Overview

New Entries

Dialog Structure	Company Code		
▽ 🗁 Company Code	Company Code	Company Name	Case Type
🗀 Reason Code	1000	IDES AG	Receivables related dis

FIGURE 4.45 Dispute case type Assignment.

4.4.10 Attribute "Category"

■ You use the attribute category to put the dispute case types into a subgroup. You can reach the configuration screen via the following menu path:

- **SAP ECC IMG menu path:** Financial Supply Chain Management → Dispute Management → Dispute Case Processing → Case Types → Create Values for Attribute "Category"

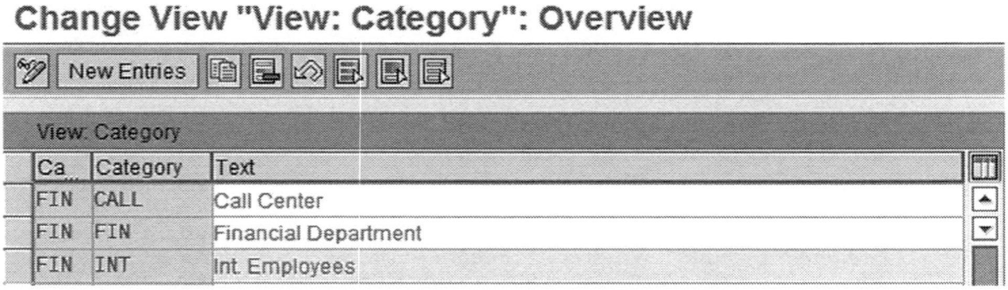

Change View "View: Category": Overview

Ca...	Category	Text
FIN	CALL	Call Center
FIN	FIN	Financial Department
FIN	INT	Int. Employees

FIGURE 4.46 SAP delivered attribute category.

■ Figure 4.46 depicts the three attribute categories delivered by SAP. Dispute cases will be classified in one of these categories. You can use SAP provided attribute categories or you create new attribute categories if the pre-delivered attribute categories don't fit your requirements.

4.4.11 Attribute Reason

■ Dispute case attributes are reasons used to define the cause of the dispute case. If attribute reason field has been flagged for a drop down list in the attribute profile, the system allows choosing attribute reasons while creating a dispute case.

■ You can reach the configuration screen by using the following menu path:

- **SAP ECC IMG menu path:** Financial Supply Chain Management → Dispute Management → Dispute Case Processing → Case Types → Create Values for Attribute Reason

Change View "Case: Reasons": Overview

Ca	Cause	Text
FIN	0000	Unknown
FIN	0001	Late Delivery
FIN	0002	Shortage / Freight Claims
FIN	0003	Payment Problems
FIN	0004	Returns
FIN	0005	Trade Promotion
FIN	0006	Damaged Goods
FIN	0007	Pricing Issue

FIGURE 4.47 SAP provided attribute reasons.

- Figure 4.47 depicts the SAP provided attribute reason code for dispute management. You can use these reason codes or you can create your own reason code.

4.4.12 Attribute Root Cause Code

- Like attribute reason code, you use attribute root cause code to classify dispute cases based on the cause of the dispute case. To use attribute root cause code, you need to flag the route cause code in the attribute profile:

  - **SAP ECC IMG menu path:** Financial Supply Chain Management → Dispute Management → Dispute Case Processing → Case Types → Create Values for Attribute Root Cause Code

4.4.13 Derivation of Element Types

- In dispute management you can link various business objects, like the customer number and customer line items, to a dispute case. To link these business objects to the dispute case, the system has to determine the element type with reference to which system will add objects. You can reach the configuration screen of derivation of element type configuration screen by following:

  - **SAP ECC IMG menu path:** Financial Supply Chain Management → Dispute Management → Dispute Case Processing → Process Integration → Define Derivation of Element Types

- SAP recommends using the following element types if you are using account receivable: BKPF, BSEG, BUS4498, KNA1, and VBRK. In the case of a contact account receivable and payable element types are BUS1006 and CA_CONTACC.

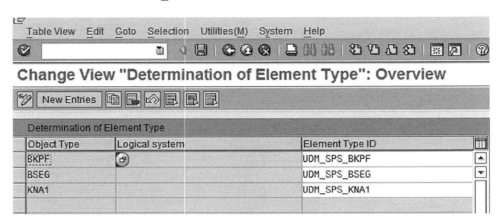

FIGURE 4.48 Standard derivation of element type.

4.4.14 Activate Process Integration for SAP Dispute Management

- SAP dispute management frequently interacts with the account receivable sub-module of financial accounting. SAP dispute management interacts only when you activate such integration. You can reach the configuration screen by using the following menu path:

  - **SAP ECC IMG menu path:** Financial Supply Chain Management → Process Integration with Accounts Receivable Accounting → Activate Process Integration for SAP Dispute Management

- This activation is cross client activation, which means if you activate in one client, it will affect other clients that resides in the same system.

Display View "BTE Application Indicator": Overview

| Menu | | | Back | Cancel | System | |

Appl.	A	Text		
FI-DM	✓	FSCM Dispute Management		▲

FIGURE 4.49 Activation of process integration.

- Figure 4.49 shows the process integration activation window. This configuration is very simple. You just need to check the box, as shown in column A.

4.4.15 Default Values for Creation of Dispute Cases

- In order to minimize data entry while creating a dispute case, SAP has provided a configuration option so that certain values can be defaulted, in addition to values derived from the case type and case category.

- You can reach the configuration screen through the following menu path:

  - **SAP ECC IMG menu path:** Financial Accounting → Accounts Receivable and Accounts Payable → SAP Financial Supply Chain Management → Process Integration with Accounts Receivable Accounting → Define Default Values for Creation of Dispute Cases

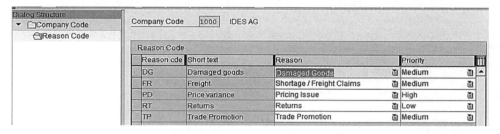

FIGURE 4.50 Default value configuration.

- Figure 4.50 depicts the default value for the dispute case priority that will be defaulted into a dispute case based on reason code. If you create a dispute case with the reason code DG or FR, the system will default dispute case priority as Medium.

4.4.16 Account Determination for Automatic Write-Off of Dispute Cases

- Sometimes you settle a dispute case by writing off the dispute-related amount. When you write off the disputed amount, the system tries to post to a G/L account, for which you need to set up account determination. In the account determination process, you designate a G/L account to which the system will post the disputed written off amount.

- If controlling is active, then you need to designate a cost center to collect the dispute related amount.

- You can reach the relevant configuration screen by navigating the following path:

  - **SAP ECC IMG menu path:** Financial Accounting → Accounts Receivable and Accounts Payable → SAP Financial Supply Chain Management → SAP Dispute Management Process Integration → Automatic Write-off of Dispute Cases → Edit Settings

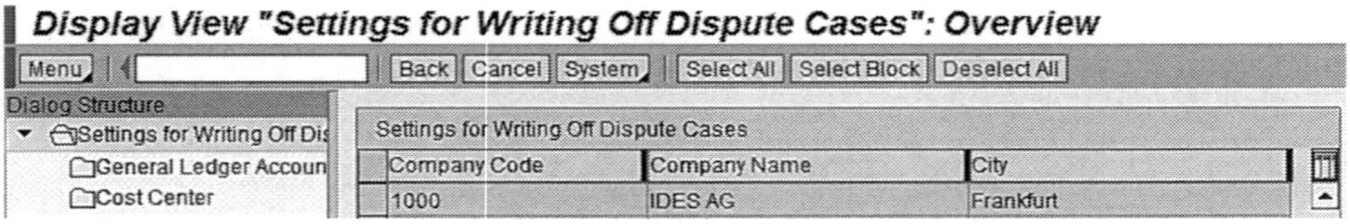

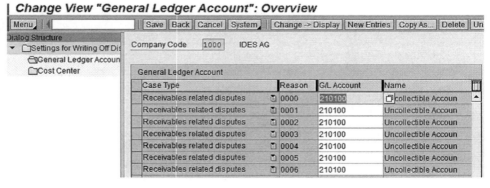

FIGURE 4.51 Account determination initial screen.

- In the initial screen of account determination, you can see that this configuration is company code specific (Figure 4.51). You need to carry out this configuration for each company individually.

- In the left hand dialog tree, you have two sub codes: one for general account determination and one for cost center determination, which is depicted in Figure 4.52.

FIGURE 4.52 General account determination.

- As you see in Figure 4.51, you can configure general account determination based on the reason code you have configured in the attribute reason code section. If the G/L account number is the same for all reason codes, you can assign different G/L accounts based on your requirements.

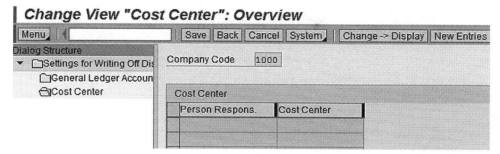

FIGURE 4.53 Cost center determination.

Figure 4.52 shows cost center assignment. You assign different cost centers based on the person responsible for the dispute case.

4.4.17 Creation of a Dispute Case

▪ In the previous section you learned how to configure dispute management. Now it is time to learn how to create and close a dispute case. You can create a dispute case in either of the following ways:

• *Through transaction Code FB03*: You can create a dispute case through transaction code FB03. Once you have displayed a financial accounting document in transaction code FB03, display the customer line item by double clicking the customer line item. You can see the customer line item as shown in Figure 4.54. You can see a button to create a dispute case, click on "Create Dispute Case." Once you clicked "Create Dispute Case" you can see a screen line (Figure 4.55), where you can see that certain fields are already populated, and certain fields have yet to be filled in. Simply fill in the desired field and choose the "Save" icon to create a dispute case. Once the dispute case is created, you can see that description of the button has changed to "Dispute Case." By choosing "Dispute Case" you can see the dispute case that you have just created (Figure 4.57).

• *Through transaction Code FBL5N*: You can create a dispute case from line item display reports. Figure 4.58 displays a customer line item report. In order to create a dispute case for a customer line item, you need to:

• Choose that line item

• Click on "dispute case" button

Display Document: Line Item 001

Additional Data | Create Dispute Case

Customer	1033	Karsson High Tech Markt		G/L Acc	140000
CoCode	1000	Lochhausenerstrasse 46			
IDES AG		Muenchen		Doc. No.	1400000000

Line Item 1 / Invoice / 01

| Amount | 30.14 | EUR |
| Tax Code | | |

Additional Data

Bus. Area	5000			
Disc. base	30.14	Disc. amount	0.00	EUR
Payt Terms	ZB01	Days/percent	14 3.000 % 30 2.000 % 45
Bline Date	05.01.2012	Invoice ref.	/ / 0
Pmnt Block			
Payment cur.		Pmnt/c amnt	0.00
Payment Ref.	0090036384		
Dunn. block		Dunning key	
Last dunned	0	Dunning Area	
Contract	/	Flow Type	
Assignment	0080015383		
Text			Long text

FIGURE 4.54 Create dispute case: T. Code: FB03.

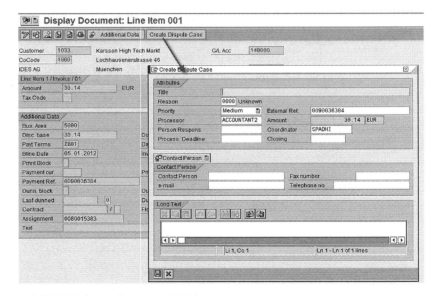

FIGURE 4.55 Create dispute case initial screen.

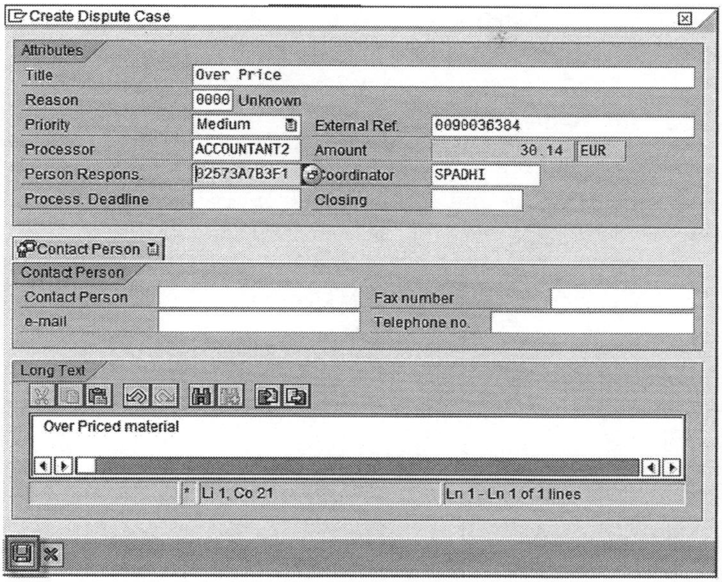

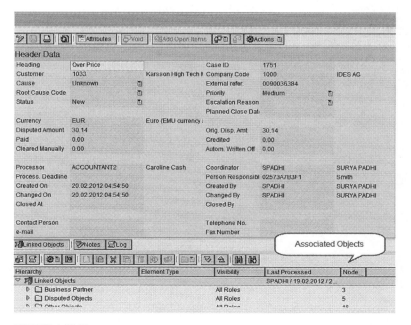

FIGURE 4.56 SAP dispute case.

FIGURE 4.57 Dispute case.

- Once you choose the "dispute case" button, the system will open a dispute case pop up window, as shown in Figure 4.55. Next, you fill in the desired information and save the information. As a result of "save" the system will create a dispute case.

- *Through transaction code F-32 / F-28*: You can create a dispute case while posting an incoming payment from customers. If you have received a short payment from a customer against your receivable, you can create a residual payment from the short payment and create a dispute case from the residual payment.

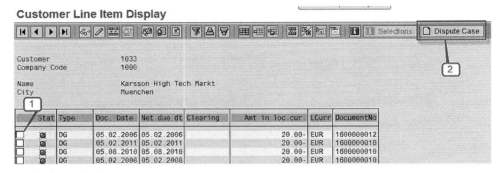

FIGURE 4.58 Customer line item display report.

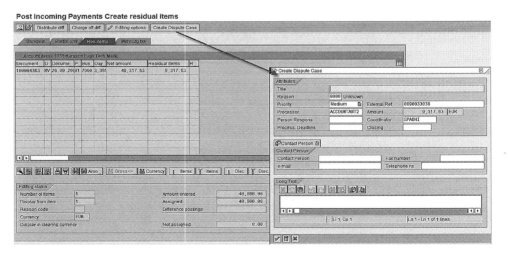

FIGURE 4.59 Dispute case while posting incoming payment.

- For example you are received an incoming payment EUR 40,000.00 against EUR 49,317.63. In the payment advice, the customer has claimed that he has received bad quality material. In this case you have posted EUR 40,000.00 against the outstanding invoice by creating a residual item as shown in Figure 4.59, and at the same time by choosing "Create Dispute Case" you are creating a dispute case. Once you have entered the desired data for the dispute case when you save the incoming payment, the system will pop up an information window as shown below information system is creating a dispute case.

Post Incoming Payments Create residual items

🧑 📝	Distribute diff.	Charge off diff.	🖉 Editing options	Create Dispute Case

Standard	Partial pmt	Res.items	Withhldg tax

Account items 1033 Karsson High Tech Markt

Document	D	Docume	P	Bus	Day	Net amount	Residual items	R
100004363	RV	26.09.20C01		7000	3,38£	49,317.63	9,317.63	

> ☞ Information   ☒
>
> 🛈 A dispute case will be created when you post the document
>
> ✔ ⑳

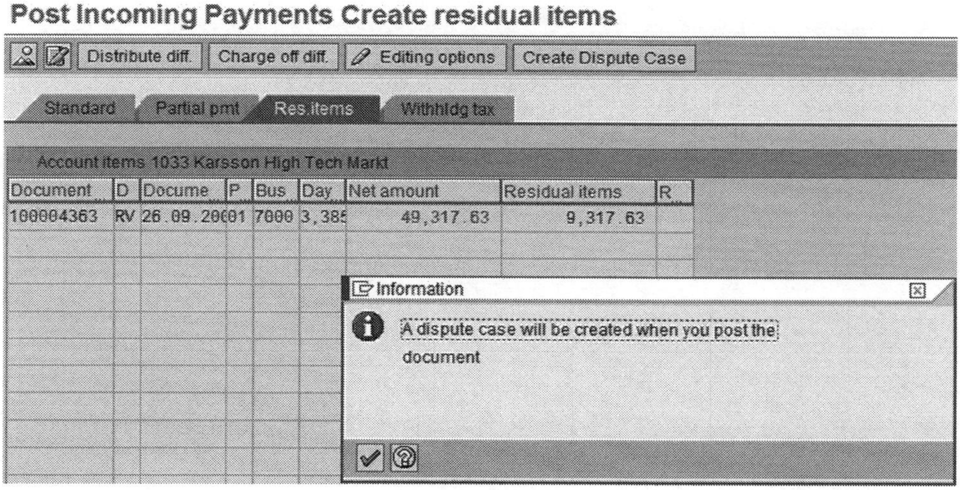

FIGURE 4.60 Pop-up information window appears.

Similarly, when you are clearing customer line items (Transaction code: F-32), you can create a residual item for a differential amount and at the same time you can create a dispute case.

- *Through transaction Code: **UDM_DISPUTE***: Up until now you have learned how to create a dispute case from financial accounting transactions. Transaction code UDM_Dispute is a dispute management transactions code to create a dispute case. With this traction you can add open line items to the existing dispute case. In our earlier case, you created a dispute case for residual line and now you can add one or more line item to the above dispute case. Execute transaction code **UDM_DISPUTE** and find the dispute case and switch the screen to change mode. Once you are in the change mode, make sure "Add Open Item" is activated. Now you can add open items by choosing "Add Open Item." Once you have chosen can "Add Open Item," the system will take you to customer line item reports, from there you can choose open items (Figure 4.61).

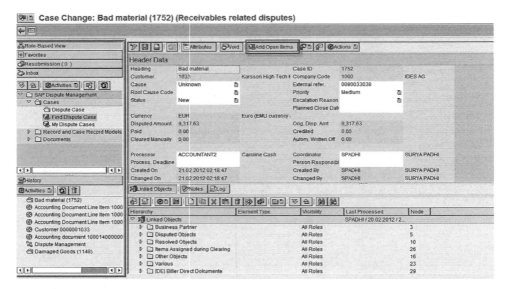

FIGURE 4.61 Adding open item to a dispute case.

- *Through transaction code FDM_AUTO_CREATE*: Like the earlier transaction code, FDM_AUTO_CREATE is a transaction code of FSCM module to create one or more dispute cases. Through this transaction code you can create dispute cases for electronic bank statement or to create mass dispute cases. SAP has provided two options: to create dispute cases for electronic bank statement and to create dispute cases for open items. Both of these options have different selection screens. In this example, you will create a dispute case for open items. Choose "Open Item" button on the screen and enter the required parameter (Figure 4.62). Once executed, you will see the system come up a "Display Log" screen (Figure 4.63) which depicts the system has created disputed cases for open line items as per selection parameters.

Automatic Creation of Dispute Cases

Automatic Incoming Payment		Open Items	

General Selections	Further Selections	Output Control	Notes in Dispute Case

Selections for Line Item

Company Code	1000	to		⇨
Document Type	DR	to		⇨
Posting Key		to		⇨
Posting Date		to		⇨
Document Date		to		⇨
Entry Date		to		⇨
Dunning Area		to		⇨
Dunning level		to		⇨
Dunning block		to		⇨
Payment Method		to		⇨
Reference key 1		to		⇨
Reference key 2		to		⇨
Reference key 3		to		⇨

FIGURE 4.62 Auto creation dispute case.

Display logs

Date/Time/User	Numb	External ID	Object txt	Sub-object text	Tran	Program	Mode	Log number
▽ 20.02.2012 21:07:46 SPADHI	46	Open Items	SAP Dispute an...	Automatic Gene...	FDM_AUT...	RFDM3000	Dialog pro...	00000000000003408849
Problem class medium	42							
Problem class Additional infor	4							

Ty	Message Text
	Customer 0000001000 (): Dispute case created for: Items 1000 1800000028 2003 001
	Customer 0000001000 (): Dispute case created for: Items 1000 1800000029 2003 001
	Customer 0000001000 (): Dispute case created for: Items 1000 1800000030 2003 001
	Customer 0000001000 (): Dispute case created for: Items 1000 1800000031 2003 001
	Customer 0000001000 (): Dispute case created for: Items 1000 1800000032 2003 001
	Customer COL001: Dispute case already exists for: Items 1000 1800000011 2006 001
	Customer COL001 (): Dispute case created for: Items 1000 1800000012 2006 001
	Customer COL001 (): Dispute case created for: Items 1000 1800000021 2006 001
	Customer COL002: Dispute case already exists for: Items 1000 1800000005 2006 001
	Customer COL002 (): Dispute case created for: Items 1000 1800000013 2006 001
	Customer COL002 (): Dispute case created for: Items 1000 1800000029 2006 001
	Customer COL003 (): Dispute case created for: Items 1000 1800000014 2006 001
	Customer COL003 (): Dispute case created for: Items 1000 1800000036 2006 001
	Customer COL004 (): Dispute case created for: Items 1000 1800000006 2006 001

FIGURE 4.63 Auto creation log.

- You can close a disputed case in two ways:

- By the clearing the line items through either an incoming payment or by through adjustment. Once the disputed line item is cleared, the system sets the disputed case status as closed.

- By writing off disputed. Once the disputed cased has been resolved and you agreed with customer for a short payment or deduction, you can write off the disputed amount. In the write off process, the system clears the disputed amount open items and sets the disputed case status as closed.

- SAP has provided transaction code UDM_AUTOWRITEOFF (Menu Path: SAP menu > Financial Supply Chain Management > Dispute Management > Periodic Processing in Dispute Case Processing > Automatic Write-Off of Dispute Cases) to write off solved disputed cases. You can execute this transaction code based on the following selection criteria:

- Case type

- Escalation reason

- Case ID

In this chapter, you have learned how Financial Supply Chain Management (FSCM) components of mySAP Financials help businesses to strengthen their cash flow through various preventive measures. You have briefly covered the main configuration steps of collection management, and also learned how to use collection management. Collection management facilitates the collection specialist by providing a readymade work list, which was generated through the predefined criteria.

Maintenance of good customer relations and early detection of customer concern is very big challenge in today's world. SAP dispute management fills this gap by providing an automated tool to handle dispute cases. In this chapter, you have learned various configuration steps and how to use SAP dispute components.

CHAPTER 5

BUSINESS PROCESSES

In This Chapter

5.1 Introduction

In this section, you will learn a few important and critical business processes. It is not possible to cover all business processes, because business processes vary by region, by rules, by trade practices, by industry, and by organization hierarchy.

The process steps and process sequence might vary depending on configuration, master data setting, business practice, and industry.

Some of these business processes are cross modules, as FICO functional consultants or business process owners it is better to have a good knowledge of how the system works and what the critical steps/paths are in each business process.

Here you will learn, some of the major process steps that generally follow to accomplish the business process.

To perform the process steps, you need to have proper configuration of different modules, which are not in the scope of this book.

5.2 Customer Down Payment and Clearing Process

Process Overview

In this business process, you will learn about the steps involved in customer down payments and subsequent adjustments of customer down payments until the settlement of the down payment.

Down payment is an advance payment towards the supply of material and services. While entering into the agreement for sale and purchase, the buyer and seller agree on certain terms and conditions. One such term and condition is down payment. In the case of the customer down payment process, the customer is expected to pay certain portions of agreed the price as an advance payment. After having received the down payment, the seller supplies the material or services to customer and bills the customer.

In subsequent steps, the seller adjusts the customer down payment towards the material. If the seller has received a full down payment for material or services, the seller clears the customer open items. If the seller only received a part of sale proceeds as a down payment, the seller will set aside these advances as either an account payment or residual payment, and expect the balance payment to complete this business scenario.

Assumptions

▪ You have implemented only mySAP ERP Financials FICO modules.

▪ Sales and distribution activities are taking place outside of mySAP ERP Financials.

Pre-Requisite

To carry out these business process scenarios, you need the following master records:

▪ C100000000 – My Customer: A customer master record.

▪ In addition to customer master record you need following G/L master records:

  • IN10000000 – Sale Proceeds: A revenue account.

  • LI10000000 – Down payment received: An alternative reconciliation account.

  • AS10000149 – Customer Receivable: Normal reconciliation Account

  • AS10000101 – Incoming check clearing account: A bank incoming clearing account.

(*G/L accounts mentioned in this section are purely fictitious and examples only*)

Business Case

A Canadian company manufactures farming equipment (company code: C100) and due to the monopoly in the market, it *asks* its customer for an equipment cost advance (down payment). When the Canadian manufacturer gets the purchase order from its customer, the sales department of the Canadian manufacturer creates a customer advance request (down payment request). Periodically, the account receivable department makes a follow up with the customer based on the customer down payment request. The Canadian manufacturer keeps the down payment in separate documents as accounts payable, until the delivery of the equipment. Once the Canadian manufacturer passes the ownership of equipment, reclassifies the down payment as accounts receivable, and receives balance of equipment cost.

Process Flow

Figure 5.1 depicts end-to-end customer down payments and the subsequent clearing of down the payment business processes and dependency.

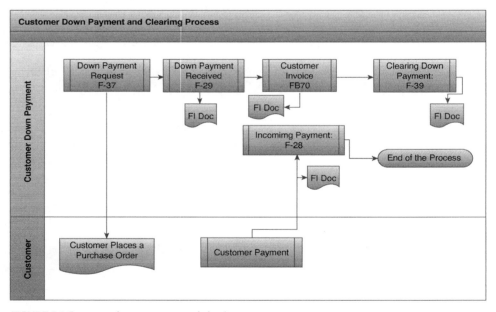

FIGURE 5.1 Customer down payment and clearing.

Process Steps

Table 5.1 depicts the various steps involved to complete this business process scenarios and the expected result from every step. Later in this section, you will learn what steps to be performed and how to perform them.

TABLE 5.1 Customer Down Payment and Clearing Process Steps

Process Step	R / O	Modules	T. Code	Expected Results
1. Down Payment Request	R	FI	F-37	Down payment request has been created
2. Down Payment Received	R	FI	F-29	Down payment has been received
3. Customer Invoice	R	FI	FB70	Customer has been billed for material
4. Clearing Down Payment	R	FI	F-39	Down payment has been cleared against aforesaid invoice
5. Incoming Payment	R	FI	F-28	Customer paid remaining balance and customer open item has been cleared

5.2.1 Down Payment Request

■ Down payment requests are noted items and meant to remind the accounts receivable department. Down payment requests neither change customer balance nor G/L balance. Down payment requests are considered for dunning purposes. In other words, you can generate a dunning notice for a down payment request and you can collect remittance through an automatic payment program. Use the following menu paths to perform this step:

- **SAP ECC Menu: Accounting → Financial Accounting → Accounts Receivable → Document Entry → Down Payment → Request**

- **Transaction Code: F-37**

■ At the end of this step, you can see a system message for the creation of an FI document. You can view the down payment document through transaction code: **FBL5N – Display/Change Line Items.**

■ The account receivable clerk of company code C100 creates a down payment request and passes the payment request to the customer for a down payment.

5.2.2 Down Payment Received

■ You can post a down payment either manually or through an automatic payment program. When a down payment is received the customer balance and alternative reconciliation account are updated. In accounts, down payments received are treated as accounts payable. The system does not post down payment received to normal reconciliation accounts. Use the following menu paths to perform this step:

- **SAP ECC Menu: Accounting → Financial Accounting → Accounts Receivable → Document Entry → Down Payment → Down Payment**

- **Transaction Code: F-29**

▪ The down payment received creates an FI account document. You can see the down payment received document through transaction code: **S_ALR_87012199 – List Of Down Payments Open On Key Date – Customers**

▪ Based on the down payment request, the account receivable clerk of company code C100 receives the down payment from the customer and gives credit to the customer.

▪ The system creates the following accounting entries:

- Dr.   AS10000101 – Incoming check clearing account

- Cr.   C100000000 – My Customer (LI10000000 – down payment received)

5.2.3 Customer Invoice

▪ Once you have sold the product, you need to invoice the customer. In this step, you create an FI document, which stays an open item until it is cleared by an incoming payment, down payment received, or credit note. Use the following menu paths to perform this step:

- **SAP ECC Menu: Accounting → Financial Accounting → Accounts Receivable → Document Entry → Invoice**

- **Transaction Code: FB70**

▪ You need to key in all the relevant information for a customer invoice posting and save the document. Once it is saved, the system displays the account document number. This document remains in the customer ledger as an open item that you will clear with a customer down payment. The system will then create a residual line item for any remaining balance.

- The sales department bills the customer and passes that information to the account department to account for accounts receivable. The system creates the following account line items:

    - Dr.   C100000000 – My Customer (AS10000149 – Customer Receivable)

    - Cr.   IN10000000 – Sale Proceeds

5.2.4 Clearing Down Payment

- In this step, the system ensures that the following activities are carried out:

    - Reclassify the special G/L transaction to normal transaction

    - Transfer the transaction from alternative reconciliation to normal reconciliation account.

    - Clear customer open items if the down payment is equal to the customer invoice. Otherwise, you can create a residual line item from the balance, which you can clear later on.

- Use the following menu paths to perform this step:

    - **SAP ECC Menu: Accounting → Financial Accounting → Accounts Receivable → Document Entry → Down Payment → Clearing**

    - **Transaction Code: F-39**

- At the end of this activity, you can see that the down payment is no longer a special G/L transaction and is transferred to a normal reconciliation account.

- The accounts receivable clerk processes the customer open items and clears the down payment against the customer invoice open items. The system clears the customer invoice with the customer down payment and creates a residual line item for the balance amount. The system creates the following line items for residual line items:

    - Dr.   C100000000 – My Customer (LI10000000 – Down Payment Received)

    - Cr.   C100000000 – My Customer (AS10000149 – Customer Receivable)

5.2.5 Incoming Payment

▪ Through incoming payment, you record customer remittance. You can record customer remittance in various ways like, manual incoming payment, lock box, or electronic bank statement. In this step, manual incoming payment has been considered. This business process is required only if you have received a partial down payment. Use the following menu paths to perform this step:

- **SAP ECC Menu: Accounting → Financial Accounting → Accounts Receivable → Document Entry → Incoming Payments**

- **Transaction Code: F-28**

▪ At the end of this step, the system will generate an FI document by clearing the customer line item.

- Dr.   AS10000101 – Incoming Check Clearing Account

- Cr.   C100000000 – My Customer (AS10000149 – Customer Receivable)

▪ Customer down payment, billing, and clearing of a down payment has now been explained.

▪ Figure 5.2 depicts accounting entries that have been generated in the previously mentioned business process scenario. The accounts and amounts mentioned below are meant for easy understanding and example purposes only.

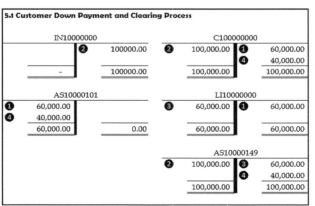

❶   Is the step number of the business process

FIGURE 5.2 Accounting entries.

5.3 Material Procurement Process

Process Overview

In your day-to-day business activities, you are procuring products and services from various vendors. With the mySAP ERP integrated system material procurement process can be handled smoothly. In this section, we will discuss a simple material procurement process under the assumption that you have implemented the MM (Material Management), QM (Quality Inspection), and FI modules. Based on shop floor requirements, the shop floor manager creates a purchase requisition for materials. Purchasing departments receive purchase requisitions and float enquiries of the required material to determine the prices from vendors. Suppliers of the material submit their quotes to the purchasing department. Based on information, the system compares prices of different suppliers. On the basis of price comparison results, the purchasing department places a purchase order for a selected vendor.

The supplier supplies the required materials and bills the customer for payment. After receiving the material, the customer put the materials through quality inspections. Based on the quality inspection result, the warehouse manager makes an informed decision about whether or not to accept the material.

Once the warehouse manager makes the decision to accept the material, the material is placed in a storage location, and will then be issued for consumption.

The account payable department creates an account payable liability and remits payment to the vendor to conclude this business process.

Assumptions

To carry out this business process scenario, it has been assumed that following modules are implemented:

1. Material Management

2. Financial Accounting

Pre-Requisite

To carry out these business process scenarios, you need following master records:

* V100000000 – My Supplier for material. A Vendor master record.

- In addition to the vendor master record you need the following G/L master records:

  - AS10000010 – Material Stock Account (Un-restricted). A material stock account, which is freely available for use.

  - AS10000011 – Material Stock Account (Restricted). A material stock account, material in this account can't issue for use.

  - LI10000100 – GR/IR Clearing Account. A control account for goods receipt and invoice receipts (GR/IR).

  - AS10000102 – Out going check-clearing account. A bank outgoing clearing account.

- M100000000 – Material for finished goods. A material master account.

Business Case

A Canadian (company code: C100) company manufactures farming equipment. To cater the needs of the manufacturing process, the company procures various materials through its centralized purchasing department.

The centralized purchasing department receives the purchase requisitions from the shop floor and processes the purchase requisitions based on the source list. If the material is new, the department asks for quotations from various suppliers.

Based on the quotation, the system does a price comparison and the purchase order is awarded to the supplier whose terms and conditions are favorable and within the company's terms and conditions.

The supplier supplies the required material, since the Canadian manufacturer has very stringent quality control policies and all material goes through the quality control process.

Based on the quality control results, the warehouse manager makes an informed decision about whether or not to accept the material.

Once the material is accepted by the warehouse manager, the Canadian company communicates the material acceptance decision to the supplier. In the subsequent step, the supplier bills for the material.

Process Flow

Figure 5.3 depicts the end to end procurement process. In this procurement process you will learn the use various steps of material management, quality management, and the finance module.

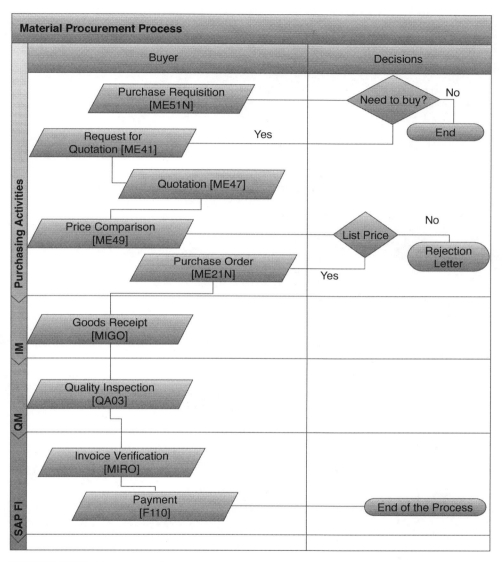

Material Procurement Process

FIGURE 5.3 Material procurement process.

Process Steps

Table 5.2 depicts the various steps involved in the material procurement cycle and the expected result from every step. Later in this section, you will briefly learn what steps are to be performed and how to perform them.

TABLE 5.2 Material Procurement Process: Process Steps

Process Step	R / O	Modules	T. Code	Expected Results
1. Purchase Requisition	R	MM	ME51N	Material requisition has been created
2. Request for Quotation	R	MM	ME41	Based on material requisition, purchasing department has created a request for quotation for vendors
3. Quotation	R	MM	ME47	Vendor quotation has been received and entered
4. Price Comparison	R	MM	ME49	System does price comparison
5. Purchase Order	R	MM	ME21	Purchasing department does an information decision and places purchase order with vendor
6. Goods Receipts	R	MM	MIGO	Warehouse department receives material and stores it for quality inspections
7. Displaying QM Inspection	O	QM	QA03	Quality inspection department performs the quality inspections.
8. Quality inspection – Accept/Reject	R	QM	QE51N	Quality inspection department makes a decision about whether the material meets the acceptable standard or not
9. Recording the Usage Decision	R	QM	QA11	Warehouse manager makes an informed decision, whether or not to accept the material.
10. Invoice Verification	R	FI	MIRO	Account payable department creates liability for material supplied by vendor
11. Vendor Payment	R	FI	F110	Treasury department pays vendor invoices

5.3.1 Purchase Requisition

- A purchase requisition is a formal request to the purchasing department to procure material or services. The purchase requisition passes information such as what materials are required, when they are required, and how much is required. Use the following menu paths to perform this step:

  - **SAP ECC Menu: Logistics → Materials Management → Purchasing → Purchase Requisition → Create**

  - **Transaction Code: ME51N**

- Purchase requisitions are created under a purchasing document type. SAP comes with standard document type NB – Purch. Requis. Stand. Check your configuration through menu path: IMG → Materials Management → Purchasing → Purchase Requisition → Define Document Types

- The shop floor manager of company code C100 creates the purchase requisition for material M100000000.

5.3.2 Request for Quotation

- The request for a quotation is a formal request from the buyer to the seller asking for a quotation. If you have issued a request for quotation to several sellers, you can have the system determine the favorable price submitted by a seller and automatically generates rejection letters for the unfavorable sellers. Use the following menu paths to perform this step:

  - **SAP ECC Menu: Logistics → Materials Management → Purchasing → RFQ/quotation → Request for Quotation → Create**

  - **Transaction Code: ME41**

- You can create a request for quotation manually with reference to an existing RFQ, requisition, or outline purchase agreement. Request for quotations are created under a purchasing document type. Check your configuration by using the following menu path: IMG → Materials Management → Purchasing → RFQ/Quotation → Define Document Types

- Based on the purchase requisition, the purchasing department creates a request for quotation. Depending on configuration, the system generates a request for quotation outputs such as fax and IDOC.

5.3.3 Quotation

- In this step of the material procurement process, you will maintain all quotations you have received against the request for the quotation step. If you have issued an RFQ to several vendors, the system can determine the most favorable quotation submitted and automatically generate letters of rejection to the unsuccessful bidders. You can also store the prices and terms of delivery from certain quotations in an information record for future use. Use the following menu paths to perform this step:

- **SAP ECC Menu: Logistics → Materials Management → Purchasing → RFQ/Quotation → Quotation → Maintain**

- **Transaction Code: ME47**

■ The purchasing department of company code C100 receives quotations from suppliers and enters this quotation into the system. Based on information entered, the system does a price comparison.

5.3.4 Price Comparison

■ You can compare the prices among the quotations received from various sellers. The comparison list ranks the quotations by item from the lowest to highest price. Use the following menu paths to perform this step:

- **SAP ECC Menu: Logistics → Materials Management → Purchasing → RFQ/Quotation → Quotation → Price Comparison**

- **Transaction Code: ME49**

■ In this activity, the purchasing department executes the application to get comparative information on the quotations they have entered in the last step. Based on this information, the purchase organization makes a decision for vendor selection.

5.3.5 Purchase Order

■ The purchase order is a formal request from the buyer to the seller for the supply of goods and/or services as specified in the purchase order. At the end of this activity, the system will generate a purchase order that can be sent to the seller via mail. Use the following menu paths to perform this step:

- **SAP ECC Menu: Logistics → Materials Management → Purchasing → Purchase Order → Create → Vendor/Supplying Plant Known**

- **Transaction Code: ME21**

■ Based on output determination, the system generates a purchase order as hard copy, mail, or IDOC.

■ After the quotation price comparison, the purchasing department places the purchase order with vendor V100000000 for the supply of material M100000000.

5.3.6 Good Receipts

▪ As a result of a fulfillment of purchase order, the system expects a goods receipt of the material ordered from the vendor. A goods movement is entered into the system referencing this purchase order and the system creates a material document. The material document triggers a financial account posting and the system creates a financial document. The material document increases the stock while the financial document updates the stock account. Since the material is subject to inspection, the system posts stock to an un-restricted stock account. Use the following menu paths to perform this step:

• **SAP ECC Menu: Logistics → Materials Management → Inventory Management → Goods Movement → Goods Receipt → For Purchase Order → PO Number Known**

• **Transaction Code: MIGO.**

▪ The system determines the G/L account based on account determination. You configure the account determination through transaction code: OBYC or the menu path: IMG → Materials Management → General Settings for Materials Management → Valuation and Account Assignment → Account Determination → Account Determination Without Wizard → Configure Automatic Postings for transaction key GBB and BSX.

▪ The warehouse manager receives the material supplied by vendor V100000000 and stores it in the store location, which is subject to quality inspection. The system created the following accounting line items:

• Dr.   AS10000011 – Material Stock Account (Restricted)

• Cr.   LI10000100 – GR / IR Clearing Account

5.3.7 Displaying QM Inspection

▪ Depending on the business process, material received in the previous step may have a restricted status or un-restricted status. If the QM module is in use, generally once the material is received it will have restricted status. You must perform the Quality Inspection for each material using transaction QE51N. You must also record a usage decision using transaction QA11. If you wish to bypass the Quality Inspection requirements, you can do so by using the batch change status transaction (MSC2N). Use the following menu paths to perform this step:

- **SAP ECC Menu: Logistics → Quality Management → Quality Inspection → Inspection Lot → Processing → Display**
- **Transaction Code: QA03**

5.3.8 Quality Inspection – Accept/Reject

- In the previous step, you have placed the material for inspection. While the inspection is pending, the material will have restricted status. In this step, a quality inspection will be performed by the relevant department and the result would be recorded in the system.

- Based on the inspection result, material will either be accepted or rejected. Use the following menu paths to perform this step:

  - **SAP ECC Menu: Logistics → Quality Management → Quality Inspection → Inspection Result → Results Recording**
  - **Transaction Code: QE51N**

- Material M100000000 passed through quality inspection and is accepted for use in the production process.

5.3.9 Recording the Usage Decision

- When the results recording is complete, the usage decision for the material can be made. Normally, this corresponds to the releasing of the raw material for production. Use the following menu paths to perform this step:

  - **SAP ECC Menu: Logistics → Quality Management → Quality Inspection → Inspection Lot → Usage Decision → Record**
  - **Transaction Code: QA11**

- Once you accept the material, the stock will automatically be posted to unrestricted stock, which can be used in the production process.

- When material is rejected, the system will create a material document with movement type 122 (return to vendor). You can see the material document with help of T. Code: MB51. The goods receipt is cancelled and the system creates the following accounting line items:

  - Dr.   AS10000010 – Material Stock Account (Un-restricted)
  - Cr.   AS10000011 – Material Stock Account (Restricted)

5.3.10 Invoice Verification

▪ At the end of the purchasing and inventory management process, your accounting department might have received an invoice from the vendor for payment. In the invoice verification process, the accounts payable department ensures that invoices are correct with respect to the quantity of material and cost of material. At the end of the invoice verification process, the system will generate a MM document and account document. Use the following menu paths to perform this step:

- **SAP ECC Menu: Logistics → Materials Management → Logistics Invoice Verification → Document Entry → Enter Invoice**

- **Transaction Code: MIRO**

▪ Generally, the invoice verification process follows either a two way or three way match. While doing invoice verification, if any discrepancies occur and fall within the tolerances created in the customizing area (yellow traffic light), the invoice can be posted, but it is blocked for payment and must be released (T.Code: MRBR) before it can be paid.

▪ If any discrepancies occur which fall outside these tolerances, the invoice cannot be posted. The system creates the following accounting line items:

- Dr.   LI10000100 – GR / IR Clearing Account
- Cr.   V100000000 – My Supplier for material (LI10000010 – Vendor Reconciliation Account)

5.3.11 Vendor Payment

▪ The last step of this process is the payment to the vendor for material. You can pay the vendor through either manual payment or through automatic payment. Manual payment is preferable when you are paying to a single vendor, while automatic payment program is preferable when you let the system determine open items to be payable. Use the following menu paths to perform this step:

- **SAP ECC Menu: Accounting → Financial Accounting → Accounts Payable → Periodic Processing → Payments**

- **Transaction Code: F110**

▪ Outgoing payments create an accounting document called payment document and clears the vendor open line items. The system created the following accounting line items:

- Dr. V100000000 – My Supplier for material ((LI10000010 – Vendor Reconciliation Account)

- Cr. AS10000102 – Bank of America-Outgoing Clearing Account

■ With this the procurement, the process comes to end. Figure 5.4 depicts the accounting entries generated in various steps of the business process scenario.

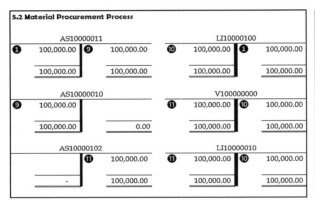

❶ Is the step number of the business process

FIGURE 5.4 Accounting entries.

5.4 Cross-Company Stock Transfer

Process Overview

In this section, you will learn about cross-company business processes. This business process is dependent on various configuration steps of FICO and MM modules and some of them are described in the previous chapters of this book.

In this business process, stock transfers from one plant to another plant, where both plants belong to different company codes.

One company code will initiate the purchase order, where the supplying plant will be another company code's plant.

The supplying plant delivers material based on the purchase order of the receiving plant. Upon receipt of goods, the receiving plant creates a goods receipt. The supplying plant bills the receiving plant, which automatically creates invoice receipts in the receiving company code. Thus, due-to-due from inter-company ties to each other, which can be settled later on.

Assumptions

To complete these inter-company stock transfer scenarios, it has been assumed that material management and finance modules are in use. Necessary master data has been maintained.

Pre-Requisite

To carry out these business process scenarios, the following master records are used:

- In receiving company code, for example C100, create following master data

  - V10000C200 – Vendor – Company code C200

  - AS10000010 – Material Stock Account (Un-restricted). A material stock account, which is freely available for use

  - LI10000100 – GR/IR Clearing Account. A control account for goods receipt and invoice receipts (GR/IR)

  - M100000000 – Material for finished goods. A material master account

- In supplying company code, for example C200, create the following master data:

  - C10000C100 – Customer – Company code C100

  - EX10000202 – Cost of goods sold – Internal Sales

  - AS10000010 – Material Stock Account (Un-restricted). A material stock account, which is freely available for use

  - IN10000000 – Sale Proceeds

Business Case

Let us assume that company code C100 want material M100000000 for its manufacturing process, which is available through company code C200. Based on the purchase order of company C100, company code C200 delivers the required material. Company code C200 creates outbound delivery of material, while company code C100 creates an inbound delivery of material M100000000.

In subsequent steps, company code C200 creates inter-company billing document, which posts to company code C100 and creates inter-company payable.

Both company codes are configured in the same landscape and configured in such a way that the system carries out some of the steps.

Process Flow

Figure 5.5 shows the steps involved and the data flow of inter company stock transfer.

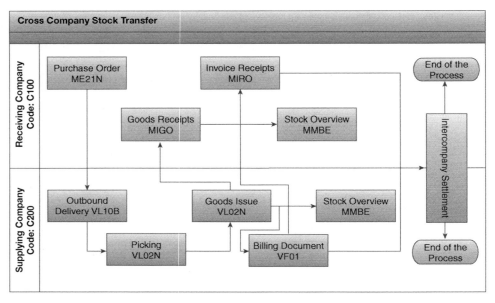

FIGURE 5.5 Cross-company code stock transfer.

Process Steps

Table 5.3 depicts the steps involved in the cross-company code stock transfer process. Depending on your business case, you may have few or more steps.

TABLE 5.3 Cross-Company Stock Transfer: Process Steps

Process Step	R / O	Modules	T. Code	Expected Results
1. Create Purchase Order	R	MM	ME21N	Purchase order has been created in company code C100
2. Create Outbound Delivery for Purchase Order	R	MM	VL10B	Delivery document has been created in company code C200

TABLE 5.3 (*continued*)

Process Step	R / O	Modules	T. Code	Expected Results
3. Pick Outbound Delivery	R	MM	VL02N	Material has been isolated for outbound delivery in company code C200
4. Post Goods Issue for Delivery	R	MM	VL02N	Goods issue has been posted and system has created a FI posting in company code C200
5. Check Status of Stock Transfer	R	MM	MMBE	Stock has been reviewed to confirm that stock has been transferred
6. Post Goods Receipt for Stock Transport Order	R	MM	MIGO	A stock receipt has been carried out and system has created a financial posting in company code C100
7. Billing	R	SD	VF01	Receiving company has been billed for material by company code C200
8. Invoice receipts	R	FI	MIRO	Receiving company code C100 booked invoice for material received

5.4.1 Create Purchase Order

■ In this step, company code C100 created a purchase order for the supply of material from the supplying plant C200. Use the following menu paths to perform this step:

- **SAP ECC Menu: Logistics → Materials Management → Purchasing → Purchase Order → Create → Vendor/Supplying Plant Known**

- **Transaction Code: ME21N**

■ Purchase orders are created under the purchasing document type. SAP comes with pre-delivered document type NB for purchase orders. You can also configure your own purchasing document types by using the following menu path: IMG Materials Management → Purchasing → Purchase Order → Define Document Types.

■ In this step, company code C100 creates a purchase for supply of M100000000 from company code C200. The output of this step is a purchase order. You can print, mail, and fax the purchase order based on the output determination configuration.

5.4.2 Create Outbound Delivery for Purchase Order

■ Based on the purchase order created in the last step, you create a delivery document. You configure these dependency through the menu path IMG → Materials Management → Purchasing → Purchase Order → Set Up Stock Transport Order → Assign Delivery Type and Checking Rule. Use the following menu paths to perform this step:

- **SAP ECC Menu: Logistics → Sales and Distribution → Shipping and Transportation → Outbound Delivery → Create → Collective Processing of Documents Due for Delivery → Purchase Orders**

- **Transaction Code: VL10B**

■ The system performs the following activities while creating an outbound delivery:

- **Completeness:** The system checks delivery blocks and incompleteness of outbound delivery of material.

- **Material availability**: Determines the delivery quantity of an item and checks the availability of the material

- **Batch determination**: If the material is subject to batch control, the system carries out batch determination.

- **Freight cost and route determination**: The system carries out route determination of material to be delivered and calculates associated cost.

- **Packing**: Packs the outbound delivery according to the reference order.

■ After receiving the purchase order from company code C100, company code C200 creates outbound delivery of material M100000000, assuming that company C200 maintains sufficient stock to fulfill company code C100 material requirement.

5.4.3 Pick Outbound Delivery

■ The picking process that involves taking goods from a storage location and staging the right quantity in a picking area where the goods will be prepared for shipping. Use the following menu paths to perform this step:

- **SAP ECC Menu: Logistics → Sales and Distribution → Shipping and Transportation → Outbound Delivery → Change → Single Document**

- **Transaction Code: VL02N**

▪ At the end of the picking process, a picking status will be recorded against each material scheduled for delivery. The picking status indicates where the item is in the picking process.

▪ The warehouse clerk of company code C200 performs this step in order to post outbound delivery.

5.4.4 Post Goods Issue for Delivery

▪ After the picking process, material will be shipped to the customer from the warehouse. In the post goods issue step, you will record such material movement.

▪ You can post goods issue:

- For individual outbound delivery

- For several outbound deliveries as collective processing

- For several outbound deliveries in background processing

▪ Use the following menu paths to perform this step:

- **SAP ECC Menu: Logistics → Sales and Distribution → Shipping and Transportation → Post Goods Issue → Outbound Delivery Single Document**

- **Transaction Code: VL02N**

▪ The outbound deliveries form the basis of goods issue posting. The data required for goods issue posting is copied from the outbound deliveries described previously.

▪ Once you post goods issue for an outbound delivery, the system carries out the following activities on the basis of the goods issue document:

- Warehouse stock of the material is reduced by the delivery quantity

- Value changes are posted to the balance sheet account in inventory accounting

- Requirements are reduced by the delivery quantity

- The serial number status is updated

- Goods issue posting is automatically recorded in the document flow

- Stock determination is executed for the vendor's consignment stock

- A worklist for the proof of delivery is generated

■ Warehouse clerk of company code C200 posts goods issue for material M100000000. As a result of post goods issue, the system reduces the stock of material in company code C200 and creates a material document, followed by an accounting document. The system creates the following accounting entries:

- Dr.   EX10000202 – Cost of goods sold – Internal Sales

- Cr.   AS10000010 – Material Stock Account

5.4.5 Check Status of Stock Transfer

■ To know the stock status, you can enter plant and subject material and the system will come up with a screen that explains the status of the stock transfer as stock in transit.

■ Use the following menu paths to perform this step:

- **SAP ECC Menu: Logistics → Materials Management → Inventory Management → Environment → Stock → Stock Overview**

- **Transaction Code: MMBE**

■ This is an optional step, where you view stock movement at supplier company code.

5.4.6 Post Goods Receipt for Stock Transport Order

■ Goods receipt is a process where you record the inbound movement of material into the warehouse. You can use goods receipts for goods received from external vendors as well as in-house production of goods or materials. All goods receipts result in an increase of stock in the warehouse.

■ The following kinds of goods receipts are considered in the SAP system:

- Goods receipt with reference to a purchase order

- Goods receipt with reference to a production order

- Goods receipt with reference to a delivery

- Goods receipts with reference to customer return

▪ In this step, you will perform goods receipts based on delivery document created – earlier.

▪ Use the follow menu paths to perform this step:

- **SAP ECC Menu: Logistics → Materials Management → Inventory Management → Goods Movement → Goods Receipt → For Purchase Order → PO Number Unknown**

- **Transaction Code: MIGO**

▪ In the goods receipts process, the system carries out the following activities:

- Check the order and material to make sure the delivery is possible

- Assign a storage location

- Update order with goods receipts

▪ Figure 5.6 shows the activities the system performs while posting goods issue.

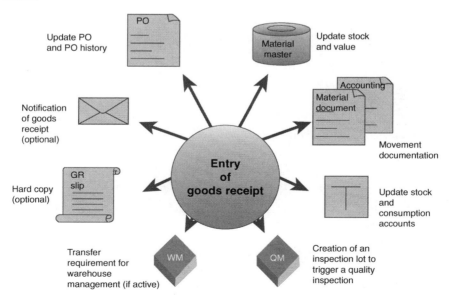

FIGURE 5.6 Goods receipts activities.

- Once you posted goods receipts, the system does not allow changing the quantity, material, and movement type fields of the material document. If you need to correct these fields then you need to reverse the material document.

- Company code C100 post goods receipts of material with reference to delivery document created in – earlier. Once a goods receipt is posted, you can review the stock position in company code C100 by following step. The system creates a material document and an FI document. You can see the material document through transaction code MB03 or menu path: SAP Menu → Logistics → Materials Management → Inventory Management → Material Document → Display

- In this activity, the system generates an accounting document in company code C200 with the following line items:

  - Dr.   AS10000010 – Material Stock Account
  - Cr.   LI10000100 – GR / IR Clearing Account

5.4.7 Billing Document

- In this step, the supplying company creates inter-company billing. SAP comes with pre-delivered sales document type IV for inter-company billing. You can create a billing document manually or through a batch job. In this step, manual creation of the billing document has been considered. You can reach out this functionality through the following menu paths:

  - **SAP ECC Menu: SAP Menu → Logistics → Sales and Distribution → Billing → Billing Document → Create**

  - **Transaction Code: VF01**

- The billing step creates a billing document in sales and distribution modules, and an FI document in FI modules. From the billing document display transaction code VF03, you can view the document flow by following environment → display document flow.

- Company code C200 creates a billing document for material supplied to company code C100. This step creates a financial posting as shown below:

  - Dr.   C10000C100 – Customer – Company code C100
  - Cr.   IN10000000 – Sale Proceeds

- Depending on the configuration, this step may internally post a vendor invoice in the receiving company code. But in our business process scenario, manual posting has been considered.

5.4.8 Invoice Verification

- In the invoice verification step, the receiving company creates account payable liability for the material received from the supplier.

- Use the following menu paths to perform this step:

  - **SAP ECC Menu: Logistics → Materials Management → Logistics Invoice Verification → Document Entry → Enter Invoice**

  - **Transaction Code: MIRO**

- Generally, the invoice verification process follows either a two way or three way match. While doing the invoice verification, if any discrepancies occur and lie within the tolerances created in the customizing area (yellow traffic light), then the invoice can be posted. However, it is blocked for payment and must be released (T.Code : MRBR) before it can be paid.

- If any discrepancies occur which lie outside these tolerances, the invoice cannot be posted. The system created the following accounting line items:

  - Dr.   V10000C200 – Vendor – Company code C200

  - Cr.   V100000000 – My Supplier for material

- In this business process scenario, you have learned how to process an inter-company stock transfer. During the execution of steps, the system generates accounting entries as shown in Figure 5.7.

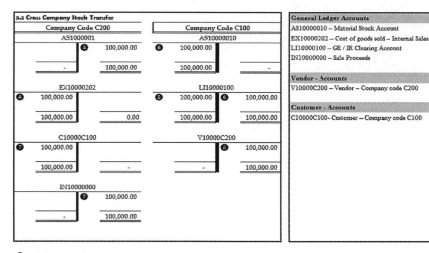

❶   Is the step number of the business process

FIGURE 5.7 Accounting entries.

5.5 Direct Shipping Process with Shipping Notification

Process Overview

In this section, you will study a business scenario where the customer places an order with the supplier for a certain quantity of material. The supplier of the material neither manufactures nor carries the stock of material requested by the customer.

In order to fulfill the customer order, the supplier passes the customer order information to a third party supplier with an instruction to ship the requested materials to the customer directly and bill the supplier for material.

The third party supplies the requested material to the customer and informs the supplier that he has supplied requested material to customer.

Once the materials are supplied by the third party to the customer, the third party bills the supplier for material. In turn, the supplier bills the customer for material supplied by the third party.

Advantages

- Reduction in inventory management cost such as carrying cost of inventory

- Fulfilling customer sales order without maintaining stock

- Billing customer based on shipping notification from vendor

Assumptions

Material Management, Sales and Destruction modules, and FI modules are already implemented and configured to cater to this business process requirement.

Pre-Requisite

To carry out these business process scenarios, you need the following master records:

- C100000000 – My Customer. A customer master record.

- V100000000 – My Supplier for material. A Vendor master record.

- In addition to vendor master & customer master record we need following G/L master records

  - AS10000010 – Material Stock Account (Un-restricted). A material stock account.

  - LI10000100 – GR / IR Clearing Account. A control account for goods receipt and invoice receipts (GR / IR).

- EX10000201 – Cost of goods sold – External Sales. A cost of goods sold account.

- IN10000000 – Sale Proceeds. A revenue account.

- M100000001 – Material for trading goods. A material master account.

Business Case

In this business scenario, company code C100 receives a purchase order from customer C100000000 for the supply of material M100000001. Company code C100 neither produces nor stocks material M100000001. Company code C100 places a purchase order with V100000000 for the supply of material M100000001, with an instruction to deliver the material to customer C100000000 directly. Vendor V100000000 ships material M100000001 and sends notification of shipment to customer C100000000 and bills to company code C100. After receiving the information for the shipment of material M100000001, company code C100 bills to customer C100000000. Company code receives money from the customer C100000000 and pays to vendor V100000000.

The following process flow describes the various processes and steps involved to cover these scenarios.

Process Flow

Figure 5.8 depicts the process flow and steps involved in this business process scenario.

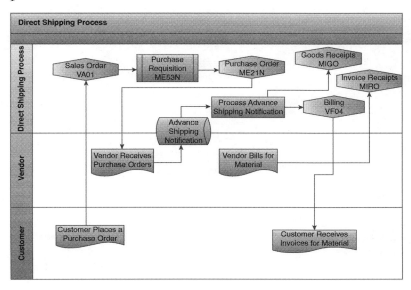

FIGURE 5.8 Direct shipping process with shipping notification.

Process Steps

Table 5.4 depicts the steps involved to accomplish this business process.

TABLE 5.4 Direct Shipping Process with Shipping Notification: Process Steps

Process Step	R / O	Modules	T. Code	Expected Results
1. Create Sales Order	R	SD	VA01	Based on customer purchase order, sales order has been created. The system automatically generates the purchase requisition
2. Display Purchase Requisitions	O	MM	ME57N	In this activity you will review
3. Create Purchase Order	R	MM	ME21N	Purchase order has been created
4. Process ASN	R		WE16	Advance shipping notification processed
5. Post Statistical Goods Receipt	R	MM	MIGO	Based on advance shipping, goods receipts have been processed
6. Invoice Verification	R	MM	MIRO	Account payable department process vendor invoices. The system creates both MM and FI documents in this step.
7. Outgoing Payment	R	FI	F110	Vendor has been paid and vendor open line item is offset by payment document
8. Billing	R	SD	VF04	Customer has been billed
9. Incoming Payment	R	FI	F-28	Incoming payment has been posted

5.5.1 Create Sales Order

▪ A sales order is a binding agreement between the seller and the buyer, where the seller agrees to sell specified quantities at an agreed price. The sales order automatically generates a purchase requisition for the purchase of material M100000001. Use the following menu paths to perform this step:

- **SAP ECC Menu: SAP Menu → Logistics → Sales and Distribution → Sales → Order → Create**

- **Transaction Code: VA01**

▪ The material that will be supplied by third party is classified under item category group "BANS" (third party item) through material type. Item category "TAS" is assigned to item category group "BANS."

- When you create a sales order, you need to assign the item category "TAS" in the sales order line item. Item category TAS initiates the creation of a purchase order for third party.

- You can create your own item category through the menu path: Sales and Distribution → Sales → Sales Documents → Sales Document Item → Define Item Categories or transaction code: VOV7

- Company code C100 creates a sales order after receiving the purchase order from C100000000 for material M100000001. The sales order triggers the creation of the purchase requisition for procurement of material.

- Depending on the configuration of the output determination, the system generates a sales order. You can configure the output determination through transaction code VV13 or menu path: SAP Menu → Logistics → Agency Business → Environment → Master Data → Customer → Messages → Sales Document → Display

5.5.2 View Purchase Requisition

- A purchase requisition is a formal request to the purchasing department to procure material or services. A purchase requisition passes information such as what are materials are required, when they are required, and how much is required. Use the following menu paths to perform this step:

  - **SAP ECC Menu: SAP Menu → Logistics → Materials Management → Purchasing → Purchase Requisition → View**

  - **Transaction Code: ME53N**

- In this business scenario based on the configuration, the system automatically generates purchase requisitions. You can view the system-generated purchase requisitions by following either of the previously stated access options.

- The purchasing department of company code C100 has created a purchase requisition for material M100000001 to procure the requisite material from vendor V100000000.

5.5.3 Create Purchase Order

- A purchase order is a formal request from the buyer to the seller for the supply of goods and/or services as specified in the purchase order. At the end of this activity, the system will generate a purchase order that can be sent to the seller via mail. Use the following menu paths to perform this step:

- **SAP ECC Menu: SAP Menu → Logistics → Materials Management → Purchasing → Purchase Order → Create → Vendor/Supplying Plant Known.**

- **Transaction Code: ME21N**

▪ The input to create a purchase order is the purchase requisition. Based on the configuration, you can create a purchase order with reference to the purchase requisition. The output of this step is the purchase order. The purchase order can create a commitment posting in CO but does not create an FI posting. You can change and view the purchase order through transaction code ME22N and ME23N, respectively. Company code C100 creates a purchase order P1000000 and sends it to vendor V100000000 for the supply of material M100000001 with a instruction that material M100000001 will be shipped to customer C100000000.

5.5.4 Processing the Inbound ASN

▪ In this step, you can upload the ASN (Advanced Shipping Notification) file received from the vendor. Generally, your system might have configured it in such a way that ASN files are processed automatically by the system. This step is optional and will be taken care of by your technical colleagues. Use the following menu paths to perform this step:

- **SAP ECC Menu: SAP Menu → Logistics → Sales and Distribution → Foreign Trade/Customs → Communication / Printing → Communication / Printing → Environment → IDoc / EDI Basis → Test → Inbound procg of orig.inb.file**

- **Transaction Code: WE16**

▪ You can upload the ASN file received from vendor V100000000. Generally, your system might have configured such way that ASN files processed automatically by the system. This step is optional and will be taken care your technical colleagues. Follow above menu paths to perform this step.

▪ Vendor V100000000 transmits an advance shipping notice through IDOCs, which is loaded into the company code C100 system.

5.5.5 Goods Receipt

- Once you receive an advance shipping notification from the vendor, you will create an indicative goods receipt as an acknowledgement. Use the following menu paths to perform this step:

  - **SAP ECC Menu: SAP Menu → Logistics → Materials Management → Inventory Management → Goods Movement → Goods Receipt → For Purchase Order → PO Number Known**

  - **Transaction Code: MIGO**

- In this step, the system will create an MM document and FI document. If the system has created a commitment at the same time as the creation of the purchase order, and goods receipts process, the system will confirm the commitment to confirm liability.

- You can view the material document through either transaction code MB51 or menu path Logistics → Materials Management → Inventory Management → Environment → List Displays → Material Documents.

- After receiving of the advance shipping notification from vendor V100000000 for the supply of material M100000001 to customer C100000000, company code C100 will make an indicative goods receipt of material M100000001 with reference to ASN. As this is not a real goods receipt, the goods receipt is directly posted into a consumption account instead of a stock account.

- In financial accounting, the system creates the following accounting line items:

  - Dr. EX10000201 – Cost of goods sold – External Sales
  - Cr. LI10000100 – GR/IR Clearing Account

5.5.6 Billing

- In this step, you will create an SD billing document for the customer. Based on output determination, the system can print customer invoices, mail, or fax. You can create the billing document with reference to the sales order or the delivery document. In this case, the system creates a billing document based on the sales order. Use the following menu paths to perform this step:

- **SAP ECC Menu: Logistics → Sales and Distribution → Billing → Billing Document → Process Billing Due List**

- **Transaction Code: VF04**

▪ The system will display a billing due list. Choose the appropriate line item and click on "individual line billing document" to create a customer invoice. The outcome of the process is a billing document, which in turn will create an FI document. If COPA is active, the billing data will be transferred to COPA.

▪ Material M100000001 is delivered to customer C100000000 by vendor V100000000. In this step, company code C100 will invoice customer C100000000 for material M100000001 based on the sales order. The input of this process is the sales ordered in step 1 and shipping notification received in step 4.

▪ In FI, the system creates the following accounting line items:

- Dr   C100000000 – My Customer

- Cr   IN10000000 – Sale Proceeds

5.5.7 Invoice Verification

▪ In the invoice verification process, the account payable user posts the invoice for material that is supplied by your vendor to the customer. Based on the configuration and master data maintenance, the system will carry out a two-way or three-way match. Input of this step is the purchase order created in step 3 and the goods receipts posted in step 5. The invoice verification process provides a link between the material management module, financial accounting, and controlling modules.

▪ Use the following menu paths to perform this step:

- **SAP ECC Menu: SAP Menu → Logistics → Materials Management → Logistics Invoice Verification → Document Entry → Enter Invoice**

- **Transaction Code: MIRO**

▪ The outputs of this step are material document for invoice verification, the FI document, and the controlling document.

▪ In this step, company code C100 will post the invoice received from vendor V100000000, which will create a liability in favor of vendor V100000000.

- In FI, the system creates the following accounting line items:

  - Dr.   LI10000100 – GR/IR Clearing Account
  - Cr.   V100000000 – My supplier for material

- In this business process, you have understood the various steps involved in the direct shipment process. This business scenario is a cross-module business process that involves material management, sales and distribution, and FI modules. The end-to-end process ends with the recording of the incoming customer payment and outgoing vendor payment. The incoming customer payment and outgoing vendor payment are already covered in various steps of this chapter. At the end of the business, you can see that the system has generated accounting entries as shown in Figure 5.9.

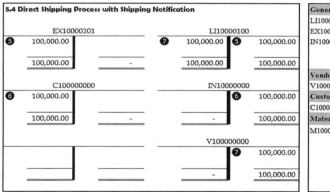
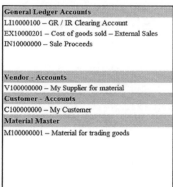

❶ Is the step number of the business process

FIGURE 5.9 Accounting entries.

5.6 Indirect Shipping Process

Process Overview

In the indirect shipment process, scenarios cover a business process where the supplier of the material does not carry stock of the required material. As soon as the supplier receives a sales order from the customer, the supplier places a purchase order with a third party.

The third party supplies the requested material to the supplier and subsequently, the supplier ships the material to customer.

The third party bills the supplier for material it has supplied, and the supplier bills the customer for the material it has shipped.

Due to the tight integration of sales and distribution, material management and finance modules data entered in one module are available in other modules, and make the business process very smooth.

Advantages

There are many advantages of this business process, such as:

1. The supplier needs to worry about carring stock, thus avoiding the associated cost of inventory management.

2. The customer gets the required specific material on time, because this reduces the time involved in multiple inventory handling.

Assumptions

Like other business processes, it is assumed that you have implemented the required modules and maintained the required master data to carry out this business process.

Pre-Requisite

To carry out these business process scenarios, you need the following master records:

▪ C100000000 – My Customer. A customer master record-to-record sale of product.

▪ V100000000 – My Supplier for material. A vendor master record.

▪ In addition to the vendor master and customer master records, you need the following G/L master records:

   • AS10000010 – Material Stock Account. A material stock account.

   • LI10000100 – GR/IR Clearing Account. A control account for goods receipt and invoice receipts (GR/IR).

   • EX10000201 – Cost of goods sold – External Sales. A cost of goods sold account.

   • IN10000000 – Sale Proceeds. A revenue account.

▪ M100000001 – Material for trading goods. A material master account.

Business Case

Customer C1000000000 places a purchase order for material M100000001 with supplier company code C100. Company code C100 neither manufactures nor carries stock material M100000001. In order to fulfill customer order, company code C100 places an order with its vendor V100000000 for the supply of material M100000001.

In indirect shipping scenarios, company code C100 procures material M100000001 from vendor V100000000, receives material at its transit warehouse, and ships the material from the transit warehouse to customer C1000000000. In this business scenario, you will learn all the steps necessary to accomplish business requirements that cover material management, sales and distribution, and FI modules.

Process Flow

Figure 5.10 depicts the process flow of indirect shipment business process scenario.

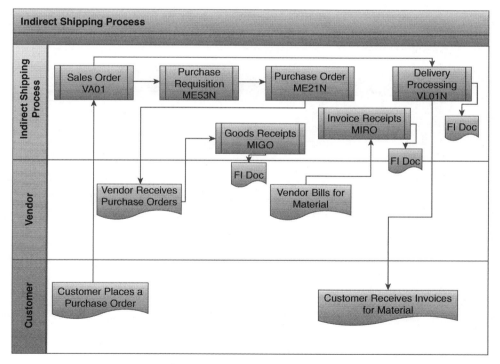

FIGURE 5.10 Indirect shipment process flow.

Process Steps

Table 5.5 outlines the various activities involved in the business process scenario. It also describes the outcomes of each and every step. Later in this section, you will briefly learn how to process these steps.

TABLE 5.5 Indirect shipping: Process Steps

Process Step	R / O	Modules	T. Code	Expected Results
1. Sales Order	R	SD	VA01	Based on customer purchase order, sales order has been created
2. Purchase Requisition	R	MM	ME53N	Purchase requisition has been generated based on sales order
3. Purchase Order	R	MM	ME21N	Purchase requisition has been converted into purchase order
4. Goods Receipt	R	Logistic	MIGO	Goods receipts have been created
5. Delivery Processing	R	Logistic	VL01N	Outbound delivery has been created based on sales order
6. Billing	R	SD	VF01	Customer has been billed for material supplied
7. Invoice Verification	R	FI	MIRO	Account payable liability has been created based on vendor invoice

5.6.1 Sales Order

- A sales order is a binding agreement between sellers and buyers where the seller agrees to sell specified quantities at an agreed price. The sales order automatically generates a purchase requisition based on item category assignment to material type of the subject material. Use the following menu paths to perform this step:

  - **SAP ECC Menu: SAP Menu → Logistics → Sales and Distribution → Sales → Order → Create**

  - **Transaction Code: VA01**

- In the business scenario, creation of sales is the first step. At this point, company code C100 has a purchase order from customer C100000000 towards the supply of material M100000001. Since company code C100 doesn't carry stock of material M100000001, company code C100 is expecting that as the system creates a sales order, the system should create a purchase requisition.

- The sales department of company code C100 will input the customer's purchase order information in order to create a sales order for material M100000001. Based on the item category of the sales order, the system will automatically generate a purchase requisition.

5.6.2 Purchase Requisition

- A purchase requisition is a formal request to the purchasing department to procure material or services. The purchase requisition included information such as what materials are required, when they are required, and how much is required. In this business scenario based on the sales order, the system automatically creates a purchase requisition based on the sales order item category. In this step, you can view the system-generated purchase requisition. Use the following menu paths to perform this step:

  - **SAP ECC Menu: SAP Menu → Logistics → Materials Management → Purchasing → Purchase Requisition → View**

  - **Transaction Code: ME53N**

- In this step, the purchase department of company code C100 can review the purchase requisition generated by the system. In the next step, you will create a purchase order for supply of material, referencing this purchase requisition.

5.6.3 Purchase Order

- In the step 1, the system has created purchase requisition while creating the sales order. With reference to the purchase requisition, you can create a purchase order. A purchase order is a binding agreement with your vendor, where the purchaser agrees to purchase a certain quantity of a specific material with certain terms and conditions. Use the following menu paths to perform this step:

  - **SAP ECC Menu: SAP Menu → Logistics → Materials Management → Purchasing → Purchase Order → Create → Vendor/Supplying Plant Known**

  - **Transaction Code: ME21N**

- The purchasing department of company code C100 creates a purchase order with reference to the purchase requisition for supply material M100000001. A purchase order can be mailed or faxed to the vendor for the supply of material M100000001 to company code C100 at the end of this step.

5.6.4 Goods Receipt

- A goods receipt is an activity of inventory management that increases stock in hand of an entity. You can carry out a goods receipt against a purchase order (from the external supplier) or against a production order (in house production). Use the following menu paths to perform this step:

- **SAP ECC Menu: SAP Menu → Logistics → Materials Management → Inventory Management → Goods Movement → Goods Receipt → For Purchase Order → PO Number Known**

- **Transaction Code: MIGO**

▪ In response to the purchase order of company code C100, vendor V100000000 shipped material M100000001. Since company code C100 receives this material against the purchase order, the materials are kept in a separate storage location for shipment to the customer. The goods receipt process updates the PO history, which helps to track purchase order. The goods receipt created an accounting document with following line items:

- Dr.   AS10000010 – Material Stock Account
- Cr.   LI10000100 – GR/IR Clearing Account

5.6.5 Delivery Processing

▪ This step is a part of the sales and distribution modules. In this step, you will initiate the material delivery process. In the delivery process, there are two different activities involved in this step: (1) create outbound delivery and (2) post goods issued for delivery.

▪ Once you post the goods issued for an outbound delivery, the system carries out the following activities on the basis of the goods issue document:

- Warehouse stock of the material is reduced by the delivery quantity

- Value changes are posted to the balance sheet account in inventory accounting

- Requirements are reduced by the delivery quantity

- The serial number status is updated

- Goods issue posting is automatically recorded in the document flow

- Stock determination is executed for the vendor's consignment stock

- A worklist for the proof of delivery is generated

- Use the following menu paths to perform this step:

  - **SAP ECC Menu: SAP Menu → Logistics → Sales and Distribution → Shipping and Transportation → Outbound Delivery → Create → Single Document → With Reference to Sales Order**

  - **Transaction Code: VL01N**

- The warehouse clerk of company code C100 creates an outbound delivery and at the same time, the goods issue is posted for the material shipment. In the post goods issue step, the system creates an accounting document as follows:

  - Dr.   EX10000201 – Cost of goods sold – External Sales

  - Cr.   AS10000010 – Material Stock Account

5.6.6 Billing Processing

- Billing is an activity in the sales and distribution process where you are making another entity liable to pay for the goods and services. This is the last stage of the sales and distribution module. Use the following menu paths to perform this step:

  - **SAP ECC Menu: SAP Menu → Logistics → Sales and Distribution → Billing → Billing Document → Create**

  - **Transaction Code: VF01**

- Once the billing document is created, the system will generate a corresponding FI document, which in turn creates a customer open item. A customer open item can be cleared either through an incoming payment, against down payment, or against the vendor open item (if the customer is also a vendor). After this step, the FI module comes in the picture to collect the receivable from the customer.

- In this step, company code C100 will bill to customer C100000000 for material M100000001. At the end of this activity, the system will generate an SD document called a billing document and an FI document with following line items:

  - Dr.   C100000000 – My Customer

  - Cr.   IN10000000 – Sale Proceeds

5.6.7 Invoice Verification

■ Invoice verification is the last step of the procurement process. In this step, you record the vendor invoice and create a financial liability for the material you have received from your supplier. The invoice verification process correlates with the purchase order, which is a material document that you have created with the goods receipts. Depending on the configuration check, the system does two-way or three-way checks to ensure that the invoice submitted by the vendor is in accordance with the price of the purchase order and the quantity of material is as per the purchase order.

■ Use the following menu paths to perform this step:

- **SAP ECC Menu: SAP Menu → Logistics → Materials Management → Logistics Invoice Verification → Document Entry → Enter Invoice**

- **Transaction Code: MIRO**

■ If the system encounters a price difference or a quantity difference during the invoice verification, than the system expects user invention in order to confirm the variance. In these process, the systems creates a material document and a financial posting.

■ The account payable department of company code C100 has received the vendor invoice and posted the invoice through MIRO transaction. The system created following accounting posting during the invoice verification process:

- Dr.   LI10000100 – GR / IR Clearing Account

- Cr.   V100000000 – My Supplier for material

■ To complete the entire end-to-end process, you may include two additional steps: (1) customer incoming payment and (2) vendor outgoing payment. These steps are pretty simple and straight forward, and have already been covered in a number of occasions in this chapter. For example, (1) customer incoming payment, (2) vendor outgoing payment: Figure 5.11 depicts the summarized accounting that the system has generated while accomplishing this business processes.

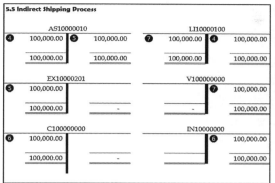

❶   Is the step number of the business process

FIGURE 5.11 Accounting entries.

5.7 Consignment Process with Customer

Process Overview

In this business process scenario, you will study how the consignment processes work with the customer.

Based on a sale order, material has been shipped to the customer, but it is still owned by the supplier. Periodically, the customer withdraws material from the consignment stock and informs the supplier. Based on the customer's information, the supplier bills the customer for the sale of material and fulfills consignment stock

If the customer does not want any more the material, supplier brings back the balance material from customer.

Some of the important concepts of this business processes include:

1. Material is in the possession of the customer and is still owned by the manufacturer.

2. The customer consumes the material from the stock in his possession, called consignment stock, and informs the supplier of such consumption.

3. Based on customer's information, the supplier bills the customer for material consumed and replaces the consignment stock.

4. After completion of the consignment agreement, the company brings back the unconsumed material.

Advantages

The consignment process has the following advantages over normal sales:

1. There are advantages in freight cost, because material can be shipped to the customer site in bulk.

2. Since the material is available at the customer's site, the material is accessible to the customer at the customer's convenience.

3. Generally, consignment agreement is a long-term agreement and there will low administrative handling costs of the material.

Assumptions

When defining the business process scenarios it has been assumed that:

1. You have implemented sales and distribution, finance, and material management of module of SAP.

2. You have configured and maintained the required master data as mentioned in the pre-requisite.

Pre-Requisite

In order to complete these business process scenarios, we need following master data:

- C100000000 – My Customer. A customer master data with whom the supplier deals with.

- M100000001 – Material for trading goods. A material master for consignment goods.

- In addition to previous customer and material master, you need at least the following G/L master records:

  - EX10000201 – Cost of goods sold – External sales
  - IN10000000 – Sale proceeds
  - AS10000010 – Material stock account
  - AS10000012 – Consignment stock account
  - AS10000101 – Incoming check clearing account

Business Case

Company C100 is a trader of material M100000000 and keeps stock of materials in its warehouse. Based on the customer's sales order, company code C100 supplies materials to various customers. Recently, company code C100 received a very large sales order from customer C100000000 for the supply of material M100000000 for one year. This sales order comes with a special condition that customer C100000000 needs an un-interrupted supply of the material for which company code C100 should maintain a stock level at the customer's site. In order to fulfill this sales order, company code C100 came up with a consignment material concept. In the consignment material process, company code C100 delivered materials to customers, but it will only bill when the customer consumes this material. In this process, customer C100000000 periodically informs company code C100 for the consumption of material M100000000. Based on the customer's information, company code C100 bills customer C100000000 and replaces the material consumed by the customer.

After completion of a one year period, company code C100 brings back unconsumed stock and puts these back in its warehouse.

Process Flow

Figure 5.12 depicts the process steps involved to accomplish this business process scenario. In this business process scenario, you will learn how the data flows between tightly integrated modules such as sales and distribution, material management, and financial accounting.

Depending on the business practice, industry, and accounting, you may have one or more steps.

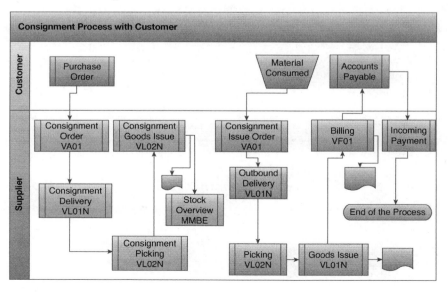

 **Accounting Document**

FIGURE 5.12 Consignment process with customer.

Process Steps

Table 5.6 explains the process steps and expected output of each process step of this business scenario.

TABLE 5.6 Consignment Process with Customer: Process Steps

Process Step	R / O	Modules	T. Code	Expected Results
1. Consignment Order	R	SD	VA01	Consignment fill up order has been created. You can use the standard SAP KB sales order type for this step.
2. Consignment Delivery	R	SD	VL01N	Delivery document has been created, while creating delivery order, the system checks for material availability
3. Consignment Picking	O	MM	VL02N	Picking has been carried out
4. Consignment Goods issue		LE	VL02N	Goods issue document has been created in MM and FI
5. Stock Overview		LE	MMBE	Stocks balance should been reduced
6. Consignment Issue		SD	VA01	Consignment issue order has been created. You can use standard sales order type KE for this steps
7. Outbound Delivery		LE	VL01N	Delivery document has been created in logistic
8. Picking		LE	VL02N	Picking has been created
9. Goods issue		LE	VL02N	Goods issue document has been created in MM and FI document posted
10. Customer Billing		SD	VF01	Customer has been billed through billing document
11. Incoming Payment		FI	F-28	Customer incoming payment has been recorded and open items of the customer have been cleared
12. Consignment Pick-up		SD	VA01	Consignment pick up document has been created. You can use standard document type KA for this purpose
13. Delivery		LE	VL01N	Return delivery document has been created
14. Goods Receipt		LE	VL02N	Return goods issue document has been created

5.7.1 Consignment Order

- Once the customer purchase order is received, you need to create a sales order called consignment order. A consignment order is a special type of sales order. The creation of a consignment order is the first step of this process. Once you create a consignment order, the system carries out an availability check of material. You need to use a different sales order type for this. Follow Sales and Distribution → Sales → Sales Documents → Sales Document Header → Define Sales Order Type or VOV8 to create sales order document type. Use the following menu paths to perform this step:

- **SAP ECC Menu: Logistics → Sales and Distribution → Sales → Order → Create**

- **Transaction Code: VA01**

■ Company code C100 has received a purchase order from customer C100000000 and creates a consignment order. Though this is not a real sales order, but you need it to initiate the consignment process. Based on the configuration, the system generates output of this sales order type.

5.7.2 Consignment Delivery

■ Delivery is one of the most important steps of the logistic execution process. The outbound process consists of picking, packing, and goods issue. You create an outbound delivery document with reference or without reference to the sales order. Use the follow menu paths to perform this step:

- **SAP ECC Menu: Logistics → Logistics Execution → Outbound Process → Goods Issue for Outbound Delivery → Outbound Delivery → Create → Single Document → With Reference to Sales Order**

- **Transaction Code: VL01N**

■ In this process, the system creates a deliver document. Based on the configuration, the system checks for material availability, and if the material is available, the system confirms the delivery of material.

5.7.3 Consignment Picking

■ In the consignment picking process, you make available the required material ready for shipping to the customer site. This is an optional step, needed in case you have not activated lean warehouse management. From the previous step, you can jump to the post goods issue step without this step. If you have activated batch management and/or serial number management before this step, you may end up with additional steps like assignment of serial number and assignment of batch numbers. Use the following menu paths to perform this step:

- **SAP ECC Menu: Logistics → Logistics Execution → Outbound Process → Goods Issue for Outbound Delivery → Outbound Delivery → Change → Single Document**

- **Transaction Code: VL02N**

■ Company code C100 doesn't activate batch management and serial number management. In this step, the warehouse clerk of company code C100 segregates material M100000001 and puts them in the shipping point.

5.7.4 Consignment Goods Issue

■ After picking, you can post goods issue. In the post goods issue step, the system reclassifies the stock from un-restricted use to special stock called consignment stock. Depending on the business practice, you might have configured it to generate an account document or not to generate an account document. Use the following menu paths to perform this step:

- **SAP ECC Menu: Logistics → Logistics Execution → Outbound Process → Goods Issue for Outbound Delivery → Post Goods Issue → Outbound. Delivery Single Document**

- **Transaction Code: VL02N**

■ The warehouse clerk of company code C100 posted a goods issue and the goods shipped to customer. Since stocks are shipped to the customer site and stored in the consignment storage location, as per the business practice, these stocks are shown separately in the financial statement. The system generates an account document as follows:

- Cr.   AS10000010 – Material Stock Account

- Dr.   AS10000012 – Consignment Stock Account

■ You can see the document flow of this activity by following Menu → Environment → Document Flow.

■ *Note: You can perform this activity through delivery monitor. Logistics → Sales and Distribution → Shipping and Transportation → Outbound Delivery → Lists and Logs → Outbound Delivery Monitor or VL06O.*

5.7.5 Stock Overview

■ Stock overview is an optional step. This step facilitates viewing stock movement but does not generate an account document or a material document. Use the following menu paths to perform this step:

- **SAP ECC Menu: Logistics → Materials Management → Inventory Management → Environment → Stock → Stock Overview**

- **Transaction Code: MMBE**

■ You can view consignment stock by following SAP Menu → Logistics → Materials Management → Purchasing → Master Data → Subsequent Settlement → Vendor Rebate Arrangements → Environment → Condition/Arrangement → Conditions: Sales → Bonus Buy → Environment → Pricing → Environment → Value Assignment → Inventory managemen → Environment → Consignment → Customer Consignment or **MB58**

5.7.6 Consignment Issue

■ From the consignment stock, the customer draws material as per his requirement. Periodically, the customer informs the supplier regarding withdrawal of material from the consignment stock. The customer passes this consumption information through electronic media like EDI or hard copy. In our business process scenario, the customer passes this information through hard copy at regular intervals.

■ The consignment issue order initiates the process of sales material consumed by the customer. When you create a consignment issue note for the consignment storage location, the system checks material availability for that storage location. Use the following menu paths to perform this step:

- **SAP ECC Menu: Logistics → Sales and Distribution → Sales → Order → Create**

- **Transaction Code: VA01**

■ Unlike the earlier step, while creating consignment issue note, the system carries out a pricing procedure.

■ Company code C100 received the consumption report from customer C100000000 and creates a consignment issue note based on the quantity consumed. In the subsequent step, the warehouse clerk creates an outbound delivery of material M100000001.

■ You can change the consignment note by using the following menu path SAP → Logistics → Sales and Distribution → Sales → Order → Create or **VA02**.

■ Based on configuration, the system determines the output of a confirmed consignment issue note. You can view the output determination setting through transaction code **VV11** or SAP Menu → Logistics → Materials Management → Purchasing → Master Data → Subsequent Settlement → Customer Rebate Arrangements → Environment → Customer → Messages → Sales Document → Create for output type **BA00**.

5.7.7 Outbound Delivery

■ Delivery is one of the most important steps of the logistic execution process. The outbound process consists of picking, packing, and a goods issue. You create an outbound delivery document with or without reference to the sales order. Use the following menu paths to perform this step:

- **SAP ECC Menu: Logistics → Logistics Execution → Outbound Process → Goods Issue for Outbound Delivery → Outbound Delivery → Create → Single Document → With Reference to Sales Order**

- **Transaction Code: VL01N**

■ Based on the consignment note created in the previous step, we have created a delivery document. While creating a delivery document, the system carries out a material availability check. If the material is available, the system confirms and creates a delivery document.

■ With reference to the consignment note in this step, company code C100 creates a delivery document. As the material in the customer site has already been consumed by the customer, company code C100 carries out this step to regularize the system process.

5.7.8 Picking

■ In the picking process, you make the required material available and ready for shipping to the customer site. This is an optional step, needed in case you have not activated the lean warehouse management. From the previous step, you can jump to the post goods issue step without going through this step. If you have activated batch management and/or serial number management before this step, you may end up with additional steps like assignment of serial number and assignment of batch numbers. There is no real movement of material in this step because material has already been consumed, however, in order to effect the consignment sale you need to follow the system process steps. Use the following menu paths to perform this step:

- **SAP ECC Menu: Logistics → Logistics Execution → Outbound Process → Goods Issue for Outbound Delivery → Outbound Delivery → Change → Single Document**

- **Transaction Code: VL02N**

■ The warehouse clerk of company code C100 created the picking list based on the delivery document created earlier. In the next step, the warehouse clerk creates a goods issue posting.

5.7.9 Goods Issue

■ In the goods issue step, you post goods issue for outbound delivery. This step has two significant roles: (1) ownership of material transferred to customer and (2) the system creates financial transactions. In this business scenario, you will issue stock from the consignment stock. Use the following menu paths to perform this step:

- **SAP ECC Menu: Logistics → Logistics Execution → Outbound Process → Goods Issue for Outbound Delivery → Post Goods Issue → Outb. Delivery Single Doc**

- **Transaction Code: VL02N**

■ The system creates the financial document by debiting the cost of the goods sold and crediting the stock account.

■ Company code C100 has posted goods issue based on the delivery document created earlier. While creating the post goods issue document, the system created following accounting line items:

- Dr.   EX10000201 – Cost of goods sold – External Sales

- Cr.   AS10000012 – Consignment Stock Account

■ You can also post goods issue though VL06O or SAP Menu → Logistics → Sales and Distribution → Shipping and Transportation → Outbound Delivery → Lists and Logs → Outbound Delivery Monitor

■ You can check your stock through **MMBE** or SAP Menu → Logistics → Materials Management → Inventory Management → Environment → Stock → Stock Overview.

5.7.10 Customer Billing

■ After material shipment, you need to bill the customer for the material. In this step, you will carry out your billing activities. Billing activities create financial documents by creating accounts receivable open items. Use the following menu paths to perform this step:

- **SAP ECC Menu: Logistics → Logistics Execution → Outbound Process → Goods Issue for Outbound Delivery → Billing → Billing document → Create**

- **Transaction Code: VF01**

■ Based on the system configuration, the system determines the output of these activities. Output can be anything from hard copy of the customer invoice through IDOC, which is transmitted to the customer in electronic media. You can view the output determination through transaction code **VV33** for message type RD00.

■ In this process, the system creates two documents: (1) the billing document for sales and distribution module and (2) a financial document. Based on the sales distribution account determination, the system determines the correct G/L accounts and creates a financial document.

■ The account receivable department of company code C100 created a billing document based on the billing due list and the system created following accounting line items:

- Cr.   IN10000000 – Sale Proceeds

- Dr.   C100000000 – My Customer

■ You can view the entire document flow starting from sales order through the billing document if you navigate Menu → environment → display document flow of display standard order (Transaction code VA03).

5.7.11 Incoming Payment

■ Incoming payment is the final step of the business process and completes the entire business process. You can post an incoming payment through various ways such as: (1) a manual incoming payment, (2) through automatic payment, (3) through lock box process (*refer to the*), or (4) through an in-house cash center.

■ You will learn about a manual incoming payment, where the customer remits payment directly to the account receivable department.

- **SAP ECC Menu: SAP menu → Accounting → Financial Accounting → Accounts Receivable → Document Entry → Incoming Payments**

- **Transaction Code: F-28**

▪ The account receivable clerk of company code C100 receives the check from customer C100000000 and clears the customer items. With this process, the system creates the following accounting line items:

- Dr.   AS10000101 – Incoming check clearing account

- Cr.   C100000000 – My customer

▪ The following few steps cover the process for the return of consignment material that is not consumed by the customer due to the completion of the consignment agreement or defective material.

5.7.12 Consignment Pick-up

▪ After the completion of the consignment agreement, whatever stock is left over at the customer's site needs to be shipped back to your own warehouse. To pick up the consignment stock from the customer site, you need to create a consignment pick up order. For a consignment pick up order you can use a different type of sales document. You can configure the sales document type through transaction code **VOV8** or IMG → Sales and Distribution → Sales → Sales Documents → Sales Document Header → Define Sales Document Types

▪ Use the following menu paths to perform this step:

- **SAP ECC Menu: Logistics → Sales and Distribution → Sales → Order → Create**

- **Transaction Code: VA01**

▪ Once you save the consignment order, the system creates a consignment pick up order.

5.7.13 Return Delivery

▪ In the previous step, you created a consignment pick up order. Using the consignment pick up order you will create a return delivery order. Like the previous step, you will use a different material document type normally known as "LR". You can configure your own document type by following IMG → Logistics Execution → Shipping → Deliveries → Define Delivery Types or transaction code **0VLK**. Like the delivery document, the system carries out a material availability check before creating a delivery document. Use the following menu paths to perform this step:

- **SAP ECC Menu: Logistics → Logistics Execution → Outbound Process → Goods Issue for Outbound Delivery → Outbound Delivery → Create → Single Document → With Reference to Sales Order**

- **Transaction Code: VL01N**

5.7.14 Goods Receipt

- Based on the delivery document, once you receive the material from the customer site, you carry out a goods receipt. The goods receipt classifies the stock from the consignment stock as unrestricted stock. Depending on your system configuration, this may or may not create an account document.

- Use the following menu paths to perform this step:

  - **SAP ECC Menu:** *Logistics → Logistics Execution → Outbound Process → Goods Issue for Outbound Delivery → Post Goods Issue → Outb. Delivery Single Doc.*

  - **Transaction Code: VL02N**

- If the system is configured to create an account document, you may see a document with a line item just opposite from the account document you generated while shipping the material to the customer site as consignment material.

5.8 Cross-Company-Code Sales Processing

Process Overview

This business process is for the direct shipping of material from the vendor to the customer. In this case, the vendor is another company code of the same corporate entity.

This business case best suits a business environment where sales are made from a centralized sales organization, which is represented by a separate legal entity and manufacturing facilities are residing in different company codes.

In this process, when you create a sales order, you mention a plant that belongs to a different company code. Once the sales order is created and saved, the system runs MRP at the supplying plant level for material availability.

Based on the receiving plant sales order, the supplying plant creates an outbound delivery of the required material to the customer.

In the subsequent step, the supplying plant creates an inter-company billing document and the receiving plant creates a customer invoice to conclude the business process.

Advantages

With this type business process, you can avail the following advantages:

▪ You can reduce the material handling cost by reducing the multiple shipment and material handling

▪ Due to the direct shipment from supplying plant to the customer, you can reduce transit time

▪ In case of the centralized sales organization, one company code will be handling multiple plants, thus the corporate entity can avail the benefit of the specialized sales service.

Assumptions

To execute this business process, it has been assumed that you have implemented: (1) the sales and distribution module, (2) the material management module, and (3) the finance module of mySAP ERP Financials.

Pre-Requisite

In this business process, the following master data records are used:

▪ **G/L Master Records:**

- AS10000010 – Material Stock Account

- AS10000101 – Incoming check clearing account

- AS10000200 – Inter company AR / AP (C100)

- AS10000201 – Inter company AR / AP (C200)

- EX10000201 – Cost of goods sold – External Sales

▪ **Customer Master Records:**

- C100000000 – My customer

■ **Material Master Records:**

• M100000000 – Material for finished goods

Business Case

A Canadian (company code C100) company manufactures farming equipment and sells its product through a centralized sales organization (company code C200). From a legal point of view, both are treated as legal entities. Company code C200 is a manufacturing unit and does not carry out sales activity.

The sales organization of company code C200 receives a sales order from its customer. To fulfill the customer order, company C200 passes the sales order information to the manufacturing unit called company code C100. While creating the sales order, the sales organization mentions the supplying plant, which is C200.

The supplying plant directly dispatches the material to the customer and raises an inter-company invoice for company code C200.

Company code C200 bills its customer C100000000 for materials supplied by the manufacturing plant of company code C100.

Process Flow

Figure 5.13 depicts the cross-company code sales order process data flow and the steps involved.

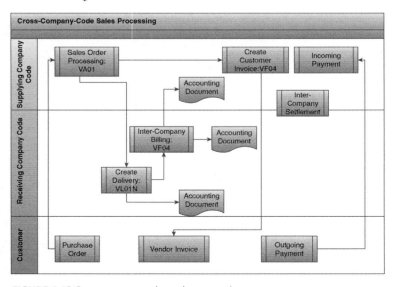

FIGURE 5.13 Cross-company sales order processing.

Process Steps

Table 5.7 depicts the process steps involved in this business process scenario. You can see the dependencies between these steps.

TABLE 5.7 Cross-Company Code Sales Process Steps

Process Step	R / O	Modules	T. Code	Expected Results
1. Sales Order Processing	R	SD	VA01	Sales order has been created by company code C200
2. Create Delivery	R	Logistics	VL01N	Delivery document has been created by company code C100
3. Create Customer Invoice	R	SD	VF04	Customer has been billed for material by company code C200
4. Intercompany Billing	R	SD	VF04	Company code C100 has created an intercompany billing document and financial document posted in both company codes

5.8.1 Sales Order Processing

- The sales organization receives a purchase order from the customer and consequently creates a sales order for the sale of material. While creating the sales order, you will key the supplying company code.

- Use the following menu paths to perform this step:

  - **SAP ECC Menu: SAP Menu → Logistics → Sales and Distribution → Sales → Order → Create.**

  - **Transaction Code: VA01**

- This sales order initiates an MRP run in the supplying plant. Depending on the availability of material at the plant of company code C100, the system determines the source of the material to be supplied.

- Company code C200 received a purchase from its customer C100000000 – My Customer for supply of material M100000000 – Material for finished goods.

5.8.2 Create Delivery

- In the delivery process, the system checks the availability of the material and completes the material delivery process. Material delivery process has already been discussed in number of occasions in our previous business process scenarios.

- Use the following menu paths to perform this step:

- **SAP ECC Menu: Logistics → Logistics Execution → Outbound Process → Goods Issue for Outbound Delivery → Outbound Delivery → Create → Single Document → With Reference to Sales Order**

- **Transaction Code: VL01N**

■ The material delivery process creates a material document and a financial document. The system creates the following account line items:

- AS10000010 – Material Stock Account

- EX10000202 – Cost of goods sold – Internal Sales

5.8.3 Create Customer Invoice

■ Once the material is shipped by the supplying plant to the customer, you can bill your customer based on the delivery document created by the supplying plant. In the billing process, the system creates an SD document as well as a financial document.

■ Use the following menu paths to perform this step:

- **SAP ECC Menu: SAP Menu → Logistics → Sales and Distribution → Billing → Billing Document → Process Billing Due List**

- **Transaction Code: VF04**

■ Depending on the revenue account determination, the system creates financial account entries.

■ Company code C200 created a customer billing document for material supplied by company code C100. Based on the output determination configuration, the system generates the billing document output. Refer to your output determination configuration via transaction code: **V/43** or menu path: IMG → Sales and Distribution → Basic Functions → Output Control → Output Determination → Output Determination Using the Condition Technique → Maintain Output Determination for Sales Documents → Assign Output Determination Procedures → Allocate Sales Document Header. The simplest account entries of this step are:

- Dr.   C100000000 – My Customer

- Cr.   IN10000000 – Sale Proceeds

5.8.4 Intercompany Billing

■ In our previous steps, the customer has been billed for the material supplied by the manufacturing facility of another company code. Now the supplying plant company code initiates an intercompany billing document for the receiving plant/sales organization. SAP comes with document type "IV" pre-delivered document type for intercompany billing, however, you can create your own document type for intercompany billing.

■ Use the following menu paths to perform this step:

- **SAP ECC Menu: SAP Menu → Logistics → Sales and Distribution → Billing → Billing Document → Process Billing Due List**

- **Transaction Code: VF04**

■ Now the question is how the system will determine who should be debited for the material. The system determines the internal customer based on the configuration you have through transaction code: SPRO or the menu path: IMG → Sales and Distribution → Billing → Inter-Company Billing → Define Internal Customer Number By Sales Organization for sales organization of supplying company code and its assignment to the internal customer, i.e. receiving company code. The inter-company billing process creates an accounting document in both the supplying company code and the receiving company code. Refer to transaction code: **WEL1** or menu path: Sales and Distribution → Billing → Intercompany Billing → Automatic Posting to Vendor Account (SAP-EDI) → Assign Vendor for automatic internal vendor determination.

■ Company code C100 created an intercompany billing document. Due to the internal vendor and internal customer configuration, the system posted an account document in company code C100 and company code C200. The system created the following accounting entries in company code C100:

- Dr.   AS10000201 – Inter company AR/AP (C200)

- Cr.   IN10000000 – Sale Proceeds

■ In company code C200:

- EX10000201 – Cost of goods sold – External Sales

- AS10000200 – Inter company AR/AP (C100)

■ You can view the inter-company billing document via transaction code: VF03 or menu path: Logistics → Sales and Distribution → Billing → Billing Document → Display. To view the account document you can navigate through the billing document or transaction code: FB03 or menu path: Accounting → Financial Accounting → General Ledger → Document → Display

■ This business comes to an end after the settlement of internal due to and due from accounts and customer incoming payments to the receiving plant. These two steps can be handled as vendor outgoing payments and customer incoming payments, which are already covered in our other business process scenarios. Figure 5.14 depicts the accounting entries that have been generated in various steps.

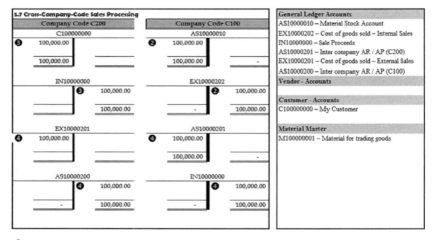

● Is the step number of the business process

FIGURE 5.14 Accounting entries.

5.9 Sales from Stock with SD Credit Management

Process Overview

In this business process scenario, you will learn the standard sales process where sales are made to the customer from the stock where SD credit control is active. In these business scenarios, we will cover all the important steps and a few optional steps to accomplish end-to-end scenarios.

This process starts with the enterprise's response to the customer's request for quotation subsequently converting the request for quotation to a sales order. During the sales order process, there are various events that take place such as availability checking, pricing conditions, and customer credit history. Finally, the material is delivered to the customer and the customer is billed for the material. To conclude this transaction, the customer pays the invoice.

Assumptions

- Material management, sales and distribution, credit control, and FI module are in use.

- There is enough stock available to fulfill the sales order.

Pre-Requisite

In this business process we will use the following master data. Before proceeding further, ensure that:

- C100000000 – My Customer

- IN10000000 – Sale Proceeds

- EX10000201 – Cost of goods sold – External Sales

- AS10000010 – Material Stock Account

- M100000000 – Material for finished goods (Material Master)

Business Case

Company code C100 receives the request for a quote for the supply of material M100000000 from customer C100000000. In response to the buyer request for quotation, company code C100 transmits quotation to customer C100000000. Customer C100000000 does the necessary price comparison and places a purchase order with company code C100. After receiving the purchase order, company code C100 creates the sales order. Due to the market credit risk, company code C100 has implemented an SD credit control. While creating the sales order, the system checks customer liability against the predefined credit limit.

As per company code C100's business practice, if the customer's total items fall within the credit limit, including the current sales order, the system releases the sales order for the subsequent delivery. If customer liability crosses the credit limit, the system blocks the sales order for further investigation.

Once the credit manager is satisfies with the customer liability, he approves the sales order by way of releasing the sales order.

Once the sales order is confirmed, the system generates picking slips for material M100000000 and the warehouse clerk stages the material M100000000 for outbound delivery.

To conclude the sales and distribution process, the system generates a billing document and the customer remits the money to complete the sales cycle.

Process Flow

Figure 5.15 shows the data flow and inter dependency of various process steps and how the data flows from one module to another.

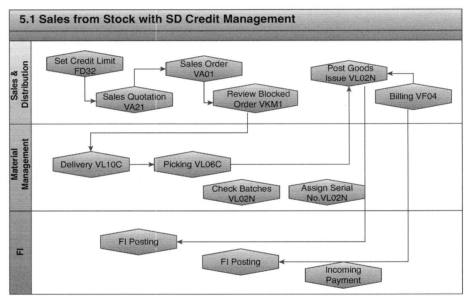

FIGURE 5.15 Sales from stock with SD credit management.

Process Steps

In Table 5.8, you will learn about the various steps involved in the end-to-end sales cycle. The complete end-to-end process involves the handoff between sales and distribution, material management, and FI modules. As mySAP ERP is an integrated application, the data flows from one module to another to accomplish the business processes. This business process may be simpler or complex depending on the business environment and the general business practice. Table 5.8 considers the commonly adopted process steps in the SAP environment.

TABLE 5.8 Sales from Stock with SD Credit Management: Process Steps

Process Step	R / O	Modules	T. Code	Expected Results
1. Set Credit Limit	R	SD	FD32	Credit Limit for customer C100000000 has been set for credit control area
2. Sales Quotation	O	SD	VA21	Sales quotation has been created
3. Sales Order Entry	R	SD	VA01	Sales Order has been created
4. Review Blocked Sales Orders	R	SD	VKM1	Sales order has been released from credit control block
5. Delivery Creation	R	SD	VL10C	Delivery is created. The system has created a material document
6. Picking (optional)	O	SD	VL02N	Material is picked and staged for shipment
7. Check Batches	O	SD	VL02N	Ensuring whether batch numbers are assigned or not
8. Assign Serial Numbers	O	SD	VL02N	Serial number is assigned
9. Post Goods Issue	R	SD	VL06O	The goods issue is posted. This creates SD and FI documents
10. Billing	R	SD	VF04	Customer has been billed for material delivered and the system has created SD and FI documents
11. Incoming Payment	FI	FI	F-28	Customer incoming payment processed and customer open items has been cleared

5.9.1 Set a Credit Limit

■ In this step, you will maintain credit for a customer. mySAP ERP Financials provides two credit limits: (1) total amount: this limit is the maximum credit for all credit control areas and (2) individual limit: the monetary limit specific to a credit control area. Here you can see the credit utilization of business partner. Use the following menu paths to perform this step:

- **SAP Menu Path: Accounting → Financial Accounting → Accounts Receivable → Credit Management → Master Data → Change**

- **Transaction Code: FD32**

■ If you don't maintain the credit limit in this transaction code, the system defaults the credit limit from the credit control areas. The output of this activity is setting the credit limit for customer C100000000 to $120,000.00.

5.9.2 Sales Quotation Entry

- Sales quotation is a document that depicts the material cost and other terms and conditions to the prospective buyer of the goods and services. In this step, you create a sales quotation after receiving the request for a quote from the customer. A sales quotation can be created with reference to an existing inquiry or from another quotation. The sales quote contains the material and quantity to be supplied, and other terms and conditions of the sale. Use the following menu paths to perform this step:

  - **SAP Menu Path: Logistics → Sales and Distribution → Sales → Quotation → Create**

  - **Transaction Code: VA21**

- Company code C100 received a request for a quote from customer C100000000 for material M100000000. Since company code C100 deals with other customers for material M100000000, company code C100 created a sales order with reference to another quotation. Depending on the configuration, the sales quotation can be transmitted to the customer through either fax, mail, or EDI. You can display the sales quote through Transaction Code: **VA23**. Sometimes the customer may reject a sales quote fully or partially. You can reject a sales order through Transaction Code: **VA22**.

- Proceed to next step, assuming that customer C100000000 has approved the quote of company code C100 for material M100000000.

5.9.3 Sales Order Entry

- A sales order is a binding contract between the seller and the purchaser towards the supply of specific materials and services in a specific period of time. While creating the sales order, the system validates the material's availability, pricing, MRP planning, delivery scheduling, shipping point, and credit limit check.

- The system copies and proposes various pieces of information from the material and customer master information to the sales order, which reduces sales data entry activities. The system determines the sales area and shipping point from "sold to parties" or "ship to parties" of the customer master records:

- **SAP Menu Path: Logistics → Sales and Distribution → Sales → Order → Create**

- **Transaction Code: VA01**

▪ Assuming that company code C100 has sufficient stock to fulfill the sales order, it creates a sales order for material M100000000.

▪ Assuming that the customer has other open items while creating this sales order and including this sales order, the customer payable amount crosses the pre-defined credit limit. The system blocks the sales order for further processing. In the next step, you will learn how to release a blocked sales order.

▪ mySAP ERP Financials provides functionality to change sales order (Transaction Code: **VA02**), display (Transaction Code: **VA03**).

5.9.4 Review Blocked Sales Orders

▪ In order to have control over receivables, the system checks the credit utilization of a customer at various points in time. If an activity fails the credit check, the system blocks the activity for further processing. You can configure the system behavior and credit check points in the credit management module.

▪ The credit manager can review, release, or reject a sales order after careful analysis of the business case. In this activity credit manager can: (1) release the sales and distribution document, (2) reject the credit and cancel the sales and distribution document, (3) forward the blocked sales and distribution document to another processor, and (4) recheck the blocked sales and distribution document.

- **SAP Menu Path: Logistics → Sales and Distribution → Credit Management → Exceptions → Blocked SD Documents**

- **Transaction Code: VKM1**

▪ After careful analysis of the sales order and customer open items, the credit manager of C100 releases the sales order for further processing.

5.9.5 Delivery Processing

▪ In this activity, after the sales order is analyzed and depending on the availability of stock, the system creates a delivery document. The delivery process initiates the picking process for the confirmed order. In case of insufficient stock, the system doesn't confirm delivery and therefore, the system doesn't start the picking process.

■ In the delivery process, you can change the delivery date or you can consolidate several sales orders, which can be delivered in a single delivery.

- **SAP Menu Path: Logistics → Logistic Execution → Outbound Process → Goods Issue for Outbound Delivery → Outbound Delivery → Create → Collective Processing of Documents Due for Delivery → Sales Order Items**

- **Transaction Code: VL10C**

■ In this business scenario, it has been assumed that company code C100 maintains sufficient stock to fulfill the customer's order. The warehouse clerk of company code C100 schedules the delivery of material M100000000. The system creates a delivery document, which instructs the warehouse clerk to isolate the material for outbound delivery.

■ In case of batch management, the system creates a batch and assign the batch numbers.

5.9.6 Picking

■ The picking process involves taking the material listed in the delivery document and placing it in the right place so that the material can be shipped to the customer. Depending on the business process, the picking process may involve labeling and a performance test, if necessary. The picking process creates the picking transfer orders. You can create a picking transfer order through either the subsequent-function update-mode of the outbound delivery or the delivery monitor.

■ The delivery monitor provides information about completed deliveries and uncompleted deliveries. Through the delivery monitor, you can monitor inbound as well as outbound deliveries.

■ In this step, the delivery monitor is used to create a transfer order:

- **SAP Menu Path: Logistics → Sales and Distribution → Shipping and Transportation → Outbound Delivery → Lists and Logs → Outbound Delivery Monitor**

- **Transaction Code: VL06O**

■ At the end of this process, the warehouse clerk of company code C100 will have a picking list for the material that has been requested in the delivery document.

5.9.7 Check Batches

▪ In this step, you can confirm the batch number assignment to the material line items. This is an optional step and is only valid if batch management is active.

- **SAP Menu Path: Logistics → Sales and Distribution → Shipping and Transportation → Outbound Delivery → Change → Single Document**

- **Transaction Code: VL02N**

▪ The warehouse clerk has verified batch numbers.

5.9.8 Assign Serial Numbers

▪ The serial number is used to identify a product and provide an overview of material you have sold. You can use the serial number for a number of business reasons among of which are:

- You can use the serial number for a service contact, which helps you to identify the material for which you are providing service.

- For a customer return, to ensure that the customer is returning the material supplied by you.

▪ This step is optional and applicable if you have activated the serial number management. The system assigns the serial number while creating the delivery document. The purpose of this step is to ensure that the serial number is assigned to the material scheduled for delivery.

- **SAP Menu Path: Logistics → Sales and Distribution → Shipping and Transportation → Outbound Delivery → Change → Single Document**

- **Transaction Code: VL02N**

▪ The warehouse clerk has confirmed serial numbers.

5.9.9 Post Goods Issue

▪ After the picking process, the material will be shipped to the customer from the warehouse. In the post goods issue step, you will record such material movement.

▪ You can post goods issue:

- For individual outbound delivery

- For several outbound deliveries as collective processing

- For several outbound deliveries in background processing

- **SAP Menu Path: Logistics → Logistics Execution → Outbound Process → Goods Issue for Outbound Delivery → Outbound Delivery → Lists and Logs → Outbound Delivery Monitor**

- **Transaction Code: VL06O**

  Or

- **Menu path: Logistics → Sales and Distribution → Shipping and Transportation → Post Goods Issue → Outbound Delivery Single Document**

- **Transaction Code: VL02N**

■ The outbound deliveries form the basis of the goods issue posting. The data required for the goods issue posting is copied from the outbound deliveries described previously.

■ Once you post a goods issue for an outbound delivery, the system carries out the following activities on the basis of the goods issue document:

- Warehouse stock of the material is reduced by the delivery quantity

- Value changes are posted to the balance sheet account in inventory accounting

- Requirements are reduced by the delivery quantity

- The serial number status is updated

■ In this process, the system generates a delivery document, which in turn creates an FI document. Normally, the following accounting entries occur in FI:

- Dr.   EX10000201 – Cost of goods sold – External Sales

- Cr.   AS10000010 – Material Stock Account

■ The warehouse clerk of company code C100 posted a goods issue of material M100000000 as part of the sales process. Based on the account determination of transaction BSX, the inventory is credited, while transaction GBB offset entry is debited. Refer to transaction code OBYC or menu path: for material management account determination.

5.9.10 Billing

- Billing is an activity in the sales and distribution process where you are making another liable to pay for the goods and services. This is the last stage of the sales and distribution module. In this step, company code C100 will bill customer C100000000 for material M100000000. At the end of this activity, the system will generate an SD document called a billing document and an FI document. The billing process can be initiated individually when you enter any of the reference numbers like sales order or delivery document. You can also call up a function that will display the list delivery document due for billing. In this step, we will call billing due list:

  - **SAP Menu Path: Logistics → Sales and Distribution → Billing → Billing Document → Process Billing Due List**

  - **Transaction Code: VF04**

- Once the billing document is created, the system will generate a corresponding FI document, which in turn creates a customer open item. The customer open item can be cleared through either an incoming payment, against a down payment, or against a vendor open item (if customer is also a vendor). After this step, the FI module comes into picture to collect the receivable from the customer.

- The billing document creates an FI document. Normally, an FI document contains the following line items.

  - Dr.   C100000000 – My Customer

  - Cr.   IN10000000 – Sale Proceeds

- The accounts receivable department of company code C100 runs a daily billing due list to the bill customer. Once the billing document is created, it can be transmitted to the customer in various ways, as per the business practice.

5.9.11 Posting Incoming Payment

- In the incoming payment process, you record the customer payment toward the material or services you sold to the customer. The incoming customer payment clears the customer open items and allows cash discounts, if any:

- **SAP Menu Path: Accounting → Financial Accounting → Accounts Receivable → Document Entry → Incoming Payments**

- **Transaction Code: F-28**

▪ The accounts receivable department of company code C100 records the incoming customer payment and clears the customer open items. The incoming payment generates the following accounting entries:

  - AS10000101 – Incoming Check Clearing Account

  - C100000000 – My Customer

▪ Figure 5.16 depicts the summarized accounting entries that the system has generated while processing the steps listed above.

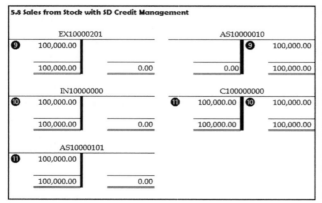

●   Is the step number of the business process

FIGURE 5.16 Accounting entries.

5.10 External Outgoing Payment (In-House Cash Center)

Process Overview

In this business process, you will learn how you can use the in-house cash functionality of mySAP ERP Financials to make the payment to the supplier of the material and services. This scenario fits best when a corporation has multiple subsidiaries and cash is being managed at the head office. The subsidiary company deals with the vendors/suppliers for the purchase of material and services during the day-to-day transactions. However, the payment is done by the shared service department, which handles the centralized payment.

The process starts at the subsidiary with the posting of the vendor invoice. Subsequently, the subsidiary runs a payment run, which clears the vendor open items with a payment document and generates a payment request in the form of IDOCs instead of checks.

IDOCs are transmitted to an in-house cash center (IHC), where payment requests are processed via a payment run. A payment run at IHC generates a real payment for vendors.

Periodically, IHC generates an internal bank statement, which creates an inter-company payable and receivable in IHC and in the subsidiary.

Assumptions

You have activated the financial supply chain component of mySAP ERP Financials.

Pre-Requisite

▪ You need the following master records in the subsidiary company code:

- EX10000101 – My IT Expenses

- LI10000300 – IHC account

- AS10000302 – IHC/AP (C200)

- V100000001 – My Supplier for IT

▪ You need the following master records in the head office company code:

- AS10000401 – Clears account for clearing partner

- AS10000402 – Current account subsidiary (C100)

- AS10000403 – IHC cash payment clearing account

- AS10000404 – Outgoing IHC clearing account

- AS10000405 – In-house cash receivable/payable account

Business Case

Company code C100 is a subsidiary of company code C200. Company code C200 provides shared services for other subsidiaries, including company code C100. These shared services include managing centralized purchasing, centralized payment, and IT services. For effective cash management, company code C200 uses the in-house cash functionality. All payment of subsidiaries are processed and paid through in-house cash.

Company code C100 purchases materials and services from various suppliers, such as V100000001. Company code C100 periodically runs a payment run in order to generate a payment request for in-house cash. Every Friday, in-house cash center converts these payment requests into payment through another payment run at the in-house cash center. On Friday, checks and wire payments are transmitted to vendors including vendor V100000001.

The treasury department of company code C200 generates an internal bank statement. The internal bank statement is processed at the in-house cash as well as the subsidiary, which clears open items in the clearing account, and clears open items in inter-company receivable and payable accounts.

Process Flow

Figure 5.17 depicts the subsidiary, in-house cash center, and head office data flow and accounting documents being generated. In our landscape, the in-house cash center resides in the head office company code, which is a different legal entity from the subsidiary.

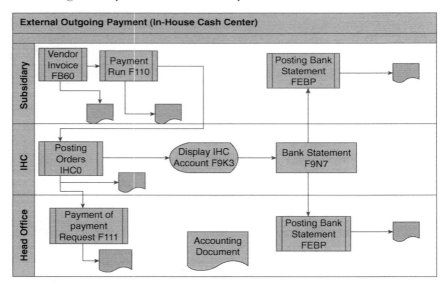

FIGURE 5.17 In-house cash data flow.

Process Steps

You will go through all the steps listed in the following table to complete this business scenario. This business scenario may be much simpler or complex depending on the modules in use, assignment authorization objects assigned to the processor, and business practice.

TABLE 5.9 External Outgoing Payment (IHC) Process Steps

Process Step	R / O	Modules	T. Code	Expected Results
1. Vendor Invoice Posting	R	FI	FB60	Vendor invoice has been posted and accounting document created in company code C100
2. Outgoing Payment	R	FI	F110	Vendor open item cleared and payment order generated by company code C100
3. Posting Payment Orders	R	FSCM	IHC0	Payment order posted at In-House Cash Center. IHC resides in company code C200
4. Payment of Payment Request	R	FI	F111	Payment orders are paid by IHC center, which resides in company C200
5. Displaying IHC Account Balance	R	FSCM	F9K3	In house cash balance confirmation
6. Creating Bank Statement	R	FSCM	F9N7	Bank statement generated at IHC
7. Posting Bank Statement	R	FSCM	FEBP	Bank statement posted

5.10.1 Vendor Invoice Posting

- In this business scenario this is the first step that initiates the business process flow. In order to record purchases you have made from external vendors, you invoke this transaction:

  - **SAP Menu Path: Accounting → Financial Accounting → Accounts Payable → Document Entry → Invoice**

  - **Transaction Code: FB60**

- In order to facilitate the IT enhancement requirement, company code C100 engaged vendor V100000001 to IT services. Vendor V100000001 periodically bills company code C100 for services rendered. In this step, company code C100 records these IT services. At the end this step, the system generates the following accounting entries:

  - Dr.   EX10000101 – My IT Expenses

  - Cr.   V100000001 – My Supplier for IT

5.10.2 Outgoing Payment

- In the outgoing payment process, you initiate the payment process for a vendor payment. You can initiate the payment process either through a manual process or an automatic process. The outgoing payment can be check, ACH, wire, or bills of exchange. In this scenario, it has been decided to pay the vendor through an automatic payment process:

- **SAP Menu Path: Accounting → Financial Accounting → Accounts Payable → Periodic Processing → Payments**

- **Transaction Code: F110**

▪ The outcome of this process is a payment document that clears the vendor's open items and creates payment advice for the in-house cash center. Since the ultimate payment to the vendor will be made through in-house cash, in this step the system will generate payment requests as IDOCs for in-house cash centers.

▪ The accounts payable department of company code C100 periodically runs an automatic payment program. The automatic payment program clears the vendor's open items and generates a payment request for the in-house cash center through IDOCs through the payment document. These IDOCs are then transmitted to the IHC. In this step, the system generates the following accounting line items in company code C100.

- Dr.   V100000001 – My Supplier for IT

- Cr.   LI10000300 – In-house cash clearing account

▪ You can see IDOCs through transaction code WE02 with IDOC message type "PAYEXT."

5.10.3 Posting Payment Orders

▪ The IHC received the payment request that were created in the last step. In this IHC, the clerk displays the payment orders and posts these payment orders. These payment requests are posted to the current account of the subsidiary at the IHC.

- **SAP Menu Path: Accounting → Financial Supply Chain Management → In- House Cash → Account Management → IHC Payment Orders → Payment Order Browser**

- **Transaction Code: IHC0**

▪ In this step, when the IHC clerk processes the payment request, the system creates the following accounting entries in the IHC of the head office:

- Dr.   AS10000402 – Current Account Subsidiary (C100)

- Cr.   AS10000401 – Clears Account for Clearing Partner

- The IHC clerk of company code C200 processed the payment request of company code C100. The system debited the current account for the subsidiary account and credited the current account for the clearing account.

5.10.4 Payment of Payment Request

- In payment of the payment request step, you process the payment request for payment to the ultimate vendor. In this step the, system aggregates all payment requests received from all subsidiaries and generates a consolidated check for vendor:

  - **SAP Menu Path: Accounting → Financial Accounting → Banks → Outgoings → Automatic Payment → Payment Requests**

  - **Transaction Code: F111**

- In this step, the system generates the account document with following line items:

  - Dr. AS10000403 – IHC cash payment clearing account

  - Cr. AS10000404 – Outgoing IHC clearing account

- The IHC of company code C200 ran a payment run. The payment run picked all payments requested created and posted earlier and created a consolidated check for individual vendors.

5.10.5 Displaying IHC Account Balance

- In the previous step, you have seen that the IHC paid the payment requests that came from the subsidiaries. Now it is time for the IHC to inform the subsidiaries that the payment has been made on their behalf. In this step, the IHC clerk displays the account statement from the in-house cash prospective. This gives an overview of the money receivable by the in-house cash center from different subsidiaries.

  - **SAP Menu Path: Accounting → Financial Supply Chain Management → In- House Cash → Account → Display**

  - **Transaction Code: F9K3**

- This step is optional for the IHC. This step gives a comfort to the IHC clerk. In the subsequent step, the IHC clerk generates bank statements for subsidiaries.

5.10.6 Creating a Bank Statement

- In this step, you can generate a bank statement for the subsidiary. You need to post this bank statement to the IHC as well as the subsidiary. Based on your landscape you may perform one or more SAP or non-SAP steps to transmit the bank statement you generated in this step:

  - **SAP Menu Path: Accounting → Financial Supply Chain Management → In-House Cash → Periodic Processing → Bank Statement → New Run → Single Run**

  - **Transaction Code: F9N7**

- You can create a bank statement for one or more subsidiaries. If you want to create more than one bank statement, you can do so through transaction code F9N1.

- The IHC clerk of company code C200 generated the bank statement for subsidiary C100. As both company codes C200 and C100 reside in the same system, the system generated IDOC with the message type FINSTA transmitted to company code C100.

5.10.7 Posting a Bank Statement

- Once the bank statements are generated at the IHC, you need to post these bank statements to the head office and the subsidiary.

  - **SAP Menu Path: Accounting → Financial Supply Chain Management → Cash and Liquidity Management → Cash Management → Incomings → Electronic Bank Statement → Post**

  - **Transaction Code: FEBP**

- Once the bank statements are generated at the IHC, you need to post these bank statements to company code C200 and company code C100. This step will create an intercompany receivable and payable in company code C200 and company code C100. You will perform this step twice: one for the subsidiary company and another for the head office.

- In this step, the system creates the following accounting line item:

  - In company code C200

    - Cr.   AS10000403 – IHC cash payment clearing account

    - Dr.   AS10000200 – Inter company AR/AP (C100)

- In company code C100

    - Dr.   LI10000300 – IHC clearing account

    - Cr.   AS10000201 – Inter company AR / AP (C200)

■ In the earlier business scenario you learned how you can process external payments to vendors through the IHC.

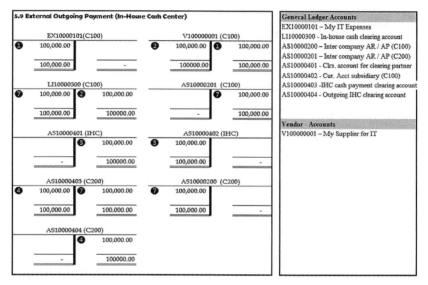

❶   Is the step number of the business process

FIGURE 5.18 Accounting entries.

5.11 External Incoming Payment (In-House Cash Center)

Process Overview

This business scenario covers the business process where the IHC that resides in the head office receives the customer payment on behalf of one or more subsidiaries. This business process best suits a case where the head office manages centralized cash and all incoming and outgoing payments are passed through IHC. The money received by the head office is initially posted to an IHC and then posted to a cash concentrated account. In order to reconcile the customer balance and the preparation of subsidiary financial statement, the IHC generates an internal bank statement in electronic format. These bank statements are processed in the head office as well as the subsidiary, which creates an inter-company payable and receivable in both the head office and subsidiary books.

Assumptions

You have activated the financial supply chain component of mySAP ERP Financials.

Pre-Requisite

▪ You need following the master records in subsidiary company code C100:

- IN10000001 – Sale Proceeds (Software)

- LI10000300 – IHC clearing account

- AS10000201 – Inter company AR/AP (C200)

- C100000000 – My Customer

▪ You need following the master records in head office company code C200:

- AS10000401 – Clears account for clearing partner

- AS10000402 – Current account for subsidiary

- AS10000020: In-house cash payment clearing account (a balance sheet account)

- AS10000406 – Incoming IHC clearing account

- AS10000405 – In-house cash receivable/payable account

Business Case

In the course of a normal day, company code C100's day-to-day business sales in-house developed software applications to various customers. For better cash management, company code C200 manages the cash of all subsidiary companies, including company code C100 through an IHC. For all sales made by the subsidiaries, the customer remits the payment to the head office.

The head office (IHC) operates a centralized bank account for all subsidiaries and all collections received by the head office are sent for collection. On the other side, the head office (IHC) generates bank statements for the subsidiaries.

All subsidiaries upload bank statements submitted by the IHC and clears the customer's open items.

Process Flow

Figure 5.19 shows the process flow for an external incoming payment with in-house cash. You can see how various components of an integrated application work together to achieve business objects.

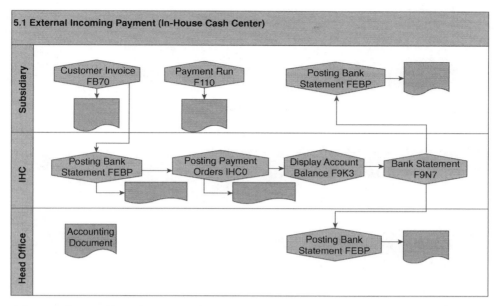

FIGURE 5.19 External incoming payment (IHC).

Process Steps

Table 5.10 outlines the various steps that you will perform in order to achieve our business requirement.

TABLE 5.10 External Incoming Payment (IHC) Process Steps

Process Step	R / O	Modules	T. Code	Expected Results
1. Customer Invoice Posting	R	FI	FB70	Company code C100 created customer invoice
2. Post the Bank Statement	R	FI	FEBP	IHC has posted bank statement for incoming payment
3. Posting of Payment Orders	R	FSCM	IHC0	In-house cash created payment orders
4. Displaying Account Balance at IHC	R	FSCM	F9K3	This is optional step. In this step you can view in-house cash balance
5. Creating Bank Statement	R	FSCM	F9N7	In-house cash center created bank statement
6. Posting Bank Statement	R	FSCM	FEBP	Bank statement has been posted at head office as well as subsidiary
7. Post Processing of Bank Statement	O	FSCM	FEBAN	Subsidiary does process processing in order to clear customer open items

5.11.1 Customer Invoice Posting

▪ This process starts at the posting of the customer invoice. When you sell your product to a customer, you book your income. Generally, if the sales and distribution module is in use, this step is not needed and FI will be posted from the sales and distribution application. With this step you will record your sale transaction:

• **SAP Menu Path: Accounting → Financial Accounting → Accounts Receivable → Document Entry → Invoice**

• **Transaction Code: FB70**

▪ At the end of this process, the system generates an account document with the following line items in subsidiary company code C100.

• Dr.   C100000000 – My Customer

• Cr.   IN10000001 – Sale Proceeds (Software)

▪ Company code C100 completed a sale of software with customer C100000000. To record the sale transaction, company code C100 debited the customer account and credited the sales income.

5.11.2 Post the Bank Statement

▪ In this step, you will post bank statements that you have received from your bank. This bank statement will be received as an IHC. It is assumed that you have a lock box setup with your banker. As per the subsidiaries directions, the customer transmits remittance to the bank's branch. At the end of the day, the bank transmits a file to the customer for the collection it has made.

• **SAP Menu Path: Accounting → Financial Supply Chain Management → Cash and Liquidity Management → Cash Management → Incomings → Electronic Bank Statement → Post**

• **Transaction Code: FEBP**

▪ IHC carries out these activities. Once the bank statements are posted, the system creates the following accounting line items:

• Cr.   AS10000406 – Incoming IHC clearing account

• Dr.   AS10000403 – IHC cash payment clearing account

▪ The IHC at company code C200 posted the bank statement that it has received from the bank. While importing the bank statement, the system debited the incoming cash clearing account by crediting the in-house cash clearing account.

5.11.3 Posting of Payment Orders

▪ Once the bank statement is posted, at the IHC, you need to generate a payment order. A payment order will be posted to the in-house cash current account maintained at the IHC for subsidiaries.

- **SAP Menu Path: Accounting → Financial Supply Chain Management → In-House Cash → Account Management → IHC Payment Orders → Payment Order Browser**

- **Transaction Code: IHC0**

▪ The system will post the following account line items in this step:

- Dr. AS10000401 – Clears account for clearing partner

- Cr. AS10000402 – Current Account for subsidiary (C100)

▪ The IHC at company code C200 in-house clerk displays the payment orders and posted the payment orders to in-house current accounts.

5.11.4 Displaying Account Balance at IHC

▪ This step is an optional step. In this step, in-house clerks overview the current accounts of subsidiaries, which give an idea about money receivable and payable by the IHCs from subsidiaries.

- **SAP Menu Path: SAP Menu Path: Accounting → Financial Supply Chain Management → In-House Cash → Account → Display**

- **Transaction Code: F9K3**

▪ This step doesn't generate any accounting documents. The IHC clerks display the account statement.

5.11.5 Creating a Bank Statement

▪ In our previous step, you learned the IHC received customer remittance from the customer and posted it in the IHC account. In this step, IHC creates internal bank statements for the subsidiaries. In the subsequent step, these internal bank statements will be posted to the subsidiaries and head office accounts.

- **SAP Menu Path: Accounting → Financial Supply Chain Management → In-House Cash → Periodic Processing → Bank Statement → New Run → Single Run**

- **Transaction Code: F9N7**

■ To pass on customer remittance information, IHC creates a bank statement and transmits it to subsidiary and head office accounts. This step doesn't generate accounting entries.

5.11.6 Posting of the Bank Statement

■ Once the IHC generates the bank statement, you need to post these statements in the subsidiary and head office. This posting creates a cross company receivable and payment in the books of the subsidiary account and head office.

- **SAP Menu Path: Accounting → Financial Supply Chain Management → Cash and Liquidity Management → Cash Management → Incomings → Electronic Bank Statement → Post**

- **Transaction Code: FEBP**

■ You need to perform this activity twice: (1) to post the bank statement in the subsidiary (2) to post the bank statement in the head office. At the end of this step, the system will generate following accounting entries:

- Subsidiary, Company code C100

  – Dr.   AS10000201 – Inter company AR/AP (C200)

  – Cr.   LI10000300 – In-house cash clearing account

- Head office, Company code C200

  – Dr.   AS10000406 – Incoming IHC clearing account

  – Cr.   AS10000200 – Inter company AR/AP (C100)

■ The treasury clerk of company code C100 and C200 processed the bank statement received from in-house cash. After these entries, the "Due to and Due from" accounts of both subsidiaries and head office are tied to each other.

5.11.7 Post Processing of the Bank Statement

■ This is the last step in this business scenario, where the account receivable clerk will perform the post processing. In the post processing step, the system will clear the customer open items by debiting the in-house cash clearing account:

- **SAP Menu Path: Accounting → Financial Supply Chain Management → Cash and Liquidity Management → Cash Management → Incomings → Electronic Bank Statement → Post process**

- **Transaction Code: FEBAN**

▪ The system creates the following account line items in subsidiaries to clear the customer account:

- Dr.   LI10000300 – In-house cash clearing account

- Cr.   C100000000 – My Customer

▪ Figure 5.20 summarizes the accounting entries generated while processing the previously-mentioned steps.

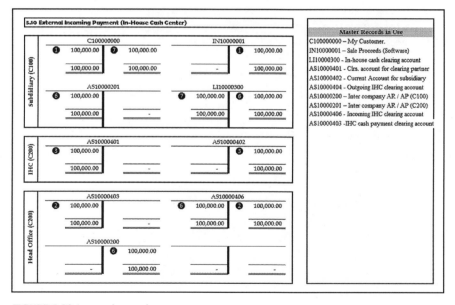

FIGURE 5.20 Accounting entries.

5.12 Internal Payments via In-House Cash Center

Process Overview

Very often one entity supplies its product and services to another entity of the same corporation. This type of transaction is called an inter-company transaction. Sooner or later inter-company transactions are settled between these units through either cash payment, services, or products.

In this business process scenario, you will study a case where one unit sells a product and services to another unit. The sales and purchases are recoded in different units, based on the customer and vendor invoices, and at the end of the month these transactions are settled with cash from the in-cash center.

Advantages

Without an IHC if you want to settle accounts between units, you need to write a check or make a wire transfer. Check and wire transfer involve bank fees for services provided by the bank. You can avoid these charges by making payment through the IHC. Other advantages of the in-cash center is that the unit doesn't need a real cash balance in its bank account to settle its due.

Assumptions

▪ Like other in-house cash you need to activate the financial supply chain component of mySAP ERP Financials.

▪ Sales and purchases in these business scenarios are handled through the finance module.

Pre-Requisite

To complete this business process scenario, you need the following master data for company code C100:

▪ AS10000407 – IHC account

▪ IN10000001 – Sale Proceeds (Software)

▪ LI10000300 – In-house cash clearing account

▪ C100000000 – My Customer

IHC reside in the head office and you have created the following master data:

IHC

▪ AS10000401 – Clears account for clearing partner

▪ AS10000402 – Current Account for subsidiary

Subsidiary company code C100 sells its products to subsidiary company code C200. You need the following master data for subsidiary company code C200:

Subsidiary – 2

- AS10000407 – IHC account

- EX10000101 – My IT Expenses

- LI10000300 – In-house cash clearing account

- V100000001 – My Supplier for IT

Business Case

Company code C100 provides IT services to company code C200. Both company code C100 and C200 belongs to the same corporate group. Company code C200 controls the centralized payment through in-house cash.

Company code C100 bills company code C200 for services it has provided, and in turn company code C200 remits payment to company code C100 through the IHC. The IHC acts as a virtual banker for both company code C100 and C200.

Process Flow

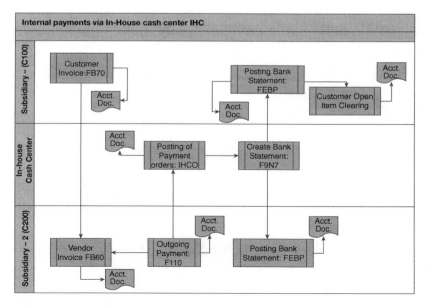

FIGURE 5.21 Internal payment via IHC.

Process Steps

Table 5.11 depicts all the steps required.

TABLE 5.11 Internal Payment via IHC Process Steps

Process Step	R / O	Modules	T. Code	Expected Results
1. Customer Invoice	R	FI	FB70	Customer invoice has been created in company code C100
2. Vendor Invoice	R	FI	FB60	Vendor invoice has been posted in company code C200
3. Outgoing Payment	R	FI	F110	Company code C200 has ran outgoing payment
4. Displaying and Posting of Payment Orders	R	FSCM	IHC0	Payment orders have been posted in IHC
5. Displaying Accounts	O	FSCM	F9K3	IHC has confirmed posting payment orders to subsidiaries clearing account
6. Creating a Bank Statement	R	FSCM	F9N7	IHC created bank statement for subsidiaries
7. Posting of the Bank Statement	R	FSCM	FEBP	Subsidiaries posted bank statement transmitted by in-house cash center

5.12.1 Customer Invoice

- In this business process scenario, posting the customer's incoming invoice is the starting point. With the sales and distribution model, you will get sales-related data from the sales and distribution module. In this business process, it has been assumed it is a non-SD related invoice. Normally in this type of situation, you will have for service-related billing. You can post the customer bill either: (1) using a separately incoming invoice or outgoing invoice or, (2) through inter-company posting. In this business process, it has been decided to post separately:

  - **SAP ECC Menu: Accounting → Financial Accounting → Accounts Receivable → Document Entry → Invoice**

  - **Transaction Code: FB70**

- Company code C100 posted a customer invoice through transaction code FB70 and transmitted the hard copy of the invoice to company code C200. The system has created the following account line items in company code C100:

- Dr.   C100000000 – My Customer

- Cr.   IN10000001 – Sale Proceeds (Software)

▣ Here customer C100000000 is subsidiary 2, i.e. company code C200. Company code will perform the vendor invoice posting in the subsequent step.

5.12.2 Vendor Invoice

▣ In our previous step, you have performed customer invoice posting. Now the information is available with the other subsidiary to perform a vendor invoice posting. You can automate this posting through either custom development or IDOCs. In this case, it has been assumed that you will receive a hard copy invoice for the services provided:

- **SAP ECC Menu: Accounting → Financial Accounting → Accounts Payable → Document Entry → Invoice**

- **Transaction Code: FB60**

▣ Company code C200 receives an invoice from company code C100 and posts a vendor invoice. In the vendor invoice posting, the system creates the following line items:

- Dr.   EX10000101 – My IT Expenses

- Cr.   V100000001 – My Supplier for IT

▣ Here you have treated vendor V100000001 as company code C100.

5.12.3 Outgoing Payment

▣ You have recoded liability for services received in our previous step. Through the outgoing payment processing, you can initiate payment processing for the vendor invoice. In this step, the system clears vendor open items and creates payment orders for IHC:

- **SAP ECC Menu: Accounting → Financial Accounting → Accounts Payable → Periodic Processing → Payments**

- **Transaction Code: F110**

▣ The accounts payable department of company code C200 initiated an outgoing payment for services provided by company code C100. In company code C200, the system created the following accounting entries, which clear the vendor outgoing payment:

- Dr.   V100000001 – My Supplier for IT

- Cr.   LI10000300 – In-house cash clearing account

■ This step doesn't create any check or ach wire file. Instead, this step creates two IDocs for the IHC with message type "PAYEXT." You can view IDocs via transaction code WE02.

5.12.4 Displaying and Posting Payment Orders

■ In the last step you created IDocs for the IHC. In this step, the treasury clerk can view IDocs that were transmitted to the IHC and post it to the subsidiary clearing account. This will be performed at IHCs:

- **SAP ECC Menu: Accounting → Financial Supply Chain Management → In-House Cash → Account Management → IHC Payment Orders → Payment Order Browser**

- **Transaction Code: IHC0**

■ In this process, the system posts to "due to" and "due from" in the subsidiaries. These entries are merely accounting entries where there is no movement of cash from one account to another account.

■ The IHC at company code C200 received IDocs that were generated in the previous step and posted to the subsidiary's clearing account. The system creates the following accounting entries at the IHC:

- Dr.   AS10000402 – Cur. Acct subsidiary (C100)

- Cr.   AS10000408 – Cur. Acct subsidiary (C200)

5.12.5 Displaying Accounts

■ This step is optional, but it is advisable before you create a bank statement for the subsidiary you check the account statement of the subsidiary. In our last step, you processed the payment orders from the subsidiary. This step will ensure that you have posted all payment orders successfully and the due to and due from subsidiaries tie to each other:

- **SAP ECC Menu: Accounting → Financial Supply Chain Management → In-House Cash → Account → Display**

- **Transaction Code: F9K3**

■ The treasury clerk of the IHC ensured that due to subsidiary company code C100 ties with the due from company code C200.

5.12.6 Creating a Bank Statement

■ In this step, you will create a bank statement for the subsidiaries. As a bank statement is needed for each subsidiary, you need to execute this transaction twice per company code. In fact, this step doesn't generate any account entries. This step creates IDocs with message type "FINSTA" for subsidiaries:

- **SAP ECC Menu: Accounting → Financial Supply Chain Management → In-House Cash → Periodic Processing → Bank Statement → New Run → Single Run**

- **Transaction Code: F9N7**

■ SAP provides transaction code F9N1 for the mass creation of bank statements. This step will be carried on by the IHC to generate bank statements for subsidiaries.

5.12.7 Posting the Bank Statement

■ In last step, you generated bank statements for the subsidiaries. Now the subsidiaries need to post the bank statements transmitted by IHC. You can execute this step individually for each company code or process them through a batch job.

■ It has been decided here to process the bank statements manually. You need to carry out this step twice, one time per company code.

■ In the case of the paying subsidiary, the system will post to the in-house clearing account by creating a liability for IHC.

■ While for the receiving company code, the system will create customer open items by creating an account receivable from IHC:

- **SAP ECC Menu: Accounting → Financial Supply Chain Management → Cash and Liquidity Management → Cash Management → Incomings → Electronic Bank Statement → Post**

- **Transaction Code: FEBP**

■ Company code C100 processed the bank statements transmitted by the IHC and the system generated the following line items for company code C100:

- Dr.   AS10000407 – IHC account

- Cr.   LI10000300 – In-house cash clearing account

- Dr.   LI10000300 – In-house cash clearing account

- Cr.   C100000000 – My Customer

▪ Company code C200 processed the bank statements transmitted by the IHC and the system generated the following line items for company code C200:

- Cr.   AS10000407 – IHC account

- Dr.   LI10000300 – In-house cash clearing account

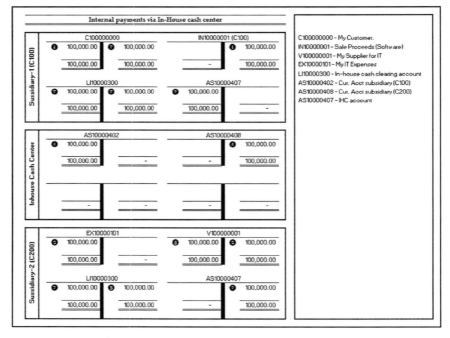

FIGURE 5.22 Internal payments.

5.13 Lock Box Process

Process Overview

Lock box service is provided by a bank to its customer for processing incoming checks or payments from a customer. In this process, the customer remits the payment to a designated post box number that is owned or maintained by the bank. At a scheduled time, the bank collects all payments collected at the lock box and processes the incoming payments.

At the agreed time, the bank transmits the information to its customer regarding the remittance it has received.

The information in this file transmitted by the bank is matched to the accounts receivable information in the R/3 system to clear the payments against the open items.

Assumptions

It has been assumed that you have implemented mySAP ERP Financials and properly configured the lock box set up.

Pre-Requisite

To complete this business, you need the following master data before posting the transaction:

- C100000000 – My Customer. Customer master data
- IN10000001 – Sale Proceeds (Software). Sales revenue account
- AS10000103 – Lock Box Clearing Account. Lock box clearing account
- AS10000101 – Incoming check clearing account. Incoming cash clearing account

Business Case

Company code C100 is a heavy equipment manufacturer and has a large customer base. In order to expedite the customer collection process it has set up a lock box at its bank. While invoicing to customers, company code C100 directs its customer's remit payment to the designated lock box maintained by the bank. Every morning, the bank collects all customer remittances from the lock box and processes these remittances.

At the end of the day, the bank transmits a feed to company code C100 containing the customer's remittances.

Company code C100 processes the file received from bank and clears customer open items.

Process Flow

Figure 5.23 depicts the process flow in the lock box process business scenarios. In this process, the customer remits payment to the lock box and processes these customer remittances. At the end of the day, the seller receives a file from the bank for remittances received from the customer. The seller processes the file and clears customer open items.

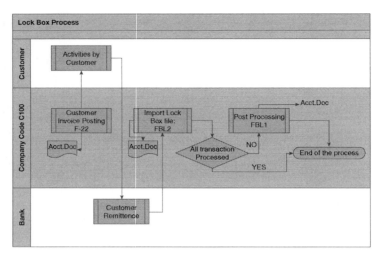

FIGURE 5.23 Lock box process.

Process Steps

Table 5.12 depicts the process steps and the expected result from each process step.

TABLE 5.12 Lock Box Process: Process Steps

Process Step	R / O	Modules	T. Code	Expected Results
Customer invoice posting	R	FI	F-22	Customer invoice has been processed
Import the lock box file	R	FI	FBL2	Lock box file has been imported
Post processing	R	FI	FBL1	Unprocessed transaction has been processed manually
Display document	O	FI	FB03	Document has been reviewed

5.13.1 Customer Invoice

■ In the business process scenarios, posting a customer invoice is the first step. If you are working in an environment where the sales and distribution application is in use, customer invoices are posted through sales and distribution modules. In this business, it is considered a non-integrated invoice posting.

- **SAP ECC Menu: Accounting → Financial Accounting → Accounts Receivable → Document Entry → Invoice-General**

- **Transaction Code: F-22**

■ In this case, you are posting a customer invoice that is not related to the sales and distribution module, such as fees for service rendered.

- Company code C100 also renders services for equipment sold to its customer as part of an annual maintenance contract. Periodically, it bills customers for maintenance activities. In this step, the system generates the following accounting entries:

  - Dr.   C100000000 – My Customer. A customer master data

  - Cr.   IN10000001 – Sale Proceeds. Revenue account

- Once the customer is billed, the customer remits payment to the designated post box on or before the due date. The bank collects and processes these customer payments. At the end of the day, the bank transmits a file (normally a BAI or BAI2 file) to company code C100.

5.13.2 Import the Lockbox Files

- Once you have received the BAI file you need to import the BAI file into the SAP application. Once imported, the system formats the file as per the desired SAP file structure and starts processing. In this step, the system generates a G/L and a customer posting. Based on the available information in the BAI file and the search result, the system clears the customer open items:

  - **SAP ECC Menu: Accounting → Financial Accounting → Banks → Incomings → Lockbox → Import**

  - **Transaction Code: FLB2**

- Once the file is available in the application servers, the accounts receivable clerk of company code C100 performs this activity. The system creates a background G/L posting and clears the customers open items. In this activity, the system generates the following accounting entries:

  - Dr.   AS10000101 – Incoming Check Clearing Account

  - Cr.   AS10000103 – Lock Box Clearing Account

  - Dr.   AS10000103 – Lock Box Clearing Account

  - Cr.   C100000000 – My Customer

5.13.3 Post Processing

- Sometimes, due to the lack of proper information, the system may not be able to process all of the incoming payments. In these circumstances, the system only creates a G/L posting and the customer collection remains in the lock box clearing account as unapplied cash. Periodically, you need manually clear the unapplied cash based on additional information. This manual clearing process is called post processing:

- **SAP ECC Menu: Accounting → Financial Accounting → Banks → Incomings → Lockbox → Post Processing**
- **Transaction Code: FLB1**

▪ Based on your experience, you can set a time frame to review the lock box-processing log and perform the post processing activities. When this is done, the system generates the following accounting entries:

- Dr.   AS10000103 – Lock Box Clearing Account
- Cr.   C100000000 – My Customer

5.13.4 Display Document

▪ In this step, you can display financial documents to see and ensure that all postings are made and the accounts are updated correctly. This is optional step:

- **SAP ECC Menu: Accounting → Financial Accounting → Accounts Receivable → Document → Display**
- **Transaction Code: FB03**

▪ Figure 5.24 summarizes the account entries that the system generated while processing the previous steps.

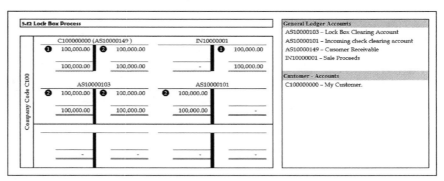

○ Is the step number of the business process

FIGURE 5.24 Accounting entries.

5.14 Bills of Exchange Receivable

Process Overview

A bill of exchange is a written order by one drawer to his bank to pay the bearer of the specified document and specific amount on or after the specific date mentioned in the document. Normally a bill of exchange consists of three parts: (1) the drawer, (2) the drawee, and (3) the payee. The drawer is the party who draws the bill of exchange for the customer. The drawee is the person who is ordered to normally pay the customer's banker. The payee is the person who is going to receive the ultimate money, i.e. the supplier or vendor. Generally, bills of exchange are used in international trade.

On or before the specified day, the payee presents the bills of exchange to the drawee for payment. Upon the presentation of the bill of exchange, the drawee pays the specified amount mentioned in the bill of exchange and later collects the money from the drawer.

Bills of exchange are used as a source for short term financing. The customer clears its vendor open items by drawing bills of exchange in favor of the vendor. Once the bill of exchange is received by the vendor, the vendor can: (1) wait and present the bills of exchange to the customer's banker for encashment, or (2) discount bills of exchange with the vendor's banker.

If the vendor discounts the bill of exchange with its banker, the vendor's banker presents the bill of exchange to the drawer on the specified day.

In this business process, you will learn a business process where you sell your material to the customer. Instead of money, the customer draws a bill of exchange in favor of you.

To keep you money flow intact, you discount those bills of exchange with your banker. In turn, your banker presents the bills of exchange to the customer's banker on the specific day.

Assumptions

It has been assumed that you have already implemented and successfully tested mySAP ERP Financials finance module.

Pre-Requisite

To achieve this business process, you need the following master data:

- C100000000 – My Customer
- IN10000001 – Sale Proceeds (Software)
- AS10000150 – Bills of Exchange Receivable (Alt.Recon)
- AS10000101 – Incoming Check Clearing Account
- LI10000400 – Contingent Liability (Bills of Exchange)

- EX10000301 – Bills of Exchange Changes

- AS10000149 – Customer Receivable

  Business Case

  Company code C100 provides its services to its customer. A customer C100000000 approached company code C100 for services with a condition that company code C100 should allow three months credit. In order to ensure customer payment and liquidity, company code C100 asked customer C100000000 to draw a bill of exchange for the services.

  Company code C100 provided services to customer C100000000 and customer C100000000 executed a bill of exchange in favor of company code C100.

  In order to maintain cash flow, company code C100 discounted the bill of exchange with its banker at 90% of face value of the bill of exchange. On the bill of exchange due date, company code C100's bank presents the bill of exchange to the customer's banker for payment.

  Process Flow

  Figure 5.25 depicts the process flow of bills of exchange receivable. To accomplish this business scenario, you will go through various steps and the system will offer a few accounting documents.

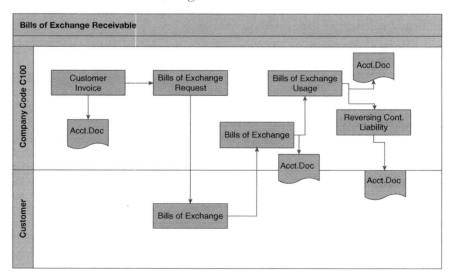

FIGURE 5.25 Bills of exchange.

Process Steps

Table 5.13 depicts the process steps to be followed to complete these business scenarios.

TABLE 5.13 Bills of Exchange Receivable Process Steps

Process Step	R / O	Modules	T. Code	Expected Results
1. Customer Invoice	R	FI	**FB70**	Company code C100 has created customer invoice
2. Bill of Exchange Payment Request	O	FI	**FBW1**	Company code C100 has created bills of exchange request
3. Bill of Exchange Payment	R	FI	**F-36**	Company code C100 has received accepted bills of exchange from customer and posted bills of exchange receivable
4. Bills of Exchange Usage	R	FI	**F-33**	Company code C100 has discounted bills of exchange with its banker for short term financing
5. Reverse Contingent Liability	R	FI	**F-20**	After he due date of bills of exchange, company code C100 reversed the bills of exchange contingent liability

5.14.1 Customer Invoice

- The starting point of this business process is the customer invoice. In case of a non-integrated SD module, you can create a customer invoice in FI. In the case of a sales and distribution related invoice, you needn't to do this step because the sales and distribution billing document will create an FI customer invoice posting. In the business process, it has been assumed that you are posting a customer invoice related to services you have rendered.

- You can create a customer invoice posting through:

  - **SAP ECC Menu: Accounting → Financial Accounting → Accounts Receivable → Document Entry → Invoice**

  - **Transaction Code: FB70**

- Alternatively, you can use transaction code F-22 or SAP ECC Menu: Accounting → Financial Accounting → Accounts Receivable → Document Entry → Invoice – General

▪ Company code C100 has posted a customer invoice for IT services it provided to customer C100000000. As a result of the customer posting, the system has created the following accounting entries:

- Dr.   C100000000 – My Customer
- Cr.   IN10000001 – Sale Proceeds (Software)

5.14.2 Bill of Exchange Payment Request

▪ Like a customer down payment request, you can create a bill of exchange payment request for your customer. A bill of exchange payment request is a noted item. As the bill of exchange is a noted item, it does not change the customer balance or clear the customer open item. Once the bill of exchange is accepted by the customer you can enter bill of exchange payment with reference to the bill of exchange payment request. You can create a bill of exchange individually through the transaction code and menu path given below, or through payment program transaction code F110. For this business, the creation of a bill of exchange is an optional step:

- **SAP ECC Menu: Accounting → Financial Accounting → Accounts Receivable → Document Entry → Bill of Exchange → Request**

- **Transaction Code: FBW1**

▪ Company code C100 created a bill of exchange payment request for the payment of services rendered through a bill of exchange.

5.14.3 Bill of Exchange Payment

▪ Once you have received the accepted copy of the bill of exchange, you can post the bill of exchange payment either with reference to the bill of exchange payment request, if you have created a request, or without reference to a bill of exchange payment request.

▪ The customer may accept a bill of exchange payment request as it is or with a changed condition. If you are posting a bill of exchange with reference to a bill of exchange payment request, then we can change the bill of exchange payment request:

- **SAP ECC Menu: Accounting → Financial Accounting → Accounts Receivable → Document Entry → Bill of Exchange → Payment**

- **Transaction Code: F-36**

- A bill of exchange payment: (1) clears customer open items, (2) clears customer noted open items for a bill of exchange payment request, and (3) creates new line items for bill of exchange receivable.

- Company code C100 has received an accepted bill of exchange from the customer and posted into the customer account. The system created the following accounting entries:

  - Dr.   C100000000 – My Customer (Alternative Recon. Account AS10000150 – Bills of Exchange Receivable)

  - Cr.   C100000000 – My Customer (Normal Recon. Account)

- After this step, you can wait for the bill of exchange due date and present the bill of exchange to the drawer, or you can go for refinancing through your banker. In order to maintain cash rotation, company code C100 chose to discount the bill of exchange with its banker.

5.14.4 Bill of Exchange Usage

- Bill of exchange usage or discounting is a financing activity. Instead of waiting for the bill of exchange due date, you can approach your banker to discount the bill of exchange. Normally, the bank keeps a certain percentage of bill of exchanges as finance changes and service charges. In this step, the system posts the incoming payment and creates contingent liability towards banks financing:

  - **SAP ECC Menu: Accounting → Financial Accounting → Accounts Receivable → Document Entry → Bill of Exchange → Discounting**

  - **Transaction Code: F-33**

- Dr.   AS10000101 – Incoming check clearing account

- Dr.   EX10000301 – Bills of Exchange Changes

- Cr.   LI10000400 – Contingent Liability (Bill of Exchange)

- Company code C100 discounts the bill exchange with its banker. After retaining 1% towards finances and services, the bank credited company code C100's account with the balance of the bill of exchange.

- Company code C100 posted the bank's service charges as business expenses and created liability for the bank's finance activity.

5.14.5 Reverse Contingent Liability

- After the expiration of the bill of exchange due date plus any grace period, you need to reverse the bill of exchange contingent liability. This step clears two open items: (1) it reverses the contingent liability you have created for the bank's financing activities and (2) it will also clear bills of exchange receivable.

- **SAP ECC Menu: Accounting → Financial Accounting → Accounts Receivable → Document Entry → Bill of Exchange → Reverse Contingent Liability**

- **Transaction Code: F-20**

- Dr.   LI10000400 – Contingent Liability (Bill of Exchange)

- Cr.   C100000000 – My Customer (Alternative Recon. Account AS10000150 – Bills of Exchange Receivable)

- Here it has been assumed your banker has presented the bill of exchange to the customer's banker and it is honored by the customer's banker.

- Figure 5.26 shows how your accounting books look at the end of the business process scenario. You can see that all of the open items created in various steps are offset by each other.

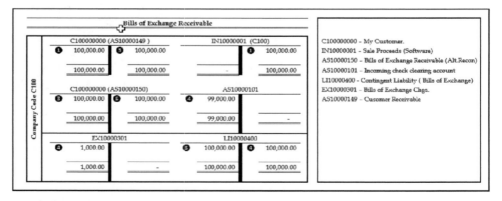

FIGURE 5.26 Bill of exchange receivable – accounting entries.

5.15 Bad Debt Provision and Write-off

Process Overview

During the course of business, you may come across a situation where your money is un-collectable or likely to be un-collectable. There are various reasons for such a conversion, including disputes over material or the financial crises of a customer. In these circumstances, in order present prudent and fair financial result of an enterprise, you need to build up provisions for doubtful debts. As the name implies, "provision for doubtful debts" means that as a prudent business practice, and based on your experience, you are considering part of customer's balance as unrecoverable.

When the money is totally un-collectable, then you will reduce your provision to the extent of money un-collectable and treat the un-collectable amount as bad debts.

There are two ways of providing bad debts: (1) the direct write off method and (2) the allowance method.

The direct method is pretty simple. In this case, you need to know that a specific amount is not collectable from a customer. You can charge the un-collectable amount to your income statement directly.

In the case of the allowance method, you need to do an estimate based on your experience and business practice. Once again, the estimate may be categorized further based on: (1) the number of days outstanding and (2) the customer's industry segment. You can estimate your un-collectable receivable based on a percentage of the invoice.

Assumptions

It is assumed that you have implemented mySAP ERP Financials FI module and maintained the necessary master data listed in the pre-requisite.

Pre-Requisite

In this business process, you will use the following master data. Ensure that you have created these master data before proceeding further:

- C100000000 (AS10000149) – My Customer
- IN10000001 – Sale Proceeds (Software)
- EX10000400 – Doubtful Debts Provided
- AS10000152 – Reserve for Doubtful Debts

Business Case

During the normal business process, company code C100 has provided IT services to customer C100000000. The services charges are payable after 30 days of the invoice date. In spite of rigorous follow-ups, customer C100000000 didn't pay company code C100. As per the business practice, if the amount is uncollected for more than six months, the business needs to provide 10% of the uncollected amount as bad debt provisions.

On the eighth month after the invoice due date, company code C100 receives communication from the liquidator of customer C100000000 for a waiver of liability as per the liquidation settlement. Company code writes off 100% of the customer balance as bed debts.

Process Flow

Figure 5.27 depicts the activity flows of these business process scenarios.

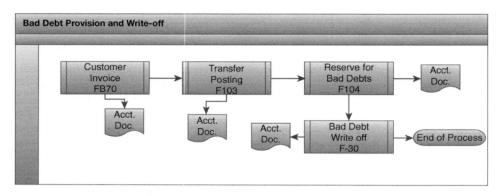

FIGURE 5.27 Bad debt provision and write-off.

Process Steps

In Table 5.14 you can see the activities you need to perform to accomplish this business process. It also depicts what the expected outcome is in each step.

TABLE 5.14 Bad Debts Provision and Write-off Process Steps

Process Step	R / O	Modules	T. Code	Expected Results
1. Posting Customer Invoice	R	FI	FB70	Customer invoice has been posted
2. Receivables Transfer Posting	R	FI	F103	Customer balance has been classified as special G/L transactions
3. Reserve for Bad Debt	R	FI	F104	Bad debt reserve has been created
4. Writing Off Doubtful Receivables	R	FI	F-30	Bad debts have been written off

5.15.1 Posting Customer Invoice

- This business process starts with the customer invoice posting. When you sell your product and services, you bill your customer for the product and services. Normally, if you use sales and distribution module in conjunction with the finance module, all inventory related billing will be triggered in the sales and distribution module. In those cases, you need not perform this step. However, in some cases you sell non-inventory material and services. In those cases, you post the customer invoice in the FI module. It has been assumed that you are billing the customer for services:

  - **SAP ECC Menu: Accounting → Financial Accounting → Accounts Receivable → Document Entry → Invoice**

  - **Transaction Code: FB70**

- Refer to the business process scenarios for sales and distribution related billing.

- Company code C100 posted a customer invoice for IT services provided to customer. As a result of the customer invoice posting, the system has created the following accounting entries:

  - Dr. C100000000 (AS10000149) – My Customer, where AS10000149 is the customer reconciliation account

  - Cr. IN10000001 – Sale Proceeds (Software)

5.15.2 Receivables Transfer Posting

- In this step you will make provisions for doubtful debts. Based on your configuration, the system will calculate a bad debts provision and transfer the provision to alternative reconciliation. You can reach the reserve for bad debts configuration through menu path: **IMG → Financial Accounting → Financial Accounting Global Settings → Accounts Receivable and Accounts Payable → Business Transactions → Closing → Valuate → Reserve for Bad Debt**.

- In this step you will classify your receivables from normal transactions to a special G/L transaction with a special G/L indicator "E" through either of the following navigations:

  - **SAP ECC Menu: Accounting → Financial Accounting → Accounts Receivable → Periodic Processing → Closing → Valuate → Receivables Transfer Posting (Gross)**

  - **Transaction Code: F103**

- Company code C100 has executed the transfer posting and the system has created the following accounting line items:

  - Dr.   C100000000 (AS10000149) – C100000000 – My Customer, where AS10000149 is the customer reconciliation account.

  - Cr.   C100000000 (AS10000151) – C100000000 – My Customer, where AS10000151 is the reserve for doubtful debts.

5.15.3 Reserve for Bad Debt

- Here you will calculate the reserve for doubtful debts and create a reserve for it. Based on your configuration, the system will calculate the amount to be set aside as a reserve for doubtful debts:

  - **SAP ECC Menu: Accounting → Financial Accounting → Accounts Receivable → Periodic Processing → Closing → Valuate → Reserve for Bad Debt (Gross)**

  - **Transaction Code: F104**

- Once you have carried out the transfer posting, you can create a bad debts reserve through either of the previous navigation options. The system reads all open items with the special G/L indicator "E" and creates a provision as per the percentage defined in your configuration. You can reach the configuration screen through either transaction code **OB04**: or menu path: IMG → Financial Accounting → Financial Accounting Global Settings → Accounts Receivable and Accounts Payable → Business Transactions → Closing → Valuate → Reserve for Bad Debt → Define Methods. The system determines the G/L account based on the account determination you have configured in the transaction code: **OBXD** or menu path: IMG → Financial Accounting → Financial Accounting Global Settings → Accounts Receivable and Accounts Payable → Business Transactions → Closing → Valuate → Reserve for Bad Debt → Define Accounts for Reserve for Bad Debt

- Once you have received the money or written off bad debts, in your subsequent run of this transaction code the system automatically resets the reserve and doubtful debts are provided.

- Company code C100 has created a reserve for doubtful debts and posted the following accounting line items:

  - Dr.   EX10000400 – Doubtful Debts Provided

  - Cr.   AS10000152 – Reserve for Doubtful Debts

5.15.4 Writing off Doubtful Receivables

- Once you have confirmed that you are not going to receive the money due from the customer, you need to write it off from the customer account. In your last step, you only created provisions for probable loss, while still making follow-ups with the customer for payment. You can carry out these activities by following either of the navigation options:

  - **SAP ECC Menu: Accounting → Financial Accounting → Accounts Receivable → Document Entry → Other → Transfer with Clearing**

  - **Transaction Code: F-30**

- Once you have written off bad debts, on your subsequent run to create/recalculate a reserve, the system automatically recalculates the bad debts reserve after considering the amount you have written off.

- Company code C100 has written off a customer balance because customer C100000000 filed bankruptcy and there is a little hope of getting the money. The system has generated the following accounting entries.

- In this business process scenario, you have started with customer invoicing, and then built bad debts reserve for a long outstanding customer balance. Finally, you have written off the customer balance as bed debts.

- Through the entries life cycle of business process scenarios, you have posted the following accounting entries.

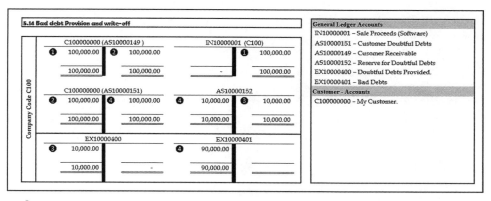

❶ Represents entries passed in step – 1 of this business process

FIGURE 5.28 Bad debt provision and write-off: accounting entries.

5.16 Assets Acquisition with Material Management

Process Overview

Assets acquisition with MM is an integrated business process scenario of the FI and MM modules. In this business process, the acquisition process is initiated in the MM module by creating a purchase requisition. Once the purchase requisition is approved for purchase of the required asset, the purchasing department creates a purchase order and communicates to the vendor for the supply of the required assets. The integrated assets acquisition business process more or less follows the same process flow of material procurement.

When you create a purchase requisition you can create it with the account assignment category to an asset. When you create a purchase requisition with an account assignment category as assets, the system expects that you will choose an asset number in the account assignment tab. That means you need to create an asset master before the creation of the purchase requisition. It is advisable to create the purchase requisition without an account assignment.

The purchase order creation function gives the option to create an asset master through the create purchase order window.

Assumptions

For this business process scenario, you need the following application component of the mySAP ERP Financials application:

- Assets management as well as assets accounting

- Accounts receivable and accounts payable

- G/L accounting

- Material management

Pre-Requisite

To accomplish the business process scenario, you need the following master data:

- V100000000 – My Supplier for material. A vendor master data

- AS10000500 – Asset Equipment (Asset Master Record). An asset master data

- LI10000100 – GR/IR clearing account. A G/L master data

- AS10000102 – Outgoing check clearing account. A G/L master data

Business Case

As a business practice, all purchases of company codes are routed through the material management module. This business process starts with initiation of the purchase requisition. Once the purchase requisition is accepted, the purchasing department places a purchase order for the purchase of assets. The receiving department does a goods receipt for the assets, and the finance department does an invoice receipt to settle the vendor invoice.

Process Flow

Figure 5.29 depicts the process flow of assets acquisition through the material management module. This process flew is similar to other material procurement processes.

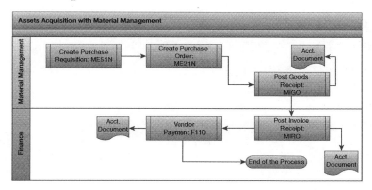

FIGURE 5.29 Assets acquistion with material management.

Process Steps

Table 5.15 depicts the process steps of the business process scenario.

TABLE 5.15 Assets Acquisition with Material Management Process Steps

Process Step	R / O	Modules	T. Code	Expected Results
1. Creating the purchase requisition	R	FI	ME51N	Purchase requisition has been created
2. Creating the purchase order	R	FI	ME21	Purchase order has been created for purchase of assets
3. Posting the goods receipt	R	FI	MIGO	Goods receipts for assets have been posted
4. Posting the invoice receipt:	R	FI	MIRO	Vendor invoice has been posted
5. Displaying in reporting	R	FI	AW01N	You have confirmed assets posting and verified planned depreciation
6. Vendor payment	R	FI	F110	Vendor has been paid and open items are cleared

5.16.1 Create Purchase Requisition

- A purchase requisition is a formal request to the purchasing department to procure the material or services. The purchase requisition passes on information such as what materials are required, when are they required, and how much is required. Use the following menu paths to perform this step:

  - **SAP ECC Menu: Logistics → Materials Management → Purchasing → Purchase Requisition → Create**

  - **Transaction Code: ME51N**

- You can create a purchase requisition with or without assigning an account assignment category.

- The shop floor of company code C100 created a purchase requisition for the purchase of equipment for the shop floor.

5.16.2 Create Purchase Order

- The second step of this business process is the creation of the purchase order. A purchase order is a formal request from the buyer to the seller for the supply of goods and/or services, as specified in the purchase order. At the end of this activity, the system will generate a purchase order, which can be sent to the seller via mail. Between the creation of the purchase requisition and the purchase order, you may or may not have addition steps 5.1. Use the following menu paths to perform this step:

  - **SAP ECC Menu: Logistics → Materials Management → Purchasing → Purchase Order → Create → Vendor/Supplying Plant Known**

  - **Transaction Code: ME21**

- While creating the purchase order, you need to choose the account assignment category as "A" and choose an asset master in the account assignment tab. Through the purchase order creation screen, you can create an assets master if the asset is a new asset.

- Company code C100 has placed a purchase order with vendor V100000000 for the purchase of manufacturing equipment.

5.16.3 Posting the Goods Receipt

- As a result of the fulfillment of the purchase order, the system expects a goods receipt for the ordered material from the vendor. A goods movement is entered into the system, referencing PO, and a goods receipt material document is posted. Based on the assets master, a G/L account will be determined. When you post the goods receipt for assets, the system capitalizes the assets and determines the depreciation start date based on period control you maintain in deprecation key assigned to the assets master. Use the following menu paths to perform this step:

- **SAP ECC Menu: Logistics → Materials Management → Inventory Management → Goods Movement → Goods Receipt → For Purchase Order → PO Number Known**

- **Transaction Code: MIGO**

▪ Company code C100 received assets AS10000500 from V100000000 and posted the goods receipt with reference to the purchase order. Based on the account determination, the system determined the G/L master record. This step creates a material document and a financial entry. A simple account entry would be as follows:

- Dr.   AS10000500 – Asset Equipment (Asset Master Record)

- Cr.   LI10000100 – GR/IR Clearing Account

5.16.4 Posting the Invoice Receipt

▪ At the end of the purchasing and inventory management process, your accounting department might have received a vendor for payment. In the invoice verification process, the accounts payable department ensures that all invoices are correct with respect to quantity of material and cost of material. At the end of the invoice verification process, the system will generate an MM document and account document. Use the following menu paths to perform this step:

- **SAP ECC Menu: Logistics → Materials Management → Logistics Invoice Verification → Document Entry → Enter Invoice**

- **Transaction Code: MIRO**

▪ Generally, the invoice verification process follows either a two-way or three-way match.

▪ In this step, company code C100 posted a vendor invoice for asset AS10000500 and the system created the following account entries:

- Dr.   LI10000100 – GR/IR Clearing Account

- Cr.   V100000000 – My Supplier for material

5.16.5 Display Report

- Once the goods receipts are posted, you can execute this report to see what amount was capitalized and how the system has calculated planned deprecation. This is an optional step. There are numerous reports available in Information Systems → Accounting → Financial Accounting → Fixed Assets where you can see assets values based on different criteria. It is not possible to give all reports, so we chose a favorite report, where we can see all the related activities and associated master data. Use the following navigation option as shown below:

  - **SAP ECC Menu: Accounting → Financial Accounting → Fixed Assets → Asset → Asset Explorer**

  - **Transaction Code: AW01N**

- As previously stated, this is a display report. Through this transaction you can see all transactions posted to an asset, associated depreciation keys, and all associated organizational objects like cost centers, vendors, and G/L master records.

5.16.6 Vendor Payment

- The last step of this process is payment to the vendor for material. You can pay the vendor either through a manual payment or through an automatic payment. A manual payment is preferable when you are paying to a single vendor, while the automatic payment program is preferable when you let the system determine the open items to be payable. Use the following menu paths to perform this step:

  - **SAP ECC Menu: Accounting → Financial Accounting → Accounts Payable → Periodic Processing → Payments**

  - **Transaction Code: F110**

- The outgoing payment creates an accounting document called the payment document and clears the vendor open line items. The system created the following accounting line items:

  - Dr.   V100000000 – My Supplier for material

  - Cr.   AS10000102 – Outgoing check clearing account

- Figure 5.30 describes the accounting entries we have entered and the master data used in various stages of this business process.

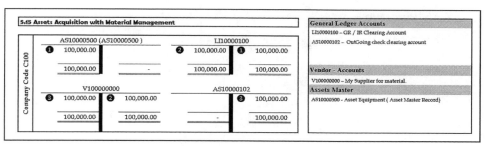

❶ Is the step number of the business process

FIGURE 5.30 Assets acquisition with material management: accounting entries.

5.17 Assets Aquisitions without Material Management

Process Overview

So far you have learned about assets acquisition with an integrated MM module. It is not always necessary to have an MM module in order to acquire assets. In this business process, you will cover a business process scenario for assets acquisition with non-integrated MM. In this process you will learn how assets accounting module is integrated with accounts payable and G/L sub-modules.

The vendor supplies assets based on the purchase order placed with the vendor. On receipt of the assets, the accounts payable department posts a vendor invoice.

When the vendor invoice posts based on period control method assigned to deprecation, the system sets a depreciation start day.

The outgoing payment clears the vendor open items.

Advantages

Compared to the MM integrated process, this business process scenario is pretty simple. Due to integrated ERP, the system data is keyed in sub-modules, which update other modules.

Assumptions

You have configured the G/L, accounts payable, and assets accounting modules of mySAP ERP Financials.

Pre-Requisite

In order to record business transactions, we need the following master data before proceeding:

- AS10000500 – Asset Equipment (Asset Master Record)

- V100000000 – My Supplier for material

- AS10000102 – Outgoing check clearing account

Business Case

Company code C100 wants to procure an automobile for its director. Company code C100 has placed a purchase order with its vendor V100000000 for the supply of an automobile (company code doesn't use material management). Vendor V100000000 supplies the automobile and bills company code C100 for the automobile.

Upon receiving the vendor invoice, company code C100 creates liability for the automobile. As per the business practice, company code C100 provides depreciation from the first day of the month the asset was acquired.

Company code C100 pays the vendor to clear its debt for the automobile.

Process Flow

Figure 5.31 depicts the process flow of the acquisition of assets without material management.

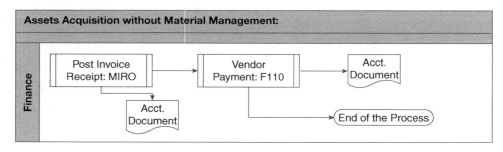

FIGURE 5.31 Assets acquisition without material management.

Process Steps

Table 5.16 depicts the steps involved in this business process scenario.

TABLE 5.16 Assets Acquisition without Material Management Process Steps

Process Step	R / O	Modules	T. Code	Expected Results
Vendor Invoice Posting	R	FI	FB60	Vendor invoice has been posted
Display Report	O	FI	AW01N	Assets reports show the correct values
Vendor Payment	R	FI	F110	Vendor has been paid

5.17.1 Posting the Vendor Invoice

- Posting the vendor invoice is the first step in this non-integrated assets acquisition business process. In our earlier business process scenarios, you already covered posting a vendor invoice in the finance module. While posting a vendor invoice, you need to key posting key 70 and the appropriate assets master. Assets management use transaction type to track assets transaction for reports. In this case key transaction type 100:

  - **SAP Menu Path: Accounting → Financial Accounting → Accounts Payable → Document Entry → Invoice**

  - **Transaction Code: FB60**

- Company code C100 received the automobile and posted the vendor invoice through the finance module. Based on the configuration, the system determined the capitalization date and depreciation start date of asset. The system created the following accounting entries:

  - Dr. AS10000500 – Asset Equipment (Asset Master Record)

  - Cr. V100000000 – My Supplier for material

5.17.2 Display Report

- You have already covered this step 0 – but it is covered once again here:

  - **SAP ECC Menu: Accounting → Financial Accounting → Fixed Assets → Asset → Asset Explorer**

  - **Transaction Code: AW01N**

- This is an optional step. Company code C100 verified the assets transaction that has been posted in the earlier step.

5.17.3 Vendor Payment

- This is the last step of this process. This step we have already discussed in a few previous steps regarding-vendor outgoing payments:

  - **SAP ECC Menu: Accounting → Financial Accounting → Accounts Payable → Periodic Processing → Payments**

  - **Transaction Code: F110**

- Company code C100 initiated an outgoing payment through the automatic payment program. The automatic payment program clears vendor open items and prints a check. The system generated the following account entries:

- • Dr.   V100000000 – My Supplier for material
- • Cr.   AS10000102 – OutGoing check clearing account

■ Figure 5.32 shows the accounting entries you have passed in various phases on this business process.

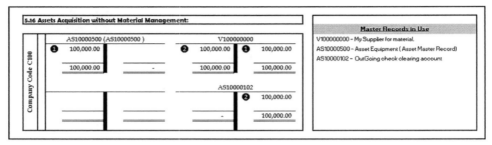

● Is the step number of the business process

FIGURE 5.32 Assets acquistion without material management: accounting entries.

5.18 Assets Retirement

Process Overview

In this business process you learn how to sell assets through the FI module.

In fact, this is the real process of selling assets. This process starts with posting the customer invoice for the sale of assets. In the subsequent step, you will record the customer incoming payment.

Advantages

In this process you need not depend on any other module. With tight integration of G/L and account receivable sub module of mySAP ERP Financials, you post in both the G/L account and accounts receivable at the same time.

Assumptions

In this business process, you will use the finance module of mySAP ERP Financials. It has been assumed that you have already implemented the finance modules. In order to record the business transaction, you need the master data mentioned in pre-requisite section andyou have already created these master data.

Pre-Requisite

You will use the following master data in this business process, so make sure that you have already created these master data before initiation of the posting process:

- AS10000500 – Asset Equipment (Asset Master Record)
- AS10000501 – Accumulated Depreciation Account
- IN10000100 – Profit on Sale of Fixed Assets
- AS10000600 – Sale of Fixed Assets Clearing Account
- C100000000 – My Customer
- AS10000101 – Incoming Check Clearing Account

Business Case

Company code C100 is a manufacturer of heavy equipment. In order to increase efficiency and productivity, they have decided to replace one piece of machinery with a new one.

In the course of the customer search, customer C100000000 agreed to purchase the equipment from company code C100.

Company code C100 sold its old equipment AS10000500 to customer C100000000 and in the subsequent step, the customer pays for the purchase of the assets.

Process Flow

Figure 5.33 depicts the process flow of assets retirement with the customer.

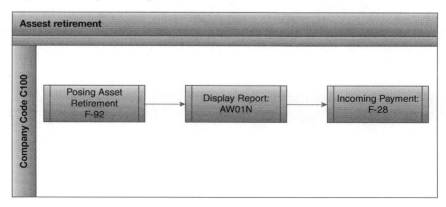

FIGURE 5.33 Assets retirement without sales and distribution.

Process Steps

Table 5.17 depicts the process steps involved.

TABLE 5.17 Assets Retirement without Sales and Distribution Module – Process Steps

Process Step	R / O	Modules	T. Code	Expected Results
1. Posting the Asset Retirement	R	FICO	F-92	Sale of assets document has been posted
2. Display Report	O	FICO	AW01N	Assets explorer has been reviewed
3. Incoming Payment	R	FICO	F-28	Customer income has been posted

5.18.1 Posting the Asset Retirement

▪ In this step, you will sell an asset with an integrated customer posting:

- **SAP ECC Menu: Accounting → Financial Accounting → Fixed Assets → Retirement → With Customer**

- **Transaction Code: F-92**

▪ While posting the assets retirement the system generates the following accounting entries:

- Dr.   C100000000 – My Customer

- Cr.   AS10000600 – Sale of Fixed Assets Clearing Account

- Dr.   AS10000600 – Sale of Fixed Assets Clearing Account

- Dr.   AS10000501 – Accumulated Depreciation Account

- Cr.   AS10000500 – Asset Equipment (G/L Master Record)

- Cr.   IN10000100 – Profit on Sale of Fixed Assets

5.18.2 Display Report

▪ Assets display was already covered earlier in this chapter. By executing this report, you can verify the sale transaction that you have carried out in previous steps:

- **SAP ECC Menu: Accounting → Financial Accounting → Accounts Payable → Periodic Processing → Payments**

- **Transaction Code: AW01N**

▪ Although this step is an optional step, it is best to confirm your sale transaction.

5.18.3 Incoming Payment

▪ You have already covered the customer incoming payment earlier in this chapter. With customer incoming payment this business process scenario comes to an end:

- **SAP Menu Path: Accounting → Financial Accounting → Accounts Receivable → Document Entry → Incoming Payments**

- **Transaction Code: F-28**

▪ The account receivable clerk received the customer payment for the sale and posted the incoming payment. As a result of the incoming payment posting, the system clears the customer open item and posts the following accounting entries:

- Dr.   AS10000101 – Incoming check clearing account

- Cr.   C100000000 – My Customer

▪ Figure 5.34 depicts the accounting entries you have entered in various phases of this business process. In real-life scenarios you may come across a different set of accounting entries.

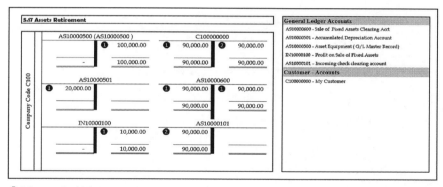

**Is the step number of the business process

FIGURE 5.34 Accounting entries.

5.19 Life Cycle of Assets Management

Process Overview

The life cycle of asset covers starts from the creation of the assets master, subsequent being put to use, and finally retiring the assets from its use. At each and every step there are various options and multiple directions are available to handle the life cycle of assets management. It is not really possible to depict all the steps, options, and deviations that are available within SAP.

In this business process scenario, you will have to learn a simple and commonly used business process, which involves the creation of an asset, depreciating the asset, and retiring the asset from commercial use.

Advantages

Due to the tight integration between various modules and sub modules, data entered in one module is available in other modules/sub modules. This reduces the data entry efforts of business users.

Assumptions

Based on business process requirements, it has been assumed that accounts payable, account receivable, G/L, and assets management components of mySAP ERP are fully functional and master data available for use.

Pre-Requisite

We need the following master data to complete this business process scenario:

- V100000000 – My Supplier for material
- AS10000102 – Outgoing Check Clearing Account
- AS10000500 – Asset Equipment (Asset Master Record)
- AS10000501 – Accumulated Depreciation Account
- EX10000500 – Depreciation Expenses Account

Business Case

Company code C100 is a manufacturer of heavy equipment and uses various assets in its manufacturing process. Due to a change in market demand, company code C100 wants to increase its manufacturing capacity.

It recently purchased a new asset (equipment), which has life for three years. As per business practice and experience, at the end of life of an asset, the asset became totally useless.

Process Flow

Figure 5.35 depicts the process flow of assets life cycle management. This process starts from the creation of master data, acquisition, and finally, retirement.

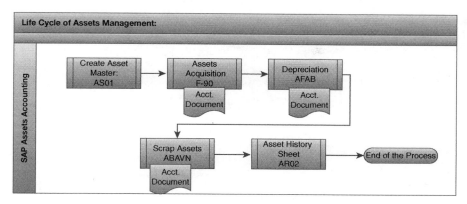

FIGURE 5.35 Life cycle of assets management.

Process Steps

Table 5.18 depicts the process steps, modules, sub-modules and expected results in each step of the life cycle of assets management business process.

TABLE 5.18 Life Cycle of Assets Management Process Steps

Process Step	R / O	Modules	T. Code	Expected Results
1. Create Asset Master Record	R	FI	AS01	Asset master has been created
2. Assets Acquisition	R	FI	F-90	Asset acquisition transaction has been posted
3. Asset Depreciation	R	FI	AFAB	Depreciation has provided for assets
4. Retirement by Scraping	R	FI	ABAVN	Assets have been retired from commercial use
5. Assets History Sheet	O	FI	AR02	Assets history sheet has been executed to validate asset transaction and for financial reporting

5.19.1 Create Asset Master Record

▪ Like the vendor/customer master you need an assets master to post a transaction. You create an assets master under an asset class and a sub-asset master under the asset. Creation of an asset master is the first step in this business process:

- **SAP ECC Menu: Accounting → Financial Accounting → Fixed Assets → Asset → Create**

- **Transaction Code: AS01**

- Company code C100 is planning to replace its old equipment with new advanced technology equipment. Company code C100 has created a new assets master AS10000500 for its new proposed assets.

5.19.2 Assets Acquisition

- The assets acquisition process you have covered in your previous business process scenarios and the acquisition can be an integrated or non-integrated purchase, depending on the business process and module that was implemented.

- Based on the period control method, the system determines the depreciation start date of an asset:

  - **SAP ECC Menu: Accounting → Financial Accounting → Fixed Assets → Posting → Acquisition → External Acquisition → With Vendor**

  - **Transaction Code: F-90**

- Company code C100 purchased new equipment to increase plant capacity. As per the period control method, the system determined the depreciation start date of the new asset. The system has created the following accounting entries for purchase asset (assuming this is non-integrated purchase):

  - Dr.   AS10000500 – Asset Equipment (G/L Master Record)

  - Cr.   V100000000 – My Supplier for material

5.19.3 Assets Depreciation

- Once you put an asset to use, you need to provide depreciation on the assets. Based on the depreciation key assigned to assets master, the system calculates the depreciation on assets and creates the accounting document:

  - **SAP ECC Menu: Accounting → Financial Accounting → Fixed Assets → Periodic Processing → Depreciation Run → Execute**

  - **Transaction Code: AFAB**

- Company code C100 executed a depreciation run for new asset along with other asset as part of a month end process. The system created the following accounting entries:

  - EX10000500 – Depreciation Expenses Account

  - AS10000501 – Accumulated Depreciation Account

5.19.4 Retirement by Scraping

■ After the useful life of the asset, you need to retire the asset. You can retire an asset in many ways such as sale to a customer or scraping. In this business process, you are scraping the assets. In the scrapping process, you will write off the book values of the asset:

- **SAP ECC Menu: Accounting → Financial Accounting → Fixed Assets → Posting → Retirement → Asset Retirement by Scrapping**

- **Transaction Code: ABAVN**

■ Company code C100 scrapped the assets it has acquired. In the scrapping process, the system has generated the following accounting entries:

- Dr. AS10000501 – Accumulated Depreciation Account

- Cr. AS10000500 – Asset Equipment (G/L Master Record)

- Dr. EX10000500 – Assets Scrapped

5.19.5 Assets History Sheet

■ Assets history sheet is one of the most important reports for month-end and year-end closing. It groups assets together based on transaction types by providing assets information in a summarized way:

- **SAP ECC Menu: Information Systems → Accounting → Fixed Assets → Asset History Sheet**

- **Transaction Code: AR02**

■ This is a reporting activity that does not create any account documents.

■ In the foresaid business process steps, the system has carried out various accounting entries as indicated in Figure 5.36.

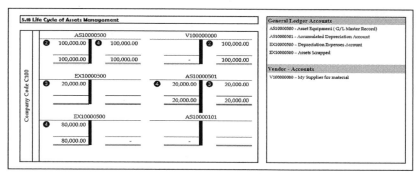

❶ Is the step number of the business process

FIGURE 5.36 Accounting entries.

5.20 Collection Management Cycle

Process Overview

The collection management application component of the FSCM modules concentrate on smoothing the customer collection process so that businesses run in the best way without losing customer balances. Without the collection management application component of FSCM, the accounts receivable module takes pains for the manual preparation of a customer overdue list and customer contacts.

The collection management application component provides a tool for tracking customer balances for overdue bills, and records the follow up activities.

Advantages

Due to the integration of the collection management application component with accounts receivable, the disputes management application component get its data from the accounts receivable module for preparation of the work list for follow up, and records the follow up process.

Assumptions

To use this business process, you need to implement the collection management application component of FSCM module in addition to the finance module's accounts receivable and G/L.

Pre-Requisite

In this business process scenario, you will use the following master data. Ensure that you have created these master data before proceeding further:

- EX10000201 – Cost of goods sold – External Sales
- AS10000010 – Material Stock Account
- IN10000000 – Sale Proceeds
- AS10000101 – Incoming Check Clearing Account. A G/L master
- C100000000 – My Customer. A customer master

Business Case

Company code C100 is a heavy equipment manufacturer and has a very big customer base. In order to expedite the collection process and minimize bad debts, it implemented the collection management application component of the FSCM module.

Once the customer is billed for the material, customer line items are transferred to collection management application component from the accounts receivable module at the end of the day. Based on the due dates, the customer line items are listed in the collection work list. Based on the work list, the collection specialist establishes contact with the customers and makes the necessary follow-ups for collection.

Process Flow

Figure 5.37 depicts the process flows of the collection management process.

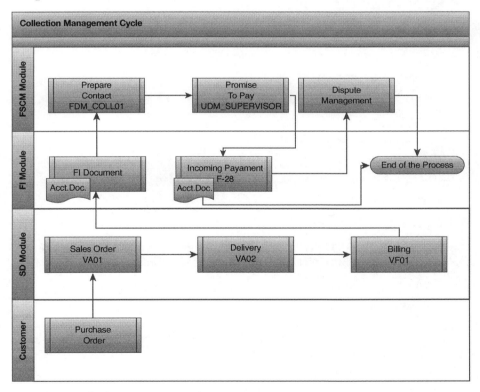

FIGURE 5.37 Collection management cycle.

Process Steps

Table 5.19 depicts the process steps you will be covering to accomplish this business process scenario, and the expected outcomes.

TABLE 5.19 Collection Managment Cycle: Process Steps

Process Step	R / O	Modules	T. Code	Expected Results
1. Creating a Sales Order	R	SD		Sales order has been created
2. Creating a Delivery	R	SD		Delivery has been created
3. Creating an Invoice	R	SD		Customer has been billed
4. Prepare Contact	R	FSCM		Customer has been contacted
5. Creating a Promise to Pay	R	FSCM		A customer promise has been created
6. Post Incoming Payment	R	FI		Incoming payment has been posted

5.20.1 Creating a Sales Order

■ To initiate the sales process, you need to create a sales order. You can create a sales order with reference to the quote or purchase order received from your customer. Sometimes you may create a sales order based on telephone call of a customer:

- **SAP ECC Menu: Logistics → Sales and Distribution → Sales → Order → Create**

- **Transaction Code: VA01**

■ Company code C100 created a sales order based on the purchase order it has received from one its valued customer C100000000 for material M100000000.

5.20.2 Creating a Delivery

■ Once you have created the sales order, the next step is delivering the material as specified in the sales order. In this step you create a delivery:

- **SAP ECC Menu: Logistics → Sales and Distribution → Sales → Order → Change**

- **Transaction Code: VA02**

■ Company code C100 created outbound delivery of material M100000000 to customer. In this step, the system generates the following accounting:

- Dr.　　EX10000201 – Cost of goods sold – External Sales

- Cr.　　AS10000010 – Material Stock Account

5.20.3 Creating an Invoice

▪ After the delivery of material you need to bill the customer for the material. In this step, the system creates a billing document and an accounting document. Based on the output determination, the system creates a billing output line printing, mail, or fax of the billing document:

- **SAP ECC Menu: Logistics → Sales and Distribution → Billing → Billing Document → Create**

- **Transaction Code: VF01**

▪ Company code C100 billed to customer, and as per the payment terms, the payment is due 15 days after the billing date. The system creates SD and accounting document as an outcome of this activity. The system has created the following accounting line items:

- Dr.   C100000000 – My Customer

- Cr.   IN10000000 – Sale Proceeds

5.20.4 Prepare Contact

▪ Based on the collection processor's work list, the collection specialist establishes contacts with the customer. To establish customer contacts, the specialist accesses the process receivables. Based on customer feedback, the specialist either creates a promise to pay, dispute case, or resubmission.

▪ Once customer contact has been established, the customer contact is summarized and documented for future references:

- **SAP ECC Menu: Accounting → Financial Supply Chain Management → Collections Management → Integration with Accounts Receivable Accounting → Edit Receivables (Old)**

- **Transaction Code: FDM_COLL01**

▪ The collection specialist of company code C100 establishes customer contact by calling the customer's accounts payable representative. Based on the customer's feedback, the specialist creates a promise to pay or a dispute case.

5.20.5 Creating a Promise to Pay

■ Once the specialist reaches customer's contact person, the customer representative sometimes makes a commitment to pay an outstanding payable on certain data. Based on the customer's commitment, the specialist creates a promise to pay for the line item or items:

- **SAP ECC Menu: Accounting → Financial Supply Chain Management → Collections Management → Worklists → All Worklists**

- **Transaction Code: UDM_SUPERVISOR**

The Collection specialist of company code C100 established contact with customer C100000000 for the outstanding payment of material M100000000. The accounts payable manager of customer C100000000 promised to release the payment by the 15th of the current month. Based on the customer's promise, the specialist created a promise to pay of the open customer's outstanding.

5.20.6 Post Incoming Payment

■ The last step of the sales process is posting an incoming payment. Once you have received the incoming payment you need to post to the customer account. Based on the amount you have received against the customers outstanding, you can clear the customer's open item or post on an account:

- **SAP ECC Menu: Accounting → Financial Accounting → Accounts Receivable → Document Entry → Incoming Payments**

- **Transaction Code: F-28**

■ On the promised date customer C100000000 has paid the amount payable for material M100000000. The accounts receivable clerk posted the incoming payment to the customer and cleared the customer open items. When you post the incoming payment, the system generated an account document with following line items:

- AS10000101 – Incoming Check Clearing Account

- C100000000 – My Customer

▪ Figure 5.38 depicts accounting entries that the system has generated while processing the above steps.

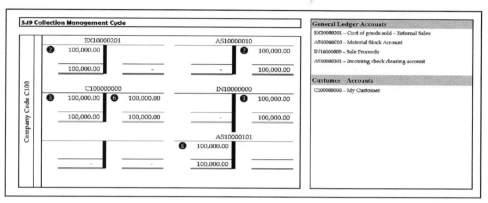

● Is the step number of the business process

FIGURE 5.38 Accounting entries.

5.21 Dispute Case Creation and Settlement

Process Overview

In this business process scenario, you will learn how the financial supply chain management's dispute management works with the financial module of mySAP ERP Financials. Due to the tight integration of FSCM dispute management module with FI account receivable module, it is possible to optimize the dispute resolution process with your business partners. The SAP Dispute Management component contains functions for processing receivables-related dispute cases. It supplements the logistics process gap between the invoice and payment if there are discrepancies with the customer.

In this business process scenario, you will start with the sales order, create the customer invoice and payment follow-up, open a dispute case based on the customer's concern, and finally, resolve the dispute.

Advantages

Without this integrated process, the accounts receivable department will end up doing manual steps for dispute resolution. Due to FSCM integration with accounts receivable functionality, it becomes easy to handle customer disputes and speed-up the customer's collection process.

Assumptions

To accomplish this business process you need to install and implement mySAP ERP Financials FSCM, FI, and SD modules.

Pre-Requisite

In this business process scenario you need the following master data to complete the business process:

- EX10000201 – Cost of goods sold – External Sales

- AS10000010 – Material Stock Account

- IN10000000 – Sale Proceeds

- AS10000101 – Incoming check clearing account. A G/L master

- C100000000 – My Customer. A customer master

- EX10000700 – Customer balance write off – Delay

Business Case

Company code C100 has a huge customer as part of marketing activities. In order to build good customer relations they provide timely attention to customer's concern and expedite the collection process implemented by financial supply chain management module of mySAP ERP Financials. Once company code C100 has received the customer's purchase order, it creates a sales order for the supply of the stipulated material at an agreed price and supplies the desired material to the customer. Before the due date, the customer remitted the payment for the material after retaining a couple of dollars. After a follow up about the unaccounted deduction customer informed them that the materials were not delivered on time. After a review with the sales and logistic department, it has been confirmed that there was a delay in the supply of the material.

Process Flow

Figure 5.39 depicts the process flow of a dispute case creation and settlement. From Figure 5.39, you can understand how the financial supply management module is integrated with the account receivable module.

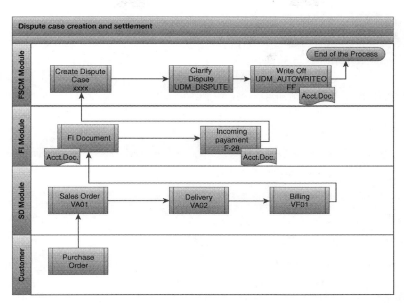

FIGURE 5.39 Dispute case creation and settlement.

Process Steps

Table 5.20 describes the process steps of the dispute case management business process.

TABLE 5.20 Dispute Case Creation and Settlement: Process Steps

Process Step	R / O	Modules	T. Code	Expected Results
1. Creating a Sales Order	R	SD	VA01	Sales order has been created
2. Creating a Delivery	R	SD	VA02	Material delivery created for the above sales order
3. Creating an Invoice	R	SD	VF01	Invoice has been created for the above delivery
4. Post Incoming Payment	R	FI	F-28	Incoming check has been posted
5. Create a Dispute Case	R	FI		A dispute case has been created for short payment
6. Clarifying the Dispute and Documenting the Resolution	R	FSCM	UDM_DISPUTE	Account receivable department has been followed up dispute for resolution
7. Writing off and Closing the Dispute Case	R	FSCM	UDM_ AUTOWRITEOFF	Dispute amount has been written off

5.21.1 Creating a Sales Order

* In this business process, you are dealing with the integrated sales process, which starts with the creation of a sales order in the sales and distribution module. After receiving the purchase order from the customer, the sales department creates a sales order. The sales order depicts the material to be supplied and the terms and conditions for the supply of the material:

  * **SAP ECC Menu: Logistics → Sales and Distribution → Sales → Order → Create**

  * **Transaction Code: VA01**

* Company code C100 creates a sales order for the supply of material M10000000 to customer C100000000.

5.21.2 Creating a Delivery

* Once you have created the sales order, the next step is to supply the material at an agreed date. In this step, you will create a material delivery, which means the material will be physically moved from the warehouse for outbound delivery:

  * **SAP ECC Menu: Logistics → Sales and Distribution → Sales → Order → Change**

  * **Transaction Code: VA02**

* Due to unavoidable circumstance, company code C100 delivered the material a few days later than the agreed date. In this step, company code C100 posted a post goods issue, which in turn creates an accounting document. The system then created the following accounting document:

  * Dr.   EX10000201 – Cost of goods sold – External Sales

  * Cr.   AS10000010 – Material Stock Account

* You may follow normal delivery process as mentioned in the earlier business process scenarios.

5.21.3 Creating an Invoice

* Once the material is supplied to the customer, you need to bill the customer for the materials. In this step, you bill the customer depending on the output determination the system creates for billing output.

Billing output depicts the material supplied and, as part of payment terms, when the bill is due for payment:

- **SAP ECC Menu: Logistics → Sales and Distribution → Billing → Billing Document → Create**

- **Transaction Code: VF01**

▪ Company code C100 billed the customer and, as per the payment terms, the bill is due 15 days days after the billing date. The system creates SD and an accounting document as an outcome of these activities. The system has created the following accounting line items:

- Dr.   C100000000 – My Customer

- Cr.   IN10000000 – Sale Proceeds

5.21.4 Post Incoming Payment

▪ Once you have billed the customer, the customer remits on the payment owed to you on the due date. The customer may retain part of the payment for a variety of reasons. When the customer retains part of the payment, you can post the incoming payment as a partial payment or residual payment, and then make a follow up for the short payment:

- **SAP ECC Menu: Accounting → Financial Accounting → Accounts Receivable → Document Entry → Incoming Payments**

- **Transaction Code: F-28**

▪ On due date, company code C100 has received payment from the customer. While posting the incoming payment it has been observed that the customer is $200.00 short towards the material supplied. As per the business practice, company code posted the incoming payment a residual payment and the system has created the following accounting line items:

- AS10000101 – Incoming check clearing account

- C100000000 – My Customer

5.21.5 Create a Dispute Case

▪ When you receive a short payment or if you don't receive any payment from the customer, the account department does a follow-up with the customer for the short payment or non-payment. Based on the information you receive from the customer, the account receivable department creates a dispute case for the uncollected amount. You can create a dispute case in different ways. In this case, the accounts receivable department creates a dispute case for customer line item management:

- **SAP ECC Menu: Accounting → Financial Accounting → Accounts Receivable → Account → FBL5N – Display/Change Line Items**

- **Transaction Code:FBL5N**

■ Company code C100 posted the short payment as a residual line item. The accounts receivable department of company code C100 followed up with customer C100000000 regarding the short payment and found out that the customer retained $200.00 for the late delivery of material. Based on the customer's information, the account receivable department created a dispute case for $200.00.

5.21.6 Clarifying the Dispute

■ Based on the available information, dispute cases are assigned to a dispute case processor. The dispute case processor further investigates the dispute and provides a resolution for the dispute case:

- **SAP ECC Menu: Accounting → Financial Supply Chain Management → Dispute Management → Dispute Case Processing**

- **Transaction Code: UDM_DISPUTE**

■ While creating a dispute case, the accounts receivable department assigned the dispute case to a logistic dispute case processor. On further inquiry, the dispute case processor found that there was a real delay in supply of the material and accepted the deduction.

5.21.7 Writing of and Closing the Dispute Case

■ Once you accepted the fault and reconciled the deduction made by the customer, the next step is to write off the amount as expenses. You can do this either though batch processing or manually running the following transaction code:

- **SAP ECC Menu: Accounting → Financial Supply Chain Management → Dispute Management → Periodic Processing**

in Dispute Case Processing → Automatic Write-Off of Dispute Cases

- **Transaction Code: UDM_AUTOWRITEOFF**

▪ Based on the dispute case processor's information, Company code C100 decided to write off the customer deduction as expenses. In this process of write-off, the system created the following account lines:

- Dr.   EX10000700 – Customer balance write off – Delay

- Cr.   C100000000 – My Customer

▪ In this business process scenario, you learn how the dispute management component of FSCM module works with G/L and the accounts receivable component of the Finance modules. The dispute management component of the FSCM module works with data that you have entered in the accounts receivable component of the financial module. In the process, the system creates the following accounting entries as shown in the Figure 5.40.

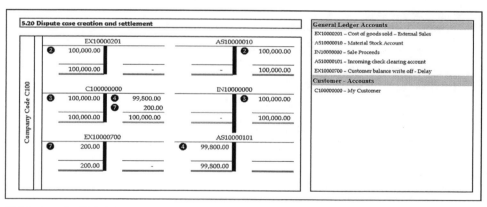

● Is the step number of the business process

FIGURE 5.40 Accounting entries.

5.22 Foreign Currency Valuation

Process Overview

Financial statements are generally created in the local currency. Due to market globalization, enterprises often maintain various balance sheet accounts in foreign currency, such as a loan account or foreign currency bank account. For your closing activities, you need to convert these accounts into the local currency. On other side you may be dealing with foreign customers or vendors for the supply of goods and services. Since you prepare the financial statement based on local currency, you need to convert these foreign currency transactions while settling open items for the financial statement.

Assumptions

It has been assumed that you have implemented the G/L component of mySAP ERP Financials and created the necessary mater data listed in the pre-requisite.

Pre-Requisite

In this business process we will use the following master data. Ensure that you have created these master data before posting any transactions:

- AS10000101 – Incoming check clearing account

- LI10000500 – Term Loan (In USD)

- LI10000501 – Term Loan (In USD) – Adjustment

- EX10000600 – Unrealized Loss Foreign Exchange

- EX10000601 – Realized Loss Foreign Exchange

- AS10000102 – Outgoing check clearing account

Note: You need to set up G/L master LI10000500 – Term Loan (In USD) currency as USD.

Business Case

In order to support the capacity expansion program, a Canadian heavy equipment manufacturer made a financing arrangement with a U.S. bank for $1 million. As the loan amount is payable in USD, the Canadian company will maintain the term loan account in USD, while its operating currency is CAD. At the month ends closing, the Canadian company code runs the foreign exchange valuation program to evaluate its liability in Canadian currencies.

Process Flow

Figure 5.41 depicts the process flow of the foreign exchange valuation business process.

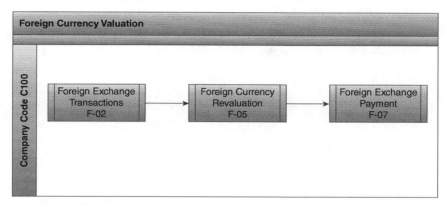

FIGURE 5.41 Foreign exchange valuation.

Process Steps

Table 5.21 depicts the steps involved in this business scenario and their dependencies.

TABLE 5.21 Foreign Currency Valuation: Process Steps

Process Step	R / O	Modules	T. Code	Expected Results
1. Posting Foreign Currency Transaction	R	FI	F-02	Transaction posted with document currency as USD
2. Foreign Currency Revaluation	R	FI	F.05	Foreign currency valuation has been performed and exchange difference has been posted to unrealized accounts
3. Foreign Currency Payment	R	FI		Term loan installment has been paid in foreign currency and realized gain or loss is posted.

5.22.1 Posting a Foreign Currency Transaction

▪ This process starts with the posting of a foreign currency document. When an account is maintained in local currency, you can post to that account with any currency. If the account is maintained in a currency other than the company code currency, you can't post to that G/L account in anything other than the G/L currency:

- **SAP ECC Menu: Accounting → Financial Accounting → General Ledger → Document Entry → General Posting**

- **Transaction Code: F-02**

- In this case, company code C100 posted a USD term loan to a USD term loan account. The system has created the following line items and recorded the transaction in USD:
  - Dr. AS10000101 – Incoming check clearing account
  - Cr. LI10000500 – Term Loan (In USD)

5.22.2 Foreign Currency Revaluation

- If you are dealing with multiple currencies, at the end of the month you may have customer and vendor open items in foreign currencies and foreign currency balances. In order to incorporate these open items in your financial statement, you need to valuate these open items.

- SAP provides options to carry over the valuation to future periods or you can reverse the valuation difference in the specified period:
  - **SAP ECC Menu: Accounting → Financial Accounting → General Ledger → Periodic Processing → Closing → Valuate → Foreign Currency Valuation**
  - **Transaction Code: F.05**

- As per company code C100's business practice, foreign transactions will be evaluated at the month end and will be reversed at the beginning of the next month. Company code C100 ran the revolution program for C100 and created the following accounting entries:
  - Cr. LI10000501 – Term Loan (In USD) – Adjustment
  - Dr   EX10000600 – Unrealized Loss Foreign Exchange

- In the subsequent period, the system can post a reversal document of the above document:
  - Dr. LI10000501 – Term Loan (In USD) – Adjustment
  - Cr   EX10000600 – Unrealized Loss Foreign Exchange

5.22.3 Foreign Currency Payment

- While making the settlement of customer/vendor /G/L open items in a foreign currency, the system translates the document currency to the local currency and post exchange rate differences to the realized accounts:
  - **SAP ECC Menu: Accounting → Financial Accounting → General Ledger → Posting → Outgoing Payments**
  - **Transaction Code: F-07**

- After a few years, company code C100 clears the term loaded in USD. As the rate of exchange is different at the time of payment, the system has calculated foreign exchange loss and posted to the realized loss account.

- In this entire business process, the system has generated the following accounting entries as shown in Figure 5.42.

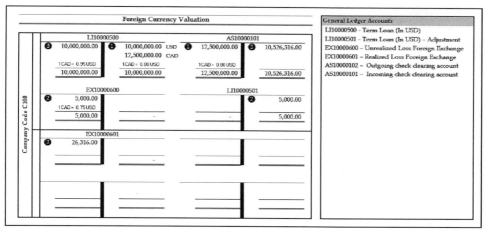

❶ Is the step number of the business process

FIGURE 5.42 Accounting entries.

5.23 Closing Process: Sales and Distribution

Process Overview

In order to have a smooth finance close, you need to close the feeder system first. Closing the activities of sales and distribution process ensures that the sales processes are completed successfully and data are transmitted to the financial system for correct accounting.

Assumptions

It has been assumed that you have implemented the sales and distribution system and posted transactions.

Business Case

Company code C100 is a manufacturing unit and sells its products throughout the country. For smooth closing, it has identified the following activities.

Process Steps

You have carried out the following important closing process steps of sales and distribution process.

TABLE 5.22 Closing Process Sales and Distribution: Process Steps

Process Step	R / O	Modules	T. Code	Expected Results
1. Review Blocked Sales Orders	R	SD	VKM1	Reviewed blocked sales order
2. Review Incomplete Sales Orders		SD	V.02	Reviewed incomplete sales order
3. Review Sales Documents Blocked for Delivery		SD	VA14L	Reviewed sales blocked delivery documents
4. Review Sales Orders Due for Delivery		SD	VL10C	Reviewed sales order due for delivery
5. Review Log of Collective Delivery Creation:		SD	V_SA	Reviewed log for collective delivery creation log
6. Review Incomplete Sales Documents		SD	V_UC	Reviewed incomplete sales document
7. Review Outbound Deliveries for Goods Issue		SD	VL060	Reviewed outbound deliveries for goods issue
8. Review Sales Documents Blocked for Billing		SD	V23	Reviewed sales document blocked for billing
9. Review Billing Due List		SD	VF04	Reviewed billing due list
10. Review Log of Collective Invoice Creation		SD	V.21	Reviewed log of collective invoice creation
11. Review List of Blocked (for accounting) Billing Documents		SD	VFX3	Reviewed blocked billing document for accounting
12. Calculation of Work in Process (Service Provider)		SD	KKAK	Reviewed work in process of sales order
13. Settling the Sales Order to Profitability Analysis (Service Provider)		SD	VA88	Settlement of sales order to COPA has been performed

5.23.1 Review Blocked Sales Orders

▪ If you are using SD credit control, your sales order might have blocked while a credit check is performed by the system. You need to review the sales order and take the appropriate corrective actions:

- **Menu Path: Logistics → Sales and Distribution → Credit Management → Exceptions → Blocked SD Documents**

- **Transaction Code: VKM1**

▪ The accounts receivable department of company code C100 has performed this step and the sales orders are released after corrective action was taken by the marketing department and accounting department.

5.23.2 Review Incomplete Sales Orders

▪ In this step, the sales department reviews erred or incomplete sales orders in the system. There are various reasons for clearing the existing system errors out of the sales orders, such as proper jurisdiction code has been set for tax calculation and communication between SAP and external tax system has been terminated while creating sales:

- **Menu Path: Menu Path: Logistics → Sales and Distribution → Orders → Incomplete Orders**

- **Transaction Code: V.02**

▪ It is very important to fix erred sales orders. Until and unless you fix these errors you can't deliver goods, which may impact your year-end sales target.

▪ As a preventive measure, company code C100 takes this step at the end of the day to ensure the system has created all sales orders and communicated to the logistic department for picking of related stock for onward delivery.

5.23.3 Review Sales Documents Blocked for Delivery

▪ Like the sales order, the system also blocks delivery documents which hit the credit control limit set by the credit control department. It is good practice to periodically review these blocked delivery documents so that you can complete your sales cycle. After corrective action, you need to release these delivery documents for further processing:

- **Menu Path: Logistics → Sales and Distribution → Credit Management → Sales and Distribution Documents → Sales and Distribution Documents Blocked for Delivery**

- **Transaction Code: VA14L**

■ At the end of each day, the sales department of company code C100 does a delivery block checking. After getting confirmation from the credit control department, it releases the delivery block.

5.23.4 Review Sales Orders Due for Delivery

■ On the scheduled delivery date of the sales order, you need to create delivery schedule lines. Once the material is available, schedule line items are due for shipping. You need to review the sales order due for delivery by running manually through delivery list by using either of the following navigation options:

- **Menu Path: Logistics → Logistics Execution → Outbound Process → Goods Issue for Outbound Delivery → Outbound Delivery → Create → Collective Processing of Documents Due for Delivery → Sales Order Items**

- **Transaction Code: VL10C**

■ At the end of the day, company code C100 creates the delivery due list for the next business day.

5.23.5 Review Log of Collective Delivery Creation

■ You can create a sales order delivery document individually or through batch processing. When you are handling a large number of delivery documents, it is advisable to create the delivery documents through collective processing. Sometimes, due to various reasons, the system doesn't create the delivery document. In order to prevent potential delay in delivery, you need to periodically review the collecting delivery creation log. The delivery creation log depicts what happened while creating the delivery document, so that you can rectify these errors:

- **Menu Path: Logistics → Sales and Distribution →Shipping and Transportation → Outbound Delivery → Lists and Logs → Collective Processing Log**

- **Transaction Code: V_SA**

■ The sales department of company code C100 reviews the collective processing log at end of the day and take corrective action in order to prevent the delay of the delivery document, which delays the ultimate delivery of the material.

5.23.6 Review Incomplete SD Documents

▪ In this activity, you will review all incomplete SD documents. There are many circumstances that prevent you from completing SD documents, such as if the system could not determine the proper G/L accounts or G/L accounts are blocked for posting. To complete the sales process, it is necessary that the sales and distribution system creates the appropriate financial entries:

- **Menu Path: Logistics → Sales and Distribution → Shipping and Transportation → Outbound Delivery → Lists and Logs → Incomplete Outbound Deliveries**

- **Transaction Code: V_UC**

▪ Company code C100 periodically reviews incomplete billing documents and takes the appropriate action to complete the SD documents.

5.23.7 Review Outbound Deliveries for Goods Issue

▪ You post the goods issue to complete the sales process. It is possible that you might have skipped posting the goods issue for some of your deliveries. In order to ensure that you have posted a goods issue for all of your deliveries, you need to review outbound deliveries for which you have not posted goods issue:

- **Menu Path: Logistics → Logistics Execution → Outbound Process → Goods Issue for Outbound Delivery → Outbound Delivery → Lists and Logs → Outbound Delivery Monitor**

- **Transaction Code: VL06O**

▪ Company code C100 periodically reviews the outbound deliveries and subsequent post goods issue process in order to ensure that all deliveries have been billed properly.

5.23.8 Review Sales Documents Blocked for Billing

▪ Depending on the credit control configuration, the system blocks billing documents. In these circumstances you need to take corrective action after analyzing the reason for blocking of the billing document:

- **Menu Path: Logistics → Sales and Distribution → Sales → Information System → Worklists → Sales Documents Blocked For Billing**

- **Transaction Code: V23**

5.23.9 Review Billing Due List

■ Generally, you create a billing due list through batch processing. Sometimes, due to system constraints or hick ups, it is possible that the system didn't generate the billing due list. Periodically reviewing the billing due list log prevents potential loss of sales revenue and delivery delays can be avoided:

- **Menu Path: Logistics → Sales and Distribution → Billing → Billing Document → Process Billing Due List**
- **Transaction Code: VF04**

5.23.10 Review Log of Collective Invoice Creation

■ At scheduled times, the sales department creates a customer invoice through batch processing. By reviewing invoice creation log, you ensure that the system has created all invoices due. This avoids delays in customer's collection:

- **Menu Path: Logistics → Sales and Distribution → Billing → Information System → Billing Documents → Log of Collective Run**
- **Transaction Code: V.21**

5.23.11 Review List Blocked (for Accounting) Billing Documents

■ Billing documents created in the sales and distribution module automatically are transmitted to the financial system. Sometimes it doesn't happen, due to various reasons. In those circumstances, it is necessary to investigate and fix the issues so that your financial system will link up with your sales and distribution system. To avoid such gaps, you need to periodically review the following navigation options and take corrective actions.

- **Menu Path: Logistics → Sales and Distribution → Billing → Billing Document → Billing → Billing Document → Blocked Billing Docs**
- **Transaction Code: VFX3**

5.23.12 Calculation of Work in Process (Service Provider)

■ Periodically, you need to evaluate the sales order progression based on planned and actual costs with expected review:

- **Menu Path: Logistics → Sales and Distribution → Sales → Product Cost by Sales Order → Period-End Closing → Single Functions → Results Analysis → Execute → Collective Processing**

- **Transaction Code: KKAK**

5.23.13 Settling the Sales Order to Profitability Analysis (Service Provider)

- As you are aware, profitability analysis gets most of its data from the feeder system sales and distribution modules. For customer-specific orders, you can collect cost and revenues initially in the sales order, and thereafter you transfer these costs to CO-PA (Controlling Profitability Analysis) for analysis. You can automate sales order settlements to CO-PA through batch jobs:

  - **Menu Path: Logistics → Sales and Distribution → Sales → Order → Subsequent Functions → Settlement**

  - **Transaction Code: VA88**

5.24 Closing Process–Accounts Receivable

Process Overview

Like G/L accounting, you need to perform specific tasks for smooth account receivable closing. The steps, or activates, mentioned in this business process may not coincide with your real-life environment.

It is not necessary to follow the sequence in which these are mentioned in this section. Some steps can be performed in parallel.

Some steps are necessary for month end, while another will fall under the year-end process.

Assumptions

It has been assumed that you have implemented mySAP ERP Financials and performed your day-to-day activities.

Pre-Requisite

You have posted transactions during you normal day-to-day activities.

Business Case

As part of the closing process, company code C100 has identified specific processes that should be carried out.

Process Steps

Table 5.23 lists the closing process steps of accounts received. It is not necessary that you should perform these in the order mentioned the table.

TABLE 5.23 Closing Process – Accounts Receivable: Process Steps

Process Step	R / O	Modules	T. Code	Expected Results
1. Clearing of open items	O	FICO	F-32	Open item has been cleared
2. Dunning	O	FICO	F150	Dunning letter has been sent to customer
3. Arrears Interest Calculation	O	FICO	F.2B	Arrear interest has been calculated
4. Recurring Entries	O	FICO	F.14	Recurring entries have been posted
5. Foreign currency valuation of open items	O	FICO	F.05 FAGL_ FC_VAL	Foreign currency valuation has been carried out
6. Regrouping of Accounts Receivable	O	FICO	F101 FAGLF101	Customer balance has been regrouped
7. Printing Account Statements	O	FICO	F.27	Customer account statement has been printed
8. Balance Confirmations – Customers/Vendors	O	FICO	F.17	Customer balance confirmation has been printed
9. Balance carry forward	R	FICO	F.07	Customer balance carry forward has been carried out

5.24.1 Clearing Open Items

- Clearing account receivable open items follows the same process that you followed for accounts payable. As you have already covered clearing of vendor open items earlier in this chapter, you can refer to the account payable functionalities:

    - **SAP ECC Menu: Accounting → Financial Accounting → Accounts Receivable → Account → Clear**

    - **Transaction Code: F-32**

5.24.2 Dunning

- As we discussed in the accounts payable, dunning is a process that sends a reminder to the customer as a follow up for collection. The system generates dunning letters based on the configuration that you have done through transaction code FBMP:

- **SAP ECC Menu: Accounting → Financial Accounting → Accounts Receivable → Periodic Processing → Dunning**

- **Transaction Code: F150**

5.24.3 Arrears Interest Calculation

▪ Arrear interest calculation is similar to other accounts payable functionalities. You have already covered arrear interest calculation in the account payable business process earlier in this chapter:

- **SAP ECC Menu: Accounting → Financial Accounting → Accounts Receivable → Periodic Processing → Interest Calculation → Calculate Interest on Arrears → With Open Items**

- **Transaction Code: F.2B**

5.24.4 Recurring Entries

▪ Like account payable recurring entries, you can post recurring entries for accounts receivable. Recurring entries were already covered earlier in this chapter. You can follow the same process that you have followed for accounts payable:

- **SAP ECC Menu: Accounting → Financial Accounting → Accounts Receivable → Periodic Processing → Recurring Entries → Execute**

- **Transaction Code: F.14**

5.24.5 Foreign Currency Valuation of Open Items

▪ For foreign currency valuation you need to follow the same process that you have followed for G/L and accounts payable. A single transaction code takes care of accounts receivable, accounts payable, and G/L accounts. Foreign currency valuation is already discussed earlier in this chapter:

- **SAP ECC Menu: Accounting → Financial Accounting → Accounts Payable → Periodic Processing → Closing Valuate → Valuation of Open Items in Foreign Currency.**

- **Transaction Code: F.05**

▪ If you have activated the SAP G/L functionality then you need to use the following menu path for foreign currency valuation:

- **SAP ECC Menu: Accounting → Financial Accounting → Accounts Payable → Periodic Processing → Closing Valuate → Foreign Currency Valuation of Open Items (New).**

- **Transaction Code: FAGL_FC_VAL**

5.24.6 Regrouping of Accounts Receivable

■ The regrouping of accounts receivable and accounts payable is to be carried out with a single transaction code. SAP provides different set-off fields for vendors and customers:

- **SAP ECC Menu: Accounting → Financial Accounting → Accounts Receivable → Periodic Processing → Closing → Reclassify → Reclassify Receivables/Payables Dunning**

- **Transaction Code: F101**

■ If you have activated SAP G/L functionality, you can regroup and reclassify through the following navigation options:

- **SAP ECC Menu: Accounting → Financial Accounting → Accounts Receivable → Periodic Processing → Closing → Reclassify → Sorting/Reclassification (New)**

- **Transaction Code: FAGLF101**

5.24.7 Printing Account Statements

■ Periodically, you need to review the accounts payable balance as well as provide accounting statements to your vendor. In this functionality, you can print accounting statement of customers:

- **SAP ECC Menu: Accounting → Financial Accounting → Accounts Receivable → Periodic Processing → Print Correspondence → Periodic Account Statements**

- **Transaction Code: F.27**

5.24.8 Balance Confirmation – Customers

■ In order to substantiate your financial statements, you need to get confirmation from the vendor for the amount payable to them. In addition, as a backup paper for financial statements, balance confirmation serves as a dispute resolution between two parties of a business transaction:

- **SAP ECC Menu: Accounting → Financial Accounting → Accounts Receivable → Periodic Processing → Closing → Check/Count → Balance Confirmation: Print**

- **Transaction Code: F.17**

5.24.9 Balance Carry Forward

- Once you have finalized your financial statements, you need to carry forward customer balances to the next fiscal year:

  - **SAP ECC Menu: Accounting → Financial Accounting → Accounts Receivable → Periodic Processing → Closing → Carry Forward → Balance Carry Forward**

  - **Transaction Code: F.07**

5.25 Closing Process–Accounts Payable

Process Overview

Like G/L accounting, you need to perform specific tasks for smooth account payable closing. Steps or activates mentioned in this business process may not coincide with your real-life environment.

It is not necessary to follow the sequence in which these steps are mentioned in this section. Some steps can be performed in parallel.

Some steps are necessary for month end, while others fall under the year-end process.

Assumptions

It has been assumed that you have implemented mySAP ERP Financials and performed your day-to-day activities.

Pre-Requisite

You have posted transactions during your normal day=today activities.

Business Case

As part of the closing process, company code C100 has identified specific processes that are to be carried out.

Process Steps

Table 5.24 shows what we generally follow while closing accounts payable as a part of closing activities.

TABLE 5.24 Closing Process – Accounts Payable: Process Steps

Process Step	R / O	Modules	T. Code	Expected Results
1. Clearing of open items		FICO	F-44	Vendor open item has been cleared
2. Dunning		FICO	F150	Dunning has been sent to vendor who owes money
3. Arrears Interest Calculation		FICO	F.4B	Interest has been calculated on outstanding open items
4. Recurring Entries		FICO	F.14	Recurring items has been posted
5. Regrouping of Accounts Payable		FICO	F101 FAGLF101	Accounts payable balance has been regrouped
6. Printing Account Statements		FICO	F.27	Account statement has been printed
7. Balance Confirmations – Vendors		FICO	F.18	Balance confirmation has been mailed to vendor

5.25.1 Clearing of Open Items

■ Earlier in this chapter, you covered how to clear G/L open items. This step is similar to the process you have discussed in G/L accounting. SAP provides various selection criteria to select and clear vendor open line items. You can automate this step through batch processing so that the accounts payable department will be free from this activity:

- **SAP ECC Menu: Accounting → Financial Accounting → Accounts Payable → Account → Clear**

- **Transaction Code: F-44**

5.25.2 Dunning

■ Dunning is the process of sending reminder letters to vendors for balance payable to you. Sometimes, the vendor has a debit balance and you need to follow up to collect money or material from the vendor. In this process, we will discuss accounts receivable sections in detail:

- **SAP ECC Menu: Accounting → Financial Accounting → Accounts Payable → Periodic Processing → Dunning**

- **Transaction Code: F150**

5.25.3 Arrears Interest Calculation

■ SAP comes with two types of interest calculation: (1) balance interest calculation and (2) arrear interest calculation. Refer to Chapter 2 for definitions and differences between balance interest and arrear interest calculations. In this case, we will learn about arrear interest calculations:

- **SAP ECC Menu: Accounting → Financial Accounting → Accounts Payable → Periodic Processing → Interest Calculation → Calculate Interest on Arrears → With Open Items**

- **Transaction Code: F.4B**

5.25.4 Recurring Entries

- Recurring entries of the closing process for G/L accounting were covered earlier in this chapter. The recurring entry process is same for G/L accounts, accounts payable, and accounts received. As this was already covered we will not be discussing this process in great detail:

- **SAP ECC Menu: Accounting → Financial Accounting → Accounts Payable → Periodic Processing → Recurring Entries → Execute**

- **Transaction Code: F.14**

5.25.5 Regrouping of Accounts Payable

- You can regroup accounts payable balances and reclassify them with debit balance to be treated as assets in the financial statement, while accounts payable with a credit balance will be treated as liability in the financial statement. This type of adjustment presents the financial statement in a proper way. The reversal entry of this type of adjustment will happen at a future period:

- **SAP ECC Menu: Accounting → Financial Accounting → Accounts Payable → Periodic Processing → Closing → Reclassify → Reclassify Receivables/Payables Dunning**

- **Transaction Code: F101**

- If you have activated SAP G/L functionality, you can regroup and reclassify through the following new navigation options:

- **SAP ECC Menu: Accounting → Financial Accounting → Accounts Payable → Periodic Processing → Closing → Reclassify → Sorting/Reclassification (New)**

- **Transaction Code: FAGLF101**

5.25.6 Printing Account Statements

▪ Periodically, you need to review the account payable balance as well as provide accounting statements to your vendor. In this functionality, you can print accounting statements of vendors:

- **SAP ECC Menu: Accounting → Financial Accounting → Accounts Payable → Periodic Processing → Print Correspondence → Periodic Account Statements**
- **Transaction Code: F.27**

5.25.7 Balance Confirmation – Vendors

▪ In order to substantiate your financial statements, you need to get confirmation from the vendor for the amount payable to them. In addition, as a backup for the financial statements, balance confirmation serves as dispute resolution between two parties of a business transaction:

- **SAP ECC Menu: Accounting → Financial Accounting → Accounts Payable → Periodic Processing → Print Correspondence → Balance Confirmation → Print Letters.**
- **Transaction Code: F.18**

5.26 Closing Process–Assets Management

Process Overview

Before preparing your financial statement, you need to close assets accounting. The closing process of assets accounting covers checking of assets master, depreciation run, and technical closing assets accounting.

Pre-Requisite

It has been assumed that you have implemented assets accounting and posted the transition in current or previous year.

Business Case

In order to close the books of the account, company code C100 performs the following steps to close assets accounting.

Process Steps

The closing process of assets management covers the following steps. In your real working environment you may have few or more steps. Table 5.25 covers the important steps of the closing process.

TABLE 5.25 Closing Process Assets Management: Process Steps

Process Step	R / O	Modules	T. Code	Expected Results
1. Check incomplete assets	R	FI	AUVA	Completeness of assets has been checked
2. Manual depreciation	R	FI	AFAB	Manual depreciation has been provided
3. Posting normal depreciation	R	FI	AFAB	Normal depreciation has been posted
4. Fiscal year change	R	FI	AJRW	Fiscal year ending has been carried out
5. earend closing	R	FI	AJAB	Old fiscal year has been closed

5.26.1 Check Incomplete Assets

- It is important to check the completeness of assets before your closing process. Incomplete assets are asset masters that were created either by the system or manually in which important information are missing. If incomplete, assets exist in your system:

  - This prevents closing the fiscal year

  - You cannot post depreciation

  - You can retire incomplete assets

- You can check incomplete master data through either of the following navigation options:

  - **SAP ECC Menu: Accounting → Financial Accounting → Fixed Assets → Environment → Closing → Problem Analysis → Incomplete Assets**

  - **Transaction Code: AUVA**

5.26.2 Manual Depreciation

- SAP provides the functionality to provide planned and/or unplanned depreciation. Planned depreciation is determined by the depreciation key, while unplanned depreciation is based on circumstances and business needs. Periodically, management reviews and makes the decision about whether or not assets are being depreciated as per the business requirement.

- If the planned depreciation is not enough, management goes for unplanned depreciation.

- **SAP ECC Menu: Accounting → Financial Accounting → Fixed Assets → Periodic Processing → Depreciation Run → Execute**
- **Transaction Code: AFAB**

5.26.3 Posting the Depreciation

■ When you create an asset under an assets class, the depreciation key is inherited to the assets master. The depreciation key in the master, the capitalization date, and depreciation start date drives the depreciation calculation.

■ When you run periodic depreciation, the system calculates depreciation based on the depreciation key and posts to G/L:

- **SAP ECC Menu: Accounting → Financial Accounting → Fixed Assets → Periodic Processing → Depreciation Run → Execute**
- **Transaction Code: AFAB**

5.26.4 Fiscal Year Change

■ In fiscal year change, you open new a fiscal year for assets accounting. Through the fiscal year change you can forward assets balances from the old fiscal year to the new fiscal year:

- **SAP ECC Menu: Accounting → Financial Accounting → Fixed Assets → Periodic Processing → Fiscal Year Change**
- **Transaction Code: AJRW**

5.26.5 Year-End Closing

■ In the year-end closing process you close the old fiscal year. Once you close a fiscal year, the system doesn't allow adding assets values in the old fiscal year:

- **SAP ECC Menu: Accounting → Financial Accounting → Fixed Assets → Periodic Processing → Fiscal Year Change → Year-End Closing → Execute**
- **Transaction Code: AJAB**

5.27 Closing Process–G/L Accounting

Process Overview

In this section, we will learn about the various closing activities that we need to perform for our day-end, month-end, and year-end closing. These are the few steps we generally perform for our day-to-day closing activities. These steps need not follow the sequence presented here. Some activities can be performed in parallel.

Assumptions

It has been assumed that you have implemented mySAP ERP Financials and performed your day-to-day activities.

Pre-Requisite

You have posted transactions during your normal day-to-day activities.

Business Case

As part of the closing process, company code C100 has identified specific processes that are to be carried out.

Process Steps

Table 5.26 depicts the G/L closing steps for general ledger accounting.

TABLE 5.26 Month End Process – General Ledger Accounting: Process Steps

Process Step	R / O	Modules	T. Code	Expected Results
1. Review of Parked Document	O	FICO	FBV0	Parking document has been reviewed either posted or deleted
2. Clearing of Open Items	O	FICO	F-03	G/L open items has been cleared
3. Recurring Entries	O	FICO	FBD1	Recurring document has been posted
4. Automatic Clearing of GR/IR Account	O	FICO	F.13	Open items of GR/IR has been cleared
5. Regrouping GR/IR Accounts	O	FICO	F.19	Balance open item of GR/IR has been classified and posted to adjustment account for balance sheet purpose and reversed in the subsequent period
6. Foreign Currency Valuation	O	FICO	F.05 FAGL_FC_VAL	G/L account has been revalued and foreign exchange has been posted to unrealized accounts
7. Balance Sheets and P&L Statements	O	FICO	S_ALR_87012249	Balance sheet and income statement has been generated
8. Balance Carry Forward	O	FICO	F.16 FAGLGVTR	G/L balances of balance sheet were carried forward and retained account has been posted

5.27.1 Review of a Parked Document

■ In the day-to-day activities, the accounting department parks and posts journal entries. There is a probability the document is parked and not posted on a particular point of time. For smooth closing of an account it becomes necessary to review parked documents. The following circumstances lead you to review parked document:

- Parked document may not be necessary to post or may be supplemented by another document

- User forgot to complete the parked document

- Approver forget to approve parked document

■ In these cases either you can post these document after the necessary correction. If these document are not needed you can delete them:

- **SAP ECC Menu: Accounting → Financial Accounting → General Ledger → Document → Parked Documents → Post/ Delete**

- **Transaction Code: FBV0**

5.27.2 Clearing Open Items

■ As part of the closing process, we clear the open items account periodically. Normally, you set up an automatic clearing process to know the debit and credit open items, which fulfill the open item clearing attributes like assignment numbers or amount. The automatic open item clearing process does not clear open items that do not fulfill the criteria. In those cases, you need to invoke the manual clearing process. In the manual clearing process, the SAP application provides various selection criteria based on which we can select open items:

- **SAP ECC Menu: Accounting → Financial Accounting → General Ledger → Account → Clear**

- **Transaction Code: F-03**

■ In this step, you can residue items by clearing unbalanced Dr. and Cr. items. Clearing open items is one of the important preconditions for the archiving process. If you are working in a multi-currency environment, the system creates foreign exchange differences while clearing open items.

5.27.3 Recurring Entries

▪ You post recurring entries for your standing orders such as monthly rent and loan installments. mySAP ERP Financials provides the functionality to automate these types of accounting entries. You can use a recurring posting even on a weekly basis.

▪ The recurring entries functionality relieves the accounting department to look after non-standard accounting entries. You can automate recurring entries through batch jobs so that the system takes care of the accounting entries for you.

▪ We use recurring entries where the account, amount, and posting keys are fixed:

- **SAP ECC Menu: Accounting → Financial Accounting → (e.g.) Accounts Payable → Document Entry → Reference Documents → Recurring Entry Document**

- **Transaction Code: FBD1**

▪ Company code C100, runs a recurring entry periodically to post lease premiums and rental insurance premiums.

5.27.4 Automatic Clearing of GR/IR Account

▪ You maintain a GR/IR account to capture the time difference between goods receipts and invoice receipts. At the end of the month, obviously you will have some balance for which you are expecting invoices or goods. While making GR and IR, the system credits and debits to the GR/IR accounts independently. We run this transaction in order to offset debit open item with credit open items. Generally, we run this transaction code through a batch job:

- **SAP ECC Menu: Accounting → Financial Accounting → General Ledger → Periodic Processing → Automatic Clearing → Without Specification of Clearing Currency**

- **Transaction Code: F.13**

5.27.5 Regrouping GR/IR Accounts

▪ As you learned previously, we maintain GR/IR account to track time differences between goods receipts and invoice receipts. At a particular point of time you will have open items represented by goods receipts for which we are waiting on invoices, and invoice receipts awaiting goods. From the accounts point of view, invoice receipt open items are considered assets because we have not received material and goods receipts open items are considered a liability. For our closing activity we need to regroup these open items by transferring these open items to different accounts. You can use either of the following navigation options:

- **SAP ECC Menu: Accounting → Financial Accounting → General Ledger → Periodic Processing → Closing → Regroup → GR/IR Clearing**

- **Transaction Code: F.19**

5.27.6 Foreign Currency Valuation

▪ Foreign currency valuation has already been covered earlier in this chapter. – We run foreign currency valuation programs to valuate foreign currency open items or foreign currency G/ L balances:

- **SAP ECC Menu: Accounting → Financial Accounting → General Ledger → Periodic Processing → Closing → Valuate → Foreign Currency Valuation**

- **Transaction Code: F.05**

▪ If you are using mySAP ERP Financials 6.0 and activated SAP the G/L functionality, you need to carry out a foreign currency valuation by using either of the following navigation options:

- **Accounting → Financial Accounting → General Ledger → Periodic Processing → Closing → Valuate → Foreign Currency Valuation (New)**

- **Transaction Code: FAGL_FC_VAL**

5.27.7 Balance Sheets and P&L Statements

▪ After the closing activity you generate a financial statement. The financial statement generally covers balance sheet, profit and loss account (or income statement), and cash flow statement:

- **SAP ECC Menu: Accounting → Financial Accounting → General Ledger → Information System → General Ledger Reports → Balance Sheet/ Profit and Loss Statement/ Cash**

Flow → General → Actual/Actual Comparisons → Actual/
Actual Comparison for Year

- **Transaction Code: S_ALR_87012249**

5.27.8 Balance Carry Forward

- Once you have finalized your financial statement, you need to carry forward the G/L balances to the next fiscal year. Carry forward balance sheet balances to next the fiscal year, while for income statements, G/L accounts balance carry forward program calculate the net balance of income and expenses. The G/L account transfers the net balance to a retained earning account:

  - **SAP ECC Menu: Accounting → Financial Accounting → General ledger → Periodic processing → Closing → Carry forward → Balances**

  - **Transaction Code: F.16**

- If you are using mySAP ERP Financials and activated the SAP G/L functionality, you need to carry forward G/L balances through either of the following navigation options:

  - **SAP ECC Menu: Accounting → Financial Accounting → General Ledger → Periodic Processing → Closing → Carrying Forward → Balance Carry Forward (New)**

  - **Transaction Code: FAGLGVTR**

In this chapter, you have covered various integrated and non-integrated business processes, which are module dependent and module independent.

CHAPTER 6

REPORTING

In previous chapters you learned how to configure the mySAP ERP Financials and how to use these configured components. The next question is how to generate reports and display data that you have captured in various activities. To mitigate these challenges SAP has provided the following tools:

- Display transaction or master data

- Display table data

- Execution of reports

Display transaction or master data: Wherever SAP has provided options to create a new record, it has also provided the functionality to display reports.

These functionalities normally display single transactions. Generally, the user community will have access to these functionalities. A few examples of these functionalities are:

- Transaction Code *FB03*: By invoking the transaction code FB03 you can display a document for a company code.

- Transaction Code *FS00*: This transaction code is the central point for the creation, display, and change of G/L master records. Within this transaction code SAP has provided options to create, display, or change. You can choose the appropriate options.

- Transaction Code *FK03*: Displays company code data and general data of the vendor master data.

- Transaction Code *FD03*: Displays company code data and general data of the customer master data.

- Transaction Code *AW01N*: Displays assets master and associated objects with assets.

Display table data with every transaction you post, and every master you create are stored in a table. In order to browse these table data, you need to know the table name where these data are stored. Some of the important tables are: Financial Accounting:

- BSEG   Accounting Document Segment
- BKPF   Accounting Document Header
- SKA1   G/L Account Master (Chart of Accounts)
- SKAT   G/L Account Master Record (Chart of Accounts – Description)
- SKB1   G/L account master (company code)
- ANEK   Document Header Asset Posting
- ANEP   Asset Line Items
- BNKA   Bank master record

Material Management:

- MARA – General Material Data
- MARC – Plant Data for Material

- MBEW – Material Valuation

- MKPF – Header – Material Document

Sales and Distribution:

- VBRK – Billing: Header Data

- VBRP – Billing: Item Data

You can browse these table data by invoking transaction code SE16N or SE16.

Execution of reports: SAP has provided hundreds of pre-delivered reports for modules and sub-modules. You can reach these reports in the information system note of the SAP application modules. In addition to these pre-delivered reports, user communities often demand varieties of reports for control, review, and to comply with reporting requirements.

To cater to customer needs, SAP has provided various reporting tools. With these reporting tools you can develop new custom reports and enhance SAP delivered reports. These reporting tools include:

- *ABAP Query*: SAP ABAP Query is one of the easiest tools to query information from. You can use this tool in almost every component of the SAP applications. You can reach ABAP query menu by navigating: SAP menu > Tools > ABAP Workbench > Utilities > ABAP Query Report

- *Report Painter/Report Writer*: Report painter/report writer reports are used to create reports such as financial statements, sales reports, and inventory reports. You can reach report painter/report writer by navigating the SAM Menu > Information systems > Ad hoc reports > Report painter >

- *Drilldown Reporting*: Drilldown reporting offers the greatest flexibility of all the reporting tool. SAP offers two types of drill down reports: (1) basic reports and (2) form reports. You can reach the drilldown report creation menu path by navigating from the SAP menu > Accounting > Controlling > Profitability analysis > Information system > Define report > Create

In this chapter, you learn more about the report writer and report painter reporting tool functionalities.

Report Writer: You can use report writer to build reports from multiple applications. In report writer you can use sets, variables, formulas, cells, and key figures to build a complex report.

Report Painter: Report painter uses a graphical report structure that forms the basis for report definition. With report painter's intuitive WYSI-WYG (What-You-See-Is-What-You-Get) approach to report design, you define a report on a form that displays the rows and columns as they will appear in the report output.

You can open, edit, and change the painter reports in report writer, but not vice versa. The report writer/report painter tools use the same reporting engine for the execution of reports.

Both report painter/report writer tools use total tables to displays data, which you can use in following application components of the SAP application.

- Total table CCSS for Cost Center Accounting (CO-CCA), Internal Orders (CO-OPA), and Activity Based Costing (CO-ABC) and Cost element reports in Project Systems (PS).

- Total table GLFUNCT for cost-of-sales accounting.

- Total table GLPCT and GLPCOP for Profit Center Accounting (CO-PCA/EC-PCA).

- Total table FILC for Legal Consolidations (FI-LC).

- Total table COFIT for the Controlling Reconciliation Ledger (CO-CEL).

- Total table ZZXXXXXX custom tables for the Special Purpose Ledger (FI-SL).

- Total table FIMC for Enterprise Controlling module (EC-LC).

- Total table GLT0 for Financial Accounting (G/L) and business area (FI-GL).

- Total Table KKBC, KKBE, and KKBU for Product Costing module.

Report painter and report writer use the following new components:

- *Sets*: A set represents a logical grouping of characteristic values. For example, the current asset may be represented by various G/L masters.

You can group all current assets together under one set, so that you can have one set ID instead of a number of different G/L accounts. A set is always represented by a set ID.

- *Libraries*: Libraries contains characteristics and key figures that can be used in report writer and report painter. The foundation of any report writer and report painter report is a library.

- *Reports*: A report represents the header, footer, rows, columns, and overall data selection of a report painter/report writer report.

- *Report Groups*: With the help of a report group you can group together more than one report. They can then execute at the same time and user can navigate from one report to another.

While creating a report painter/report writer report you will come across the following terminology:

- *Key Figures*: The key figure represents the currency and/or quantity of a report. SAP has provided few key figures for each application components, including: (1) local currency amount for profit center accounting, (2) costs for cost center accounting, and (3) net value for billing line items.

- *Characteristics*: Characteristics are the fields, other than currency or quantity, needed to build the report. These include, company code, plant, sales organization, G/L account, cost center, and period.

- *Rows*: The rows of a report painter/report writer report contain characteristics that determine how the rows will appear in the report.

- *Columns*: The columns of a report painter report must have key figures. If needed, columns may also contain characteristics.

- *General Data Selection*: The general data selection area contains the additional characteristics that should control the data included in the report. Any required fields that are not in the rows or columns are also included in the general data selection.

In order to create a report painter/report writer report, you need to follow a sequence of steps described in Figure 6.1.

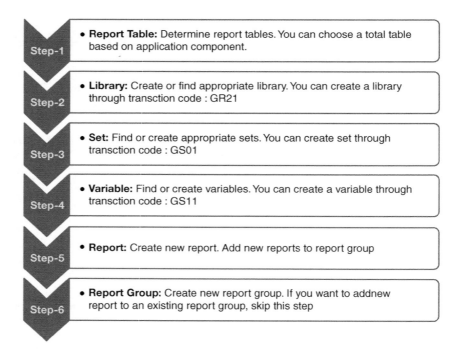

FIGURE 6.1 Report painter/report writer steps.

Let us study the steps to better understand the report painter and report writer functionalities. Let us take a business case where the business wants a report that will depict trial balances on a particular day, as seen in Table 6.1.

TABLE 6.1 Trial Balances Example

Trial Balance of Company Code BR01 as ...	
G/L Accounts – Descriptions	**Amount (in $)**
	Total Revenue
3000000000	Interest income
3000000001	P & L on sale of FA
3000000002	FA Cls Account
3000000003	Sales Account
	Total Expenses
4000000000	Cash Discount Exp
4000000001	Depreciation Exp

TABLE 6.1 (*continued*)

Trial Balance of Company Code BR01 as ...	
G/L Accounts – Descriptions	**Amount (in $)**
4000000002	Salaries Account	
4000000004	Wages Account	
4000000005	Vacation Bonus	
4000000006	Yearly Bonus	
4000000007	Misc Periodic Cost	
4000000008	Telephone Expenses	
4000000009	Electricity Expenses	
4000000010	IT Expenses	
4000000011	FX Realized G/L	
	Total Assets	
1000000000	BofAmerica	
1000000001	HSBC Bank	
1000000002	CITI BANK	
1000000003	Spl. G/L Recon Account	
1000000004	ASST-LAND	
1000000101	CITI Bank-LBOX-Incom	
1000002000	FX Unrealized G/L	
	Total Liabilities	
2000000000	Ven Recon Account	
2000000001	FA Cls Account	
2000000002	Other Payable Account	
Total	

Reports Tables: Before you start building a report you must know what type of report you want. Choices include G/L reports, special ledger reports, or profit center reports. The choice of table depends on what type of report you want. You can't build a report painter/report writer report for all tables. SAP has provided the following total tables to build report painter/report writer reports:

- Total table CCSS for Cost Center Accounting (CO-CCA), Internal Orders (CO-OPA), Activity Based Costing (CO-ABC), and cost element reports in Project Systems (PS).

- Total table GLFUNCT for cost-of-sales accounting.

- Total table GLPCT and GLPCOP for Profit Center Accounting (CO-PCA/EC-PCA).

- Total table FILC for Legal Consolidations (FI-LC).

- Total table COFIT for the Controlling Reconciliation Ledger (CO-CEL).

- Total table ZZXXXXXX custom tables for the Special Purpose Ledger (FI-SL).

- Total table FIMC for Enterprise Controlling module (EC-LC).

- Total table GLT0 for Financial Accounting (G/L) and business area (FI-GL).

- Total Table KKBC, KKBE, and KKBU for Product Costing module.

In this example, you have decided to build a trial balance for a company code, which means your table choice is G/L total table GLT0. You can see the attributes of the GLT0 table through the table browser transaction code SE16N.

General Table Display

	Background	Number of Entries				All Entries		

Table	GLT0			G/L account master record transaction figures
Text table				☐ No texts
Layout				
Maximum no. of hits	500			☐ Maintain entries

Selection Criteria						
Fld name	O	Fr.Value	To value	More	Output	Technical name
Client						RCLNT
Ledger	☒			⇨	☑	RLDNR
Record Type	☒			⇨	☑	RRCTY
Version	☒			⇨	☑	RVERS
Company Code	☒			⇨	☑	BUKRS
Fiscal Year	☒			⇨	☑	RYEAR
Account Number	☒			⇨	☑	RACCT
Business Area	☒			⇨	☑	RBUSA
Currency	☒			⇨	☑	RTCUR
Debit/Credit	☒			⇨	☑	DRCRK
Period	☒			⇨	☑	RPMAX
Transactn curr.	☒			⇨	☑	TSLVT
Transactn curr.	☒			⇨	☑	TSL01
Transactn curr.	☒			⇨	☑	TSL02
Transactn curr.	☒			⇨	☑	TSL03
Transactn curr.	☒			⇨	☑	TSL04
Transactn curr.	☒			⇨	☑	TSL05

FIGURE 6.2 Table browser SE16N.

With the help of a data browser you can view the table's attributes, available fields, and number of transactions. Now you have selected to use G/L total table GLT0. The next step is to create a library.

Library: A report library is the container of characteristics for the key figures. SAP comes with pre-delivered libraries for all total tables. However, you can create your own report library. You can create a report library by following the menu path: Information systems → Ad hoc reports → Report painter → Report Writer → Libraries → Create (Transaction Code GR21). In this example, you will learn how to create a library.

Executing transaction code GR21, you will create a library window without any value in the fields, seen in the following figure.

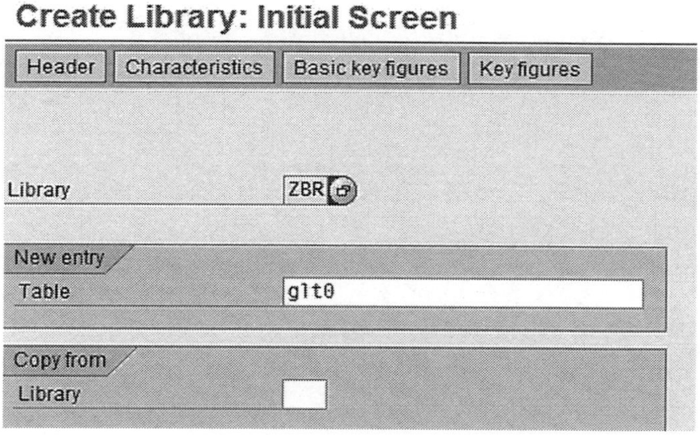

Create Library: Initial Screen

Header	Characteristics	Basic key figures	Key figures

Library   ZBR

New entry
Table   glt0

Copy from
Library

FIGURE 6.3 Create report library.

As you base decided to create a library for table GLT0, you have keyed GLT0 in the table field and given the library name as ZBR, shown in Figure 6.3. You can use any name starting with Z.

Click on [✓] to create the library. Figure 6.4 shows the library header screen.

Give the report library a name and choose the [💾] icon to save the report library that you are creating.

Once the library is saved, you can see the available characteristics and key figures by executing transaction code GR22, which changes the report library transaction code. To see the available characteristics, choose Characteristics . Figure 6.6 shows the available characteristics

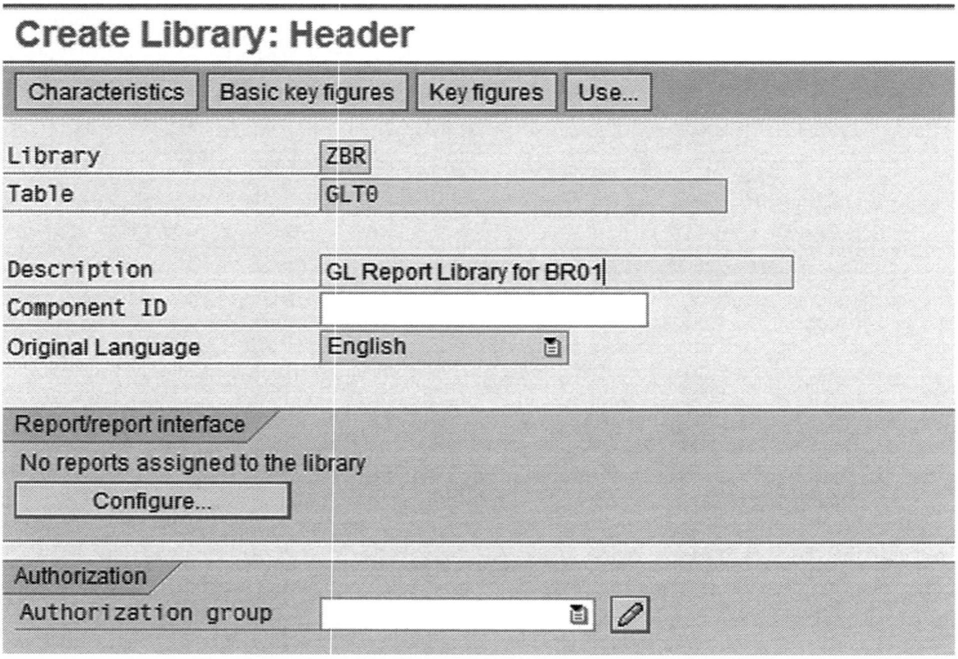

Create Library: Header

| Characteristics | Basic key figures | Key figures | Use... |

Library	ZBR
Table	GLT0

Description	GL Report Library for BR01
Component ID	
Original Language	English

Report/report interface

No reports assigned to the library

Configure...

Authorization

Authorization group

FIGURE 6.4 Report library header.

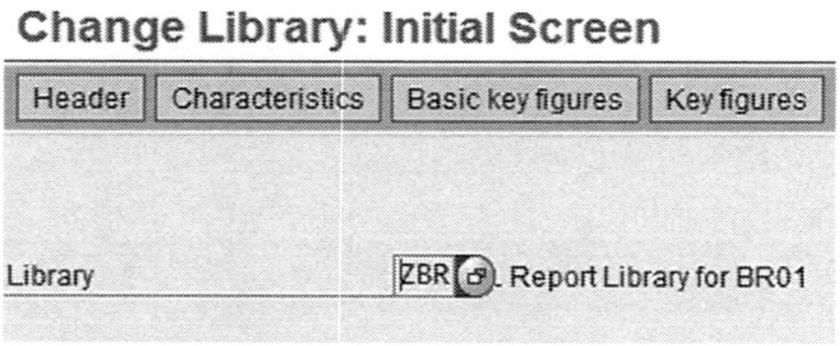

Change Library: Initial Screen

| Header | Characteristics | Basic key figures | Key figures |

Library   ZBR Report Library for BR01

FIGURE 6.5 Report library change window.

You can activate or deactivate these characteristics by checking or un-checking the check mark box next to the technical name of the characteristics. You can assign default steps to any of the characteristics.

Similarly, you can see the available key figures by choosing Basic key figures . Figure 6.7 shows the basic key figures available for the total table GLT0.

In this step, you learned how to create a library and review the available characteristics and key figures. In the next step, you will learn how to create set and how it is used.

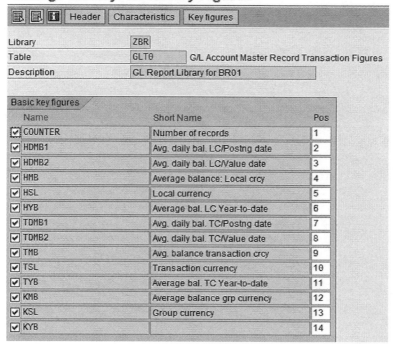

Change Library: Characteristics

| | | | Set | Header | Basic key figures | Key figures |

Library	ZBR
Table	GLT0 G/L Account Master Record Transaction Figures
Description	GL Report Library for BR01

Characteristics

	Name	Default set	Short text	Pos
☑	RLDNR		Ledger	1
☑	RRCTY		Record Type	2
☑	RVERS		Version	3
☑	BUKRS		Company Code	4
☑	RYEAR		Fiscal Year	5
☑	RPMAX		Period	6
☑	RACCT		Account Number	
☐	RBUSA		Business Area	
☐	RTCUR		Currency Key	
☐	DRCRK		Debit/Credit Indicator	
☐	CSPRED		Distribution key for currency amounts	

FIGURE 6.6 Report library characteristics.

Change Library: Basic Key Figures

| | | | Header | Characteristics | Key figures |

Library	ZBR
Table	GLT0 G/L Account Master Record Transaction Figures
Description	GL Report Library for BR01

Basic key figures

	Name	Short Name	Pos
☑	COUNTER	Number of records	1
☑	HDMB1	Avg. daily bal. LC/Postng date	2
☑	HDMB2	Avg. daily bal. LC/Value date	3
☑	HMB	Average balance: Local crcy	4
☑	HSL	Local currency	5
☑	HYB	Average bal. LC Year-to-date	6
☑	TDMB1	Avg. daily bal. TC/Postng date	7
☑	TDMB2	Avg. daily bal. TC/Value date	8
☑	TMB	Avg. balance transaction crcy	9
☑	TSL	Transaction currency	10
☑	TYB	Average bal. TC Year-to-date	11
☑	KMB	Average balance grp currency	12
☑	KSL	Group currency	13
☑	KYB		14

FIGURE 6.7 Basic key figures.

Sets: Sets represent a grouping of characteristics. Sets help maintain the characteristics and make reporting easier. You can create sets by navigating menu path Information systems → Ad hoc reports → Report painter → Report Writer → Set → Create (Transaction: GS01). In this example, you will create four sets: (1) Assets accounts i.e. ZBR01ASS, (2) Liabilities Accounts i.e. ZBR01LIB, (3) Income Incomes i.e. ZBR01INC, and (4) Expenses Incomes i.e. ZBR01EXP.

Execute transaction code GS01 to create a set. The first set you are going to create is for your liability accounts. Once you have executed transaction code GS01, you will get the initial screen, as shown in Figure 6.8.

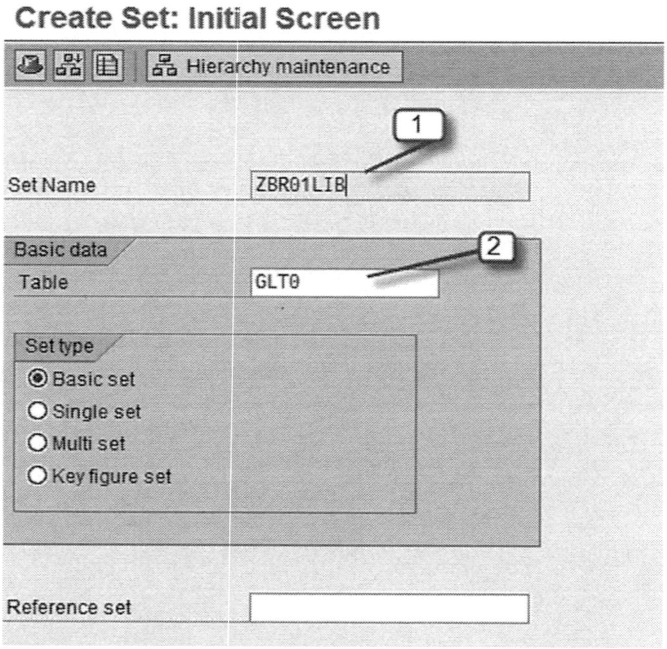

Create Set: Initial Screen

FIGURE 6.8 Create set initial screen.

1. Enter a set name starting with the letter Z.

2. Enter the total table name and accept other default values. Hit *enter* to navigate to the next screen, shown in Figure 6.9.

3. Enter the account number and technical field name "RACCT" or choose the account number from the drop down list. Choose ☑ to proceed to the next screen.

4. Enter the set values as shown in Figure 6.10. Here you can enter the values in the "from and to" fields. If you are maintaining an account number range, once the new account is created, the system will take care of the new values.

5. Maintain a description of the account number range for your reference.

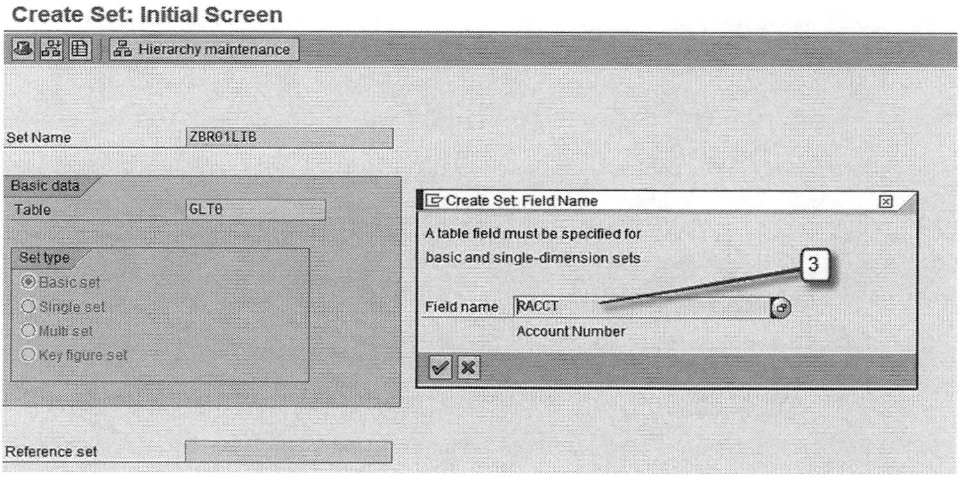

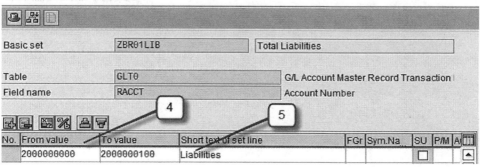

FIGURE 6.9 Create set initial screen two.

FIGURE 6.10 Set values.

Similarly, you can create other sets specified below:

- ZBR01ASS – Assets – 1000000000 through 1000002000

- ZBR01INC – Income – Account Numbers 3000000000 through 3000000100

- ZBR01EXP – Expenses – Account Numbers 4000000000 through 4000000100

You can build set hierarchies by grouping sets under one group.

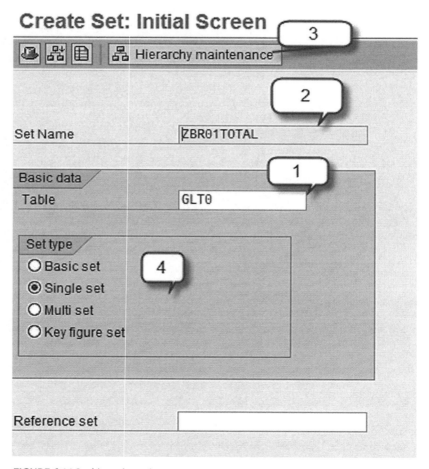

FIGURE 6.11 Set hierarchy maintenance.

To build set hierarchies follow the steps given below:

1. Enter higher level set ID

2. Enter total table name

3. Choose hierarchy maintenance, as shown in Figure 6.11.

4. Multiset

Choose ✅ to continue and the system will come up with the next screen, shown in Figure 6.12.

Now you can choose the sets that you created earlier in the order you want to display them.

To save the set hierarchy, choose 💾.

Change Set: Subordinate Sets

Single set	ZBR01TOTAL	All Accounts

Table	GLT0	G/L Account Master Record Transaction
Field name	RACCT	Account Number

No.	Set Name	Set short text	FGr	Sym.Na	SU	P/M	
001	ZBR01INC	Income			☐		
002	ZBR01EXP	Expenses			☐		
003	ZBR01ASS	Assets Account			☐		
004	ZBR01LIB	Liabilities			☐		

FIGURE 6.12 Set hierarchy maintenance.

You will learn how to use the sets while creating reports.

Variable: Within report painter/reports writer, variables are used for calculating the period and year based on the selection parameters. For example, you want to compare the current year results with the previous year results. You can create a variable that is the current fiscal year minus one. In the report selection screen you will input the current year and the system will derive results from the previous year. You can create a variable by navigating the SAP application menu path: Information systems → Ad hoc reports → Report painter → Report Writer → Variable → Create (Transaction Code: GS11).

Display Formula Variable: Basic Data

Formula variable	0BRYEAR

Table	GLT0	G/L Account Master Record Transaction Figures
Field name	RYEAR	Fiscal Year

Description	Fiscal year

Proposal

Formula	'#S001'

Entry fields on selection screens

☐ Internal variable

FIGURE 6.13 Variable fiscal year.

Figure 6.13 shows the SAP-delivered fiscal year variable. As the year is not using variables in this example, you can proceed to the next section to create a report group.

Reports: In this example, you are going to learn how to build a report painter report. You can reach the report painter create menu by navigating the SAP application menu: Information Systems → Ad hoc reports → Report painter → Report → Create.

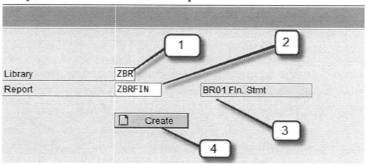

Report Painter: Create Report

Library	ZBR	①
Report	ZBRFIN	BR01 Fin. Stmt ② ③

☐ Create ④

FIGURE 6.14 Report painter initial screen.

1. Key in the report library ID that you created earlier.

2. Key in the report name ID.

3. Enter the report description.

4. Choose create to create a report.

The system will come up with a new screen as shown in Figure 6.15.

Report Painter: Create Report

| Report | ZBRFIN | BR01 FIn. Stmt |
| Section | 0001 | |

Format group:	0	0	0	0
Lead column	Column 1	Column 2	Column 3	Column 4
Row 1	XXX,XXX,XXX	XXX,XXX,XXX	XXX,XXX,XXX	XXX,XXX,XXX
Row 2	XXX,XXX,XXX	XXX,XXX,XXX	XXX,XXX,XXX	XXX,XXX,XXX
Row 3	XXX,XXX,XXX	XXX,XXX,XXX	XXX,XXX,XXX	XXX,XXX,XXX
Row 4	XXX,XXX,XXX	XXX,XXX,XXX	XXX,XXX,XXX	XXX,XXX,XXX

FIGURE 6.15 Report painter screen.

Figure 6.15 depicts the report painter report screen. Most of the time you spend in this screen will be to build row values, column values, and other attributes of report painter report.

In your first step towards report painter report you will build report rows.

1. Double click on "Lead column" as indicated in Figure 6.16. The system will come up with the "Report Painter: Create Report" window".

2. Fill in the short, medium, and long text. This text will appear in your report row header as per your report header selection.

3. Once you done with text field, choose ✔ to continue.

Report Row Values: In this section, you will learn how to build report values and how to use the set values you have earlier.

1. Double click on the first row shown in Figure 6.17 and if the system asks, select "characteristics." From the available characteristics that appear in the right hand screen, bring "Account Number" to left side of the window.

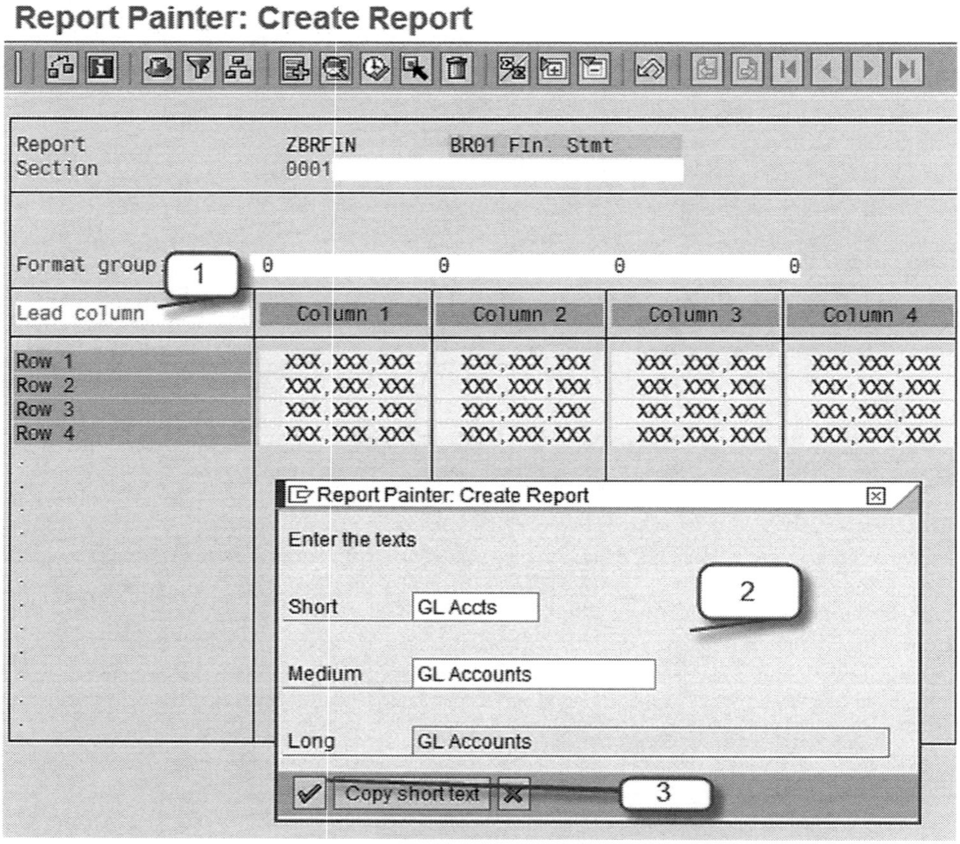

Report Painter: Create Report

FIGURE 6.16 Report painter row header.

2. Since you are going to use a set in this case, select the check mark as indicated in Figure 6.17.

3. Select set "ZBR01INC" for income G/L from the drop down list.

4. Choose check to see any potential error.

5. Choose confirm to accept the values.

Once you are done with the first row, double click on the second row and follow steps one to five. Once you have completed all four rows you will see a screen like Figure 6.18.

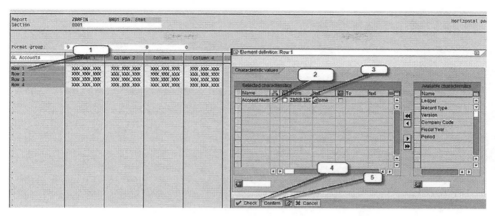

FIGURE 6.17 Report painter row values.

Report Painter: Create Report

Report	ZBRFIN	BR01 FIn. Stmt		
Section	0001			

Format group:	0	0	0	0
GL Accounts	Column 1	Column 2	Column 3	Column 4	...
Income	XXX,XXX,XXX	XXX,XXX,XXX	XXX,XXX,XXX	XXX,XXX,XXX	
Expenses	XXX,XXX,XXX	XXX,XXX,XXX	XXX,XXX,XXX	XXX,XXX,XXX	
Assets Account	XXX,XXX,XXX	XXX,XXX,XXX	XXX,XXX,XXX	XXX,XXX,XXX	
Liabilities	XXX,XXX,XXX	XXX,XXX,XXX	XXX,XXX,XXX	XXX,XXX,XXX	

FIGURE 6.18 Report painter report rows.

In the last two steps, you defined the report header and report rows with values. Now you are going to switch your attention from report rows to the report columns.

As you are going to build a one column report, you need to delete three columns from the report. To delete a column, right click your mouse you see a list menu, show in Figure 6.19.

Report Painter: Create Report

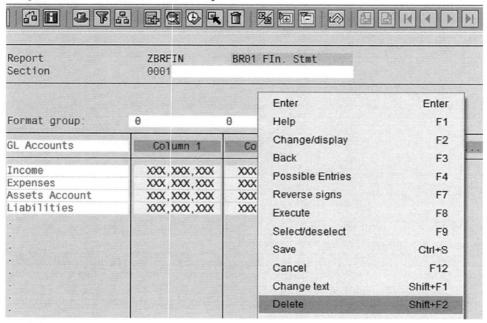

FIGURE 6.19 Delete report columns.

Once you have deleted three columns, you will be left with one column where you will define values, shown in Figure 6.20.

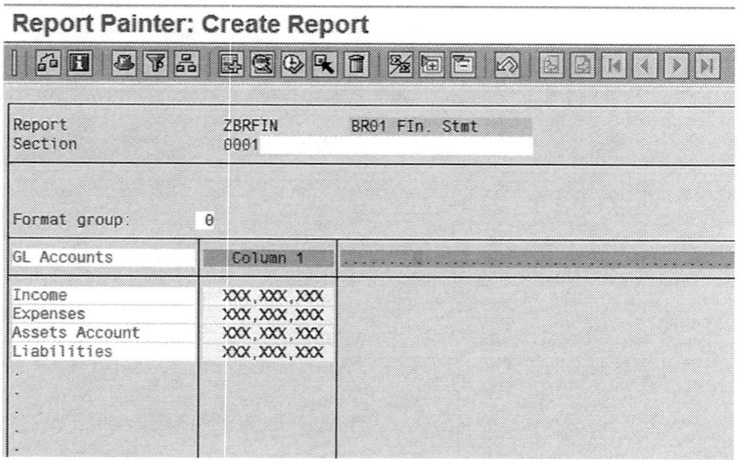

Report Painter: Create Report

FIGURE 6.20 Report painter column.

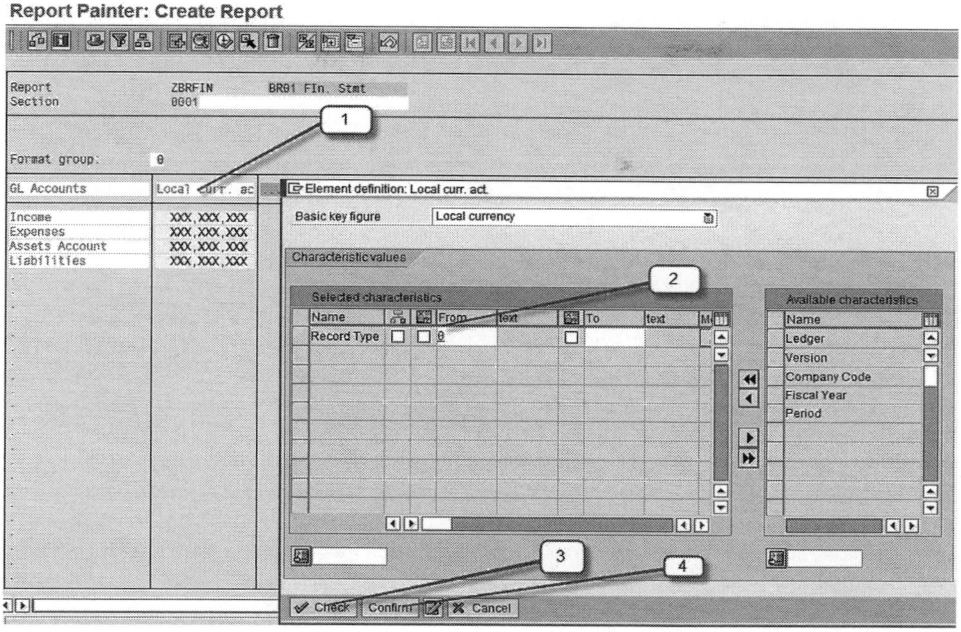

Report Painter: Create Report

FIGURE 6.21 Column values.

Now you will define the column values:

1. Double click on the column.

2. Bring the record type from the right hand window to the left hand window.

3. Check for potential errors.

4. Choose "Confirm" to see potential errors.

To maintain the column header, double click on the column header and maintain the short, medium, and long text that you defined for the row header.

Now it is time to build a selection screen and default parameters from your reports.

Choose "General Data Selection" as shown in Figure 6.22. Once you select the general data section, you will see a pop up window with a general data selection, as shown Figure 6.23.

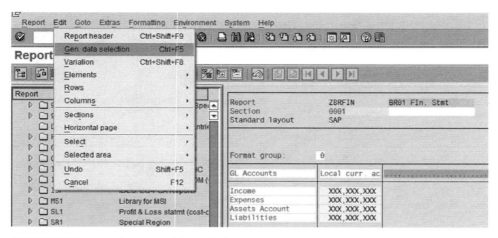

FIGURE 6.22 Report painter general data selection.

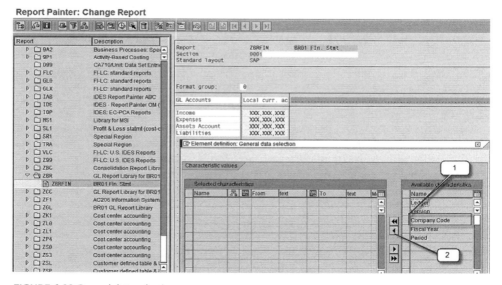

FIGURE 6.23 General data selection parameter.

1. From the right hand window, select company code, ledger, period, and version.

2. Bring them to the left hand screen.

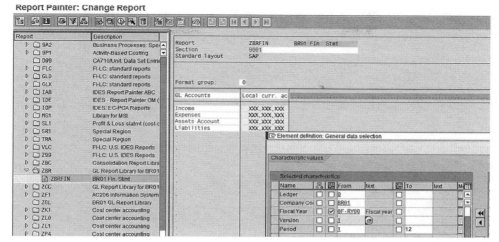

FIGURE 6.24 General data selection values.

Once the parameters are available, you need to maintain the values, as shown in Figure 6.24.

- *Ledger*: Select 0, actual values are stored in the ledger 0.

- *Company Code*: Select or enter BR01. As you are building a specific report for company code BR01, by entering value BR01 you are hard coding the company code value.

- *Fiscal Year*: Since this report is fiscal year dependent and you want the user to key in a fiscal year in the selection screen, you need to assign a variable. To assign a variable, choose thee check variable check box, as shown in Figure 6.24, and assign variable "0F-RY00" as the pre-defined variable for fiscal year.

- *Version*: Select version 1

- *Period***:** Enter from period and to period.

Now you almost done with the report, with a few exceptions like the report header andcolumn width.

Now you need to assign you newly developed report to a report group. You can assign the report to a report group by navigating environment > Assign report group as shown in Figure 6.25.

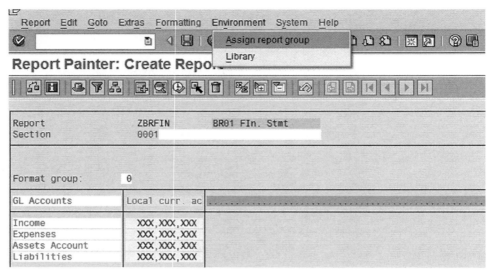

FIGURE 6.25 Assign report group 1.

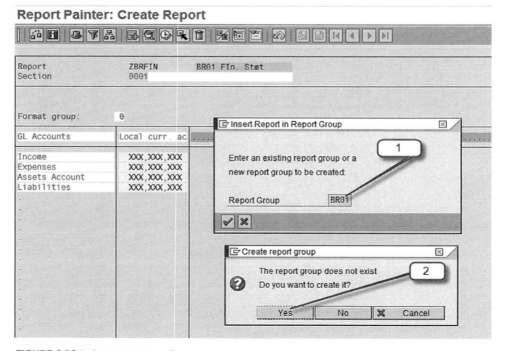

FIGURE 6.26 Assign report group 2.

In I "insert in report group" enter the report group name. If your report group name is new, the system will come up with a new window called "create report group" as shown in Figure 6.26. Next, you need to follow the screen given in report group section.

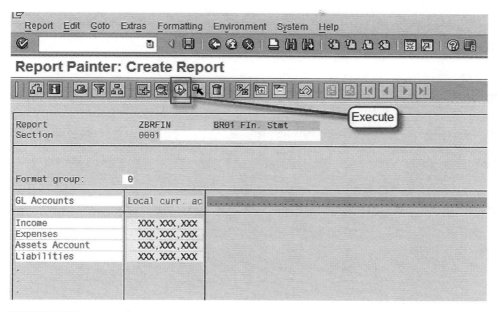

FIGURE 6.27 Execution of report.

Once you assigned the report to a report group, you can execute the report painter report from your development screen, shown in Figure 6.27.

If the system encounters any errors, the system will pop up with a message window, shown in Figure 6.37... (Figure 6.37 shows the execution results before the maintenance of general data selection show in Figure 6.24.)

Once you have executed the report, the system will come up with Figure 6.28, which is your report selection screen. As you have selected a variable, the system is expecting an input value. Key in fiscal year 2011 and execute.

Without any further cosmetic changes, the system will come up with an initial report as shown in Figure 6.29.

Figure 6.29 depicts the total of all the G/L accounts that are grouped in the four sets used in the respective rows. Now you are likely wondering

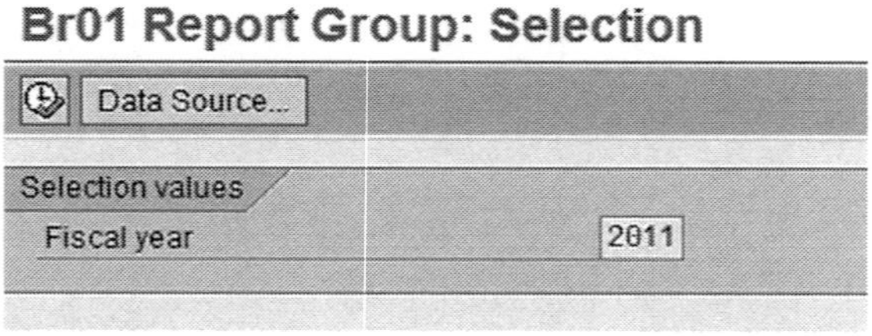

Br01 Report Group: Selection

Data Source...	
Selection values	
Fiscal year	2011

FIGURE 6.28 Report selection screen.

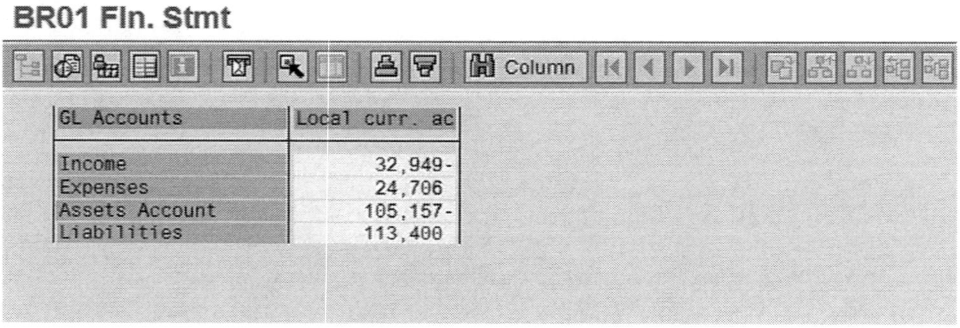

BR01 Fin. Stmt

GL Accounts	Local curr. ac
Income	32,949-
Expenses	24,706
Assets Account	105,157-
Liabilities	113,400

FIGURE 6.29 Report 1.

how to show the individual general balances and G/L accounts included in these balances.

You can see these by enabling the explode option available in characteristic values. Refer Figure 6.17 and move to the right of the account number row and you will find the explode option, as shown Figure 6.30. Choose explode from the selection list and check the confirm to accept setting box. You need to do this for all the rows for which you want to see individual values.

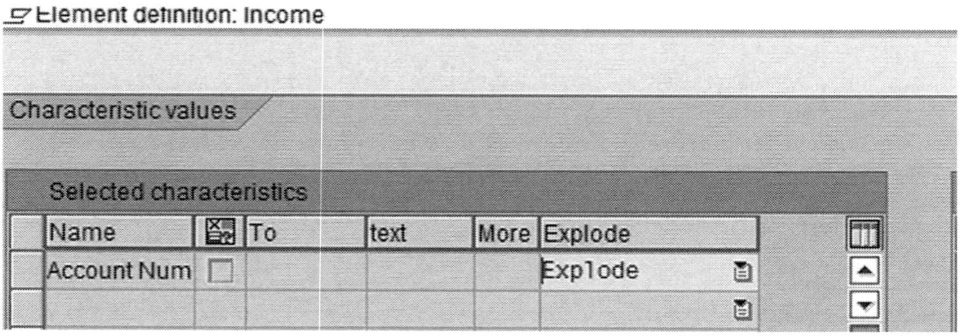

Element definition: Income

Characteristic values					
Selected characteristics					
Name	To	text	More	Explode	
Account Num				Explode	

FIGURE 6.30 Explode options.

Once you enable the explode option and execute your report, you will see all G/Ls associated in the ledger and their individual values, shown in Figure 6.31.

BR01 Fin. Stmt

GL Accounts		Local curr. ac
3000000000	int.in	49-
3000000001	P & L	500-
3000000002	FA Cls	
3000000003	Sales	32,400-
* Income		32,949-
4000000000	Expens	439-
4000000001	Expens	125
4000000002	Expens	1,000
4000000004	Expens	500
4000000008	Expens	700
4000000009	Expens	400
4000000010	Expens	23,220
4000000011	Expens	800-
* Expenses		24,706
1000000000	Balanc	139,932-
1000000003	Balanc	
1000000004	Balanc	3,000
1000000005	Balanc	
1000000007	Balanc	125-
1000000008	Balanc	24,500
1000000009	Balanc	
1000000101	Balanc	7,400
* Assets Account		105,157-
2000000000	Liabil	
2000000002	Liabil	113,400
* Liabilities		113,400

FIGURE 6.31 Report after explode enable.

The report shown in Figure 6.31 doesn't show a total row. You are going to build a total row with help of the formula builder. Double click on the blank row after Liabilities and the system will come up with a "select element type" window. Now you have two options: (1) characteristics i.e., G/L accounts and (2) formula i.e., you can build a row with formula builder by using one or more characteristics.

When you choose "formula" in the check box, the system will bring up the screen shown in Figure 6.33. In this screen, as you need to add all four rows together.

Select row ID Y001 and operator + and then go on to the other rows. Finally, you will see a screen shown in Figure 6.33. Check and confirm to

Report Painter: Change Report

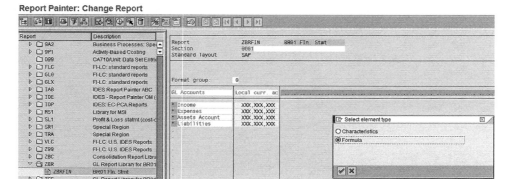

FIGURE 6.32 Use of formula.

Report Painter: Change Report

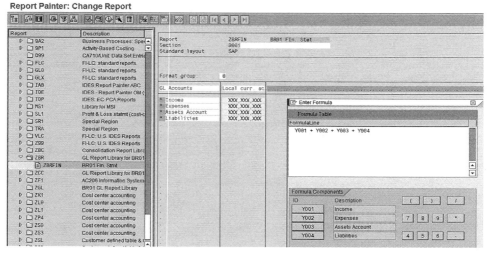

FIGURE 6.33 Use of formula 2.

accept the values. Once you are done with the total row, you can execute the report.

Now you can see the total row at the end of the report, as shown in Figure 6.34.

Report Group: You can create a report group from report development, or you can choose the application navigation path: Information Systems > Ad Hoc Reports > Report Painter > Report Writer > Report Group > Create (Transaction Code: GR51)

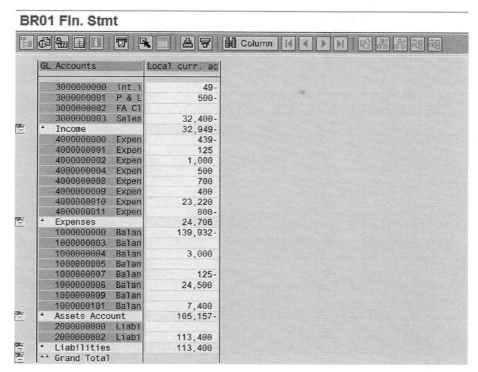

FIGURE 6.34 Report 3.

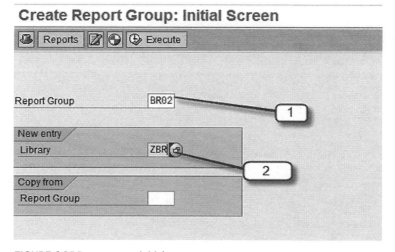

FIGURE 6.35 Report group initial screen.

In the initial screen of the report group, enter the report group ID and the report library that you created earlier. Once you enter the report group ID and library ID choose ✅ to continue. Now you can see the "Create Report Group: Header" screen, shown in Figure 6.36.

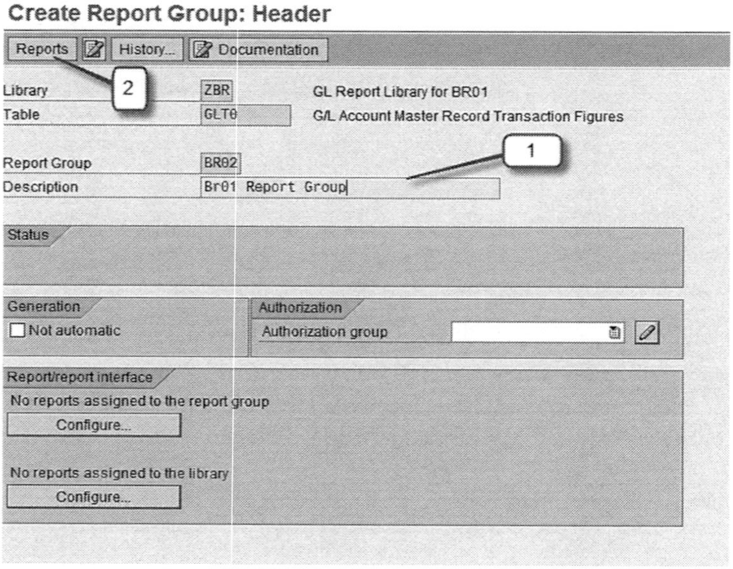

Create Report Group: Header

Reports 🗒	History...	🗒 Documentation

| Library | 2 | ZBR | GL Report Library for BR01 |
| Table | | GLT0 | G/L Account Master Record Transaction Figures |

| Report Group | BR02 | |
| Description | Br01 Report Group | 1 |

Status

| Generation | Authorization | |
| ☐ Not automatic | Authorization group | 🗓 🖉 |

Report/report interface
No reports assigned to the report group
Configure...

No reports assigned to the library
Configure...

FIGURE 6.36 Report group header.

Maintain the report group description and assign the report by choosing report icon, as shown in Figure 6.36.

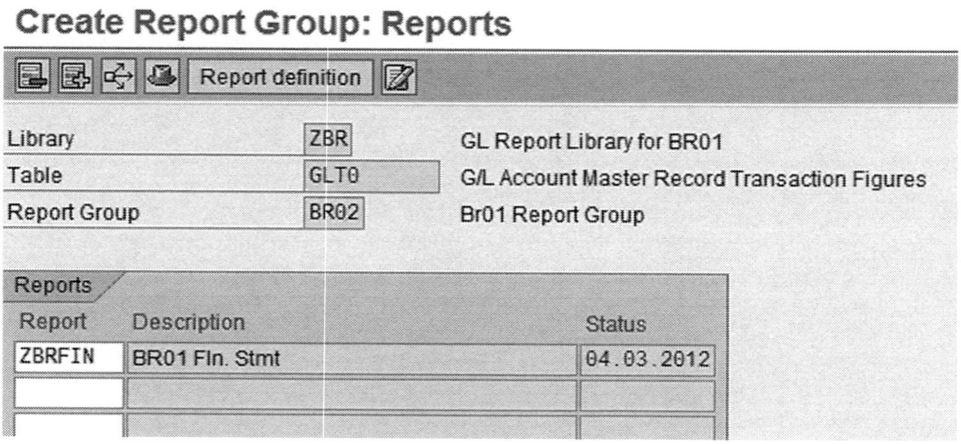

Create Report Group: Reports

🗒 🗒 🕸 🗒	Report definition 🗒

Library	ZBR	GL Report Library for BR01
Table	GLT0	G/L Account Master Record Transaction Figures
Report Group	BR02	Br01 Report Group

Reports		
Report	Description	Status
ZBRFIN	BR01 Fln. Stmt	04.03.2012

FIGURE 6.37 Group reports.

You can assign more than one report to a report group and one report can be assigned to more the one report group.

Sometimes while running a report, you can come across error messages. These error messages are pretty straight forward and come up with a message that is self-explanatory.

Execute Report Group: Initial Screen

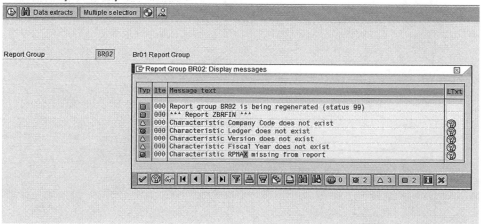

FIGURE 6.38 Error reports.

Once the reports are executable, you can run these reports through transaction code: GR55 or following application Information Systems > Ad Hoc Reports > Report Painter > Report Writer > Report Group > Execute

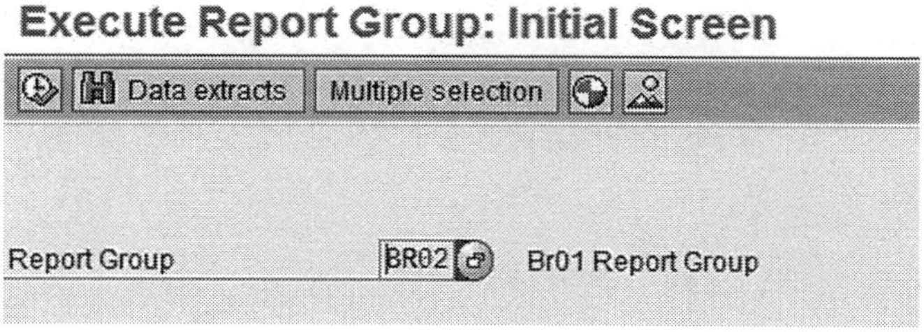

Execute Report Group: Initial Screen

| | Data extracts | Multiple selection | | |

Report Group   BR02   Br01 Report Group

FIGURE 6.39 Report execution initial screen.

Figure 6.39 depicts the report group execution screen, where the system expects the report group ID. Key in the report ID and choose the execution icon.

Br01 Report Group: Selection

Data Source...	
Selection values	
Fiscal year	2011

FIGURE 6.40 Report selection screen.

Figure 6.40 depicts the report selection screen that you have just built. Enter fiscal year 2011 and hit the execute icon to execute the report.

Once you have executed the report, you can see the report that you have just built.

BR01 Fin. Stmt

GL Accounts		Local curr. ac
3000000000	int.1	49-
3000000001	P & L	500-
3000000002	FA C1	
3000000003	Sales	32,400-
* Income		32,949-
4000000000	Expen	439-
4000000001	Expen	125
4000000002	Expen	1,000
4000000004	Expen	500
4000000008	Expen	700
4000000009	Expen	400
4000000010	Expen	23,220
4000000011	Expen	800-
* Expenses		24,706
1000000000	Balan	139,932-
1000000003	Balan	
1000000004	Balan	3,000
1000000005	Balan	
1000000007	Balan	125-
1000000008	Balan	24,500
1000000009	Balan	
1000000101	Balan	7,400
* Assets Account		105,157-
2000000000	Liabi	
2000000002	Liabi	113,400
* Liabilities		113,400
** Grand Total		

FIGURE 6.41 Report.

You now know how to create report painter reports and can do some of the cosmetic changes like the report header and aligning the column width.

INDEX